The Catholic Biblical Quarterly
Monograph Series
33

The Antithesis
of the Ages

Paul's Reconfiguration
of Torah

BY

Stephan K. Davis

The Catholic Biblical Quarterly
Monograph Series
33

©2002 The Catholic Biblical Association of America,
Washington, DC 20064

Portions of chapters 1, 3, 5, and 7 first appeared as
"Primordial Wisdom, Eschatological Word: The Eternal Torah and Paul," in the
Proceedings of the Eastern Great Lakes and Midwest Biblical Societies
17 (1997): 83–94. Used by permission of the copyright holder.

Produced in the United States of America

Library of Congress Cataloging-in-Publication Data

Davis, Stephan K., 1959-
  The antithesis of the ages : Paul's reconfiguration of Torah / by
Stephan K. Davis.
        p.   cm. — (The Catholic biblical quarterly. Monograph series)
  ISBN 0-915170-32-9
1. Paul, the Apostle, Saint—Views on Jewish law. 2. Bible. N.T.
Epistles of Paul—Theology. 3. Jewish law—History. I. Title. II.
Series.
  BS2655.L35 .D38 2002
  227'.06—dc21
                                                2001007936

To my treasures,
Lynda Joyce, Noah, and Hana

Contents

Acknowledgments

This book first appeared as a Marquette University dissertation. It is difficult to overstate the influence of the dissertation's director, Carol Stockhausen. From our first acquaintance in an Intertextuality seminar, Carol pointed me in the right direction, inspired me at every turn, allowed me to glean from her own unpublished work, and exposed my mistaken judgments. Her influence is most apparent in my Pauline studies, chapters four through six.

Each of my Marquette readers has stimulated me and improved the quality of this study: Hieromonk Alexander Golitzin, William Kurz, S.J., Julian Hills, Deirdre Dempsey.

Many dear friends have contributed in various ways, but I must single out Dr. Ian C. Levy, who enthusiastically read and discussed these ideas, and Brandon Knight, who made numerous methodological suggestions.

I am honored to have the Catholic Biblical Quarterly Monograph Series publish this volume. My thanks to Mark S. Smith and the associate editors for accepting the manuscript and improving the final form.

Finally, I must express my gratitude to the Marquette University Theology Department for awarding me a dissertation fellowship in 1996-97, and for nominating me for the Reverend John P. Raynor, S. J., Fellowship, which I received for 1997-98. These generous awards made it possible for me to devote myself fully to this study.

CHAPTER 1

Introduction to the Antithesis
of the Ages

In order to frame the topic and introduce the perspective of this study, I ask the reader to consider Martin Hengel's provocative statement that within early Jewish theology "eschatology formed the only regulative force by which the omnipotence of the Torah, dominating the present and anchored in the cosmos, could possibly be limited."[1] Perhaps suspicious minds may find in these words an anti-Torah bias that implies Torah should be limited in some way, but the statement also hints at the heart of Paul's theological characterization of Torah.[2] "The Antithesis of the Ages" means that the primary Pauline Torah/Christ polarity is inherently an antithesis of history and eschatology, of "this

---

[1] M. Hengel, *Judaism and Hellenism* (2 vols.; Minneapolis: Fortress, 1974) 1.312.

[2] "Torah" without the definite article is grammatical in Jewish theologies, but in this study it reflects the early Jewish development of Torah as a quasi-personal intermediary. The choice to isolate "Torah" rather than "Nomos" is admittedly arbitrary since Paul never in fact uses the Hebrew term. My intention in using "Torah" is merely to underscore the Jewish background of Paul's idea of the Law. Jewish scholars have long protested that νόμος ("law") is a poor translation equivalent of תורה, which is more properly rendered "instruction" (e.g., S. Schecter, *Aspects of Rabbinic Theology* [New York: Schocken, 1909] 117, and S. Sandmel, *The Genius of Paul* [New York: Farrar, Straus, and Cudahy, 1958] 46–47; see also C. H. Dodd, *The Bible and the Greeks* [London: Hodder and Stoughton, 1934] 30–37, and A. F. Segal, "Torah and *Nomos* in Recent Scholarly Discussion," *SR* 13 [1984] 19–27).

age" (עולם הזה) and the "age to come" (עולם הבא). For Paul, Christ was God's primordial Wisdom and eschatological Word, whereas Torah belongs solely to history. Torah was neither the agent of creation nor would it mediate eschatological judgment.[3] Christ assumed roles in Pauline theology that many early Jewish texts assigned to Torah, the cosmic entity.

The tension between Torah and eschatology echoes Albert Schweitzer's earlier assertion of the "incompatibility of Law and eschatology." Schweitzer contended that, in contradistinction to Paul, "Judaism refused to acknowledge" this incompatibility, and "Post-Exilic Judaism and Rabbinism" were characterized by their efforts to "unite these incompatibles."[4] Schweitzer's analysis is typical of pre-paradigm shift Pauline scholarship in which Christian scholars denigrate the Mosaic Law in favor of a fanciful projection of the contrary and superior religion of the Hebrew prophets.[5] But the idea of Paul's theological perception of a tension or incompatibility between Law

[3] The history/eschatology contrast is used for want of better terminology. Although there are native Pauline contrast sets, such as the τὸ καταργούμενον/τὸ μένον antipodes in 2 Cor 3:11, these are incomplete rather than polyvalent signs like "history" and "eschatology." "History" and "historical" are intended to signify the עולם הזה, what Paul referred to as "the present evil age" (Gal 1:4). Non-protological biblical narratives are thus "history" whether or not they meet modern critical criteria for that designation. "Eschatology" and "eschatological" generally correspond to עולם הבא. I have no special term for the transitional events and periods, nor do I presuppose belief in a preliminary messianic age for the pre-rabbinic period. "Eschatological" will have to be elastic enough to cover the variables.

[4] A. Schweitzer, *The Mysticism of Paul the Apostle* (New York: Seabury, 1931) 189–90.

[5] Both the idea of a "paradigm shift" in Pauline scholarship, and the repudiation of the Law/prophets polarity (especially characteristic of past German-Lutheran scholars) are identified with E. P. Sanders, *Paul and Palestinian Judaism* (Philadelphia: Fortress, 1977). See especially T. L. Donaldson, *Paul and the Gentiles: Remapping the Apostle's Convictional World* (Minneapolis: Fortress, 1997) 3–27, and the previous use of "paradigm shift" in 309 n. 1. Schweitzer anticipated at least the first of Donaldson's three elements in the emerging paradigm: justification by faith is a "subsidiary crater, which has formed within the rim of the main crater—the mystical doctrine of redemption through the being-in-Christ" (*Mysticism*, 225). Sanders comments that German scholarship has generally ignored Schweitzer's arguments against justification by faith as the center of Pauline theology, although they "have never been effectively countered" (*Paul and Palestinian Judaism*, 434, 440).

and eschatology should not be dismissed too quickly. One will find that Schweitzer, despite his inadequate treatment of Law in the "messianic era" (§1.2.1), had a clearer idea of the eschatology that Paul inherited from early Jewish theology than is generally found in subsequent scholarship. The eschatological Paul is Schweitzer's legacy. This study can be understood as an attempt to unpack Schweitzer's idea of the "incompatibility between Law and eschatology" in order to demonstrate how this insight helps to clarify Paul's Christian view of Torah.[6]

Puzzles as perplexing as Paul-and-Torah resist simple solutions based on a new or unique interpretation of ancient texts. This puzzle resists even the most ingenious interpreter, yet new studies emerge yearly with widely divergent theses: Paul did not view the Law as abolished; only parts of the Law were abolished; the law was abolished for gentiles, but not Jews; the Law was abolished for those in Christ, whether Jew or gentile. Given the enigmatic nature of the topic, it is wise to resist the seduction of an all too simple solution. On the other hand, a change in perspective may be all that is needed to recognize a real solution. From the angle proposed in this study, I not only focus on what the Pauline writings have to say about Torah, but also on which "Torah"—that is, which early Jewish theological conception of Torah—Paul was addressing.

1.1 The Eternal Torah and Paul

Although my thesis is multifaceted, it can be summarized simply: when Paul wrote negatively about Torah he was not addressing Torah *per se*, but rather a particular mode of envisioning Torah that is identifiable in many early Jewish texts.[7] I refer to the conception of Torah that Paul opposed as the "eternal Torah," but it might also be termed the

---

[6] Obviously "Christian" here and elsewhere in this study is an anachronism. The term is simply intended to identify the phase in Paul's thought after his "ἀποκάλυψις of Jesus Christ" (Gal 1:12).

[7] To avoid unnecessary confusion, I use "early Jewish" and "post-biblical" as they are normally understood. These rubrics include proto-rabbinic traditions and the NT, but not the subsequent Christian and rabbinic literature. For the complexities of our terminology regarding this period, see the insightful treatment of G. Boccaccini, *Middle Judaism* (Minneapolis: Fortress, 1990) 7–25.

"cosmic Torah" or the "ontological Torah."[8] The eternal Torah is not merely a revelatory book, a group of books, or a set of laws; it is Torah as God's cosmic force, an entity that acts as an intermediary between God and humanity. The eternal Torah is the Word or Wisdom by which God created the world, and the instrument of final judgment.

Paul-and-Torah theories should coordinate his three kinds of assertions about Torah. First, Paul wrote negatively about Torah. He identified the Law with the age of sin and death, asserting that the Law was unable to defeat these powers (e.g., Rom 8:2–3). The Law was little more than a guardian (Gal 3:25), and was even given to increase sin (Rom 5:20). Paul wrote of the "letter that kills," referring to the Mosaic tablets (2 Cor 3:6). Finally and perhaps most enigmatically, Paul asserted that Christ was the τέλος of the Law (Rom 10:4). Second, Paul also wrote positively about Torah. The Law was spiritual (Rom 7:14) and holy (Rom 7:12). He thought of himself as affirming Torah (Rom 3:31), and encouraged Christians to stay in that position in which they were "called," either Greek or Jew, slave or free (1 Cor 7:17–20). Third, phrases like the "law of Christ" (1 Cor 9:21; Gal 6:2; Rom 8:2) suggest to some scholars that Paul believed in a messianic Torah that replaced the Torah of Moses.[9]

From this three-fold presentation of the Paul-and-Torah riddle, the simplest, almost syllogistic solution is that he affirmed that Torah was given by God and good (positive), but he denied some aspects of early Jewish Torah theology (negative), and transferred to Christ those functions and titles that he denied to Torah (replacement). This is, in fact, the position I would defend were I dealing comprehensively with each relevant Pauline text. This study is focused on the link between Paul's rejection of the eternal Torah and his replacement of Torah with Christ.

I prefer to describe Paul's negative assertions about Torah as a "reconfiguration" of early Jewish Torah theology rather than a "denial" because he is denying only the "eternal Torah" elements

---

[8] Hengel uses the label "*'ontologischen' Toraverständnisses*" for the theological development to which I am referring (see e.g., *Judentum und Hellenismus* [WUNT 10; Tübingen: Mohr, 1969] 311).

[9] J. D. G. Dunn summarizes the Paul-and-Torah dilemma in terms of similar positive and negative assertions (*The Theology of Paul the Apostle* [Grand Rapids: Eerdmans, 1998] 129–31), without acknowledging the elements of replacement essential to this study.

rather than Torah itself. Forgive the pun, but if one could think of the early Jewish Torah as a mosaic of biblical and post-biblical tesserae, Paul removed the tesserae from this mosaic that represent Torah as the primordial Wisdom and eschatological judge. Paul modifies the mosaic, but he does not destroy it.

The tesserae extracted from the Torah mosaic were not simply discarded. Paul pieced them into his Christ mosaic. Why? The Pauline corpus does not provide all the answers because the principal problem lies at the convictional level rather than the rhetorical.[10] One can make educated guesses based on the theological values that Pauline discourse manifests. Perhaps the simplest value is christological: the eternal Torah occupied a theological "space" that necessarily belonged to Christ. One might also expect that Paul's replacement of Torah is related to his understanding of the inclusion of the gentiles into the eschatological people of God without the necessity of adhering to Jewish requirements, such as circumcision—the issue that dominates Galatians, and to a lesser extent Romans.[11] The gentiles are a problem within Jewish theologies because the גוים/ἔθνη represent Israel's mythic and real-time enemies. Their role as snare or enemy in Jewish sacred memory develops in some early Jewish texts into the gentiles' eschatological condemnation.[12] Even "righteous gentile" notions are fraught

[10] Donaldson identifies Paul's "convictional world" as the "set of basic convictions (about Christ, Israel, the Torah, the Gentiles, and so on) that seldom emerge explicitly but nevertheless provide the tacit 'semantic universe' in which the text in all its aspects has its being" (*Paul and the Gentiles*, 34). The convictional level often lies below the rhetorical level in Pauline discourse.

[11] The Corinthian correspondence does not exhibit the same preoccupation with the inclusion of gentiles, but it does deal with corollary issues: gentile morality and religious practices.

[12] I cannot be as categorical as J. Jeremias, who states that "the attitude of late Judaism towards non-Jews was uncompromisingly severe" (*Jesus' Promise to the Nations* [London: SCM, 1958] 40). There is ambiguity concerning the status of gentiles, as T. L. Donaldson summarizes: "The Judaism of Paul's day had developed a range of attitudes toward the Gentiles and their status with respect to God. At one end, there existed tolerant and open strands of universalism, including the recognition of 'righteous Gentiles' and the (probably closely associated) eschatological pilgrimage tradition. At the other extreme, there was the rigid and exclusive covenantal soteriology represented by *Jub.* 15:26. which assigns to perdition all but those who were circumcised on the eighth day. Lying somewhere in between was proselytism" ("'Riches for the Gentiles' (Rom. 11.12): Israel's Rejection and Paul's Gentile Mission," *JBL* 112 [1993] 95). The

with the problem of gentile religiosity that violates the first commandment; traditional Jewish theologies might accept righteous gentiles so long as they are not religious. The biblical tradition of an eschatological gentile "pilgrimage" to Zion provides hope for some gentiles, but the nature and role of the gentile group drawn to Zion are open to interpretation. What are the qualifications of these gentiles? Would they come to serve the Jews, or join them as fellow heirs?

---

ambiguity is maintained in early Jewish texts that concern the eschatological fate of gentiles. There is also the explicit association of a gentile rejection of Torah with its eschatological condemnation of them (*2 Apoc. Bar.* 48:47; see also *Pss. Sol.* 8:23), or even judgment without a rejection tradition (*L.A.B.* 11:2). The rabbinic development (see below) reinforces these texts. Conversely, if "righteous" in *T. Naph.* 8:3 refers to righteous gentiles rather than "exiled" Jewry, then there is hope for a special group of gentiles (although the terms of their righteousness are unspecified). The ambiguity is also reflected in rabbinic literature: ". . . righteous among the nations of the world who have a share in the world to come" (*t. Sanh.* 13:2). The positive outlook for some gentiles must be held in balance with its antipode: "The Babylonian Talmud concludes that the nations were then doomed irreversibly for the 'pit of destruction', for they should have learnt the (written) *Torah* but failed to do so" (S. Stern, *Jewish Identity in Early Rabbinic Writings* [AGJU 23; Leiden: Brill, 1994] 212; the text referred to is *b. Sot.* 35b). This conclusion is based on the traditions that Moses translated the Torah into 70 languages (*m. Sot.* 7.5; on Deut 27:1–8), and that every nation sent representatives to copy from these translations (*t. Sot.* 8.6; *y. Sot.* 7.5; *b. Sot.* 35b); similar traditions have Torah given in 70 languages at Sinai, for all the world's comprehension (*b. Shab.* 88b; *Exod. Rab.* 5.9). Another often repeated tradition is based on Deut 33:2: "He said, 'The Lord came (בא) from Sinai, and dawned (זרח) from Seir upon us; he shone forth (הופיע) from Mount Paran, he came from the ten thousands of holy ones, with flaming fire at his right hand.'" *Sifre* 343 is an elaborate version: "*And he said: the Lord came from Sinai*: When God revealed Himself to give the Torah to Israel, He revealed Himself not only to Israel but to all the nations. He went first to the children of Esau and asked them, 'Will you accept the Torah?'" The Torah was similarly offered to the sons of Esau, the Ammonites, Moabites, Ishmaelites; each people has a characteristic sin that makes them unable to accept. "And thus it was with every other nation—he asked them all, 'Will you accept the Torah?', as it is said, *All the kings of the earth shall give Thee thanks, O Lord, for they have heard the words of Thy mouth* (Ps 138:4). One might think (from this verse) that they heard and accepted (His offer); therefore Scripture states elsewhere, *And I will execute vengeance in anger and fury upon the nations, because they hearkened not* (Mic 5:14). It was not enough for them that they did not hearken—they were not even able to observe the seven commandments that the children of Noah had accepted upon themselves, and they cast them off. When the holy one, blessed be He, saw that, He surrendered them to Israel" (R. Hammer, tr., *Sifre: A Tannaitic Commentary on the Book of Deuteronomy* [New Haven: Yale University Press, 1986]).

Although eschatology is not investigated explicitly in this study, Zion eschatology is regarded as a hermeneutical key to Paul-and-Torah: it is the eschatological scenario that he envisioned.[13] His διακονία on behalf of the ἔθνη and attitude to Torah are bound to his interpretation of the Isaianic Zion tradition. Paul believed that gentiles ἐν χριστῷ were pilgrims to the "Jerusalem above" (i.e., eschatological Zion), and that their faith was δικαιοσύνη before God irrespective of their relationship to the Torah given in history to Israel.[14] This is considerably different from Jewish theologies that portrayed the gentiles rejecting Torah in the pre-patriarchal period and/or the present, and therefore receiving eschatological condemnation as their reward. As Schweitzer asserted earlier in this century, one cannot understand Paul without recognizing his eschatological orientation. It is not the "mere thatness" of the eschaton's dawning that is at issue in Paul, but correlative ideas: the nature of the transitional age, who participates in the eschaton, how this participation is accomplished and experienced, and the relationship between Jewish sacred history (Moses, Torah, Israel) and eschatological universalism.

Because it is present at, and in some cases the instrument of, final judgment, the eternal Torah overlaps eschatology. Paul opposed the eternal element of Torah, and applied the primordial and eschatological elements to Christ.[15] Torah was still a positive gift of God in an

[13] I use "Zion eschatology" as the descriptive referent for the eschatological pilgrimage tradition (see Donaldson, *Paul and the Gentiles*, 69–74). Some scholars (e.g., E. P. Sanders) describe early Jewish eschatology in terms of "restoration," but I think the "restoration" element can overwhelm the mystical, supernal nature of Pauline eschatology. Even the apocalyptic restoration of *Urzeit* conditions usually means the emergence of a heavenly paradise more perfect than biblical Eden.

[14] Although this study owes a great deal to L. Gaston, I do not mean this as an endorsement of his thesis that Paul's argument against Torah only concerned the gentiles, whereas the status of Jews was determined by covenantal nomism (see *Paul and the Torah* [Vancouver: University of British Columbia Press, 1987]). Irrespective of the extent to which he maintained Torah observance, Paul certainly included himself, a Jew, among those "dead to the law" (Gal 3:19; Rom 7:4). There is little reason to suspect that Paul himself is the one exception to Gaston's rule. On the other hand, what is the point of Rom 11:25–26—especially in light of Paul's argument in the early chapters of Romans of the universal (Jew *and* gentile) need for deliverance from sin and death—unless Paul saw Jews' status within the covenant as the precondition for σωτηρία?

[15] Compare the judgment of F. Thielman: "Paul does not, as is frequently said, limit the law to a particular time and therefore deny the Jewish doctrine of the eternality of

otherwise fading, oppressive world, but it was impotent to conquer the powers of this world. If Torah is not the means of transcendence, gentiles do not have to go through Torah to participate in the eschaton that has mystically dawned.

The antithesis of Christ and Torah involves the transference of Torah's cosmic attributes to Christ, based on the difference between this age and the age to come. Torah was God's exclusive historical revelation for Israel, whereas Christ was eschatological revelation for all the people of God, Jew and gentile alike. The relationship between Christ and reconfigured Torah may be described as an antithesis in the same way that "this age" (עולם הזה) and the "age to come" (עולם הבא) are, since Paul understood the age of Torah to have ended with the coming of the superior, unmediated revelation through the Spirit of Christ. But the real "anti-theses" are Christ and the eternal Torah.

The roots of my thesis may be traced to two pioneering articles by C. Bugge and Hans Windisch on the relationship of Torah and Wisdom to Christ. Windisch is largely responsible for gathering what has become the standard pool of Wisdom texts (see §2.1–4) and perceiving that Paul applied the attributes of Wisdom in these texts to Christ.[16] Before Windisch, Bugge recognized that Torah was depicted in early Jewish literature as a hypostasis that existed before all of creation. According to Bugge, Paul inherited (from Stephen's speech in Acts 7) the notion that Jesus as Messiah had taken the central place of Torah. Paul understood Torah as a temporally limited (zeitgeschichtlich beschränkte) form of Messiah. Like a river that flows into a sea and is transformed, Torah flows into Christ. Christ thus contains (einmünden) all of Torah.[17] The transformation as replacement element of Bugge's theory would reemerge particularly in the theories of W. D. Davies and Peter Stuhlmacher who envision Paul advocating an eschatological Christ-Torah that inscrutably replaces yet does not negate the Mosaic Torah.[18]

---

the law," but ". . . he affirms the existence of the law in the eschatological age" (From Plight to Solution: A Jewish Framework for Understanding Paul's View of the Law in Romans and Galatians [NovTSup 61; Leiden: Brill, 1989] 76).

[16] H. Windisch, "Die göttliche Weisheit der Juden und die paulinische Christologie," Neutestamentliche Studien für Georg Heinrici (eds. A. Deissmann and H. Windisch; Leipzig: Hinrichs, 1914) 220–34.

[17] C. Bugge, "Das Gesetz und Christus nach der Anschauung der ältesten Christengemeinde," ZNW 4 (1903) 89–110.

[18] For Davies, see §1.2.2; Stuhlmacher, §1.2.4. Schweitzer (§1.2.1) also thought of an eternal Torah that was nonetheless replaced in the messianic age.

Bugge's early identification of Torah the hypostasis anticipates Hengel's narrative of the emergence of the cosmic, or "ontological Torah" in early Jewish literature.[19] Torah achieves this status by means of a wholesale transfer to it of the attributes of hypostasized Wisdom in biblical texts like Prov 8:22–31 and Job 28:20–27.[20] Hengel views hypostases as a subcategory of the "middle-forms" (intermediate beings), which during the hellenistic period "increased in both Palestinian Judaism and that of the Diaspora."[21] By transference from other "forces" in Jewish and hellenistic literature, Torah became a cosmic force which existed before all else. An ontological Torah therefore is not primarily a revelatory text or tradition; rather, it is a mediating force, even *the* "mediator of creation and revelation between God and world."[22]

Lloyd Gaston keenly observes the impact of such elevated ideas of Torah:

> As soon as the Torah is identified with *wisdom,* then all nations are under the laws of creation, but as soon as wisdom is identified with *Torah,* then the nations must keep all the laws given to Israel without being part of the covenant God made with Israel.[23]

---

[19] Hengel, *Judaism and Hellenism*, 1. 169–75. According to Hengel, the aggrandizement of Torah is attributable to socio-historical factors, specifically the "controversy with Hellenism [that] made the Torah the centre point of Judaism" through the arousal of "zeal for the law" (1. 312).

[20] Whether חכמה in these texts may be truly labeled a hypostasis is of course debatable, but both Bugge and Hengel (for related but different reasons) have understood that Torah was thought of in this way. My thesis is not bound to the applicability of the term "hypostasis" to the Torah that Paul opposed.

[21] Hengel, *Judaism and Hellenism*, 1.155.

[22] Hengel, *Judaism and Hellenism*, 1.171 (emphasis removed). For more on Jewish mediator figures, see A. F. Segal, *Two Powers in Heaven: Early Rabbinic Reports About Christianity and Gnosticism* (SJLA 25; Leiden: Brill, 1977); H.-F. Weiss, *Untersuchungen zur Kosmologie des hellenistischen und palästinischen Judentums* (TU 97; Berlin: Akademie-Verlag, 1966); A. Chester, *Divine Revelation and Divine Titles in the Pentateuchal Targumim* (Tübingen: Mohr [Siebeck], 1986), and "Jewish Messianic Expectations and Mediatorial Figures and Pauline Christology," in *Paulus und das antike Judentum* (eds. M. Hengel and U. Heckel; Tübingen: Mohr [Siebeck], 1991) 17–89; J. Fossum, *The Name of God and the Angel of the Lord: Samaritan and Jewish Concepts of Intermediation and the Origin of Gnosticism* (WUNT 36; Tübingen: Mohr [Siebeck], 1985). G. F. Moore ("Intermediaries in Jewish Theology: Memra, Shekinah, Metatron," *HTR* 15 [1922] 41–85) argues against Memra and Shekinah as mediators in rabbinic texts.

[23] Gaston, *Paul and Torah*, 27.

This fact, coupled with the tradition that all the nations (גוים/ἔθνη) were offered the Torah before Sinai but Israel alone accepted it, makes difficult the situation of gentiles—like Paul's converts—who desire to be "righteous." Gaston finds most first-century Jewish texts envisioning Torah's condemnation of gentiles. Thus, whereas Torah is for Jews the expression of God's covenantal grace, for gentiles outside of the covenant "Torah as law functions in an exclusively negative way, to condemn."[24] Gentiles without circumcision could not rely on their status within the covenant, so Gaston reasons that they were prone to anxious scrupulosity. For gentiles, Torah, the Law, would have been a negative entity: "Those outside the covenant are completely subject to the Lordship of Sin and Death, who use the process of the powers administering the law. This is the Gentile predicament."[25] The Law was therefore threatening, an instrument of gentile oppression.

Although Gaston correctly perceives the problem of the gentile in early Jewish theology, and the role that heightened views of Torah played in the gentile problem, the final step in his Paul-and-the-Law theory is its fatal flaw: because the arguments in the epistles are directed to the gentile predicament under the Law, they *only* address the status of gentiles. He contends that Paul "has no quarrel with the Jewish understanding of Torah as it applies to Israel."[26] Paul only intended that gentile believers were free from Torah observance. To Gaston one may object that although Paul maintained the privileged status of Israel in history, he nonetheless argued emphatically, especially in Romans, for a universal plight of Jew and gentile that necessitated the universal solution, Christ, and for the equality of all people in Christ. Moreover, the Antioch incident narrated in Galatians 2 suggests that there were no barriers in Paul's mind. Thus, Gaston's radical distinction between Jew and gentile obligation is unwarranted.

1.2 The Eschatological Torah and its Critics

The thesis of this book may also be associated with those Pauline interpreters who have proposed that, like other early Jewish thinkers, Paul

---

[24] Gaston, *Paul and Torah*, 28.

[25] Gaston, *Paul and Torah*, 10.

[26] Gaston, *Paul and Torah*, 14; this contention is developed in "Israel's Misstep in the Eyes of Paul," 135–50.

envisioned an eschatological change in or replacement of Torah. W. D. Davies has been perhaps the most persistent advocate of the eschatological Torah, but such scholars as Schweitzer, Hans J. Schoeps and Peter Stuhlmacher have also explained Paul in terms of the eschatological replacement of the Sinai Torah. These scholars have perceived, in different ways, the tension in Paul between Torah and eschatology, that Christ has replaced Torah. Their fatal flaw has been to assume that Paul was generally consistent with early Jewish theology in believing that the Messiah would assume this role. As the critics of the theory have argued, there is simply no evidence for an early Jewish expectation of Torah's replacement. Moreover, an eschatological replacement of Torah is inconsistent with the doctrine of Torah's immutability. Therefore it is not necessary to rehabilitate the eschatological Torah theory as it has been presented by Davies, et al. But there is a kernel of truth here warranting a reformulation of the eschatological Torah theory that does justice both to early Jewish Torah theology and to Pauline discourse (see §1.2.6).[27]

1.2.1 Paul's Eschatological Mysticism

Albert Schweitzer is uniquely responsible for the eschatological interpretation of Paul necessary to eschatological Torah theories. The uniqueness of Schweitzer's perspective is found in his advocacy of Jewish apocalyptic eschatology as the center of Pauline theology, and his conception of Pauline mysticism.[28] Paul's "eschatological mysticism" means that while the outward characteristics of this age have

[27] Eschatological Torah theories get little or no notice in even the best analyses of Paul-and-Torah scholarship. For example, S. Westerholm's fine study, *Israel's Law and the Church's Faith: Paul and His Recent Interpreters* (Grand Rapids: Eerdmans, 1988), does not consider this approach to Paul-and-Torah, nor does Westerholm note the work of Davies and Stuhlmacher beyond the odd footnote. In J. Toew's exceptional survey, "The Law in Paul's Letter to the Romans: A Study of Romans 9.30–10.13" (Ph.D. diss., Northwestern University, 1977), Davies and Schoeps are well accounted for as the figureheads of the "quest for a more Jewish Paul," but Toews does not focus intently or critically on their presumption of the messianic Torah doctrine.

[28] Commenting on the exact relationship between Pauline mysticism, the sacraments, and eschatology, Schweitzer writes, "The one thing certain is that no other way of explanation is possible than that which leads from the circumference of his future hope to the central idea of his 'theology'" (*Paul and His Interpreters* [New York: Schocken, 1912] 243).

not changed, Christ's death and resurrection have inaugurated invisibly the age to come. The age to come is accessible to those "in Christ," through the Spirit. Both emphases are apparent in Schweitzer's thinking on Paul and the Law: Paul held to a Jewish traditional expectation of the eschatological abrogation of the Torah; Paul thought those "in Christ" were mystically free from the reign of the Law, even though they still lived in its domain.

Schweitzer's logic works like this: Judaism held that the Law would not be valid in the messianic Age (despite the fact that it was eternal), and since Paul believed the messianic age had dawned for those "in Christ," for those in Christ the Law was invalid. The special circumstance of the overlapping of ages between Christ's death and return results in the peculiarities and difficulties of Paul's understanding of Torah. He "assumes that, so long as the natural world endures, even down into the messianic period, angelic powers stand between man and God and render direct relations between the two impossible."[29] Because Christ's death and resurrection have dealt this world a mortal blow, these angelic powers have no dominion over, nor can they "accuse" before God, those "in Christ." The inverse is true as well: if one is under angelic control of some sort, then one cannot be in Christ.[30] The same thing could be said of the Law, for it "belongs to that natural world which lies under the dominion of the Angels."[31]

Schweitzer understood Gal 3:19 to mean that the Law was given by angels to subject humans to their rule:

> Why then the law? It was added because of transgressions (τῶν παραβάσεων χάριν προσετέθη), till the offspring should come to whom the promise had been made; and it was ordained by angels through an intermediary (διαταγεὶς δι' ἀγγέλων ἐν χειρὶ μεσίτου).

Submission to the Law, accepting its circumcision, is equated not with obedience to God but with submission to angelic dominion.[32] The

---

[29] Schweitzer, *Mysticism*, 10. See *Paul and His Interpreters*, 167, for this notion of the dominion of powers in W. Wrede.

[30] Schweitzer, *Mysticism*, 12–13.

[31] Schweitzer, *Mysticism*, 188.

[32] Schweitzer, *Mysticism*, 68–71. It seems more likely that Paul incorporated the idea of the angelic mediation of Torah as part of an antithesis between mediated and unmediated revelation. As a seer Paul had access to heavenly secrets, and as a Jew in

Law's dominion is coterminous with this world, so those who have ascended to a Christ-mysticism, and have thereby taken part in the "supernatural world," belong to a reality in which the Law is not valid.

If Torah is limited to "this present evil age" as Paul calls it (Gal 1:4), or the "natural world" in Schweitzer's terminology, then Torah does not endure into the eschatological age. Schweitzer assumed that in the messianic age the Law would no longer be valid: "That the Law comes to an end when the Messianic reign begins is for Jewish thought self-evident."[33] One might conclude from this that the Law is neither immutable, nor eternal. Schweitzer acknowledged this implication, but he rationalized it: "That the Law is eternal does not necessarily mean that it is of eternal application."[34] Although he perceived the "incompatibility of Law and eschatology," Schweitzer nevertheless assumed that for Paul the Law was eternal.[35] An eternal Law that is incompatible with eschatology borders on the oxymoronic. Schweitzer insightfully recognized that Paul's eschatology was incompatible with the Law. But he assumed that Paul could not have abandoned the Jewish idea of an eternal Torah and thus did not see that it was specifically the notion of the eternal Torah, rather than Torah itself, that Paul found incompatible. In contradistinction to Schweitzer, I read Paul as having denied the eternal Torah, one of the more pervasive axioms in early Jewish literature.

1.2.2 Christ as New Torah

W. D. Davies opposed Schweitzer's view that for Paul the Law was invalid for those who mystically experienced the messianic kingdom. Davies agreed that Paul believed he was living in the messianic age, and the Apostle shared the rabbinic belief that the Messiah would bring a new Torah:

> As far back as Jeremiah [31:33] we find the view that in the Messianic Age the Torah would be spontaneously obeyed by every individual.

Christ he communicated with God directly through the Spirit, so the mediated Torah revelation was by nature secondary. Torah was not the word spoken directly by God.

[33] Schweitzer, *Mysticism*, 69. "The supernatural character of the Kingdom therefore makes it in practice impossible for Late-Judaism to conceive of the Kingdom as the Kingdom of the Law" (*Mysticism*, 192; also see p.73).

[34] Schweitzer, *Mysticism*, 192.

[35] Schweitzer, *Mysticism*, 189.

So too in the pre-Christian pseudepigrapha it was taught that the Messiah when he came would be wise and an exponent of the Torah. . . . Later Rabbinic literature reveals the same attitude, and although those passages which explicitly speak of the Messiah as the bringer of a New Torah . . . are late, we cannot doubt that they reflect earlier beliefs, because there must have been controversies among the Rabbis as to the role of the Torah in the Messianic Age at all periods. . . . When the Rabbis taught, moreover, that the Messiah when he came would bring a new Law, they thought of that Law as new not in the sense that it would be contrary to the Law of Moses but that it would explain it more fully.[36]

Like Schweitzer, Davies thought Judaism expected the messianic age to bring some sort of change in Torah. But whereas Schweitzer argued that being "in Christ" invalidated the Law, despite the fact that Torah was eternal, Davies concluded that Paul's Christian life-style was still Pharisaic, so the Law could not have become indifferent to him.[37]

To verify his interpretation Davies searched for the expectation in early Jewish literature of a new or altered Torah in the age to come. The only texts that supported the idea where rabbinic, much later than the Pauline epistles. The most impressive text is based on Isa 26:2: "Open the gates, that the righteous nation which keeps faith may enter in." In Hebrew the last two words are שֹׁמֵר אֱמֻנִים, "(the one) keeping faith." In the *Yalqut* the words are understood as if they were שֶׁאָמַר אֲמֵנִים, "which say Amen." The comment to this verse has God seated, expounding a "new Torah" (תּוֹרָה חֲדָשָׁה), which would be given through the Messiah. Davies found here an "explicit reference to a Messianic Torah new in kind."[38] "New in kind" is important for Davies since the rest of the relevant texts concern changes in the Torah of the messianic age, or an increased ability in Torah observance. Because of the paucity and ambiguity of texts, Davies indecisively concluded that NT-era Judaism *may have* expected some sort of eschato-

---

[36] Davies, *Paul and Rabbinic Judaism* (4th ed.; Philadelphia: Fortress, 1980) 72.

[37] Davies, *Paul and Rabbinic Judaism*, 71.

[38] W. D. Davies, *The Setting of the Sermon on the Mount* (Cambridge: Cambridge University Press, 1964) 176–77. Except for updated material on Qumran, Davies' treatment of early Jewish eschatological Torah expectation in *The Setting of the Sermon on the Mount* replicates his *Torah in the Messianic Age and/or Age to Come* (JBLMS 7; Philadelphia: SBL, 1952).

logical change in Torah.[39] Somehow the immutability of Torah was unaffected.

Davies thought Paul interpreted Christ in the light of traditional Jewish notions of Torah. Paul had replaced Torah with Christ. This theory depended on the pre-Christian Jewish association of Wisdom, especially as it appears in Proverbs 1–8, with God's creation, and Torah. The first words of Genesis, בראשית, were related to Wisdom in Prov 8:22: "Yhwh possessed me ראשית of his ways." Also important is Prov 3:19: "Yhwh created the earth by wisdom (בחכמה)." These texts establish the link between Wisdom and creation, and the Mosaic Law is explicitly associated with Wisdom in Sir 24:23 and Bar 4:1. In the NT, Christ is identified with Wisdom explicitly in 1 Cor 1:24 ("Christ is the wisdom and power of God"), but the most important text is Col 1:15–20, which Davies took as Pauline.[40] Davies' point of reference is C. F. Burney's 1926 study that showed how these lines exhaust the range of interpretation of בראשית (LXX = ἐν ἀρχῇ): the preposition ב could mean "in, by, into" and ראשית could be "beginning, sum-total, head, first fruits."[41] By means of a ראשית/Wisdom linkage, the בראשית of Gen 1:1 is applied in Colossians to Christ. For Davies, the Christ/Wisdom association is, in effect, Christ equals Torah.[42]

What Davies thought he had accomplished, so I infer, was a precedent for Paul's Christ, the new Torah. The new Torah did not necessarily invalidate the Sinai Torah. Davies' model was the Matthean Christ who preached a new Torah yet did not defy the Mosaic Torah: "It would not be unnatural for Paul also to believe that loyalty to the new law of Christ did not involve disloyalty to the Torah of his fathers."[43] Jesus' words formed for Paul a Law of Christ, on which

[39] For example, see Davies, *The Setting of the Sermon on the Mount*, 170.

[40] Davies, *Paul and Rabbinic Judaism*, 151.

[41] C. F. Burney, "Christ as the Αρχη of Creation," *JTS* 27 (1926) 160–77; Davies, *Paul and Rabbinic Judaism*, 151–52, 172.

[42] The Wisdom/Torah material will be analyzed in greater depth, in support of different theses, in chapter 2. The goal here is to represent Davies' thinking on Paul's use of Wisdom language for Christ.

[43] Davies, *Paul and Rabbinic Judaism*, 73. For Jesus as the new Torah teacher in Matthew, see Davies, *The Setting of the Sermon on the Mount*, and the subsequent studies by D. C. Allison (*The New Moses: A Matthean Typology* [Minneapolis: Augsburg Fortress, 1993]) and T. L. Donaldson (*Jesus and the Mountain. A Study in Matthean Theology* [JSNTSup 8; Sheffield: JSOT, 1985]).

was based a Christian halakah.[44] And it was not just the words of Christ which comprised Paul's new Torah; it was also Christ himself: "In a real sense conformity to Christ, His teaching and His life, has taken the place for Paul of conformity to the Jewish Torah."[45] Unfortunately for Davies, using Matthew to verify Paul is not as convincing as establishing these ideas in the Pauline corpus.

Despite the holes in his framework, Davies was on the right path in seeing Christ as the eschatological replacement of Torah. But Davies made a significant error in insisting on the coexistence in Pauline theology of the Mosaic Torah and the new Torah. The relationship between the two Torahs is hazy; the role of Christ as Torah appears unimportant. On the other hand, if the Mosaic Torah is eschatologically abrogated, and Christ is the eschatological revelation, written on the hearts of those "in Christ," the idea of a new Torah appears to be more consequential. This does not work for Davies because he views the Mosaic Torah as an important part of the life of the early Jesus-movement, even in the communities of Paul the Christian Pharisee. Without the Torah relevant and informing the Pauline communitites, in Davies' eyes Paul looks too much like an antinomian, anti-Jewish propagandist. This un-Jewish Paul is unacceptable to Davies.

1.2.3 Paul's Misunderstanding of Torah

Hans Joachim Schoeps did not devote much energy developing or defending the notion of an eschatological Torah in early Judaism. But he did repeat the belief that Paul represented Jewish eschatology about the status of the Torah in the age to come. Paul's conception of the Law stems from his eschatology, and only within this context does it make sense.[46] Schoeps accepted Schweitzer's position on the three ages (found in some rabbinic material): Paul believed he was living in the final, messianic age, which followed the age of Torah, which in turn followed the age that Schoeps labeled "*Tohuwabohu*" (= תהו ובהו; Gen 1:2). Each period lasted 2,000 years. In Schweitzer's mind it was logical to conclude that, since the Mosaic period had ended, the Law's reign had ended as well. Schoeps' language repeated the boldness with

---

[44] Davies, *Paul and Rabbinic Judaism*, 144.

[45] Davies, *Paul and Rabbinic Judaism*, 148.

[46] H. J. Schoeps, *Paul: The Theology of the Apostle in the Light of Jewish Religious History* (Philadelphia: Westminster, 1961) 168–73.

which Schweitzer expressed himself on this point: "My judgment is that Rom. 10:4 is an absolutely exact inference from the standpoint of Jewish eschatological thought."[47] For Paul the rabbi the cessation of the law was an obvious inference from Jesus' resurrection; he differed from other rabbis only in identifying Jesus as Messiah. In asserting the Law's cessation Schoeps deviated from Davies. On the other hand, he followed Davies in finding in Paul a new Torah.[48]

Anticipating later trends in Pauline scholarship, Schoeps thought Paul argued backwards from Jesus' identity as Messiah to the cessation of the Law. In other words, it was not the Law itself that prompted Paul to argue as he did, but Jesus' messiahship: "The retrospective way of thought is the real axis of his argument. Not the meaning of scripture, but Christ is the *a priori* for his judgment of the law." No other Jew could contend that Torah was a "Law unto death" (Rom 8:2–3; Gal 3:21).[49] But Paul could argue in this manner because he had assumed what he meant to prove: "For any solution apart from faith in Jesus Christ he excludes from the start."[50] Torah and Christ were competing authorities, so Torah's redemptive inadequacy had to be emphasized. Because of his deep conviction that the "Messianic age" had arrived, Paul constructed an argument based on the "features of the law which indicated that it would be cancelled in the Messianic age."[51] Schoeps' Paul was a poor exegete who impetuously attributed Torah to the angels, violated the clear sense of scripture, misunderstood the inherent connection of Law and covenant, and misguidedly used the Torah to invalidate itself.

1.2.4 The Zion Torah.

Like Davies, Peter Stuhlmacher associates Paul's idea of Torah with the Matthean Jesus. Paul mirrors the Sermon on the Mount's perspective,

---

[47] Schoeps, *Paul*, 172.

[48] Schoeps, *Paul*, 172–73. Both Davies and Schoeps point to the 17th-century Sabbatians as a Jewish messianic movement with striking parallels to early Christianity, particularly a denial of the validity of the Law correlative to what appears in Paul. See Davies, "From Schweitzer to Scholem: Reflections on Sabbatai Svi," *JBL* 95 (1976) 529–58.

[49] Schoeps, *Paul*, 175.

[50] Schoeps, *Paul*, 187.

[51] Schoeps, *Paul*, 200–201. Unfortunately, Schoeps does not offer the texts to support the eschatological abrogation of Torah.

in which Christ's love replaces Pharisaic purity. Paul is therefore not an antinomian. For Stuhlmacher the Law of Christ is an end to the Mosaic Law (Rom 10:4), but this is understood in a limited way: the "cultic Torah" is "fulfilled and abolished."[52] More importantly, Stuhlmacher builds upon Hartmut Gese's "Zion Torah." The Zion Torah is the eschatological counterpart of the Sinai revelation. Mt. Zion, "the world mountain," eschatologically replaced Sinai as the locus of revelation, and "Israel has been replaced by all the peoples."[53] Gese's scenario parallels what other scholars term "universalism," the idea that in the eschatological age Israel's special status as God's people will be extended to the non-Jewish nations.[54] Isa 2:2–4 (// Mic 4:1–4) contains most of the components of Gese's Zion Torah:

> It shall come to pass in the latter days that the mountain of the house of the Lord shall be established as the highest of the mountains, and shall be raised above the hills; and all the nations shall flow to it, and many peoples shall come, and say: "Come, let us go up to the mountain of the Lord, to the house of the God of Jacob; that he may teach us his ways and that we may walk in his paths." For out of Zion shall go forth the law, and the word of the Lord from Jerusalem. He shall judge between the nations, and shall decide for many peoples; and they shall beat their swords into plowshares, and their spears into

[52] P. Stuhlmacher, "Paul's Understanding of the Law in the Letter to the Romans," *SEÅ* 50 (1985) 100–101.

[53] H. Gese, "The Law," *Essays on Biblical Theology* (Minneapolis: Augsburg, 1981) 83. It should be noted that the context of Gese and Stuhlmacher's Zion Torah is pan-biblical theology, not strictly early Jewish expectation.

[54] For this sense of "universalism," see Schweitzer, *Mysticism*; more recently, S. McKnight, *A Light among the Gentiles: Jewish Missionary Activity in the Second Temple Period* (Minneapolis: Fortress, 1991) 13–14; A. F. Segal, "Universalism in Judaism and Christianity," *Paul in His Hellenistic Context* (ed. T. Engberg-Pederson; Minneapolis: Augsburg Fortress, 1995) 1–29; M. Nanos, *The Mystery of Romans* (Minneapolis: Augsburg Fortress, 1996). Pauline theology is built upon Isaianic Zion eschatology, which includes universalism and revelation. Other elements of Zion eschatology: Mt. Zion was the eschatological counterpart of both the paradise garden of Genesis 2–3, the place of God's throne (*Endzeit/Urzeit* typology) and Sinai, the mountain of revelation (historical eschatological typology). "Zion eschatology" is also used by Donaldson (*Jesus and the Mountain*; "Proselytes or 'Righteous Gentiles'? The Status of Gentiles in Eschatological Pilgrimage Patterns of Thought," *JSP* 7 [1990] 3–27). I use it specifically to avoid the abstract, non-descriptive "universalism," not to accept Donaldson's explication of the biblical Zion tradition.

pruning hooks; nation shall not lift up sword against nation, neither shall they learn war any more.[55]

Gese also identifies as Zion Torah texts the "statutes (חֻקִּים) not good" of Ezek 20:25–26, which establish that the Sinai revelation is relational and dynamic, rather than invariable; the new covenant written on the heart of Jer 31:31–34; the new heart and new spirit of Ezek 36:26–27; the eschatological feast "for all peoples" on "this mountain" (Isa 25:6). Finally, for Gese Psalm 50 represents a "qualitative change in Torah," a denial of the Sinai Torah's blood sacrifices in favor of the תודה ("thank-offering"), from which Gese derives the idea of an eschatological *todah*-meal: following the critique of sacrifices, there is the command to "sacrifice to God a תודה" (Ps 50:14). The climax of Psalm 50 again exalts the תודה:

> He who brings תודה as his sacrifice honors me;
> to him who orders his way aright I will show the salvation of God.
> (Ps 50:23)

This תודה is combined with the eschatological feast of Isa 25:6, although there is no mention of תודה: "On this mountain the Lord of hosts will make for all peoples a feast."[56]

Stuhlmacher's version of the Zion Torah is fourfold: (1) Israel can adequately observe Torah only through a Spirit-wrought personal transformation and new creation; (2) Israel would one day dwell in peace and walk in righteousness to God's statutes; (3) there would be a new revelation of the Torah that would replace—in some vague, seemingly indefinable sense—the Sinai Torah; (4) Israel would experience their peaceful existence under the Messiah's rule in Jerusalem, bound together by the new Torah, the Zion revelation.[57] The precise relation-

---

[55] All biblical quotations are from the RSV.

[56] Gese, "Law," 82–83; see also "Psalm 50 und das alttestamentliche Gesetzesverständnis," *Rechtfertigung* (ed. J. Friedman, W. Pöhlmann, and P. Stuhlmacher; Tübingen: Mohr, Göttingen: Vandenhoeck und Ruprecht, 1976) 57–77.

[57] P. Stuhlmacher, *Biblische Theologie des Neuen Testaments* (2 vols.; Göttingen: Vandenhoeck und Ruprecht, 1992) 1. 257. The section "Das Gesetz bei Paulus" (253–68) clarifies the Zion Torah theory as it relates to Paul. It also contains Stuhlmacher's evaluation of other Torah theologies in the milieu. Although Stuhlmacher notes Räisänen's negative analysis of the Zion Torah theory (see below), he does not respond to Räisänen.

ship between the Sinai and Zion Torahs remains as hazy in Stuhl-macher as it was in Gese's paradox: "The Sinai revelation has become the eschatological Zion revelation, and the Torah of Sinai and that of Zion are different."[58] But the salient point of the Zion Torah is clear: Paul received a biblical and exegetical tradition expecting an eschato-logical transformation of the Mosaic Torah, which he saw fulfilled in Christ. "The 'Torah of Christ' is the Zion Torah."[59]

The Zion Torah theory obviously parallels Davies' conception of a new Torah, but there is a notable difference in approach. Davies had no desire to drive a wedge between Paul and Pharisaic Judaism. He searched the intertestamental and rabbinic literature for signs of conti-nuity between Paul and his predecessors. His *Paul and Rabbinic Judaism* is an attempt to use rabbinic or Pharisaic material to shed light on Paulinism, rather than using it as a legalistic foil. Gese and Stuhlmacher view Jesus and Paul, not the Pharisees, as the legitimate heirs of the Hebrew prophets. They identify two trajectories in first century Jewish theology: (1) the eschatological, which emphasized a future transformation of God's revelation; and (2) the cosmic, which looked to the Sinai Torah as the embodiment of God's eternal, immutable Law. The second trajectory is represented by the Pharisees. Under their influence early Jewish theology moved away from the Zion Torah—the expectation of an eschatological change in Torah itself became a hope in an increased capacity to observe the Sinai Torah.[60] The Pharisees are the bogeymen, while Paul simply opposed the bad use of the Law.[61] His attitude toward Torah was consistent with the rest of the NT, including Jesus.

---

[58] Gese, "Law," 82.

[59] P. Stuhlmacher, "The Law as a Topic of Biblical Theology," *Reconciliation, Law, and Righteousness: Essays in Biblical Theology* (Philadelphia: Fortress, 1986) 126.

[60] Stuhlmacher points to the *Book of Jubilees* and the *Damascus Document* as examples of early Jewish writings that betray some expansion of the Sinai Torah, yet do not contain a new Torah eschatology. He identifies in *Jubilees* a refrain that later will become common in "Pharisaic" Judaism: "In Jubilees 1 the promise of Ezek. 36:22–28 is applied to the renewal of the righteous to full obedience to the torah and to a true knowledge of God which is associated with the day of new creation" ("The Law as a Topic of Biblical Theology," 116).

[61] This portrayal of the first-century Pharisees is increasingly unacceptable for two

1.2.5 The Critics

Robert Banks and Heikki Räisänen have written thorough and devastating critiques of the eschatological Torah theories. Both critiques appeal to the plain meaning or authorial intent of the main biblical texts. For example, Banks argues that since תורה in First Isaiah (and Jeremiah) consistently refers to the prophetic message (Isa 1:10; 8:16, 20; 30:9), it should be so interpreted in Isa 2:3: the תורה that would "go out from Zion" is the prophetic word rather than an eschatological Torah.[62] Räisänen disputes the use of Jer 31:31–34 and Ezek 36:24–28 because neither text refers to the abrogation of Torah.[63]

In Banks' estimation, Davies' reliance on rabbinic texts exposes the lack of evidence for a new Torah expectation in pre-rabbinic literature. Moreover, an eschatological change in Torah runs contrary to a rabbinic dogma: "the rabbinic writings clearly presuppose the eternal validity of the Law throughout."[64] Because nearly all of Davies' texts are fraught with dating or interpretive difficulties, Banks dismisses Davies' assertion that there are some rabbinic texts that indicate a partial modification or abrogation of Torah. For example, *Lev. Rab.* 9:7

---

reasons: (1) E. P. Sanders has convincingly argued that German Lutheran portrayals of legalistic Pharisaic Judaism have actually been caricatures, stimulated by reformation images of Catholicism; (2) Pharisaism, and its link to Rabbinic Judaism, is increasingly difficult to characterize adequately—what was the nature of Pharisaism, and what power did the Pharisees exercise in emerging rabbinism? A. F. Segal (*Paul the Convert* [New Haven: Yale University Press, 1990]) makes the case for Paul as the best evidence for Pharisaism in the first century, not its foil.

[62] R. Banks, "The Eschatological Role of the Law in Pre- and Post-Christian Jewish Thought," *Reconciliation and Hope* (ed. R. Banks; Exeter: Paternoster, 1974) 174–75. The targets of Banks' critique are J. Jocz, *The Jewish People and Jesus Christ* (London: SPCK, 1949) 155–58; H. Teeple, "The Future of Law in Judaism," *The Mosaic Eschatological Prophet* (SBLMS 10; Philadelphia: Society of Biblical Literature, 1957) 14–28; and R. Longenecker, "The End of Nomism," *Paul, Apostle of Liberty* (New York: Harper and Row, 1964) 128–55.

[63] H. Räisänen, "Zion Torah and Biblical Theology: Thoughts on a Tübingen Theory," *Jesus, Paul and Torah* (JSNTSup 43; Sheffield: Sheffield Academic, 1992) 231–33.

[64] Banks, "Eschatological Role of the Law," 175. Banks cites *Exod. Rab.* 33:7 for the eternal validity of Torah as a whole, *Exod. Rab.* 6:1 and *Lev. Rab.* 19:2 for the words and letters. Banks also notes the presence of the "eternal Torah" in various intertestamental writings (see §3.1).

asserts that all sacrifices and prayers, save the thanksgiving, are to be annulled in the age to come. Banks views this text as too late to be of consequence. Furthermore, rather than denying the perpetuity of other rites, it attests to the surpassing importance of the thanksgiving prayer.[65] The rabbinic comment on Deut 17:18 in *Sifre* 160 is interesting: ". . . why does Scripture say, 'a copy of this law'? Because in the future it will be changed."[66] Banks dismisses this in favor of the "earlier" parallel passage in *t. Sanh* 4:4, which attests to a "change" in the script rather than in the content of Torah.[67] *Qoh. Rab.* 11:8 says that "the Torah which a man learns in this world is vanity compared with the Messiah's Torah," but Banks argues that the text refers to new insight into the Mosaic Torah, rather than a new Torah.[68] Since Davies' rabbinic texts are subject to other interpretations, his theory therefore "loses most of its plausibility when a different construction is placed upon them."[69]

At least one of Davies' texts is prematurely dismissed: "With joy you will draw water from the wells of salvation" (Isa 12:3). The MT and targumic versions read as follows:

ושאבתם מים בששׂן ממעיני הישׁועה (MT)

ותקבלון אלפן חדת בחדוא מבחירי צדקא (targum)[70]

---

[65] Banks, "Eschatological Role of the Law," 177–78.

[66] The full text: "'And it shall be, when he sitteth upon the throne of his kingdom'— if he does all that has been said here in this matter, he is worthy of sitting on the throne of his kingdom—'that he shall write him'—for himself, and not pride himself on that of his ancestors—'a copy (of this law)' (17:18): This can refer only to Deuteronomy; whence do we learn that this includes also the rest of the words of the Torah? From the following 'To keep all the words of this law and these statutes, to do them' (17:19). If so, why does Scripture say, 'a copy of this law'? Because in the future it will be changed. Others say: When reading before the assemblage, only the Book of Deuteronomy should be read" (Hammer, tr., *Sifre*, 193).

[67] Banks, "Eschatological Role of the Law," 178. Banks should not dismiss *Sifre Deut* 160 without asking whether the royal context of Deut 17:18—the *future* king—was read as messianic. Thus the difference in the two rabbinic texts may reflect a dispute over whether Deut 17:18 is messianic, and *Sifre Deut* 160 may genuinely express a messianic Torah.

[68] Banks, "Eschatological Role of the Law," 183.

[69] Banks, "Eschatological Role of the Law," 185.

[70] The text is from A. Sperber, *The Bible in Aramaic: The Latter Prophets according to Targum Jonathan* (reprinted ed.; Leiden: Brill, 1992) 27.

The targum can be rendered as, "With joy you will receive new teaching (אלפן חדת) from the chosen righteous."[71] David Daube explained אלפן חדת as a "better Law, a new and final revelation."[72] Banks accepts that the targum is "based on first-century traditions,"[73] but he contends that since the final phrase (בחירי צדקא) "must" be referring "to a group rather than a single individual," אלפן cannot be equivalent to Torah.[74] Reading בחירי as a plural is problematic, as Davies acknowledges.[75] But the targum, as an interpretation of Isaiah's "water from the wells of salvation," undoubtedly reflects the figurative relationship in early Jewish literature between well/water and Torah.[76] Banks overlooks this interpretive tradition, and perhaps for this reason reads the targum through minimalist lenses. At the very least this targum exhibits an expectation of eschatological instruction.

Banks concludes that since Davies' case is made by means of a tendentious use of rabbinic literature that post-dates the NT by centuries, and in which there is no evidence for anything other than a "new interpretation of the old Torah," a new Torah expectation in first-century Jewish theology is untenable.[77] For Banks, the eternal nature of the Torah is clearly held in biblical texts and subsequent tradition.[78]

The bulk of Räisänen's analysis of the "Zion Torah" is devoted to showing how the theory is an artificial construction superimposed onto the Hebrew Bible, rather than an idea that appears when the key

[71] My translation, maintaining the clausal sequence of the RSV.

[72] D. Daube, "ἐξουσία in Mark 1.22 and 27," *JTS* 39 (1938) 55; cited by Davies, *Setting of the Sermon on the Mount*, 174 and n. 1.

[73] R. Banks, *Jesus and the Law in the Synoptic Tradition* (SNTSMS 28; Cambridge: Cambridge University Press, 1975) 78.

[74] Banks, "Eschatological Role of the Law," 183.

[75] It is possible that בחירי צדקא meant, "my chosen, the righteous one," although this depends on reading צדקא as a defective form of צדיקא—but see Sperber's variants (*The Bible In Aramaic*, 27).

[76] For example, CD 6:3–4, referring to the "well which the princes dug" (Num 21:18): "The well is the Torah." John 4:10–11 should also be considered here: If the woman had known who Jesus was, "you would have asked him, and he would have given you living water." See M. Fishbane, "The Well of Living Water: A Biblical Motif and its Ancient Transformations," in *Sha'arei Talmon* (ed. M. Fishbane and E. Tov with W. Fields; Winona Lake, IN: Eisenbrauns, 1992) 3–16.

[77] Banks, "Eschatological Role of the Law," 185.

[78] See Banks' chapter, "The Law—Eternal or Provisional?" in *Jesus and the Law*, 65–85.

texts are interpreted naturally. The Zion Torah *topoi* (reference to Torah, criticisms of Torah, Zion, nations, spirit, todah-meal, future, annihilation of death) do not appear together in any one text.[79] Moreover, the prophetic critique of the cult did not include the expectation of another revelation altering or replacing the Sinai Torah. Räisänen contends that Jer 31:31–34 does not refer to a change in Torah, but in a change in "people's attitude to God's law."[80] The Torah is not Jeremiah's problem, so there is no reason to read its abrogation into the text. It is the same way with Ezek 36:25–27: the people are renewed by means of a "new heart" and "new spirit," but there is no suggestion of a new Torah.[81] The "statutes not good" of Ezek 20:25 do not derive from Torah, so this text cannot support the Zion Torah theory.

Räisänen raises other issues that do not overwhelm the Zion Torah theory, but his final reproach is potentially devastating for my thesis: even if there were a strong biblical Zion Torah tradition, there is absolutely no indication that Paul accessed it. If the Zion Torah was well known, would Paul not have saved himself the grief of his readers' misunderstanding by unequivocally citing the tradition? Räisänen is adamant that Paul did not refer to or employ any of Gese and Stuhlmacher's Zion Torah texts; Jer 31:31–34 is cited only in Heb 8:7–13 and 10:16–18, but never in the accepted Pauline corpus.[82] Räisänen specifically denies the presence of Jer 31:31–34 in 2 Corinthians 3: "Paul did *not* derive his theology of the law from the promise of the new covenant in Jer 31."[83] Thus the Zion Torah theory has not explained or provided the background for Paul's view of Torah. If anything, Paul represents a break in the theological characterization of Torah rather than its renewal.[84]

1.2.6 Reprise: the Antitheses of the Ages

Banks and Räisänen have sufficiently rebuffed the notion of an eschatological Torah in early Jewish literature. I do not think one can still

---

[79] Räisänen, "Zion Torah," 241–43.

[80] Räisänen, "Zion Torah," 231.

[81] Räisänen, "Zion Torah," 233.

[82] H. Räisänen, *Paul and the Law* (2nd ed.; WUNT 29; Tübingen: Mohr [Siebeck], 1987) 240–45. Räisänen admits, however, that there may be aspects of Jer 31:31–34 present in NT eucharistic traditions, but he views the issue as unsettled.

[83] Räisänen, *Paul and the Law*, 245.

[84] Räisänen, "Zion Torah," 251.

argue with any persuasion that, in presenting his view of Torah, Paul appealed to a tradition in which there was the expectation of the Mosaic Torah's transformation or annulment. For Torah's changed status there is a dearth of evidence in biblical and post-biblical literature.[85] So why even introduce the idea if only to bury it? I think Davies and others with similar theories, and especially Gese and Stuhlmacher, have been on the right track, but have approached the issue from an angle that only leads to an impasse. The new Torah theorists have heretofore considered Paul to have been *continuing* what has proven to be a phantom tradition. And they have judged that Paul accepted the eternal Torah doctrine. I propose that Paul understood Christ as the eschatological antitype of the Sinai Torah, and the antithesis to the eternal Torah. An eternal Torah cannot be replaced, so Paul placed temporal limitations on the Sinai Torah: it belonged to this age, whereas the "Zion Torah"—Christ and/or the gospel—is God's primordial creative word and eschatological revelation. Paul transferred to Christ, the new Torah, the cosmic roles that were otherwise assigned in early Jewish theology to the Mosaic Torah.

"Antithesis" is a strong term, but it is appropriate for Paul's style (e.g., 2 Cor 3:6) and his theology. Unlike Schweitzer, Davies, Schoeps, and others, I am not proposing that Paul's perplexing evaluation of the Law is attributable to ideas inherent in early Jewish theology.[86] The scholars who have attempted to find in Paul's view of Torah the flower of an idea budding in early Jewish texts have not succeeded because they conceived of a linear development in the theology of Torah from the Hebrew Bible, through the intertestamental literature, to Paul. Paul's role in the development, however, was dialectical rather than evolutionary. He was not a passive heir to biblical or post-biblical tradition. As Räisänen contends, Paul's position on the Law is a break in the tradition.

---

[85] I am not including in this "dearth" the so-called "rewritten Bible" (e.g., *Jubilees*, *Genesis Apocryphon*) or the *Temple Scroll* (see §3.3). These writings play no role in Davies' new Torah theory, although I think analysis of them might yield insight into the sufficiency of the Mosaic Torah in pre-rabbinic Judaism.

[86] The advocates of the Zion Torah theory at least acknowledge competing theological traditions in early Jewish texts. Stuhlmacher in particular recognizes a problem in the presence in the later biblical books of both a Zion Torah expectation that includes the notion of the Sinai Torah's provisional nature, and a tradition of Torah as a "comprehensive, eternal order of creation" ("The Law as a Topic of Biblical Theology," 116).

I noted that most of Banks' and Räisänen's arguments against eschatological Torah theories were based on the substantial difference between what the biblical texts vital to these theories were intended to mean and what they meant in the theory. Both scholars maintain that the key eschatological Torah texts (Jer 31:31–34; Ezek 36:25–26; Isa 2:2–4) did not mean what the eschatological Torah theorists say they meant. Furthermore, Räisänen contends that Gese and Stuhlmacher are wrong because the texts they cite in support of their theory were never used by Paul to establish or verify his view of the Law. These objections are not the end of the matter. Räisänen retrojects modern standards of meaning onto ancient texts that do not share these standards. There is a sense in which theories like the Zion Torah are legitimate, despite the fact that the key texts, if analyzed according to their historical setting and intended meaning, as well as their relationship to one another, do not yield the theory. This legitimacy rests not with the intention of an authored text but with its reception by early Jewish readers.

Räisänen's only reflection on Paul's reception of the Zion Torah texts is that Paul did not cite them. He denies, for example, that Paul used Jer 31:31–34 and Ezek 36:25–27 in 2 Corinthians 3. I will reassert the presence and importance of these prophetic texts for Paul in chapter 6, and I will suggest that Paul alluded to the Sinai/Zion polarity in different ways. But my point here is not just that Paul did in fact use these texts. As the recipient of the traditions and as the creator of new textual relationships among the received traditions, Paul transcends any of the constraints the intended meaning of Isa 2:2–5 (or any of the other "Zion Torah" texts) may place upon him. Paul did not receive Isa 2:2–5 alone, so this text does not demand Paul's undivided exegetical attention. Paul receives the many texts as one.

Biblical authors and editors were in some sense aware of being part of the growth of the biblical tradition, primarily because of their conscious intertextual relationship to their received sacred literary tradition. On the other hand, the individual books could not have been intended to be included in the sacred collection as it emerged later. Even if authors were convinced that their writings were authoritative for their religious communities, they could not have known with which other documents, composed from what theological perspective, their compositions would be read. Lectionaries and other collections by nature skew a text. And individual books themselves take on a new life, often irrespective of authorial intent, within the sacred collection. The authorial voice is transformed when it becomes part of the choir; it takes part in the aesthetic of the whole. For example, the Deuteronomic tradition may be the dominant canonical voice of Israel's covenantal relationship with Yhwh, but it is not the only voice. The Psalter, the literary prophets and the Chronicler (not to mention the NT) modify the readers' perception of that relationship, and therefore the Deuteronomic writings are not read and interpreted as they were intended. Thus the unique Deuteronomic story of King David becomes part of the biblical story of David. The individual writings and theological traditions are not robbed of their uniqueness by their place in the sacred collection, but their autonomy in conveying their agendas is transformed. The ideological force of the individual book is subverted by its inclusion in the collection, and the reader is thereby liberated (in a sense) from a theological monolith. Individual theologies are interpreted in the light of each other; although some are privileged, no one text or book is autonomous.

For Paul this means that the boundary within which he exegetes is the whole of his sacred literature, not Jeremiah as it was intended. Paul may therefore interpret the "new covenant" of Jer 31:31–34 in relationship to the "new thing" of Isa 43:19 (also 42:9; 48:6), rather than its context in Jeremiah. Thus his exegesis is concerned with verses rather than books.[87] Although justified from a historical-critical perspective, Räisänen's negative evaluation of the Zion Torah is irrelevant if Paul in fact received the Zion Torah texts as Gese and Stuhlmacher have presented them.

1.3 An Intertextual Approach to Paul-and-Torah

In the context of the spate of studies emerging to advance our understanding of Paul's use and interpretation of biblical texts, this book is intended as an intertextual analysis of Paul's Torah theology in the light of other early Jewish Torah theologies.[88] "Intertextual" here

---

[87] J. L. Kugel remarks that midrash is exegesis of verses, not books ("Two Introductions to Midrash," in *Midrash and Literature* [ed. G. Hartman and S. Budick; New Haven: Yale University Press, 1986] 93).

[88] For the nature of Pauline citations see especially D-A. Koch, *Die Schrift als Zeuge*

refers to the impact of authors' interpretation of specific, identifiable biblical texts on their composition. By this I do not mean that items of interpreted scripture in a later text were the independent exegetical production of the author or editor. Early Jewish exegetes (including Paul) were heirs to an interpretive tradition that extends back into the biblical texts themselves.[89] The point, rather, is simply that biblical interpretation influenced the structure, language and imagery of later biblical and post-biblical texts. Michael Fishbane refers to the "creative recombination" and "complex transformations" of "earlier words or *topoi*" from biblical texts;[90] this is the defining characteristic of biblical intertextuality. Although scholars regularly recognize the presence of biblical lemmata in Pauline texts in the form of explicit citations or verbal fragments, I am aware of no other study of Paul-and-Torah that focuses on intertextuality.

Coined by Julia Kristeva, "intertextuality" is borrowed from modern literary theory. Used loosely it can mean "all the possible relations that can be established between texts," but "writers who use the term and concept of intertextuality generally imply trouble and disturbance in textual relations."[91] Literary intertextuality presumes that

---

des Evangeliums (BZHT 69; Tübingen: Mohr [Siebeck], 1986), and C. D. Stanley, *Paul and the Language of Scripture* (SNTSMS 69; Cambridge: Cambridge University Press, 1992). For the characteristics of Paul's biblical interpretation see R. B. Hays, *Echoes of Scripture in the Letters of Paul* (New Haven: Yale University Press, 1989), and C. Stockhausen, "2 Corinthians and the Principles of Pauline Exegesis," in *Paul and the Scriptures of Israel* (ed. C. A. Evans and J. A. Sanders; JSNTSup 83; SSEJC 1; Sheffield: JSOT, 1993) 143–64. Although it is only a superficial study of Pauline biblical interpretation, T. H. Lim's *Holy Scripture in the Qumran Commentaries and Pauline Letters* (Oxford: Clarendon, 1997) contains some important methodological proposals. D. I. Brewer (*Techniques and Assumptions in Jewish Exegesis before 70 CE* [SAJ 30; Tübingen: Mohr [Siebeck], 1992]) uses rabbinic material to depict the nature of pre-70 exegesis, so his conclusions are tenuous.

[89] The idea that exegetical traditions are embedded in the Hebrew Bible can be traced at least to S. Sandmel, "The Haggadah within Scripture," *JBL* 80 (1961) 105–22. See especially M. Fishbane, *Biblical Interpretation in Ancient Israel* (Oxford: Clarendon, 1985); *The Garments of Torah* (Bloomington: Indiana University, 1989) 3–18. The interpretive tradition includes the *targumim*, rewritten biblical narratives, the Qumran scrolls, early Jewish apocalypses, and the NT.

[90] Fishbane, *Biblical Interpretation in Ancient Israel*, 283. Fishbane is here characterizing inner-biblical "aggadic exegesis," but his words fit the post-biblical phenomenon well.

[91] P. D. Miscall, "Isaiah: New Heavens, New Earth, New Book," in *Reading*

every text is formed by every previous text, and that the relationship between authors and their literary precursors is tension-filled because of the predilection (however unwittingly) of authors to subvert prior texts.[92] This study is focused on *intended* intertextuality in Pauline discourse, so the imposition of a modern literary meta-theory or super-structure (whether Freudian, deconstructionist or structuralist) is obtrusive.[93] In contrast to its literary counterpart, which is often attuned to authors' blindness to the influence of previous texts, studies of biblical intertextuality examine texts that are self-consciously composed to recall and enlist, for various purposes, specific sacred intertexts. Studies of the place of biblical texts in Pauline discourse typically dwell on what Paul has done *with* rather than *to* his intertext; thus intertextual dissonance has not been part of the vocabulary. On the other hand, there is tension between unsympathetic readings of Paul (e.g., Schoeps, Räisänen) that accentuate Paul's subversion of the intended meaning of the biblical texts he enlists, and overly sympathetic readings that verge on rationalization of their hero's handling of the sacred text. Both extremes are to be avoided in this study.

Biblical intertextuality is also characterized by its fixed boundaries. It is therefore formalist in the sense that there are boundaries of influence, a relatively fixed body of sacred literature. Thus interpretation as composition takes place within a grid of "received" texts that are potentially (however artificially) interrelated. In this respect the proposed compositional model is at odds with historical-critical sensibilities. An insightful arbiter of the critical and post-critical, Daniel Boyarin summarizes the tension between the rival interpretive models: the "formalist model" views "literature as occupying an autonomous ontological realm, divorced from and 'above' the material and social

---

between Texts: Intertextuality and the Hebrew Bible (ed. D. Nolan Fewell; Louisville: Westminster John Knox, 1992) 44. For the significant distinctions between literary intertextual theory and the appropriation of "intertextuality" in biblical studies, see especially T. K. Beal, "Ideology and Intertextuality: Surplus of Meaning and Controlling the Means of Production," 27–39 in the same volume, and Hays, *Echoes of Scripture*, 1–33.

[92] This tendency among poets is behind H. Bloom's postulate of the "anxiety of influence" (see *The Anxiety of Influence* [New York: Oxford University Press, 1973]; *A Map of Misreading* [New York: Oxford University Press, 1975]; *Agon: Towards a Theory of Revisionism* [New York: Oxford University Press, 1982]).

[93] The *"antithesis of the ages"* denotes Paul's preference for antipodal structures rather than my own.

conditions of its production." The "historicist model," on the other hand, "understands the text to be wholly determined by and to be a reflection of its historical circumstances."[94] Because these are extremes, biblical intertextuality does not fit comfortably in either model. Although this study is historical-critical in nature, it intersects with literary intertextuality as nodes within post-critical hermeneutics. The intersection is apparent at two points. First, my intention is to focus solely on the relationship between texts rather than texts as clues in a historical reconstruction of the environment of Paulinism.[95] Secondly, I recognize an irony in that the status of sacred paradigmatic texts in early Jewish theology comes at the expense of their autonomy. The post-biblical reappropriation of biblical words and *topoi* is not necessarily consistent with their authorially intended meaning. As the Pauline studies herein show, intertextuality among biblical texts is often the unintended product of their juxtaposition within the collection of sacred literature. Biblical intertextuality is therefore attuned to relationships between texts that were not anticipated by their authors.

"Biblical intertextuality" is my covering term for a range of studies devoted to "the use of the Old Testament in the New Testament," "inner-biblical exegesis," "aggadic exegesis," and "midrash."[96] The labels applied to biblical and post-biblical intertextuality are still debated because the proposed terms are either limited to one body of literature, or perhaps should be.[97] The crux of the problem is adopting

---

[94] D. Boyarin, *Intertextuality and the Reading of Midrash* (Bloomington: Indiana University Press, 1990) 117.

[95] This is not to suggest that there is no theological development within the Pauline corpus, or that Paul could not clarify in Romans what was misunderstood or potentially scandalous in Galatians.

[96] "Inner-biblical exegesis" is Fishbane's label for exegetical traditions embedded in the Hebrew Bible. "Aggadic" or "haggadic exegesis" is differentiated from restrained legal "halakic exegesis." The haggadic is characterized by its attention to all the possible relationships between texts, and its incorporation of extra-biblical traditions to explicate biblical texts.

[97] J. Neusner's often cited statement cuts to the heart of the terminological problem: "It is difficult to specify what the word 'Midrash' in Hebrew expresses that the word 'exegesis' in English does not. How 'exegesis' in English differed from 'Midrash' in Hebrew, or why the Hebrew will serve better than the more familiar English, I do not know" (*What is Midrash?* [Philadelphia: Fortress, 1987] 8). Of course, the modern use of "exegesis" to signify early Jewish biblical interpretation is also problematic.

descriptive terminology that respects the family resemblance among modes of biblical interpretation in early Jewish texts, yet allows the necessary distinctions. Abstractions of the native terms מדרש and פשר function as descriptive labels for types of ancient Jewish exegesis.[98] In studies of Pauline intertextuality some scholars have taken to combining them: "midrash-pesher" means ancient Jewish biblical interpretation exhibiting exegetical traits similar to those found in the *pesharim*.[99] The interpretive traits common to the Pauline corpus and the *pesharim* include the authors' belief in themselves as eschatologically empowered exegetes, and their practice of reading the foundational events and figures of their movements as prefigured in biblical texts.[100] This latter element has been dubbed "actualization."[101]

---

[98] At the very least the term "midrash" is "native" for Paul and other early Jewish interpreters because of its biblical precedent: 2 Chr 24:27 refers to the "מדרש on the Book of the Kings" (see also 13:22); Ezra is said to have "set his heart to study (דרוש) the law of the Lord" (Ezra 7:10). פשר is, of course, the preferred term in the Qumran commentaries. It is otherwise attested in Qoh 8:1: "who knows the *interpretation* of a thing."

[99] Some of the notable applications of the *pesher* phenomenon to NT biblical interpretation: K. Stendahl defined the formula quotations in Matthew as *pesher*, whereas the "synoptic" quotes and other Matthean quotes come from the stock LXX texts of the early church (*The School of St. Matthew and its Use of the Old Testament* [2nd ed.; Philadelphia: Fortress, 1968]). E. E. Ellis, who introduced "midrash pesher" into Pauline studies (*Paul's Use of the Old Testament* [Edinburgh: Oliver and Boyd, 1957] 139–47), dubs these Pauline characteristics as *pesher*: (1) merging verses into one suggestive text; (2) adapting the grammar of texts for Christian use; (3) using readings that suit his purposes from different texts and traditions (e.g., *targumim*); (4) making new occasional interpretations (149). Building upon J. D. G. Dunn's study of Paul's *pesher* exegesis in 2 Cor 3:17 ("2 Corinthians III, 17 'The Lord is the Spirit,' *JTS* 21 [1970] 309–20), C. Stockhausen argues that the context is characterized by "'*pesher*-like' contemporization of Exodus 34:29–35" (*Moses' Veil and the Glory of the New Covenant* [AnBib 116; Rome: Pontifical Biblical Institute, 1989] 130–53; quote 152–53).

[100] The *pesharim* are widely recognized as providing valuable context for the style of NT biblical interpretation: a group or movement within early Judaism that understands itself eschatologically, and reads biblical texts as if the texts were about, or addressed to them. The labels, however, are often found distracting: "*Pesher*, meaning simply 'interpretation' or 'hermeneutic', seems sufficiently covered by these more familiar terms; *midrash-pesher* is a modern invention probably best forgotten" (M. Black, "The Christological Use of the Old Testament in the New Testament," *NTS* 18 [1971] 1).

[101] "Actualization" appears in R. Bloch's seminal article "Midrash" (in *Approaches to Ancient Judaism: Theory and Practice* [ed. W. Green; BJS 1; Missoula: Scholars Press,

Clearly there is a need among scholars to suitably define and label their material. But none of the proposed terms for Pauline or early Jewish biblical interpretation has been widely received. I am content with the rubric "midrashic exegesis" for all ancient Jewish interpretation that is attuned to what Fishbane identifies as the *"sensus plenior"* of biblical texts.[102] In this sense midrash may be defined broadly as an "interpretative stance."[103] The key to employing this terminology is forming a definition that is broad enough to cover the variables and applying it consistently. Donald Juel's description of this mode of interpretation is worthy of consideration:

> Interpretation moves from explanation to heightening the dramatic to the creation of legends that sometimes became part of an exegetical tradition. The possibilities of such creative exegesis are limited only by the imagination of the exegete. Every such comment, however, takes its cue from specific features of the text and depends upon some interpretive mechanism, whether etymology, wordplay, analogy, or the like. These interpretive mechanisms constitute what we would term *midrashic method.*[104]

These textual "cues" and "interpretive mechanisms" (such as the *middoth* that control the production of new texts) are essential features of biblical intertextuality, as is the understanding shared by early Jewish exegetes that all biblical texts are potentially related because there are no significant boundaries between verse and canon:

> . . . Each verse of the Bible is in principle as connected to its most distant fellow as to the one next door; in seeking to illuminate a verse from Genesis, the midrashist is as likely to have reference (if to any-

---

1978] 29–50) as a characteristic of the homiletical nature of rabbinic midrash. The NT and Qumran varieties are of an altogether different quality. Bloch's midrashic notion might be termed "contemporization," making the biblical text relate to the issues of the day, whereas Qumranian "actualization" might be more accurately described as "identification" (as suggested by Lim, *Holy Scripture in the Qumran Commentaries and Pauline Letters,* 49).

[102] For Fishbane attentiveness to the *"sensus plenior"* is a characteristic of "aggadic exegesis" (*Biblical Interpretation in Ancient Israel,* 283).

[103] "At bottom midrash is not a genre of interpretation but as interpretative stance, a way of reading the sacred text" (Kugel, "Two Introductions to Midrash," 91).

[104] D. Juel, *Messianic Exegesis* (Philadelphia: Fortress, 1988) 40, emphasis added.

thing) to a verse from the Psalter as to another verse in the immediate context—indeed, he sometimes delights in the remoter source.[105]

In other words, Jeremiah and Isaiah, for example, may be read as mutually informing, provided that verbal or thematic analogies are found in specific texts.

Although I am in full agreement with Juel that these interpretive characteristics are usefully labeled "midrashic," "midrash" and "midrashic" as descriptive terms are avoided in this study because the goal is to describe Paul's biblical interpretation as it pertains to the entity Torah rather than find a suitable rubric for it.[106] I consider the work of grouping types of midrashic interpretation to be largely complete. Labelling Paul's exegesis "midrashic" does not solve the lingering riddle to which this study is devoted: how does Paul exegetically arrive at his conclusions concerning the status of Torah? The term "exegesis," which appears throughout this study, is difficult as well because it is the domain of modern critical scholarship in search of the authorially intended meaning of biblical texts. To avoid confusion Pauline exegesis must be differentiated from critical exegesis.

The model of Pauline intertextuality that I operate with is adopted from Boyarin's study, *Intertextuality and the Reading of Midrash* (1990). Boyarin's chief methodological tool is sagely simple: he asks a midrashic commentary on Exodus (the *Mekhilta de-Rabbi Ishmael*), "What in the Bible's text might have motivated this gloss on this verse? Can I explain this text in such a way that this gloss makes sense as an interpretation of the verse?"[107] This question is at the heart of the early Jewish and Pauline studies that follow this chapter. Boyarin under-

---

[105] Kugel, "Two Introductions to Midrash," 93.

[106] It is difficult to avoid confusion here because "Torah" represents (1) the most sacred Jewish texts, (2) the revelation given by God at Sinai, and (3) the cosmic entity that I have named the "eternal Torah." The first and second categories overlap, although the second in no way should be limited to the first. Similarly, the second and third categories overlap, although the third cannot be limited to the boundaries of the second.

[107] Boyarin, *Intertextuality and the Reading of Midrash*, ix. There are, of course, many substantial differences between the creative enlisting of authoritative tradition in the Pauline epistles and the rabbinic midrashic texts that are by nature commentary. For example, the surface level of the Pauline corpus seems univocal, whereas rabbinic texts are multivocal.

stands that ancient Jewish interpreters isolated aspects of biblical texts that may not catch our eye today. These aspects are the textual cues that Juel identifies. It is not enough, therefore, to ask what a biblical text was intended to mean in context, and how a post-biblical interpretation of it can be understood in the light of its original meaning. A skilled modern reader of post-biblical intertexture will therefore grasp for the ancient interpreter's eye or intuition for gaps, ungrammatical constructions, potential cameos of supernatural figures, unique phraseology, and other flags or "surface irregularities" in biblical texts.[108] I use "gap" as a descriptive term for missing information in Paul's reading and composition of texts. An "ungrammaticality" is a word, phrase or idea that is not consistent with the theological vernacular. For example, Paul's phrase *"reading* the old covenant" (2 Cor 3:14) is ungrammatical; it indicates that the language of a specific biblical text, in this case Jer 31:31–32, has influenced his phraseology (§6.3.1).[109]

Fishbane has labored to show that the Hebrew Bible itself is exegetical literature, that later texts draw on and play off earlier ones. "Inner-biblical exegesis" means that the Bible is a "self-glossing book."[110] The glosses establish duality between texts. Boyarin sees rabbinic midrash as the literature which exposes the "double-voicedness of the Torah by setting up a dialectic between interpretations."[111] Moreover, the rabbis pose their conflicting "assertions as an essential part of the structure of their discourse." Midrash is self-consciously a commentary genre, whereas the Pauline epistles are not. It is therefore difficult to identify the significance of biblical texts in Paul's letters (even if he uses a citation formula), and hence the multivocality of a

[108] Kugel notes that midrashic exegetes focus on "surface irregularities" in biblical texts ("Two Introductions to Midrash," 92).

[109] A "gap" is typically associated with narratives. M. Sternberg, acknowledging the "necessity of establishing the relevance of the absent material" (i.e., the difference between relevant "gaps" and irrelevant "blanks"), defines a gap as "a lack of information about the world—an event, motive, causal link, character trait, plot structure, law of probability—contrived by temporal displacement" (*The Poetics of Biblical Narrative* [Bloomington: Indiana University Press, 1985] 235).

[110] G. Bruns, "Midrash and Allegory," in *The Literary Guide to the Bible* (ed. R. Alter and F. Kermode; Cambridge: Harvard University Press, 1986) 626; cited in Boyarin, *Intertextuality*, 15.

[111] Boyarin, *Intertextuality*, 19.

text. Unlike midrash, in Pauline texts the debate often lies below the text, in the circumstances to which the epistle is a response, or in the intertextual relationships Paul has formed. Pauline scholars locate traces of debate in features of the surface text that indicate hypothetical debate partners (e.g., rhetorical questions). Intertextual debate, the tension between text and intertext, is also evident in the Pauline corpus.[112] Because of the genre-related differences of midrash and epistle, the results of this study are more tenuous than Boyarin's, but the dialogical nature of Pauline texts is clear nonetheless. My notion of the Pauline "antithesis" draws from his characterization of the dialogical nature of biblical intertextuality. Paul raises a contrary voice to the ramifications of Torah's projection into the cosmos.

According to Boyarin, the midrashic text is "always made up of a mosaic of conscious and unconscious citation of earlier discourse."[113] When one reads Paul it is much more difficult to differentiate a "conscious citation" from the free use of words and phrases in the author's cultural lexicon. After identifying biblical fragments in a Pauline text, how does one know when Paul is intentionally working with biblical texts, and when biblical language simply pops into his head? In *Echoes of Scripture in the Letters of Paul*, Richard Hays raises the issue of free association vs. systematic exegesis. He thinks of Paul more as a spiritually dynamic prophet-poet of free association:

> The Pauline letters, read as hermeneutical events, are evocative allusive reflections on a text (Scripture) that is in turn deemed allusive rather than overt in its communication strategies. . . . Echoes linger in the air and lure the reader of Paul's letters back into the symbolic world of Scripture. Paul's allusions gesture toward precursors whose words are already heavy with tacit implication. . . . If meaning is the product of such intertextual relations, then it is—to alter the figure— not so much like a relic excavated from an ancient text as it is like a spark struck by the shovel hitting rock.[114]

---

[112] N. Dahl's article, "Contradictions in Scripture" (*Studies in Paul* [Minneapolis: Augsburg, 1977] 159–77) is the seminal study of this intertextual dissonance in Paul. See also Stockhausen, "Principles of Pauline Exegesis," and chapter 6 of this book.

[113] Boyarin, *Intertextuality and the Reading of Midrash*, 12.

[114] Hays, *Echoes of Scripture*, 155.

Although in practice Hays does not treat Paul's use of biblical words, phrases, and even sentences as mere accidents of Paul's art, from his theoretical musings and analysis of other intertextual approaches to Paul, it is hard to escape this very conclusion. But Hays is reacting to what sometimes appears to be a mere retrojection of rabbinic hermeneutical principles or Qumranian *Pesher*-exegesis onto Paul:

> He adheres neither to any single exegetical procedure, nor even to a readily specifiable inventory of procedures. . . . There is no evidence in the letters that Paul—in contrast to other ancient authors such as Philo—ever sat down with the biblical text and tried to figure out what it might mean by applying an exegetical procedure abstractable from the particular text that he was reading. Rather, he seems to have leaped—in moments of metaphorical insight—to intuitive apprehensions of the meaning of texts without the aid or encumbrance of systematic reflection about his hermeneutics.[115]

In other words, Hays challenges the very existence of "interpretive mechanisms" that allow and limit Pauline interpretation.

Hays has reacted too far in the opposite direction. On the one hand, it is unlikely that Paul consciously approached his Scripture with hermeneutical rules which he was free to apply to whatever texts met his preconceived criteria and thereby create unprecedented, non-traditional textual relationships. On the other hand, it is just as unlikely that Paul leapt from intuition to intuition, from "metaphorical insight" to metaphorical insight, without methods by which his "leaps" were guided. What Hays has not fully appreciated is the extent to which those who connect Pauline biblical interpretation with similar techniques in rabbinic texts or the Dead Sea Scrolls, have done so specifically because a family resemblance is apparent. This resemblance is demonstrable despite the diversity of literary genres in view: rabbinic midrash, the so-called *Pesharim*, Pauline epistle.

Most of the OT Apocrypha and Pseudepigrapha (and Philo, for that matter) should be included in this "family" as well, but their exegetical characteristics are so well hidden by their genre that few studies have adequately treated them as exegetical literature. There have not been many studies of, for example, biblical exegesis in Sirach or *1 Enoch*.

---

[115] Hays, *Echoes of Scripture*, 160–61.

Perhaps the problem ultimately results from the blurry distinction between tradition and exegesis: the various apocalypses, sapiential writings, and narrative developments of biblical writings that populate the intertestamental period are recognized for their traditional material, but not necessarily as exegetically engendered tradition. Menahem Kister issues a slight caution that traditions present in early Jewish texts are not necessarily based on exegesis, even if the exegetical launch point is identified; there is a "complex relationship among conscious theological innovation, casual mutation of tradition, exegetical elements, and biblical reflection."[116] More than anything else, Kister's comment exposes the lack of specificity in terms. Although I regularly use the term "exegesis" for instances of early Jewish biblical interpretation, this principle is becoming my refrain: exegesis now is not exegesis then.

Hays proposes seven criteria by which one evaluates the presence of intertextual echo in Paul: the availibility of the source text; the explicitness, or "volume" of an echo; recurrence of particular echoed biblical texts; thematic coherence, or how the allusion works with other rhetorical features in its section; historical plausibility (i.e., is this Paul the first century Jew, or Paul the Lutheran?); history of interpretation; satisfaction, or reader's judgment.[117] Of these seven, the most important for my purposes is "volume": the intertextual volume is very high in the three Pauline texts considered in this study (Romans 9:30–10:13; Galatians 3–4; 2 Corinthians 3). In each case it is clear that Paul is referring to, and using, specific and identifiable biblical texts. And, in contradistinction to Hays, for whom Paul the practiced midrashist is anathema, formal hermeneutical principles are observable in these high-volume texts.

The defining characteristics of Pauline intertextuality may be summarized as follows: Paul was generally interested in the same texts as other early Jewish theologians, though his perspective is certainly unique. In the light of Christ he reinterprets the creation accounts and the paradise narrative, the Abraham narratives, the Sinai theophanies

---

[116] M. Kister, "Observations on Aspects of Exegesis, Tradition, and Theology in Midrash, Pseudepigrapha, and other Jewish Writings," in *Tracing the Threads: Studies in the Vitality of Jewish Pseudepigrapha* (ed. J. Reeves; SBLEJL 6; Atlanta: Scholars Press, 1994) 14–15.

[117] Hays, *Echoes of Scripture*, 29–32.

and the revelation of Torah, the historical fate of Israel, the prophetic depictions of eschatological renewal, redemption and regeneration. From this subtextual matrix Paul presents Christ as God's eschatological revelation, whereas Torah was God's time-bound (i.e., not eternal) revelation, for the Jews alone, in this (fading) age. Paul was an exegete who transformed the biblical texts he worked with by isolating their semantic and/or narrative features and establishing new relationships between semantically or thematically analogous texts. He could also use a text against itself, and reject received interpretive traditions such as the eternal Torah.

1.4 Structure

The chapters that follow may be divided into two parts. The next two chapters provide the context in which Paul's view Torah is best understood. The Pauline corpus is the focus of part two, chapters four through six. One has to decide how to approach the Pauline material: by means of an exegetical analysis of each νόμος-text,[118] a selection of significant texts,[119] or the Torah content of each epistle.[120] I have chosen the second option, the case study approach. For the case studies I have selected texts that are characterized by their high "volume" of Torah-content and the prominence of biblical lemmata: Rom 9:30–10:13; Galatians 3–4; 2 Corinthians 3. The point of the case studies is to exhibit how these texts can be fruitfully interpreted as Paul's counter-claim to the elevated images of Torah described in chapters two and three.

---

[118] For an example of the text-by-text approach, see E. P. Sanders, *Paul, the Law and the Jewish People* (Philadelphia: Fortress, 1983).

[119] Although he claims to operate on a text by text basis, N. T. Wright's *The Climax of the Covenant: Christ and the Law in Pauline Theology* (Edinburgh: T. and T. Clark, 1991) is an example of a study that isolates key texts.

[120] An example of the epistle approach is F. Thielman, *Paul and the Law: A Contextual Approach* (Downers Grove: InterVarsity, 1994).

CHAPTER 2

A Narrative of Wisdom
and Torah

The day of revelation is considered as the day on which earth was wedded to heaven. The barrier between them was removed by the fact that the Torah, the heavenly bride, the daughter of the Holy One, was wedded to Israel on that day.[1]

These words of Solomon Schechter do not reveal the mechanism by which the Sinai revelation event was interpreted as the marriage of heaven and earth. The revelation narratives in Exodus, which feature the descent and theophany of Yhwh and the ascent of the privileged intermediary Moses, certainly suggest the idea of Mt. Sinai as the meeting place of heaven and earth. But the idea of Torah as the "daughter of the Holy One" does not emerge from the language of Exodus. The goal of this chapter is to identify biblical and post-biblical developments that influenced such figurations of Torah. Specifically, the focus is on the identification of Torah with the personified Wisdom of Prov 8:22–31. In the "remything" of Torah that develops from the transference of Wisdom texts, Torah is projected into the primordial narrative, assuming roles in the creation and garden stories of Genesis 1–3.[2] The interpretive trajectory that begins in biblical

---

[1] S. Schechter, *Aspects of Rabbinic Theology* (New York: Schocken, 1909) 130.

[2] M. Hengel notes the "remything of wisdom" (*Judaism and Hellenism* [2 vols.; Minneapolis: Fortress, 1974] 1. 156), which refers to the early Jewish theological appro-

texts extends at least as far as the Zoharic notion of the "garments of Torah."[3]

The early Jewish interpretive tradition that identified Wisdom and Torah makes a significant impression on early Christian theology. Although scholarship has grown accustomed to the notion of a Wisdom christology in Paul, the relationship between this tradition and Paul's view of Torah has received little attention, and no one has used it to situate his thought in early Jewish Torah theology. This chapter is a first step in addressing this oversight.

2.1 Introduction and Assumptions

The identification in early Jewish texts of personified Wisdom with Torah is now considered a matter of fact in biblical scholarship. George F. Moore anticipated the present consensus:

> The identification of revelation, and more specifically of the Mosaic Law, with divine Wisdom, was thus established in Jewish teaching at least as far back as Sirach (ca. 200 B.C.E.), and his way of introducing it makes the impression that it was commonplace in his time, when the study of the law and the cultivation of wisdom went hand in hand, and as in his case were united in the same person.[4]

Although Moore is correct in isolating the influence of Sirach in the process (§2.3), there is much less agreement on what this early Wisdom/Torah identification means. A minimalist reading of the relevant texts sees the identification of Torah with Wisdom as no more than an extension to Torah of the poetic personification of biblical Wisdom. Moore's statement represents a moderate estimation of the impact of the Wisdom/Torah tradition:

---

priation (beginning with Sirach 24) of elements of an older ANE wisdom myth, coupled with Platonic and Stoic ideas. The *remything of Torah* signifies the multi-faceted, elevated Torah tradition that Paul inherits, and especially the exegetical process by which Torah was envisioned as a cosmic entity, the first emanation from which all of creation proceeds.

[3] See especially G. Scholem, "The Meaning of the Torah in Jewish Mysticism," *Diogenes* 14 (1956) 36–47; *Major Trends in Jewish Mysticism* (New York: Schocken, 1954) 156–243.

[4] G. F. Moore, *Judaism in the First Centuries of the Christian Era* (3 vols.; Cambridge: Harvard University Press, 1927) 1. 265.

Once this equivalence was established, all that was said in the Scriptures about the nature of wisdom, its source, its fruits, and its inestimable worth, was applied to the Law, either in the larger sense of revelation, or with special reference to the law of Moses; in the same way Law acquires the vivid poetical personification that is given to Wisdom in the higher flights of the sapiential books.[5]

Thus Wisdom and Torah become mutually interpretive, which means that Wisdom texts inform about Torah. One could say the relationship is reciprocal, but Wisdom recedes into the background once it transfers its traits to Torah. Torah texts are generally not applied to Wisdom. From the maximalist perspective divine Wisdom—and thereby Torah—is viewed as an hypostasis, an independently existing entity.

Wisdom's role in creation can illustrate the difference between these approaches. There are a number of biblical expressions similar to Prov 3:19:

> The LORD *by wisdom* (בחכמה) founded the earth; by understanding he established the heavens.

This affirmation could be a poetic expression that Yhwh created the heavens and earth wisely rather than haphazardly. Conversely, it might testify to Wisdom's role as a *Schöpfungsmittler*, an agent or mediator of creation. Of course, one has to consider individual statements critically, according to their context and setting. For example, the opening lines of *Genesis Rabbah* assert that "Thus God consulted the Torah and created the world" (*Gen. Rab.* 1:1).[6] Generally speaking, the transference of Wisdom to Torah is complete in rabbinic literature, so it is no surprise that Torah is involved in God's creation.

It does not follow, however, that the midrashist viewed Torah as a hypostasis. This sort of intermediary figure that emerged in Christianity and Gnosticism was rejected in rabbinic theology because it encroached upon rabbinic standards of monotheism and God's sovereignty.[7] But as Schechter stated, Torah became envisioned as an entity with a "mystical life of its own":

---

[5] Moore, *Judaism*, 1. 265.

[6] *Midrash Rabbah Genesis* (tr. H. Freedman; London: Soncino, 1983) 1.

[7] A. F. Segal (*Two Powers in Heaven: Early Rabbinic Reports About Christianity and Gnosticism* [SJLA 25; Leiden: Brill, 1977] 60–73) relates the story of the "Simon

The Torah . . . was personified and endowed with a mystical life of its own, which emanates from God, yet is partly detached from him. Thus we find the Torah pleading for or against Israel, as on occasion of the destruction of the temple, when Torah was called to give evidence against Israel, but desisted from it at the instance of Abraham, who said unto her, "My daughter, were not my children the only ones who received thee, when thou wast rejected by other nations?" Nay, even single letters of the alphabet are endowed with a separate life, enabling them to act the same part almost as the Torah. The whole later mystical theory which degenerated into the combinations of letters to which the most important meaning is attached, takes its origin from these personifications.[8]

What Schechter described as a degeneration could also be viewed as the flowering of Torah as the communication of heavenly secrets. He was correct in identifying the personification of Torah, by means of Wisdom, as the stimulus for its investment with cosmic and mystical significance.[9]

Magus of early rabbinic texts," Elisha b. Abuya (110–35 C.E.), also dubbed Aher (אחר). He was one of four rabbis (the others are Simeon b. Zoma, Simeon b. Azzai, Akiba) who journeyed to *pardes* (paradise). Aher sees Metatron sitting on the throne (he is writing) and concludes that Metatron is enthroned and that there are two powers in heaven. Both Aher and Metatron are punished: Aher for his apostasy, Metatron for not rising when Aher was near. Segal consistently judges the core of such traditions to be far older than the amoraic age.

[8] Schechter, *Rabbinic Theology*, 129.

[9] E. R. Goodenough summarizes the place of Torah in a hellenistic Jewish theological milieu: "The Law became a difficult problem. As the Torah, the sacred teaching, it was the ἱερὸς λόγος of the Mystery; but as a set of commands concerned with physical life it was obviously of less importance than the great spiritual reality of the Light-Stream. So again a clever solution was found: the Law, as commandments, was said to be only the projection of the true Law, the Logos, into the material medium of nouns and verbs. It was the material copy of the Platonic original. As such it had its uses, and by most Jews was carefully followed. But its spiritual value was secondary altogether to that of the great Source of the written Law, the Unwritten Law, the unwritten streaming Logos-Nomos of God. Only as one came up into this, the true Law of Judaism, had one fulfilled the Law of Moses. The Patriarchs, it was said, had had access to this Law, and so had been true Jews before the legislation of Sinai. Indeed they were the model Jews, the Hierophants of the Mystery. One could be a Jew, in a sense, by obeying the copy-law. But the true Jew, according to mystic Judaism, got his Law through the mediation of the Patriarchs, especially of Moses, who had ascended the Stream to the Logos, and were God's 'loans' to help other men, Jews and proselytes, to come to the same vision.

The subject of this chapter is the development of the Wisdom/Torah tradition, from its biblical beginnings to its full expression in the rabbinic literature. This study is not concerned, however, with the original intent of the biblical texts from which the tradition arose, and the rabbinic material is relevant chiefly because it manifests the direction in which the exegetical tradition develops. In sum, the focus here is on the *reception* of the tradition in early Jewish texts. Contrary to Moore's assertion that equating Wisdom and Torah was a "commonplace" in our period, there is no way to ascertain the extent of the idea's penetration in early Jewish theology. The texts do not indicate their readership, so it is difficult to determine the popularity of individual writings. Our best evidence of a work's popularity is when it is quoted by subsequent writers. Hence the reception of the Wisdom/Torah tradition is known only from the early Jewish texts that draw from the language and imagery of the key biblical texts.

2.2 The Biblical Texts

The biblical foundation of the Wisdom/Torah tradition is the personification of Wisdom in Proverbs 1–9. Prov 8:22–31 is the most important text in the developing tradition of Wisdom as a cosmic force, but there is nothing in these lines that links Wisdom with Torah, since Torah is not mentioned. Rather, the explicit Wisdom/Torah association that emerges first in Sirach 24 is based on a cumulative semantic impression left on early Jewish interpreters by verbal and thematic analogies between many biblical texts. But Prov 8:22 is singularly important because it allowed the verbal association of the ראשית of Gen 1:1 with חכמה ("wisdom"), and thus opened the door to viewing personified Wisdom as the agent of creation.

Two clarifications are necessary at the outset. First, the biblical and post-biblical development I am referring to as the "Wisdom/Torah tradition" is not necessarily linear. In presenting the biblical material I am grouping texts not chronologically but semantically and/or thematically: texts that relate חכמה and תורה; texts that mention חכמה in some

---

Indeed some of them, especially Moses, were incarnations of the Logos, and so the saviors of those who would join the Mystery" (*By Light, Light: The Mystic Gospel of Hellenistic Judaism* [New Haven: Yale University, 1935] 8). Generally, this is an accurate depiction of the Torah mysticism that Paul confronted.

connection with creation; texts that relate חכמה to Eden. Second, each text will not have the same value for interpreters. Only a few of these biblical texts would have been regarded by early Jewish exegetes as "special," by which I mean a text that by itself would mystify, invite interpretation and speculation, or provide key verbal analogies.[10] In other words, the unexceptional text would not have been foundational for a burgeoning tradition. Such unexceptional texts would be cited mainly in commentary genres like rabbinic midrash and the so-called "pesher" from Qumran, in which collecting mutually interpretive biblical texts was important, or they might influence the language of a paraphrase.[11] My point is that these texts are auxiliary in the Wisdom/Torah tradition. They may add important elements to the relational set of Wisdom/Torah images, but without Prov 8:22–30 and its intertextual relationship to Genesis 1–3, the auxiliary texts would not have established the tradition that results in the projection of the Sinai Torah into the cosmos.

I will start with texts that contain some sort of semantic association of Wisdom and Torah. For example, in Deuteronomy 4 Israel's חכמה is in observing the חקים and משפטים ("statutes" and "ordinances"; v. 5), but the term תורה is not mentioned:

> Keep them and do them; for that will be *your wisdom* and your understanding in the sight of the peoples, who, when they hear all these statutes, will say, "Surely this great nation is a wise and understanding people." (Deut 4:6)

Jeremiah 8 has a parallelism of those who have wisdom and those who possess Torah:

---

[10] Any theophany would be "special." Some of the other "special" texts that attracted the ancient Jewish exegete: Eden's tree of life; the Rock which produced water for the ancient Hebrews in the wilderness (Exod 17:6; Num 20:8–11; Deut 8:15, 32:31; Wis 11:4; 1 Cor 10:4); Melchisedek (Gen 14:18; Ps 110:4; 11Q Melch; Heb 5:6–10, 7:1–17; 2 Enoch 71–72); the fiery chariot in the account of Elijah being taken up in a "whirlwind" (2 Kgs 2:11)—a formative scene for Jewish Merkabah, or heavenly ascent mysticism, the symbols of which overlap with those of paradise. In addition, the mysterious assumptions of Elijah (2 Kgs 2:11; Mal 4:5; 1 Macc 2:58) and Enoch (Gen 5:24; Sir 44:16) were particularly fascinating.

[11] This is not to say that these unexceptionable texts would not be used to prove a point. In the so-called "atomistic exegesis," each element of each sacred text could be interpreted, or aid in the interpretation of other texts.

How can you say, "We are wise (חכמים), and the law (תורה) of the Lord is with us"? But, behold, the false pen of the scribes has made it into a lie. (Jer 8:8)

In Ezra 7 there is an implied identification of wisdom and the Law, since the two entities seem interchangeable:

. . . according to the law (Aramaic דת) of your God, *which is in your hand.* (Ezra 7:14)[12]

. . . according to the wisdom (חכמה) of your God *which is in your hand.* (Ezra 7:25)

In the following text the close proximity of Torah and Wisdom may attest to the identification of the two entities:

My son, keep my words
and treasure up my commandments (מצותי) with you;
keep my commandments (מצותי) and live,
keep my *teachings* (תורתי) as the apple of your eye;
bind them on your fingers,
write them on the tablet of your heart.
Say to *wisdom,* "You are my sister,"
and call insight your intimate friend. (Prov 7:1–4)

The figurative presence of "tablet" (לוח) echoes the Sinai revelation narrative, and thus leaves no doubt what תורה is in view. The RSV translators regard תורתי ("my teachings"; 7:2) as a defectively written plural (for תורותי), probably in service of symmetry with מצותי (7:1), which contextually, given the plural pronouns which follow ("bind them" and "write them"; 7:3), must be plural. It should be noted, however, that there is nothing about the form תורתי itself that necessitates taking it as a plural—that is, it may simply mean "my Torah."

Wisdom and creation are related in the following texts in a manner that recalls Proverbs 1–9 and the ensuing exegetical tradition portraying Wisdom/Torah as the agent of creation:

---

[12] דת is roughly parallel to the Greek νόμος. Compare these lines from Daniel's vision: "He shall speak words against the Most High, and shall wear out the saints of the Most High, and shall think to change the times and the law (דת); and they shall be given into his hand for a time, two times, and half a time" (Dan 7:25).

It is he who made the earth by his power,
who established the world by his wisdom (בחכמתו),
and by his understanding stretched out the heavens. (Jer 51:15)

O Lord, how manifold are your works!
In wisdom (בחכמה) you have made them all;
the earth is full of your creatures. (Ps 104:24)

The phrase rendered in Ps 104:24 as "*in* wisdom" by the RSV translators, but as "*by* his wisdom" in Jer 51:15 (with an additional personal suffix), was the subject of exegetical activity in the early Jewish period and in subsequent rabbinic and Christian literature. The phrasing will be addressed below, so here I will simply introduce the issue: בחכמה is an adverbial phrase, with the Hebrew preposition ב ("in, with, by") attached to the noun. In Jer 51:15 חכמה + ב is rendered instrumentally, as it often was in early Jewish and Christian texts, "*by means of* wisdom." The instrumental interpretation of ב figures significantly in the tradition because בראשית (ראשית + ב), the phrase that opens the Hebrew Bible (Gen 1:1), was taken by some early interpreters as instrumental as well: "By means of ראשית God created the heavens and the earth." [13]

Without the influence of Prov 8:22–31, however, these texts would be taken as figurative expressions of God's creative abilities—God created "wisely"—rather than as assertions of the force by which God created. And one can only speak as Hengel does of a "Torah-ontology" because of the transference to Torah of personified Wisdom's traits, as depicted in these lines:

The Lord created me (קנני) at the beginning (ראשית) of his
    work,
the first of his acts of old.
Ages ago (מעולם) I was set up, at the first (מראש),
before the beginning of the earth (מקדמי ארץ).
When there were no depths I was brought forth,
when there were no springs abounding with water.

---

[13] The LXX regularly has ἐν where the Hebrew has ב, as is the case in Jer 51:15 and Ps 104:24. This does not mean, however, that the LXX translators decided against an instrumental interpretation of ב; rather, they maintained the ambiguity of the Hebrew, since ἐν may be used in instrumental adverbial phrases as well.

Before the mountains had been shaped, before the hills,
I was brought forth;
before he had made the earth with its fields,
or the first of the dust of the world.
When he established the heavens, I was there,
when he drew a circle on the face of the deep,
when he made firm the skies above,
when he established the fountains of the deep,
when he assigned to the sea its limit,
so that the waters might not transgress his command,
when he marked out the foundations of the earth,
then I was beside him, like a master workman (אָמוֹן);
and I was daily his delight, rejoicing before him always,
rejoicing in his inhabited world and delighting in the sons
   of men. (Prov 8:22–31)

Isolated from their reception in subsequent texts, these lines are suggestive but ambiguous: "Lady Wisdom has received great press by reason of her association with creation, but her precise role remains unclear."[14] The term אָמוֹן (v. 30) is a key element in establishing the agency of Wisdom, but it probably did not originally signify a "master workman."[15] There is no question, however, that Prov 8:22–31 was *received* as presenting Wisdom as God's agent of creation, the רֵאשִׁית of Gen 1:1.

The Hebrew of Prov 8:22 has a significant verbal analogy with the opening of the Hebrew:

(Prov 8:22) ויהוה קנני ראשית דרכו קדם מפעליו מאז

The Hebrew term רֵאשִׁית here replicates the בְּרֵאשִׁית of Gen 1:1. If the choice of רֵאשִׁית was not intended to recall the creation narrative, Gen 1:1 and Prov 8:22 were certainly taken as mutually interpretive in post-

---

[14] R. E. Murphy, "Wisdom and Creation," *JBL* 104 (1985) 5. Theories of personified Wisdom's identity, or referent, are reviewed in C. Maier, *Die "fremde Frau" in Proverbien 1–9* (OBO 144; Freiburg: Universtätsverlag, Göttingen: Vandenhoeck und Ruprecht, 1995) 7–13.

[15] The interpretation of אָמוֹן as agent or tool probably underlies Wisdom as ἡ πάντων τεχνῖτις in Wis 7:22, and Torah as the "working tool of the Holy One" in *Gen. Rab.* 1 (cited by H. Ringgren, *Word and Wisdom* [Lund: Håkan Ohlssons Boktryckeri, 1947] 102–3).

biblical literature. In some targumim the influence of Prov 8:22 is evident in the use of בחכמה ("by Wisdom") to replace or supplement ראשית.[16] The biblical precedent for the בחכמה/בראשית switch includes the following, which confirms the role of Wisdom in creation:

> The Lord *by wisdom* (בחכמה) founded the earth;
> by understanding he established the heavens. (Prov 3:19)[17]

Prov 8:22 is significant because of its intertexture with the מעשׂה בראשׂית rather than simply the semantic characteristics of ראשׂית. But ראשׂית is the linchpin that unites Wisdom with the narrative of creation, and thus becomes itself a key *sema* for both Jewish and Christian exegetes.[18] And as Wisdom is projected onto Gen 1:1 because it is identified as ראשׂית, so the phrase בראשׂית is interpreted instrumentally in light of the בחכמה phrases cited above. Because of its biblical and post-biblical association with hypostasized Wisdom, בראשׂית is suggestive of

---

[16] "Fragment" *targumim* of Gen 1:1 list בחכמה for בראשׂית (see M. L. Klein, *The Fragment-Targums of the Pentateuch* [2 vols.; AnBib 76; Rome: Biblical Institute Press, 1980]), while Neofiti includes both a temporal and a means clause: מלקדמין בחכמה ברא (A. Díez Macho, *Neophyti 1. Targum Palestinense MS de la Biblioteca Vaticana: Génesis* [Madrid: Consejo Superior de Investigaciones Científicas, 1968] 3). Targum Onqelos literally renders the MT of Gen 1:1, and thereby affirms the temporal interpretation of בראשׂית and reduces the resonance with Prov 8:22: בקדמין ברא (A. Sperber, *The Bible in Aramaic. The Pentateuch according to Targum Onkelos* [reprinted ed.; Leiden: Brill, 1992] 1).

[17] Modern exegetes might downplay בחכמה here because of its synonymous parallel relationship with בתבונה, "by understanding." The ancients, however, did not recognize that the parallelism weakened חכמה. J. L. Kugel notes the "striking contradiction" that "while in their own compositions the Rabbis showed ample awareness of the elements of biblical style, as exegetes they seem singularly blind to the same procedures. Stated bluntly, the point is this: the ways of biblical parallelism are everywhere apparent in rabbinic prayers and songs: yet nowhere do the Rabbis speak of parallelism or acknowledge it in their explanation or interpretation of biblical verses, even when—to our eyes—it is so obvious that the greatest industry seems necessary to devise a reading that does not comment on it" (*The Idea of Biblical Poetry* [New Haven: Yale University Press, 1981] 97). In other words, "rabbinic exegesis simply does not recognize the possibility of restatement" (102).

[18] The rabbis recognized this sort of interpretation of Gen 1:1 as the fount of heavenly ascent mysticism and Christian Logos-theology: who is with God in creation, at the throne, and in the wilderness (see Segal, *Two Powers in Heaven*, passim). J. W. Bowker notes that contemplation of מעשׂה בראשׂית ("narrative of creation") was forbidden ("'Merkabah' Visions and the Visions of Paul," *JSS* 16 [1971] 158).

meanings far removed from the simple temporal clause which opens English Bibles.[19]

Another text that helps to fill in the picture is Job 28:20–27. Like Prov 8:22–31, it places חכמה in the creation events:

Whence then comes wisdom?
And where is the place of understanding?
It is hid from the eyes of all living,
and concealed from the birds of the air.
Abaddon and Death say, "We have heard a rumor of it with
    our ears."
God understands the way to it,
and he knows its place.
For he looks to the ends of the earth,
and sees everything under the heavens.
When he gave to the wind its weight,
and meted out the waters by measure;
when he made a decree for the rain,
and a way for the lightning of the thunder;
then he saw it and declared it;

---

[19] Some examples that are representative of numerous other interpretations of ראשית in rabbinic midrash and early Christian literature: C. F. Burney argued that the stanzas of the Christ hymn of Col 1:15–20 drew on the multivalency of בראשית, which is rendered by ἐν ἀρχῇ in the LXX ("Christ as the APXH of Creation," *JTS* 27 [1926] 160–77; see also W. D. Davies, *Paul and Rabbinic Judaism* [4th ed.; Philadelphia: Fortress, 1980] 152). Burney's conclusions have made little penetration, however: for example, R. G. Hamerton-Kelly finds the hymn's connection to בראשית "unlikely in view of the repetition of this sequence as a formula elsewhere in the New Testament and in pagan philosophic and gnostic texts. It is, more likely, a reflection of the Stoic formula for omnipotence, transferred to the cosmic Adam, the macro-anthropos" (*Pre-existence, Wisdom, and the Son of Man; a Study of the Idea of Pre-existence in the New Testament* [Cambridge: Cambridge University Press, 1973] 172–73). Commenting on Theophilus of Antioch (2nd C.E.), Segal points out a common early Christian way of reading בראשית: "For him, 'In the beginning,' the first words of Genesis, has the meaning of 'by means of the beginning,' which is yet another name for the *logos* and characterizes it as Lord and agent of God in the creation" (Segal, *Two Powers in Heaven*, 226). H.-F. Weiss cites Johannes Philoponus (6th C.E.), who communicates the following possible interpretations of בראשית/ἐν ἀρχῇ: beginning of time; groundwork of creation; the active agent (τὸ ποιητικὸν αἴτιον); the end or goal (τὸ τελικόν); ἐν τῇ σοφίᾳ (*Untersuchungen zur Kosmologie des hellenistischen und palästinischen Judentums* [TU 97; Berlin: Akademie-Verlag, 1966] 184).

> he established it,
> and searched it out.

Notwithstanding the thematic parallels with Prov 8:22–31, in Job חכמה is not personified or hypostasized, nor is there any comparable hint of instrumentality. In post-biblical literature the impact of Job 28 may be isolated to the appearance in later "Wisdom" texts (Sir 24:5–6; Bar 3:29–30; Rom 10:7) of a descent motif that reflects Job's "Abaddon and Death" (28:22).

In addition to Wisdom's presence in creation, there are two other aspects of Wisdom in Proverbs 1–9 that figure prominently in the subsequent Wisdom/Torah tradition. The first is verbally related to a mysterious feature of the Eden narrative: "[Wisdom] is a tree of life to those who lay hold of her" (Prov 3:18a). Wisdom as the tree of life converges with the idea that it was near to God (Prov 8:30) and the later image of an archetypal paradise wherein lies God's throne.[20] According to the paradise narrative of Genesis 2–3, there were two trees in the garden: the tree of knowledge of good and evil, and the tree of life:

> And out of the ground the Lord God made to grow every tree that is pleasant to the sight and good for food, the tree of life also in the midst of the garden, and the tree of the knowledge of good and evil. (Gen 2:9)

The command "not to eat" only concerns the tree of knowledge of good and evil (Gen 2:17); there is no mention here of the tree of life. The climax of the tale has Yhwh saying,

> Behold, the man has become like one of us, knowing good and evil; and now, lest he put forth his hand and take also of the tree of life, and eat, and live for ever. (Gen 3:22)

Finally, after the expulsion of Adam and Eve,

> At the east of the garden of Eden [Yhwh] placed the cherubim, and a flaming sword which turned every way, to guard the way to the tree of life. (Gen 3:24)

---

[20] The question here concerns the manner in which tree of life texts were received and interpreted in subsequent Jewish texts, rather than their parallels in Mesopotamia, Canaan or Crete.

In the Genesis paradise story the tree of life is an unexplored detail, since neither the human characters nor the serpent react to it in any way, and yet this tale ends with God denying future access to this tree. The presence of the tree of life in Eden is the sort of mysterious feature that drew the attention of ancient Jewish and Christian exegetes.[21] They saw God's mysteries—cameo appearances of Torah or the pre-existent Christ—where modern biblical scholarship finds redactional seams or the vestiges of very ancient traditions.[22]

Prov 3:18 is thus a crucial text in the confluence of Wisdom, creation, and Eden *topoi*. The confluence will become explicit in Sirach 24. Once Wisdom's properties are transfered to Torah, Torah in turn becomes the tree of life.[23] Evidence of this aspect of Torah's figuration can be found in Targum Neofiti's extensive elaboration of Gen 3:24:

> The Law is the *tree of life* for all who study it, and anyone who observes its precepts lives and endures as (כ) the tree of life in (ל) the world to come.[24]

The targum mirrors another element in early Jewish Torah theology that is found in some of the most important Wisdom/Torah texts: Torah observance is linked to one's eschatological fate.[25] There may

---

[21] Because of the influence of Gen 3:3, in which the tree of knowledge of good and evil is "in the midst of the garden," not every ancient interpreter recognizes two trees in the narrative. The *Apocalypse of Sedrach* (2d-5th cent. C.E.), for example, only mentions the tree of life (chap. 4), whereas the *Life of Adam and Eve* (1st cent. C.E.) has the tree of knowledge in the "midst of the Garden" (*Adam and Eve* 32:1; *Apocalypse of Moses* 7). *Jubilees* (2d B.C.E.), which has a rewritten account of the Fall, does not mention two trees, nor does it identify the "tree in the midst of the garden" (*Jub.* 3:18) by name, although there is a later reference to the tree of knowledge (*Jub.* 4:30).

[22] The "tree of life in the midst of paradise" is perhaps the most important of these mysteries, or symbols, in early Christian literature because it correlates otherwise unrelated *topoi* (Sinai, throne, holy of holies, Zion, the Marah עץ in Exod 15:25) which cohere as analogues to Eden in the exegetical tradition. Other examples of these biblical mysteries were listed above.

[23] And, of course, in Christian interpretation the tree of life would be associated with Christ's cross rather than Torah. Ignatius perhaps had the tree of life in mind when he wrote of the "branches of the cross" (*Trall.* 11:2). Ephrem the Syrian, who thought that the tree of the cross had to undo all the damage done by the tree of knowledge, figuratively depicted the tree of life "shining forth from Golgotha" (*Hymns on the Virginity* 16.10).

[24] Text and translation in Díez Macho, *Neophyti 1: Génesis*, 19 and 505.

[25] The key texts are Sir 24:23; Bar 4:1; 2 *Apoc. Bar.* 48:22–24 (see below).

also be a connection between the Mishnaic maxim "make a fence around Torah" (*m. Abot* 1.1) and the image of the tree of life being guarded by cherubim and the flaming sword (Gen 3:24), although the rabbis probably meant their "fence" to keep Torah sacred and special, rather than as a denial of access.[26] Torah can also be symbolized in the "flaming sword" that prevents entrance unto the tree of life (Gen 3:24).[27] I should also add to this set of images the characterization of Eden as "the holy mountain of God" (Ezek 28:14), and the typological correlation of special biblical mountains—Eden, Sinai, Zion—and therefore also paradise, revelation, divine presence, and eschatology.[28] In summary, then, the trajectories extending from the Wisdom, creation and Eden texts permeate post-biblical interpretive tradition, and it should be no surprise when they converge, as in Sirach 24.

The second correlation between the portrayal of Wisdom in Proverbs 1–9 and the Genesis creation narratives concerns the manner of God's creating: "And God said, 'Let there be light'; and there was light" (Gen 1:3). God creates through the word, or mouth. This idea is reflected in many texts in biblical and post-biblical literature. Psalms and Isaiah contain the majority of the biblical "creation by word" texts. In the Psalter, although Psalm 19 is the principal statement of Yhwh whose word creates,[29] Ps 33:6 is the clearest affirmation of the idea:

---

[26] This may in turn reflect the interrelationship between paradise and vineyard imagery in early Judaism and Christianity, since the rabbis' "fence" could be based on the "hedge" around the vineyard (Isa 5:5), the people of God.

[27] The paradise symbols can be quite fluid in early Jewish and Christian literature: for example, any remarkable appearance of wood or lumber could be associated with the tree of life. See *L.A.B.* 11:15, in which the tree of life is that which sweetens the bitter water of Marah (Exod 15:25).

[28] "For the LORD has four (sacred) places upon the earth: the garden of Eden and the mountain of the East and this mountain which you are upon today, Mount Sinai, and Mount Zion, which will be sanctified in the new creation for the sanctification of the earth" (*Jub.* 4:26; tr. O. Wintermute, *OTP* 2.63).

[29] H. Gese notes that Psalm 19 prefigures the identification of creation and revelation present in the association of Wisdom and Torah in Sirach 24 ("Wisdom, Son of Man, and the Origins of Christology: The Consistent Development of Biblical Theology," *HBT* 3 [1981] 35). This comment is consistent with my thesis, which has Paul substituting Christ for Torah as the creative and revelatory word, thus relegating Torah as revelation to this age only. A similar case can be made for Johannine theology.

> By the word of the Lord the heavens are made,
> and all their host by the breath of his mouth.

In the following lines, the consistency of Yhwh's creative word and his revelatory word to Israel is expressed:

> He sends forth his command to the earth;
>   his word runs swiftly.
> He gives snow like wool;
>   he scatters hoarfrost like ashes.
> He casts forth his ice like morsels;
>   who can stand before his cold?
> He sends forth his word, and melts them;
>   he makes his wind blow, and the waters flow.
> He declares his word to Jacob,
>   his statutes and ordinances to Israel.
> He has not dealt thus with any other nation;
>   they do not know his ordinances.
> Praise the Lord! (Ps 147:15–20)

Because Yhwh's creative word (דבר; אמרה) in vv. 15–18 is not differentiated from the revelatory word in vv. 19–20, this text anticipates the convergence of creation and revelation symbols in Sirach 24 and later Jewish and Christian thought.

For subsequent early Jewish interpretation in which Wisdom's place in Genesis 1 is firm, the following text from Proverbs 2 confirms the link between Wisdom and word: "For the Lord gives wisdom; from his mouth come knowledge and understanding" (Prov 2:6). In addition, Torah and word occur together as parallel pairs a number of times in prophetic texts:

> Hear the word (דבר) of the Lord, you rulers of Sodom!
> Give ear to the teaching (תורה) of our God, you people of
>   Gomorrah! (Isa 1:10)

> Many peoples shall come, and say:
> "Come, let us go up to the mountain of the Lord,
> to the house of the God of Jacob;
> that he may teach us his ways
> and that we may walk in his paths."
> For out of Zion shall go forth the law (תורה),

and the word (דבר) of the Lord from Jerusalem.
(Isa 2:3; also Mic 4:2)

Hear, O earth; behold, I am bringing evil upon this people, the fruit of their devices, because they have not given heed to my words (דברי); and as for my law (תורתי), they have rejected it. (Jer 6:19)

They made their hearts like adamant lest they should hear the law (תורה) and the words (דברים) which the Lord of hosts had sent by his Spirit through the former prophets. Therefore great wrath came from the Lord of hosts. (Zech 7:12)

The important consequence of this parallelism is that for the inheritors of these texts, for whom the establishing of verbal analogies between texts was a key interpretive methodology, the circle of relationships was complete with the identification of God's word and Torah. The only missing piece in the tradition, the strong connection between Wisdom and Torah, is found in Sirach 24.

To conclude this section I note a text from the *Wisdom of Solomon* that illustrates the sort of relationships that were drawn from the biblical tradition by its early Jewish interpreters:

> O God of my fathers and Lord of mercy,
> who hast *made all things by your word* (ἐν λόγῳ σου),
> and *by your wisdom* (τῇ σοφίᾳ σου) hast formed man,
>   to have dominion over the creatures you have made,
>   and rule the world in holiness and righteousness,
>   and pronounce judgment in uprightness of soul,
> give me the *wisdom that sits by your throne*,
> and do not reject me from among your servants." (Wis 9:1–4)

Creation *by word* and *by wisdom* are parallel here because of the exegetical association of these ideas: (1) the instrumental interpretation of בראשית (Gen 1:1); (2) the interpretation of ראשית as "wisdom"; and (3) the reciprocal interpretation of Gen 1:1 and Gen 1:3, and subsequent mingling of בראשית, Wisdom, and creation by God's word. Creation by God's word, by Wisdom, or by the ראשית are interchangeable and mutually interpretive. The final underlined words (Wis 9:4) add an element to the relational set of images that anticipates christological developments and the figuration of Torah in rabbinic literature:

"Wisdom" is placed at God's throne.[30] Although Eden and/or tree of life imagery are lacking in Wisdom 9, this text converges with other traditions that place the tree of life in the immediate vicinity of the divine throne.[31]

2.3 Wisdom and Torah in Sirach 24

The Wisdom of Jesus ben-Sira (ca. 180 B.C.E.) might be termed an inter-textual composition since it is characterized by its glosses, adaptations and reconfigurations of material from biblical texts. The portrayal of Wisdom in Proverbs 1–9, especially Prov 8:22–31, is incorporated and transformed in Sirach 24.[32] Whereas Prov 8:22–31 writes Wisdom into the creation details of Gen 1:1, Sirach associates the creator Wisdom, which issues forth from the mouth of God (Prov 2:6; Sir 24:3), with the historical revelation to Israel (Sir 24:23). The word of creation is thus conflated with the word of revelation given to Israel through Moses.[33]

---

[30] For throne-speculation in the context of Jewish mediator figures, see Segal, *Two Powers in Heaven.*

[31] E. J. Schnabel notes the concept of the divine Law is undeveloped in the Book of Wisdom, especially in comparison with its development of "Wisdom," and concludes that it is "impossible" to establish "an implicit or explicit identification of wisdom and law" (*Law and Wisdom from Ben Sirach to Paul* [WUNT 216; Tübingen: Mohr [Siebeck], 1985] 134). While it is true that the Book of Wisdom does not manifest an explicit Wisdom/Torah connection, Wis 6:18, which refers to Wisdom's νόμοι, is suggestive that such a connection may have influenced its presentation of Wisdom. Wisdom may completely—that is, not in occasional allusion or echo—represent the cosmological Torah in the Book of Wisdom. In other words, everything that is asserted of Wisdom may be associated with the full-blown early Jewish notion of Torah. It may well be, then, that the Book of Wisdom, rather than Sirach 24, is the high point of the Wisdom/Torah tradition.

[32] For Sirach's dependence on Proverbs, see P. W. Skehan and A. A. Di Lella, *The Wisdom of Ben Sira* (AB 39; New York: Doubleday, 1987) 40–45.

[33] H. Gese does not limit the Wisdom/revelation link to Sirach, for he sees it in Proverbs 8 and Job 28 as well: "In creational order God mediates himself to the world, and in the knowledge of wisdom this mediation is completed. It is particularly evident at this point that the notion of wisdom, standing apart from both God and humanity, has revelatory character and corresponds to the biblical idea of revelation. Sophia appears as *mediatrix Dei*" ("Wisdom, Son of Man, and the Origins of Christology: The Consistent Development of Biblical Theology," *HBT* 3 [1981] 32). Gese also notes that Psalm 19 prefigures the association of creation and revelation in Sirach 24.

Sirach 24 merges images from the narratives of creation, the primordial garden and the Mosaic revelation around Proverbs' depiction of the role of Wisdom in creation.

As Hengel terms it, Sirach 24 represents the "remything" of Wisdom, in which Wisdom became "more and more bound up with the doctrine of creation."[34] For Hengel this transformation can best be accounted for by recourse to the incorporation of Greek thought, specifically Platonic forms, and the Stoic correlation of the universal Law with the Logos that orders the world. These lines, attributed to Zeno, reinforce Hengel's position:

> The universal law (ὁ νόμος κοινός), which is true wisdom (ὁ ὀρθὸς λόγος) premeating everything, is identical with Zeus, the director of the pervading things.[35]

Hengel notes that Platonic and Stoic ideas were not equally attractive to early Jewish thinkers, who would find more acceptable the cosmogony of the Timaeus, with the demiurge as the creator God, and the world soul as its first creation (parallel to Jewish Wisdom); Stoicism's association of God and world does not work well within Jewish systems.[36] On the other hand, Hengel sees a correspondence with Stoic ideas in both the λόγος of Aristobulus and the νόμος of Sirach.[37] Whereas I might argue that there is a happy interface in the post-biblical Wisdom books between Jewish and Greek cosmogonies, and that the "re-mything" in Sirach 24 is the interpretive conjunction of Jewish traditions, Hengel presses the Greek influence, questioning whether

---

[34] Hengel, *Judaism and Hellenism*, 1. 156.

[35] Diogenes Laertius 7.87; cited in Hengel, *Judaism and Hellenism*, 1. 160. The translation of ὁ ὀρθὸς λόγος as "true wisdom" is unfortunate given the nature of the present study, but the relevance of the text is unrelated to the appearance of "wisdom" in *Judaism and Hellenism*.

[36] The world soul "permeates the universe, surrounding it and guaranteeing rationality and harmony to the corporeal world as an invisible mediatrix" (Hengel, *Judaism and Hellenism*, 1.163).

[37] The implications of Wisdom residing exclusively in Torah may have been far-reaching: if (as is the case) the Greek "world-soul" or "Logos" were identified with Torah, there should have been a corresponding Torah mission to the non-Jewish world. Paul's criticism of the Judaisms he knew should be seen in this light, that (some) Jews "kept God's revelation to themselves" (see Rom 10:3, τὴν ἰδίαν δικαιοσύνην ζητοῦντες στῆσαι), when they should have taking Torah to the gentiles. In early Christianity, Jewish Torah-ology was transferred to Christ, and there was a missionary outreach.

the Jewish Wisdom tradition would have developed in this direction without "the necessity to ward off foreign influences."[38] Hengel must show that the ideas in Sirach 24 could not be derived from interpretation of the Jewish Bible, and how the Greek ideas he proposes help Ben Sira's cause. In contrast to Hengel, I find Sirach 24 to be fully understandable in the light of inner-biblical and post-biblical exegesis.

In his major study of inner-biblical exegesis, Michael Fishbane writes of the "wholesale transfer of spatial imagery from one narrative *topos* to another."[39] Because it is viewed by ancient Jewish exegetes as the locus of primordial and eschatological presence of God, Eden is the Bible's most prominent spatial image. Fishbane categorizes Eden typologies as retrojective or projective: a retrojective spatial typology depicts a sacred place and/or institution with Eden imagery, whereas a projective typology presents a future hope in the imagery of Eden. Sirach 24 is a good example of the retrojective form of transference, since Zion, as the site of Wisdom (Sir 24:10), is figuratively likened to Eden. Temple imagery can be linked with Eden as well: "the garden of

[38] Hengel, *Judaism and Hellenism*, 1. 162. Hengel is on much surer ground with the "seven-fold *Logos*" of Aristobulus (2d cent. B.C.E.; trans. of the Aristobulus fragments by A. Yarbro Collins, OTP 2. 831–42). The seventh day is the source of the Platonic Light, "in which all things are contemplated" (frag. 5.9); "Wisdom" is called a "lantern" in the "Peripatetic school" (frag. 5.10); "Wisdom" of Proverbs 8—which "existed before heaven and earth"—is linked with the Greek philosophical Light (frag. 5.11; notice the manner in which concepts, even from different authoritative traditions, are linked by verbal and/or thematic analogy). Hengel summarizes the pattern of associations between concepts: "By and large, Aristobulous has fused the original Jewish-Palestinian conception of personified '*hokma*' as the consort of God at the creation of the world with the biblical account of creation in Gen. 1–2:4a, with conceptions of Greek philosophical cosmology and epistemology, yet without giving up their specific features" (Hengel, *Judaism and Hellenism*, 1. 167). This "fusion" Hengel contrasts with Sirach and the Pharisees' (i.e., proto-rabbinic Judaism) link of Torah and cosmic Wisdom. In the end, by driving a wedge between Aristobulus and Sirach, Hengel somewhat betrays his dominant thesis: he himself is using "Palestinian" and "hellenistic" as poles. There is not so great a difference, however, between the Wisdom/Logos link and the Wisdom/Torah; the contrast between them is one of focus, not kind. To the early Jewish mind there is—as I suggest throughout this study—a natural link between Torah and Logos as ciphers of revelation: Wisdom "came forth from the *mouth* of the Most High" (Sir 24:3). Wisdom and Logos should not be set in opposition unless it is demonstrable.

[39] M. Fishbane, *Biblical Interpretation in Ancient Israel* (Oxford: Clarendon, 1985) 368. See also his earlier but more extensive treatment of spatial typology in *Text and Texture* (New York: Schocken, 1979) 111–20.

Eden was the holy of holies and the dwelling of the Lord" (*Jub.* 8:19). Employing the temple/Eden imagery, but in Fishbane's "projective" form, Revelation 21–22 depicts the eschatological throne of God with the attributes of Eden. In Sirach 24 the attributes of Sinai—the site of God's presence and the mountain of revelation—are transferred to Zion. The biblical precedent for Zion as revelation mountain is Isa 2:3, in which the "Torah will go out from Zion."

As yet there is no Hebrew text of Sirach 24, despite the fact that 68 percent of Sirach has been recovered in Hebrew fragments from the Cairo Genizah, Qumran, Masada, and other sites.[40] I will not seek, therefore, to identify word and phrase intertextual relationships between the Greek version of Sirach 24 and the Hebrew of Proverbs 8. Rather, my goal is to identify the biblical *topoi* Sirach utilized, especially those from Proverbs 1–9. Patrick W. Skehan confirms the intertextual nature of Sirach 24: he shows that Sirach 24 was modeled on Proverbs 8 (they have 35 common lines), although there are "strong echoes also of Deuteronomy and of Genesis."[41] For this study it is the influence of both Genesis 1–3 and Proverbs 1–9 on Sirach 24 that is important.

An interpretive key to Sirach 24 is found in its uniting of imagery relating to the paradigmic creation and revelation narratives around the personified Wisdom of Proverbs 1–9. For the sake of analysis, these sets of relational images, as they appear in Sirach 24, must be dissected. I will begin with a study by Maurice Gilbert that demonstrates how Sirach 24 includes every dimension of spatial and temporal reality.[42] The first aspect is apparent in the use of the four dimensions of Jewish cosmology:

> I dwelt in high places, and my throne was in a pillar of cloud.
> Alone I have made the circuit of the vault of heaven and have
> walked in the depths of the abyss.

---

[40] Percentage from A. A. Di Lella, "Wisdom of Ben-Sira," *ABD* 6.935.

[41] P. W. Skehan, "Structures in Poems on Wisdom: Proverbs 8 and Sirach 24," *CBQ* 41 (1979) 376–77. The basis of Skehan's comparative analysis is a Hebrew retroversion of Sirach 24, which is compared with the Hebrew of Proverbs 8. Skehan, "Structures in Poems on Wisdom," 376–77. Although he identifies these echoes, Skehan does little to verify the intertextual relationship of Sirach 24 to biblical material beyond Proverbs 8; nor does he address *topoi.*

[42] M. Gilbert, "L'éloge de la Sagesse (*Siracide* 24)," *RTL* 5 (1974) 326–48.

In the waves of the sea, in the whole earth, and in every people
and nation I have gotten a possession. (Sir 24:4–6)

The vertical poles are the "high places" and "abyss" (24:4–5), and the
horizontal poles are "sea" and "earth" (24:6). The temporal poles are
expressed with phrases that depict the beginning and end of time.[43]

From eternity, in the beginning, he created me,
and for eternity I shall not cease to exist. (24:9)

Sirach's declaration of Wisdom's inclusive influence among people
should be included here as well ("every people and nation"; 24:6).
Wisdom dominates the entire universe, but in our world it is concentrated in one place and people; thus Gilbert argues that the movement
in Sirach 24 is from descent to concentration to expansion. Zion, the
Jerusalem temple, Israel, and Torah are a "sacred center" in which the
heavenly world (the abode of Wisdom) enters our world:[44]

In the holy tabernacle I ministered before him,
and so I was established in Zion.
In the beloved city likewise he gave me a resting place,
and in Jerusalem was my dominion. (Sir 24:10–11)

All wisdom may come from God (Sir 1:1), but in Sirach 24 "all
wisdom" seems limited to that which enters this world through
Israel.[45]

---

[43] Sirach's temporal poles (πρὸ τοῦ αἰῶνος and ἕως αἰῶνος; 24:9) develop those of
Proverbs 8: Wisdom was established מעולם (LXX = πρὸ τοῦ αἰῶνος; 8:23) and would be
with God בכל־עת (8:30). Compare also Sir 1:1: "All wisdom comes from the Lord and is
with him for ever (εἰς τὸν αἰῶνα)." In Sir 42:21, πρὸ τοῦ αἰῶνος καὶ εἰς τὸν αἰῶνα represents
מעולם; there is no Hebrew clause matching εἰς τὸν αἰῶνα, although the following parallelism implies Wisdom's eternal future: "nothing can be added or taken away." Πρὸ
αἰῶνος translates מקדם in Ps 74:12. In Sir 44:13, ἕως αἰῶνος translates עד עולם, as it does
often in the LXX (e.g., Exod 12:24; Jer 25:5; Ps 18:50); cp. also עד עולם/ἕως τοῦ αἰῶνος (Sir
48:25). I assume that the temporal poles of Sir 24:9 reflect מעולם and עד עולם. Hebrew
text of Sirach in F. Vattioni, *Ecclesiastico: Testo ebraico con apparato critico e versioni
greca, latina e siriaca* (Naples: Pubblicazioni del Seminario di Semitistica, 1968).

[44] See Fishbane, *Biblical Interpretation in Ancient Israel*, 368.

[45] There is some dispute whether the concentration of divine wisdom among the
Jews should be regarded as particularism, especially with regard to the special interpreters of that wisdom to whom all must go (like Ben Sira, who is so privileged; Sir
24:30–34), or universalism, since all wisdom is God's wisdom (Sir 1:1), and the Torah is

The first line of Wisdom's speech introduces the first of the Genesis 1 *topoi*: Wisdom, which "came forth from the mouth of the Most High" (Sir 24:3a), is associated with God's primordial creative word in Gen 1:3–27; the second half of the line, in which Wisdom "covered the earth like a mist" (Sir 24:3b), recalls the mist of Gen 2:6 as well as the cloud in the wilderness narrative.[46] The revelation *topoi* (mixed with theophanic symbols) are introduced in 24:4b, in which Wisdom's throne on the pillar of cloud recalls Yhwh's presence prior to the giving of the Torah: "Yhwh went before them by day in a pillar of cloud" (Exod 13:21; also Num 12:5; Deut 31:15; Ps 98:7; Neh 9:12; see also Exod 33:9).

Despite the fact that we do not possess the Hebrew of Sirach 24, it is still possible to read the verb κατασκηνόω (Sir 24:4a) as suggesting that Wisdom's "high places" were associated with the tabernacle and Temple dwelling of Yhwh:

> Solomon said, "The Lord has said that he would dwell (κατασκηνῶ-σαι) in thick darkness. I have built thee an exalted house, a place for thee to dwell in for ever." (2 Chr 6:1–2)

Forms of σκηνή were probably attractive lexical choices in such contexts because of their assonance with words formed from שׁכן, of which the most significant is the post-biblical cipher for Yhwh's presence, *Shekinah.*[47] In the NT the prime example is found in the Johannine

---

the repository of universal wisdom. The chosen people are charged with channeling God's wisdom (Torah) to the nations, but it is still their possession, their inheritance (Sir 24:23). Hengel stresses the particularity of wisdom in the hands of the privileged few (*Judaism and Hellenism*, 1. 163), whereas R. A. Argall pleads for the universalist understanding of wisdom in Sirach (1 Enoch *and Sirach: A Comparative Literary and Conceptual Analysis of the Themes of Revelation, Creation and Judgment* [SBLEJL 8; Atlanta: Scholars Press, 1995] 56 n. 144). This problem transcends the confines of Sirach, for there is a natural tension inherent with any assertion that "I have what all of humanity needs"—is the prominent feature the one who possesses, or the others who need? There is abusable power in claims to have the one thing everyone needs. Finally, Sirach's assertion that Torah is the one instantiation of divine wisdom is positive, but there is an implied negative: all other forms of human wisdom (e.g., philosophy, sacred texts) are not.

[46] On the relationship between ὀμίχλη ("mist"; Sir 24:3; 43:22), ענן ("cloud"; Sir 43:22) and אד ("mist"?; Gen 2:6), see Gilbert, "L'éloge de la Sagesse," 342–43.

[47] Although the roots of Shekinah are in the biblical wilderness and temple narratives, perhaps the best access to the development of the tradition is through the rabbinic

prologue in which the Logos is said to have "become flesh and dwelt (ἐσκήνωσεν) among us" (John 1:14), a likely allusion to Yhwh's glory that "settled" (שׁכן) on Mt. Sinai (Exod 24:16; see also Exod 25:8; 29:45–46; 40:35), since "we beheld the glory" of the Logos. Sir 24:7–8, which depicts Wisdom as receiving her "dwelling" (κατασκήνωσον) in Israel, is consistent with the biblical presence *topoi*. Wisdom is also placed in the "holy tabernacle" (ἐν σκηνῇ ἁγίᾳ; 24:10), which in this context must refer to the heavenly version.[48]

According to Gilbert's categories, Sir 24:10 begins the "concentration" of heavenly properties in Israel with "I was established in Zion." The "expansion" begins when Wisdom "takes root" (Sir 24:12), and from there the author likens its fruitfulness to various trees, plants, spices, and aromatics. In Sir 24:13–17 there are actually 12 similes for Wisdom "established in Zion," arranged in a 2-4-4-2 chiastic pattern. Each group is introduced by ὡς: cedar, cypress, palm, olive, plane, rosebush, myrrh, incense, terebinth, and vine are likened to Wisdom individually (= 10); cassia and camel's thorn are likened together, as are galbanum, onycha and stacte (24:15). The similes derive part of their effectiveness from the way they link Wisdom imagery to two biblical narratives. First, Gilbert recognizes that the author has Exodus 30 in mind:[49] Yhwh instructs Moses to make for the holy places—including the Tent of Meeting (ἡ σκηνὴ τοῦ μαρτυρίου; Exod 30:26 LXX)—a chrism including myrrh, cinnamon (Exod 30:23; Sir 24:15) and cassia (Exod 30:23; Sir 24:16), and incense of stacte, onycha, galbanum, and frankincense (Exod 30:34; Sir 24:15). Because of the language of presence (שׁכן/σκηνή) in Sirach 24, the mingling of other *topoi* from the Exodus narrative only strengthens the association of Wisdom with the wilderness, and temple theophanies.

Second, a more profound intertextual confluence appears in these similes. I have already noted that Sirach 24 links the creation and Eden accounts of Genesis 1–3 with the Sinai revelation; the explicit drawing on Exodus 30 manifests the latter aspect. The twelve similes in turn are figurative allusions to the Eden narrative, and subsequent develop-

---

literature, especially the midrashim. See especially E. E. Urbach, *The Sages: Their Concepts and Beliefs* (2 vols.; Jerusalem: Magnes, 1975) 2. 37–65.

[48] See A. Fournier-Bidoz, "L'Arbre et la Demeure: Siracide XXIV 10–17," *VT* 34 (1984) 3–5.

[49] Gilbert, "L'éloge de la Sagesse," 332–33.

ment of the primordial paradise scenario.[50] Most commentators notice
that four of the six rivers in Sir 24:25–27 are the paradise rivers of Gen
2:10–14.[51] The rivers, as well as the other elements that recall the paradise narrative (e.g., the watering of the παράδεισον, Gen 2:10; Sir
24:30–31), deepen the earlier association of Torah with the tree of life
(Prov 3:18). In other words, Sirach establishes a three-way linkage
between Wisdom, the tree of life, and Torah.[52] Wisdom is the key
middle term in the relationship, which may be represented as follows:

  a. Wisdom → tree of life (Prov 3:18)
  b. Wisdom → Torah (Sir 24:23)
  c. Torah → tree of life

The relationship between Torah and the tree of life is figurative rather
than explicit in Sirach 24. The wealth of figures, however, makes a
clear connection with paradise. The point of the similes is evident in
comparison with similar material in John's Apocalypse and rabbinic
literature. In the vision of the new heaven and earth, and the new
Jerusalem, the seer sees that the tree of life has twelve kinds of fruit
(Rev 22:2). The twelve trees and plants of Sirach 24 probably reflect an
earlier stage of speculation on the nature of the tree of life, in which
the tree of life cannot be limited to any one type of tree. Moreover,
outside of Sirach 24 tree metaphors are applied to Wisdom: Sir 1:20

---

[50] The Hebrew term in Gen 2:8 is גַן ("garden"), rendered παράδεισος in the LXX.
The latter term, taken up in John's Apocalypse (Rev 2:7), became the common cipher
for both primordial and eschatological imagery—that is, the *Endzeit/Urzeit* typology
characteristic of apocalypses and the apocalyptic *Vorstellungswelt*.

[51] There is no sixth river in the RSV of Sir 24:27a: φῶς ("light") reflects the Hebrew
אוֹר, which may have been a misreading of an original Hebrew יְאוֹר ("Nile"). According
to Skehan, the Syriac (ܢܗܪܐ) supports יְאוֹר as the correct reading (*The Wisdom of Ben
Sira*, 330). The Syriac roots for "light" and "river" are the same, so the Greek version
may represent a deliberate skewing based on "light" as a figure for Torah (Prov 6:23).

[52] Argall understands the tree similes in Sirach 24 as reflecting the tree of knowledge
as the "world tree," but his identification is based on a comparison with the "tree of
wisdom" of *1 Enoch* 32, and the prominence of wisdom *topoi* in Sirach rather than a
close reading of Sir 24:13–22 (1 Enoch *and* Sirach, 93–94; see also 32–35, 55). The trees of
Enoch and Sirach are functionally comparable, and there is overlap in their descrip-
tions, but they do not seem to be based on the same interpretation of Genesis 2–3. There
is no mention of the tree of wisdom in Sirach, and the figurative language of Sirach 24
points to the tree of life rather the tree of knowledge. The tree of life is normally recognized as the Jewish form of the "world tree."

refers to Wisdom's root and its branches.[53] This figuration likely reflects the biblical tradition of a special tree, modeled on the archetypal tree of life, or world tree, whose branches shelter "all kinds of birds" (Ezek 17:23, Ezek 28:14–16; Ezekiel 31; Daniel 4). Evidence that the tree of life was interpreted in this manner is found in 1QHodayot 16: the "trees [עצי] of life" in the "everlasting [עולם] plantation" would become food for "all [the anima]ls of the wood," and "its trunk will be pasture for all who cross the path, and its leaves for all winged birds" (lines 6–9).

In summary form, these are the other creation/Eden *topoi* in Sirach 24: Torah is likened to overflowing rivers, specifically the four rivers of Gen 2:10–14 plus the Nile and Jordan (Sir 24:25–27). Reference is made to the "first man" (ὁ πρῶτος; Sir 24:28), which refers to the Adam of Genesis 1–3. In support of his role as a mediator, the author (or Wisdom?) likens himself to waters that nourish a garden (παράδεισος; Sir 24:30–31), which continues the Eden theme and suggests furthermore the idea of God's people as a plantation, or a vineyard.[54] Consistent with Gilbert's scheme, the water that concentrates in the garden goes out and becomes a river and then a sea (Sir 24:31).[55] There may be a final creation image in the instruction (παιδεία) that would "shine forth like the dawn" (Sir 24:32). This possibly reflects speculation on the mysterious light of the first day of creation (Gen 1:3). Ben Sira did

---

[53] For more on the Eden imagery in Sirach 24, see Fournier-Bidoz, "L'Arbre et la Demeure," 8–9.

[54] The "vineyard" is a biblical figure for the people of God (e.g., Isa 5:1–7; cf. Exod 15:17). There is a related set of images for the people as God's "plantation": for example, the language of 1QS 8, where the Qumran community is the "Eternal Plantation" (line 5) which offers up "sweet fragrances" (line 10); also Isa 61:3, where those who "mourn in Zion" are to be given a "garland instead of ashes," the "oil of gladness instead of mourning," and will be "oaks of righteousness, the planting of the Lord." Each of these images—especially plantation, fragrance and oil—are associated in Jewish and Christian literature with the paradise of Genesis 2–3.

[55] Various "water" terms are used figuratively for Torah in biblical and post-biblical literature. See M. Fishbane, "The Well of Living Water: A Biblical Motif and its Ancient Transformations," in *Sha'arei Talmon* (ed. M. Fishbane and E. Tov with W. Fields; Winona Lake, IN: Eisenbrauns, 1992) 3–16. The benefits of Torah study are likened to flowing water in this Mishnaic text: "He that occupies himself in the study of the Law for its own sake merits many things . . . to him are revealed the secrets of the Law, and is made like to a never-failing spring and like to a river that flows ever more mightily" (*m. Abot* 6:1).

not read Genesis as moderns do: the Eden narrative takes place before any celestial lights were created (Gen 2:5), so the ancient interpreter understood that God's glory illuminated the primordial world. This feature of the story is reflected in the apocalyptic *Endzeit* paradise scene:

> And night shall be no more; they need no light of lamp or sun, for the Lord God will be their light, and they shall reign for ever and ever. (Rev 22:5; cf. Isa 60:19)

Light itself is a metaphor for Torah (Prov 6:23; Wis 18:4).[56]

It is in the context of the mingling in Sirach 24 of biblical *topoi* from Genesis 1–3, the Exodus wilderness narrative, and Proverbs 1–9, that one must interpret the explicit identification of Wisdom with Torah:

> ταῦτα πάντα βίβλος διαθήκης θεοῦ ὑψίστου νόμον
> ὃν ἐνετείλατο ἡμῖν Μωυσῆς κληρονομίαν συναγωγαῖς Ιακωβ
> (Sir 24:23)

Again Ben Sira is employing biblical material: the phrase "book of the covenant" occurs a few times (Exod 24:7; 2 Kgs 23:2–3, 21; 2 Chr 34:30–31; 1 Macc 1:57),[57] but not parallel to "Law." The second half of Sir 24:23 (νόμον ὃν ἐνετείλατο ἡμῖν Μωυσῆς κληρονομίαν συναγωγαῖς Ιακωβ) is an exact citation of the LXX of Deut 33:4. The interpretation of deuteronomic revelation symbols is specific in Sir 24:23—"all this is Torah"—whereas the confluence of symbols from Exodus (tent of meeting), Wisdom, creation, and paradise are figuratively, poetically expressed. Torah is, in a sense, Ben Sira's organizing principle for the other *topoi*; although Wisdom is consistently the lead character in Sirach 24, the summarizing statement in verse 23 shows that Torah was the key all along.

---

[56] See G. Vermes, "The Torah is a Light," *VT* 8 (1958) 436–38. "Although it would not be wise to underestimate the importance of the similarity of the words,—which is even greater in Aramaic (אוריתא—אורתא) than in Hebrew,—the main emphasis should be laid on the association of meaning between light, on the one hand, and truth, divine revelation, Torah, etc., on the other" (437). Rather, the primary "association of meaning" is in the interpretive confluence of the creative word that says יהי אור (Gen 1:3) and the Torah given at Sinai.

[57] The form of "book" is always βιβλίος rather than the βίβλος of Sir 24:23.

How complete was the identification of Torah with Wisdom?[58] Was Ben Sira asserting that Torah was what Wisdom was, that Wisdom might as well be considered Torah, even before the Sinai revelation? In other words, was Torah around in the beginning, was it preexistent? G. Boccaccini has argued that Wisdom and Torah were not really identified with each other, since "identity is a transitive relation, in which the two elements bear the same properties"; "Wisdom and Law in Sirach are not interchangeable terms."[59] For Boccaccini, Sirach presents Torah as the historical instantiation of Wisdom rather than Torah itself as eternal and preexistent entity:

> The Law, as the historical embodiment of Wisdom, is the means through which one can obtain the gift of wisdom, but in the cosmic context it is but one of the rules that God in His Wisdom has established to govern human affairs on earth.[60]

Boccaccini is not convinced the preexistence of Torah was adhered to until the rabbis specifically asserted it.[61]

Although Boccaccini's problem with the notion of identity seems anachronistic because one cannot expect ancient writers to conform to modern standards of identification, and arbitrary because Sirach 24 is almost entirely poetry, about which one can demand little, his corrective is warranted in at least one respect: Sirach did not directly assert that Torah was preexistent. The language of preexistence belongs to Wisdom rather than Torah: Wisdom "was established in Zion" (Sir 24:10); she found the "resting place" she sought (Sir 24:7). On the other

---

[58] The confluence of creation and revelation in Sirach 24 is not the only means by which Ben Sira expresses Wisdom's identification with Torah. See Argall's insightful treatment of the "*Liebesgeschichte*" of Wisdom and her pursuers, especially his analysis of Sirach's quasi-sexual language of exploration and discovery—that is, study and interpretation (1 Enoch *and Sirach*, 57–73).

[59] G. Boccaccini, "The Preexistence of the Torah: A Commonplace in Second Temple Judaism or a Later Rabbinic Development?" *Henoch* 17 (1995) 331. Prof. Boccaccini generously provided me with a pre-publication copy of this paper.

[60] Boccaccini, "Preexistence of the Torah," 331. Boccaccini seems to go beyond what is actually present in Sirach; he substantiates this judgment well, however, in *Middle Judaism* (Minneapolis: Fortress, 1991) 81–98.

[61] A similar point is made by R. Penna: "The conception of a pre-existence of the Torah is rabbinic" ("Dissolution and Restoration of the Relationship of Law and Wisdom in Paul," *Paul the Apostle* [2 vols.; Collegeville: Liturgical, 1996] 2. 146).

hand, since Boccaccini does not investigate the figurative language of Sirach 24, nor ask what is behind the figuration, his verdict is limited. Sirach 24 is precisely about the presence of Torah in the beginning of creation—hence its preexistence—and at the end of this age (Sir 24:9). When Ben Sira declared that "all this is the Law," "this" represents all that Wisdom proclaimed about herself in vv. 3–22. Torah is Wisdom, rather than Wisdom became Torah. Ben Sira figuratively asserted an equivalence of Torah with God's Wisdom and creative Word. Thus their texts were mutually interpretive: if Wisdom is in creation and Eden, so too is Torah. The creative word and the revelatory word are one.

2.4 Wisdom and Torah in Baruch 3:9–4:4

The features of Baruch's poem to Wisdom overlap with Sirach 24, especially its accumulation of words, phrases, images, and whole lines from the biblical Wisdom texts (Proverbs; Job 28). For Baruch, however, Deuteronomy is the more prominent subtext. The poem begins with a parallelism of "the commandments of life" and "wisdom" (φρόνησις; Bar 3:9) that recalls Deut 4:6;[62] later in the poem there is another parallelism in which the election of God is linked with the possession of wisdom (Bar 3:27–28). The deuteronomic disobedience-punishment motif, in which Israel's unhappy circumstance is directly linked to its unfaithfulness to God's commands, is prevalent in Bar 3:9–4:4: the exile is attributed to Israel's abandoning the "fountain of wisdom," Torah (Bar 3:12). The most notable echo of Deuteronomy in Baruch's Wisdom poem is Bar 3:29–30:

Deut 30:12–14[63]
"It is not in heaven, that you should say,
'Who will go up for us to heaven,
and bring it to us, that we may

Bar 3:29–30
*"Who has gone up into heaven, and
taken her, and brought her down*

[62] In the RSV of Baruch, "wisdom"—which does not occur outside of Bar 3:9–4:4—occurs five times. Three times "wisdom" translates φρόνησις (Bar 3:9, 14, 28), and two times it translates σοφία (Bar 3:12, 23).

[63] Only the comparable lines are given in Greek. The Greek is used because there is no Hebrew text of Baruch. The italics are to facilitate identification of common language.

hear it and do it?'"

τίς ἀναβήσεται ἡμῖν εἰς τὸν οὐρανὸν
καὶ λήμψεται αὐτὴν ἡμῖν
καὶ ἀκούσαντες αὐτὴν ποιήσομεν

"Neither is it beyond the sea, that you
    should say,
'Who will go over the sea for us, and
 bring it to us, that we may hear it
and do it?'"

τίς διαπεράσει ἡμῖν εἰς τὸ πέραν τῆς
θαλάσσης καὶ λήμψεται ἡμῖν αὐτήν καὶ
ἀκουστὴν ἡμῖν ποιήσει αὐτήν καὶ
ποιήσομεν (30:13)

"But the word is very near you; it is in
your mouth and in your heart, so that
you can do it."

from the clouds?"

τίς ἀνέβη εἰς τὸν οὐρανὸν
καὶ ἔλαβεν αὐτὴν
καὶ κατεβίβασεν αὐτὴν ἐκ τῶν νεφελῶν

"Who has gone over the sea, and found
her, and will buy her for pure gold?"

τίς διέβη πέραν τῆς θαλάσσης
καὶ εὗρεν αὐτὴν καὶ οἴσει αὐτὴν
χρυσίου ἐκλεκτοῦ

("After this she appeared upon earth
and lived among men."

μετὰ τοῦτο ἐπὶ τῆς ὤφθη
καὶ ἐν τοῖς ἀνθρώποις συνανεστράφη
[Bar 3:37; 3:38 LXX])[64]

The verbal relationship is not tight between the two texts, but the use
of the phrase "going up to heaven" for Wisdom/Torah is unmistakable, especially in a Torah context, in a poem so otherwise dependent
on Deuteronomy.

In Baruch, like Job 28:23, only God knows the way to Wisdom (3:16–
32). It is in this context that Baruch understands God's gift of Torah:

He found the whole way to knowledge, and gave her to Jacob his ser-
vant and to Israel whom he loved. (Bar 3:36)

The gift of Wisdom is then explicitly identified with the Mosaic revelation (in deuteronomic language):

She is the book of the commandments of God
(ἡ βίβλος τῶν προσταγμάτων τοῦ θεοῦ),

---

[64] Bar 3:37 has often been considered a Christian interpolation, but scholarship
today generally takes it as original. It is included here because it may be an interpretation of Deut 30:14, "the word is near you."

and the law that endures for ever
(ὁ νόμος ὁ ὑπάρχων εἰς τὸν αἰῶνα).
All who hold her fast will live,
and those who forsake her will die. (Bar 4:1)

This is, of course, very much like Sir 24:23; the details are different but each of them correlates to something in the larger context of Sirach 24. The line that asserts the Law's eternality is paralleled in the second clause of Sir 24:9. The final lines of Bar 4:1 roughly echo Sir 24:22:

> Whoever obeys me will not be put to shame,
> and those who work with my help will not sin

Although both texts connect one's fate with obedience to the Law, Baruch follows Deut 30:15, 19 by associating Torah with life and death.[65]

Although there are many similarities between Sirach 24 and Bar 3:9–4:4, Wisdom in Baruch plays no role in creation, and there is no direct relationship with the ראשית of Gen 1:1 or Prov 8:22. The Wisdom/Torah connection in Baruch is therefore on a different scale: few would describe Wisdom in Baruch as a hypostasis, or a consort of God. On the other hand, Baruch goes beyond the simple association of Torah and Wisdom in Deut 4:6 since Wisdom for Baruch is cosmic, something that enters our world from above, and is found and distributed by God alone.

2.5 Wisdom in the Similitudes of Enoch

The Similitudes (also called the "Parables") of Enoch comprise chapters 37–71 of the Ethiopic Enoch book (*1 Enoch*). At Qumran Aramaic portions of each Enoch book have been discovered except the Similitudes, so they have been regarded as a later addition to *1 Enoch*. The earliest portions of the Enoch books date to perhaps the fourth century

---

[65] Both the connection between Torah and one's fate and the synonymous use of Torah and Wisdom are present in this text: "In you we have put our trust, because, behold, your Law is with us, and we know that *we do not fall* as long as we keep statutes. We shall always be blessed; at least, we did not mingle with the nations. For we are all a people of the Name; we, who received one Law from the One. And that *Law* that is among us will help us, and that excellent *wisdom* which is in us will support us" (*2 Apoc. Bar.* 48:22–24; tr. A. Klign, *OTP* 1. 633).

B.C.E., but the Similitudes are commonly dated from late first century B.C.E. to late first century C.E. The dating issue is important for NT scholarship because the Similitudes' "Son of Man" figure attests to a heavenly redeeming figure analogous to Christ in the NT. For my purposes the dating issue is not vital; it is enough that a consensus considers the Similitudes to be roughly contemporaneous with early Christianity and the production of the NT.

There is no narrative introduction to the Similitudes; they are simply presented as Enoch's second vision, which is described as a "vision of wisdom" (37:1):

> This is the *beginning of the words of wisdom* which I commenced to propound, saying to those who dwell in the earth, "Listen, you first ones, and look, you last ones, the words of the Holy One, which I teach before the Lord of the Spirits. It is good to declare these words to those of former times, but one should not withhold the *beginning of wisdom* from those of latter days. Until now such wisdom, which received as I recited (it) in accordance with the will of the Lord of the Spirits, had not been bestowed upon me before the face of the Lord of the Spirits. From him, the lot of eternal life has been given to me. Three things were imparted to me"; and I began to recount them to those who dwell upon the earth. (*1 Enoch* 37:2–5)[66]

Because the Ethiopic Enoch is either a translation of a Greek original or a Greek translation of an Aramaic or Hebrew original, convincing arguments about specific vocabulary are tenuous. But given the consistent choice in the Similitudes of "wisdom" as the cipher for Enoch's revelations, a case can be made that the language underlined in the above text reflects the biblical and post-biblical wisdom tradition. The unique phrase "vision of wisdom" is a clue that the author is in the orbit of biblical wisdom because wisdom is usually not connected with apocalyptic visions,[67] although the genres share many *topoi* and ideas.[68] Since it is treated as an entity that can be withheld (v. 3), the

---

[66] English translations of *1 Enoch* are from E. Isaac, *OTP* 1. 5–89.

[67] M. Black, *The Book of Enoch or 1 Enoch* (Leiden: Brill, 1985) 194.

[68] Establishing a connection in form and content between an apocalypse and a "wisdom book" is Argall's project in *1 Enoch and Sirach*. Von Rad has been the leading spokesperson for wisdom as the "real matrix from which apocalyptic literature originates" (*Old Testament Theology*, 2. 306).

phrase "beginning of wisdom" is conspicuous as well: R. H. Charles noted that it may represent the Hebrew ראש חכמה, in which ראש means "sum."[69] To my knowledge ראש חכמה is unprecedented.[70] It seems more likely that what is represented in Ethiopic by *re'esu* (equivalent to ראש) was originally a match for the ראשית/ἀρχή of Gen 1:1, which was interpreted as חכמה.[71] Moreover, ראשית חכמה has biblical precedent in Ps 110:10 and Prov 4:7.[72] Supporting this reading is the phrase "words of the Holy One" (*1 Enoch* 37:2), which is associated with wisdom and may allude to God's primordial creative activity.

"Wisdom" does not occur again until *1 Enoch* 42, a wisdom poem that is antithetical to Sir 24:7–8, 10–12 (and perhaps Bar 3:29–30):

> Wisdom could not find a place in which she could dwell;
> but a place was found (for her) in the heavens.
> Then Wisdom went out to dwell with the children of the people,
> but she found no dwelling place.
> (So) Wisdom returned to her place
> and she settled permanently among the angels.
> (*1 Enoch* 42:1–2)[73]

Sirach has Wisdom accessible in Zion, ultimately as Torah (Sir 24:23), but the author of the Similitudes specifically denies this. Wisdom is in heaven, and thus only the visionary may access this Wisdom. The primary role of the visionary represents a further contradiction of Sirach 24, where the author is the channel through which God's Wisdom becomes available to those outside of the "garden" (Sir 24:30-34). Con-

---

[69] R. H. Charles, *The Book of Enoch or 1 Enoch* (Oxford: Clarendon, 1912) 69. Charles also noted that תחלת חכמה (Prov 9:10) may have been the original.

[70] Although compare ראש דברך, "sum of your word" (Ps 119:160); ראש is rendered with ἀρχή in the LXX.

[71] For the Ethiopic text of *1 Enoch*, see M. Knibb, *The Ethiopic Book of Enoch* (2 vols.; Oxford: Clarendon, 1978).

[72] As Black notes (*The Book of Enoch*, 194).

[73] In the translations of Charles and Knibb, *1 Enoch* 94:5 also has wisdom as without a dwelling among people, but note that Isaac's translation does not because it follows a different Ethiopic reading. The tradition of Wisdom's inaccessibility springs from Prov 1:28: "Then they will call upon me, but I will not answer; they will seek me diligently but will not find me." The future oriented language is transformed into an apocalyptic sign of the last days: "Wisdom shall withdraw into its chamber, and it shall be sought by many but shall not be found, and unrighteousness and unrestraint shall increase on earth" (4 Ezra 5:9b–10).

versely, the author of the Similitudes may be the channel of God's Wisdom, but the inaccessability of that Wisdom through normal means necessitates the visionary. The Torah scholar of Sirach exercises control over legitimate interpretation of Wisdom as revelation, but the Enochian visionary alone views "all the hidden things" (*1 Enoch* 40:2), "all the secrets of heaven" (*1 Enoch* 41:1). Control of the means of revelation is thus absolute for the apocalypticist.[74]

The theological rift between Sirach 24 and the Similitudes is further exacerbated by the use of "Iniquity" as the antithesis of Wisdom (*1 Enoch* 42:3). Generally, this "Iniquity" contributes to the post–biblical Wisdom tradition a typically apocalyptic pessimism about present existence. More to the point, Iniquity is employed in a surprising figurative attack on Sirach's notion of Torah, and probably even on the Sinai Torah itself. Iniquity assumes the place Sirach reserved for Torah: "Iniquity"—not Wisdom—dwells with people. The application to Iniquity of water metaphors ("rain" and "dew"; v. 3) is striking as well, since they are elsewhere regularly used for Torah.

How is the Similitudes' negative appraisal of Torah as Wisdom to be understood? Although he recognizes that the specific "relationship of Enoch's wisdom to the Mosaic Torah is ambiguous,"[75] G. W. E. Nickelsburg consistently asserts that the Enochic corpus as a whole represents for its authors Torah rival to the Mosaic Torah. I shall take up the Enochian rival Torah theory in §3.4, so for now I mention it only to provide a context for *1 Enoch* 42, specifically the motivation for the figurative denigration of the Sinai Torah.

Besides the Enochian seer who is granted access to heavenly wisdom, or "secrets," the two eschatological figures of the Similitudes (who may be the same figure) are revealers of wisdom. The Son of Man (dubbed the "light of the gentiles"; *1 Enoch* 48:4) is a revealer of "the wisdom of the Lord of the Spirits to the righteous and the holy ones" (48:7). The scene is sprinkled with Wisdom/Torah *topoi*: there is a "fountain of righteousness" surrounded by many "fountains of wisdom," and those who partake of the water from the fountains are

---

[74] The tension between Enoch and Sirach over access to God's Wisdom is analogous to P. Hanson's visionary-hierocratic (*The Dawn of Apocalyptic* [rev. ed.; Philadelphia: Fortress, 1979]) or visionary-pragmatist (*The Diversity of Scripture* [Philadelphia: Fortress, 1982] 37–62) polarity; Sirach's Torah scholar plays the role of cultic authority.

[75] Nickelsburg, "Wisdom and Apocalypticism in Early Judaism: Some Points for Discussion," *SBLASP* 1994: 720.

"filled with wisdom" (48:1). The "spirit of wisdom" dwells within the "Elect One" (49:3). The Elect One is a judge (49:3), and at the resurrection of the dead he sits on the throne of glory (also 61:8; 62:2-5), and out of his mouth come "all the secrets of wisdom" (51:3):

> In those days, (the Elect One) shall sit on my throne, and from the conscience of his mouth shall come out all the secrets of wisdom, for the Lord of the Spirits has given them to him and glorified him.

Throughout *1 Enoch* "wisdom" is the cipher for Enochic revelation, but these "secrets of wisdom" are ambiguous; they do not appear, as is the case generally in *1 Enoch*, to reflect the Mosaic Torah. Therefore, one role of the Similitudes' eschatological figure(s) is to reveal heavenly wisdom, quite probably a Wisdom/Torah different or competing with that of Moses.[76] And there appears to be an *Urzeit/Endzeit* relationship in the Enoch corpus between the wisdom granted to Enoch and that which the Elect will receive through the work of the Enochic eschatological figure (cf. *1 Enoch* 81–82 with 5:8, 51:3). In *1 Enoch* 6–11, which embellishes Gen 6:1–4, there is even an intervening revelation of "eternal secrets" (9:6) by rebelling angels.[77] Thus *1 Enoch* leaves open the possibility of different revelations of wisdom, of varying value.

2.6 Wisdom and Logos in Philo

Philo could easily dominate this Wisdom narrative, but his role here is simply to demonstrate the reception in first century C.E. Jewish thought of the Wisdom/Torah tradition as I have portrayed it. The Philonic Logos is portrayed with most of the cosmic traits and functions that other biblical and post-biblical texts ascribe to Wisdom.[78] Within a Jewish theological context this should be no surprise: the circle of verbal relationships sketched in §2.2–5 shows how the early

---

[76] W. D. Davies recognizes that *1 Enoch* and Sirach are in tension on the dwelling place of Wisdom (which means, again, that "Wisdom" in *1 Enoch* is not the Sinai Torah) but continues to identify *1 Enoch*'s Wisdom with Torah (*Torah in the Messianic Age and/or Age to Come* [JBLMS 7; Philadelphia: SBL, 1952] 42–43).

[77] See Argall, 1 Enoch *and Sirach*, 24–31 and the literature cited there.

[78] B. Mack contends that Philo avoided mingling human and divine wisdom, and thus "divine wisdom was pictured only in the presence of God" ("The Christ and Jewish Wisdom," in *The Messiah* [ed. J. Charlesworth; Minneapolis: Fortress, 1992] 207). The Stoic Logos was immanent in some sense, so it was a more malleable tool than Wisdom in Philo's thinking about the cosmic order.

Jewish biblical interpreter could view דבר/λόγος as interchangeable with תורה and חכמה. Based on verbal analogies, each term has a clear and significant connection with the Genesis creation account. In this first text Philo equates Logos with Wisdom:

> Let us look too at the particular words used. "A river," it says "issues forth from Eden to water the garden." "River" is generic virtue, goodness. This issues forth out of Eden, the wisdom of God, and this is the Reason [λόγος] of God; for after that has generic virtue been made. (*Leg.* 1.65[79])

Despite the difficulties his allegorical interpretation presents, at the very least Philo's comment on Gen 2:10 confirms the first century reception of the confluence of Wisdom and Eden images. Similarly, the following excerpt demonstrates the symbolic range of Logos,[80] and establishes its potential ties to the creation narrative:

> ... God's First-born (πρωτόγονον), the Word (λόγος), who holds the eldership among the angels, their ruler (ἀρχάγγελον) as it were. And many names are his, for he is called, "the Beginning (ἀρχή)," and the Name of God, and His Word, and the Man after His image, and "he that sees," that is Israel. ... For if we have not yet become fit to be thought sons of God yet we may be sons of His invisible image, the most holy Word. For the Word is the eldest-born image (εἰκὼν λόγος ὁ πρεσβύτατος) of God. (*Conf.* 146–47[81])

Each of Philo's Greek terms represents possible interpretations of the ראשית/ἀρχή (Gen 1:1).[82] Philo regularly identifies the Logos as God's partner in creation, so the ראשית language is understandable. What one learns from Philo is how comfortably these elements of the Wisdom/ Torah tradition interface with the philosophical use of Logos: "because the *logos* is an emanation of God, Philo can also talk about

---

[79] *Philo* 1 (LCL; tr. F. Colson and G. Whitaker; Cambridge: Harvard University, 1929) 157–59.

[80] Segal accounts for the multivalency of Logos: "Philo wants the *logos* ... to serve as a simple explanation for all the angelic and human manifestations of the divine in the Old Testament" (*Two Powers in Heaven*, 169). See *Leg.* 3.177; *Conf.* 28; *Her.* 205; *Somn.* 1.115, 1.239; *Cher.* 3.35; *Mut.* 87; *Migr.* 173; *Post.* 91.

[81] *Philo* 4 (LCL; tr. F. Colson and G. Whitaker; Cambridge: Harvard University, 1932) 88–91.

[82] The argument here about Philo mirrors Burney's theory about the genesis of the Col 1:15–20 hymn (see "The APXH of Creation").

him as God's offspring, or the first-born son of God. As such, he is a kind of immortal, heavenly man or the true father of men."[83]

2.7 Conclusion

It is common these days to review the texts on which the Wisdom/ Torah tradition is based, but few researchers choose to elaborate on these texts in order to uncover the implications of the tradition. Indeed, scholarship has not progressed far beyond Hans Windisch's 1914 presentation of the textual tradition underlying the so-called Wisdom christology.[84] The texts have been a constant. This chapter has exposed aspects of the Wisdom/Torah tradition that have not appeared (to my knowledge) elsewhere.

My Wisdom narrative has been speculative, but a vague "Wisdom tradition" can yield little more without studies that fill in the details (which perhaps explains why scholars have been reticent to go beyond recitation of the texts). These speculations are not leaps in the dark, however. The depiction of Wisdom in Sirach 24 is an informing guide to the tradition: Wisdom is the creative Word of God; Sinai, the mountain of revelation, and Zion, the mountain of the temple, are cosmic centers on which heaven and earth converge; Torah is the embodiment of God's eternal Wisdom; the place where Torah pitched its tent was likened to the Paradise garden.

The next chapter investigates some implications of Wisdom and Torah's association. To what extent does Israel's Torah reflect its heavenly archetype? In the Pauline case studies that follow (chapters 4–6), the Wisdom/Torah tradition is linked to Paul's messianic reconfiguration of Torah theology: Paul's negative language about Torah is explained as his denial that Torah is divine Wisdom. In effect, Paul subverts Sirach 24 by presenting Torah as limited to this age and by applying Wisdom imagery to Christ. Paul did not oppose the Jewish Law *per se*, but he did oppose Torah as the repository of divine Wisdom. In this he was consistent with the Similitudes of Enoch.

---

[83] Segal, *Two Powers in Heaven*, 173.

[84] H. Windisch, "Die göttliche Weisheit der Juden und die paulinische Christologie," in *Neutestamentliche Studien für Georg Heinrici* (ed. A. Deissmann and H. Windisch; Leipzig: Hinrichs, 1914) 220–34.

CHAPTER 3

Torahs Eternal and Eschatological, Heavenly and Hidden

In early Jewish literature the emergence of Torah as the embodiment of divine Wisdom stimulated inquiries into the extent to which the earthly Sinai version corresponded to its heavenly archetype, and who controlled access to this well of Wisdom. Theologians also had to deal with the consequences of this "remything" of Torah for the non-Jewish world that did not possess Torah. What was the relationship between the wisdom of the nations and Torah? Was the nations' non-acceptance of Torah actually a rejection that would result in their eschatological condemnation? Modern studies of the Law in early Judaism have largely overlooked these questions.[1] It is all the more

---

[1] R. Marcus, *Law in the Apocrypha* (New York: Columbia University Press, 1927); W. D. Davies, *Torah in the Messianic Age and/or Age to Come* (JBLMS 7; Philadelphia: SBL, 1952); *The Setting of the Sermon on the Mount* (Cambridge: Cambridge University Press, 1964) 109–90; "Law in First-Century Judaism," *IDB* 3. 89–95, reprinted in *Jewish and Pauline Studies* (Philadelphia: Fortress, 1984) 3–26; "Law in the New Testament," *IDB* 3. 95–102, reprinted in *Jewish and Pauline Studies*, 227–42; "Paul and the Law: Reflections on Pitfalls in Interpretation," *Paul and Paulinism* (ed. M. Hooker and S. Wilson; London: SPCK, 1982) 4–16, reprinted in *Jewish and Pauline Studies*, 91–122; H. Teeple, *The Mosaic Eschatological Prophet* (SBLMS 10; Philadelphia: Society of Biblical Literature, 1957) 14–28; M. Limbeck, *Die Ordnung des Heils: Untersuchungen zum Gesetzesverständnis des Frühjudentums* (Düsseldorf: Patmos, 1971); R. Smend and U. Luz, *Gesetz* (KTBK 1015; Stuttgart: Kolhammer, 1981) 45–57; H. Lichtenberger, "Das Tora-Verständnis im Judentum zur Zeit des Paulus," in *Paul and the Mosaic Law* (ed. J. D. G. Dunn; WUNT 89; Tübingen: Mohr [Siebeck], 1996) 7–23.

amazing that interpreters of Paul, so often perplexed by his Torah theology, have not investigated further this element of the theological milieu in which Paul's Christian view of Torah was born—especially since it affects the eschatological fate of the gentiles, the axis of Pauline thought.

The aggrandizement of Torah by its identification with Wisdom has its ironies. On the one hand, because of its temporal and spatial extension, the eternality and immutability of Torah becomes axiomatic in Jewish theology (see §3.1).[2] But some early Jewish texts appear to challenge the sufficiency of the revelation contained in the Mosaic books. The challenge comes in three forms: an unwritten, secret or heavenly repository of revelation that supplements the written (§3.2, 5)[3]; a perfected Torah that, although it is modeled on the Pentateuch, in effect replaces it (§3.3); an alternate body of revelation that is identified with Enoch, an intermediary more ancient (and mysterious) than Moses (§3.4). Each of these challenges to the sufficiency of the Mosaic books can be interpreted in a less radical fashion. Although it is not my intention to abandon sober analysis of the pertinent texts, the perspective of this chapter is unique; since alternative interpretations are well represented in the standard assumption of Torah as the early Jewish monolith, I argue herein with little attention to other explanations of these theologoumena.[4]

---

[2] The eternality and immutability of Torah is also the working assumption among Pauline scholars, even for those who conclude that the Law in Paulinism is inoperative (A. Schweitzer), or replaced (W. D. Davies, P. Stuhlmacher). As I argue throughout this study, this assumption is mistaken. In Paul's reconfiguration of early Jewish Torah theology, Christ replaces Torah as the embodiment of Wisdom, the creative Word of God, the intermediary between God and humanity. Paul does little more than undo the elevated "Torah ontology" (Hengel) by confining Torah to this realm.

[3] Because this study is limited to early Jewish (i.e., pre-rabbinic) texts, I am not thinking here of the rabbinic "oral Torah," although it could be understood as parallel to these other developments.

[4] I respond here to the assumption that the nature of Torah was a given in early Jewish theologies, that it was beyond the sort of challenge presented in this chapter. A relevant example is H. Stegemann's difficulty in imagining "that a supplementary sixth book of the *Torah* could have been compiled and acknowledged by at least some Jewish authorities much later than the 4th century B.C.E." ("The Literary Composition of the Temple Scroll and its Status at Qumran," in *Temple Scroll Studies: Papers Presented at the International Symposium on the Temple Scroll* [ed. G. Brooke; JSPSup 7; Sheffield: JSOT, 1989] 129; also "The Origins of the Temple Scroll," in *IOSOT Congress Volume*

Not every development in early Jewish Torah theology is attributable to the Wisdom/Torah tradition. Biblical interpreters were fasci-
nated and perplexed by the form of Torah. What was recorded on the
Sinai tablets, the Decalogue or all of Torah? Was there any change in
the second set of tablets, given after the golden calf incident? The text
of Exodus contains simple answers to these two questions: The Decalogue was written on the tablets (see e.g., Exod 34:28), and there was
no difference between the two sets of tablets (Exod 34:1). But why are
the two sets of commandments inconsistent? What was the relationship between the tablets, the "book of the covenant" and "book of the
law" preserved by the side of the Ark (e.g., Deut 31:24)? Such questions
urge the ancient exegete to take a closer look at the language of these
texts. Another question about the tablets is resolved with a haggadic
creation: what happened to the tablets that Moses smashed in anger?
Two examples will demonstrate the interest of early Jewish interpreters in these issues:

(1) CD 5:2–3 refers to the ספר התורה החתום אשר היה בארון, "book of the
sealed *torah* which was in/by the Ark." Strictly speaking, the phrase is
not biblical, but it clearly recalls the placing of the "book of this
torah" next to the ark of the covenant (Deut 31:24–26). There is a striking feature in CD's language that diverts from Deuteronomy: what is
the force of the prepositional phrase בארון? It can mean "in the ark," or
"by the ark." Deut 31:26 uses מצד ארון, literally "from the side"; the literal sense is picked up by the LXX, ἐκ πλαγίων. Although בארון is
ambiguous, it seems likely that CD's Torah was sealed in the Ark, since
there is little sense to a "sealed" Torah at the side of the Ark.[5] Thus
Deuteronomy's book has become the "sealed Torah" of CD 5:2: it was
put within the Ark, and thus "sealed" for later generations (compare
Isa 8:16; Dan 8:26; 12:4, 9). The tablets in the Ark are not referred to.

(2) *Biblical Antiquities* 12 is a rewriting of Exod 32:15–19. In the biblical story Moses descends the mountain of revelation with the tablets,

---

Jerusalem [ed. J. Emerton; VTSup 40; Leiden: Brill, 1986] 254). Stegemann's comment is
evaluative of the thesis that 11QTemple was a rival Torah (§3.3), but it also shows that
for Stegemann Sirach's presentation of Torah is programmatic for early Jewish theology.

[5] B. Wacholder suggests that ארון (CD 5:3) was understood as a "sealed container,"
but this is forced and unnecessary ("The 'Sealed' Torah Versus the 'Revealed' Torah: an
Exegesis of Damascus Covenant V, 1–6 and Jeremiah 32:10–14," *RevQ* 12 [1986] 357). CD
is reflecting on the Ark's holdings, rather than its nature.

hears and then sees his people celebrating, sees the golden calf and smashes the tablets. The early Jewish interpreter was intrigued by the scenario of the tablets written with the "finger of God" (Exod 31:18; Deut 9:10) lying in pieces on the ground. Pseudo-Philo deals with the text by inserting an extra-biblical tradition that the writing on the tablets disappeared when Moses descended and viewed the golden calf (*L.A.B.* 12:5).[6] This solves the problem of what happened to the tablets after they were broken. Another option would have been to leave the words on the tablets, and have the broken pieces hidden or taken away miraculously. Pseudo-Philo makes the tablets unimportant because the words were gone.

3.1 The Eternal Torah

In early Jewish texts Torah is commonly represented as the "eternal Law." This appellation is not tied to any specific exegesis, nor is it surrounded by *topoi* from any one biblical tradition; the "eternal Law" occurs as if it were part of the theological vernacular. The phrase itself goes beyond OT usage, however, there is some precedent in biblical texts which qualify terms associated with Torah (דבר, ברית, חק) with עולם. The most common of these combinations is ברית עולם ("everlasting covenant"),[7] but the most profound come from Psalm 119 and Deutero-Isaiah. Ps 119:89 asserts that Yhwh's word is situated in heaven לעולם. Ps 119:160 is a complementary parallelism of ראש דברך אמת ("the sum of your word is truth") and לעולם כל משפט צדקך ("each of your righteous ordinances [endures] forever"). Isa 40:8 is the famous "The grass withers, the flower fades, but the word of our God will stand לעולם." Isa 59:21 reaffirms the covenant, which is characterized by

---

[6] Interestingly, Pseudo-Philo only mentions the calf, but not the singing and dancing (Exod 32:18–19). Perhaps this is indicative of Pseudo-Philo's lack of interest in this feature of the biblical text, but it may also suggest that the author/interpreter did not want the reader to misunderstand the focus of Moses' anger: the calf. In other words, singing and dancing were cultically acceptable in a proper (non-idolatrous) context, and thus were not Pseudo-Philo's issue.

[7] Gen 9:16; 17:7, 13, 19; 2 Sam 23:5; 1 Chr 16:15–17; Ps 104:10; Isa 55:3; 61:8; Jer 32:40; 50:5; Ezek 16:60; 37:36. For texts which assert a perpetual "statute" (חק), see Exod 12:24; 29:28; 30:21; Lev 6:11, 15; 7:34; 10:15; 24:9; Num 18:8, 11, 19. A provocative parallelism of חק and ברית עולם occurs in 1 Chr 16:17 and Ps 105:10.

Yhwh's "spirit upon you" and "words in your mouth from now and
עד עולם." Along with the Wisdom/Torah tradition, statements such as
these prepare the way for the idea of the eternal Torah: Torah transcends temporal limitations. The more developed idea has Torah present at the creation and the final judgment (see below).

The hinge term in the combinations highlighted above is עולם, a difficult *sema* because of its questionable derivation and specific referent:
what conception of time does it signify? Current OT scholarship recognizes that biblical עולם could not mean "eternal" in the sense of
timelessness. Ernst Jenni's perspective on עולם is widely accepted: עולם
means "remotest time, past or present."[8] James Barr adds to this the
notion of "perpetuity," which works well with combinations like
ברית עולם.[9] The semantic range of עולם is expanded by the fact that the
LXX generally rendered it by αἰών/αἰώνιος, which cover a wide range
of meanings, from "lifetime" to "eternity."[10] In post-biblical literature
עולם is also used for "world," as in the classic עולם הבא/עולם הזה polarity.[11]

The early Jewish texts which express the "eternal Torah" thus must
be measured against the degree to which biblical עולם took on new

---

[8] See Jenni, "עולם," in *Theologisches Handwörterbuch zum Alten Testament*
(2 vols.; ed. E. Jenni with C. Westermann; Munich: Kaiser, 1984) 2. 228–43. The connotations of עולם range from "durability" to "definitiveness" to "inalterability, finality"
(230).

[9] See J. Barr, *Biblical Words for Time* (Naperville: Allenson, 1962) 69–70, 117. Barr
argues that עולם should be interpreted according to context rather than preconceptions
of the ancient Hebrew notion of time: "Most important is to notice that in the sense
'the remotest time' no specification is given of how remote the time referred to is; pre-
cisions of this kind may be inferred from the context, but the word itself just tells us
that the remotest time relevant to the present subject is meant" (70). Barr uses עבד עולם
(Deut 15:17) as his test case for Jenni's "remotest time."

[10] For αἰών as "eternity" LSJ points to Plato's *Timaeus* 37d, where αἰών and αἰώνιος
are contrasted with χρόνος.

[11] The contrast between this world and the next predates rabbinic literature: "For
surely, as you endured much labor in the short time in which you live in this passing
world (ܥܠܡܐ ܗܢܐ), so you will receive great light in that world (ܥܠܡܐ) which has
no end" (2 *Apoc. Bar.* 48:50); "For they will see that world (ܥܠܡܐ) which is now invisible to them, and they will see a time which is now hidden from them" (2 *Apoc. Bar.* 51:8).
Trans. of 2 *Apocalypse of Baruch* by A. Klijn (*OTP* 1. 615–52); Syriac text edited by S.
Dedering (*The OT in Syriac According to the Peshitta Version* [Peshitta Institute, 4.3;
Leiden, Brill, 1973]).

meanings, specifically limitless time, and/or eternity. But the idea of an eternal Torah is not necessarily dependent on an expanded עולם: the phrasing of Sir 24:9—πρὸ τοῦ αἰῶνος ἀπ᾽ ἀρχῆς ἔκτισέν με καὶ ἕως αἰῶνος οὐ μὴ ἐκλίπω—provides the likely model for what is meant by "eternal."[12] It also reflects a tendency to render עולם in Greek with extended prepositional phrases in order to express "forever," thereby overcoming the potential ambiguity of עולם.[13] In other words, Sirach 24 establishes the parameters of the "eternal Torah"—Torah present in the beginning (πρὸ τοῦ αἰῶνος ἀπ᾽ ἀρχῆς) and at the eschatological judgment (ἕως αἰῶνος). Thus it is not necessary to postulate a timeless eternity in order to entertain the idea "eternal Torah." But there will still be some difficulty with its time-aspect: whereas Sirach 24 clearly reflects Genesis 1–3, it is not obvious when "eternal Torah" expressions from other early Jewish writings refer to the remote past, to a time prior to the Sinai revelation. Therefore I must define the "eternal Torah" as potentially but not necessarily including the idea of its pre-existence.

In various forms, "Eternal Torah" assertions are found in many post-biblical literary traditions (e.g., Sir 24:9; Bar 4:1; *1 Enoch* 99:2; *2 Apoc. Bar.* 48:47, 77:15; Philo *Mos.* 2.14). Two of the more remarkable expressions are found in Jewish apocalypses generally dated late first century C.E. The first text, from 4 Ezra, asserts that although the generation which possesses the Law dies, the Law itself does not:

> Hear me, O Israel
> Give heed to my words, O descendants of Jacob
> For behold I sow my Law in you,
> and you shall be glorified in it forever
> But though your fathers received the Law,
>   they did not keep it,
>   and did not observe the statutes;
> yet the fruit of the Law did not perish
>   —for it could not, because it was yours.

[12] Although Wisdom has not been introduced as Torah by Sir 24:9, the previous verse anticipates the identification: "The Creator of all things gave me a commandment. . . . Make your dwelling in Jacob, and in Israel receive your inheritance" (24:8).

[13] Ps 118:44 (LXX): "I will keep your Law διὰ παντός εἰς τὸν αἰῶνα καὶ εἰς τὸν αἰῶνα τοῦ αἰῶνος"; the Hebrew is simply ואשמרה תורתך תמיד לעולם ועד (Ps 119:44).

Yet those who received it perished, because they did not keep what
had been sown in them. And behold, it is a rule that, when the
ground has received seed, or the sea a ship, or any dish food or drink,
and when it happens that what was sown or what was launched or
what was put in was destroyed, they are destroyed, but the things
that held them remain; yet with us it has not been so. For we who
have received the Law and sinned will perish, as well as our heart
which received it; the *Law,* however, *does not perish,* but remains in
glory. (4 Ezra 9:30–37)[14]

The theology here is consistent with the biblical texts that attest to the
perpetuity of the covenant and individual statutes, but the final line
suggests something more: the Torah would endure into the eschaton.

In *2 Apocalypse of Baruch* 59 an earlier vision (ch. 53) is interpreted
by the angel Ramael. Concerning the generation of Moses, Aaron,
Miriam and Joshua (59:1), Ramael says these words:

For at that time the lamp of the *eternal Law* (ܪܫܒܠܠܝܬ ܕܢܡܘܣܐ)
which exists forever and ever[15] illuminated all those who sat in
darkness. This (lamp) will announce to those who believe the
promise of their reward and to those who deny the punishment of
the fire which is kept for them. (*2 Apoc. Bar.* 59:2)

The implication is that the Torah transcends the generation to which it
was first entrusted. This notion of Torah before Sinai is complemented
in chapter 57 (also part of Ramael's interpretation of the vision): there
is an "unwritten Law" (ܕܢܡܘܣܐ ܗܘ ܠܐ ܟܬܒ), which Abraham's generation obeyed (*2 Apoc. Bar.* 57:2). And like Sirach 24, the Law which
Moses receives on Sinai embodies heavenly wisdom: "the root of
wisdom, the richness of understanding, the fountain of knowledge"
(*2 Apoc. Bar.* 59:7).[16] The witness of the larger context makes it all the
more likely that the "eternal Law" in *2 Apocalypse of Baruch* 59 sub-
sumes the idea of the preexistent Law. Thus *2 Apocalypse of Baruch*
represents the mature version of the eternal Law: God's Wisdom, the

---

[14] Tr. B. Metzger, *OTP* 1. 545.

[15] Klijn, who follows Dedering's edition, gives no justification for "which exists forever and ever"; the Syriac is merely ܕܢܡܘܣܐ ܕܠܥܠܡ.

[16] Notice that in *2 Apocalypse of Baruch* Moses receives the heavenly wisdom in the
form of Torah whereas Enoch receives it prior to the Sinai revelation in *1 Enoch*.

Law which the Patriarchs could keep, and the standard of final judgment.[17]

The final texts I cite as evidence for the eternal Torah in early Jewish literature come from the Pseudo-Philonic *Biblical Antiquities*, a first-century C.E. reworking of portions of Israel's story that mingles biblical and traditional material. The nature of the Law is not a key issue in Pseudo-Philo; the texts below are isolated and somewhat matter-of-fact, as if they were the expression of commonly held beliefs.[18] The first citation, though without explicitly identifying Torah, reflects the Wisdom/Torah tradition, and is a witness to the preexistent Torah:

> He brought them out of there [Egypt] and brought them to Mount Sinai and brought forth for them the foundation of understanding that he had prepared from the creation of the world. (*L.A.B.* 32:7)[19]

The other citations come from Pseudo-Philo's retelling of Exodus 19; the first two are spoken by God, and establish Torah's role in eschatological judgment:

---

[17] Compare the second half of 2 *Apoc. Bar.* 59:2, which links one's fate with one's relationship to the Law, with the parallel idea in this text: "And it will happen in that time that a change of times will reveal itself openly for the eyes of everyone because they polluted themselves in all those times and caused oppression, and each one walked in his own works and did not remember the Law of the Mighty One. Therefore, a fire will consume their thoughts, and with a flame the meditations of their kidneys will be examined. For the Judge will come and will not hesitate. For each of the inhabitants of the earth knew when he acted unrighteously, and they did not know my Law because of their pride. . . . And concerning all those, their end will put them to shame, and *your Law* which they transgressed *will repay them* on your day" (2 *Apoc. Bar.* 48:38–40, 47). Add to this text the witness of Wis 6:18, Sir 24:22 and *L.A.B.* 11:1–2.

[18] Contrary to J. Levison, who implicates Torah with the prominence of covenant in Pseudo-Philo ("Torah and Covenant in Pseudo Philo's *Liber Antiquitatum Biblicarum*," in *Bund und Tora* [eds. F. Avemaria and H. Lichtenberger; WUNT 92; Tübingen: Mohr [Siebeck], 1996] 111–27). Levison is of course correct that Torah and covenant are integrally linked with each other, but I question whether the linkage is more prominent in Pseudo-Philo than other early Jewish writings, and whether it was directed at a devaluation of Torah (123). If Pseudo-Philo were reasserting the "privileged place" of Torah, there would be support for it —that is, new exegesis or argumentation through skewing of the biblical material—observable in the narrative, beyond the expression of what is generally the case in the theological milieu.

[19] Harrington's translation (*OTP* 2. 346).

> For [the sons of men] I will bring out the eternal statutes that are for those in the light but for the ungodly a punishment. (*L.A.B.* 11:1)

> I have given an *everlasting Law* into your hands and by this I will judge the whole world. (*L.A.B.* 11:2)

The final lines are the narrator's:

> Until God should establish the Law of his eternal covenant with the sons of Israel and give his eternal commandments that will not pass away. (*L.A.B.* 11:5)

This is a strong statement of Torah's endurance into the age to come.

3.2 The Heavenly Tablets

Appearing in *1 Enoch* and *Jubilees*, the idea of "heavenly tablets" is one of the more interesting *theologoumena* to emerge in post-biblical Jewish literature. Oddly enough, the heavenly tablets have not received extensive scholarly attention, perhaps because they are never explicated in early Jewish literature and in *1 Enoch* there is a degree of referential ambiguity for even the most educated modern reader. Like the "eternal Torah" they appear almost as a given, something which the intended reader would recognize and understand without the necessity of elaboration. By including a section on the heavenly tablets in this chapter on early Jewish Torah theologies, I am implying that the heavenly tablets belong to the relational set of images orbiting around the Sinai revelation. The heavenly tablets could be viewed as an analogue of the heavenly Wisdom studied in the previous chapter: as Wisdom provides a quasi-personal source from which the Sinai revelation is drawn, the heavenly tablets provide a material repository. Thus my intention is to establish the relationship of the heavenly tablets to Torah. The meaning of "heavenly tablets" can be ambiguous, but especially in *Jubilees* it refers in some sense to a heavenly archetype of the Sinai tablets.[20] Because it is ultimately not knowable from the

[20] For the heavenly tablets as "archetype" see R. Eppel, "Les tables de la Loi et les tables célestes," *RHPR* 17 (1937) 401–12. Eppel (p. 404) suggests that heavenly archetypes of special earthly realities were anticipated in the words concerning the תבנית משכן in Exodus 25: in the LXX תבנית becomes παράδειγμα (Exod 25:9) and τύπος (Exod 25:40). In Exod 26:30, the משפט ("plan") of the משכן is rendered as its εἶδος.

texts, I will not address the intriguing issue of the extent to which the archetype is represented by the earthly version. The power of the heavenly tablets image is that it both relates to the Mosaic revelation and transcends it as the celestial source of knowledge of which all has not been revealed.

The ambiguity of the heavenly tablets pertains to its use for two different but related concepts: (1) a heavenly archetype of the Sinai tablets or (2a) a book of fate or destiny, which may overlap with (2b) the idea of a "book of life." Shalom Paul refers to the tablets of the second group as "celestial ledgers,"[21] for which this fragment is a good example: "For I have read in the tablets of heaven all that shall befall you and your sons."[22] When considered from a *religionsgeschichtlich* perspective, these ledgers are almost certainly prior to the notion of "heavenly tablets" as archetypes. Paul collects extensive evidence from the OT and post-biblical literature for the idea of heavenly bookkeeping, with which the NT "book of life" (Phil 4:3; Rev 3:5; 13:8; 17:8; 20:12, 15; 21:27) is consistent.[23] Thus the environment for the tablets as celestial ledgers is good, but it applies primarily to *1 Enoch*; the heavenly tablets in *Jubilees* signify the archetype of the Sinai tablets.

The four occurrences of heavenly tablets in *1 Enoch* are ambiguous. In the Book of the Heavenly Luminaries the Angel Uriel instructs Enoch to read the heavenly tablets (*1 Enoch* 81:1), which he does:

> So I looked at the tablet(s) of heaven, read all the writing (on them), and came to understand everything. I read *that* book *and* all the deeds of humanity and all the children of the flesh upon the earth for all generations of the world. (*1 Enoch* 81:2)

The second sentence presents the heavenly tablets as a book of destiny. I have highlighted "that" and "and" because they are omitted in two of the major Ethiopic witnesses. Without these two small words, this

---

[21] S. Paul, "Heavenly Tablets and the Book of Life," *JANESCU* 5 (1973) 345–53.

[22] The *Prayer of Joseph*, fragment B; see also fragment C. Translated by J. Smith, *OTP* 2. 714.

[23] Exod 32:32–33; Isa 4:3; 34:16–17; 65:6; Jer 17:13; 22:30; Mal 3:16; Pss 40:8; 56:9; 69:29; 87:6; 139:16; Dan 7:10; 10:21; 12:1; *1 Enoch* 47:3; *Jub.* 30:19–23; *Apocalypse of Zephaniah* 3:15–4:13; 14:5; 4QDib Ham; 4Q180:3; Luke 10:20; Heb 12:23; *m. Abot* 3:20; *b. Rosh ha-Sh.* 16b; *t. Arak.* 10b. Paul includes the heavenly tablets of *1 Enoch* in this list of celestial ledgers ("Heavenly Tablets," 349). According to Rev 13:8 and 17:8 names in the "book of life" were recorded "before the foundation of the world."

text possibly refers to two writings: the heavenly tablets and a book of destiny. Preferring the alternate reading, both Michael Knibb and Matthew Black translate the disputed clause "I read the book."[24] In the context of Ethiopic Enoch as a whole, the content of Enochic visionary experience is often cosmological speculation and eschatological judgment (e.g., *1 Enoch* 82:1–3), both of which could be derived from heavenly tablets but were not part of the Mosaic Torah. The book of deeds here could refer to writings mentioned in the Dream Visions (*1 Enoch* 83–90): "sealed books" (90:20) and a "book of destruction" (90:17; see also 89:68, 71, 76). The heavenly tablets are understood in a similar way in the "Epistle of Enoch" (*1 Enoch* 92–105), where a book of destiny is clearly in view:

> For I know this mystery; I have read the tablets of heaven and have seen the holy writings, and I have understood the writing in them; they are inscribed concerning you. For all good things, and joy and honor are prepared for and written down for the souls of those who died in righteousness. (*1 Enoch* 103:2–3)

Here the tablets seem to be in a parallelism with "the holy writings" (103:2). Are they synonymous or complementary? There is no justification in this text for differentiating the heavenly tablets as book of destiny from the tablets as archetype.

The heavenly tablets can mean a repository of knowledge about the future:

> After that there shall occur still greater oppression than that which was fulfilled upon the earth the first time; for I do know the mysteries of the holy ones; for he, the Lord has revealed (them) to me and made me know—and I have read (them) in the heavenly tablets. (*1 Enoch* 106:19)

In the Apocalypse of Weeks (*1 Enoch* 91:12–17; 91:1–10), a synopsis of significant events in Israel's religious history past and future organized into "weeks," the heavenly tablets are part of the prologue indicating from whence the apocalypse comes:

> I will speak these things, my children, verily I, Enoch, myself, and let you know (about it) according to that which was revealed to me from

---

[24] M. Knibb, *The Ethiopic Book of Enoch* (2 vols.; Oxford: Clarendon, 1978) 2. 186; M. Black, *The Book of Enoch or 1 Enoch* (Leiden: Brill, 1985) 70. So also R. Charles, *The Book of Enoch or 1 Enoch* (Oxford: Clarendon, 1912) 172.

the heavenly vision, that which I have learned from the words of the holy angels, and understood from the heavenly tablets. (*1 Enoch* 93:2)

The content of this revelation is more specific than the previously cited text because most of it has already occurred. The material in weeks 1–6 refers to biblical narrative, so it may be that the heavenly tablets in this text mean pre-Sinai revelation: they explain how the antediluvian Enoch knew what was not yet revealed or recorded in biblical history. But again there is nothing firm from which to distinguish between the tablets as a record of destiny and as the archetype for the Mosaic Torah.

The heavenly tablets are not ambiguous in the *Book of Jubilees* (19x). *Jubilees* presents Jewish statutes and cultic practices as eternal, rather than mere custom.[25] For this reason, in its rewriting of the Genesis patriarchal narratives, the Patriarchs are portrayed as knowing and performing the law in their day, before the giving of the Sinai Torah. In this context the heavenly tablets play a crucial role. Because of the heavenly tablets the author of *Jubilees* may argue that the Jewish laws predate the Sinai revelation, but they are not merely natural laws, for they are specific, inscribed laws, not an abstract Wisdom which becomes specific when it is revealed and becomes Torah. According to *Jubilees* these are the things inscribed on the heavenly tablets: the shame of nakedness (3:31); a prohibition against striking a neighbor (4:5); a development on the eye-for-an eye principle (4:32); the just judgment of evil (5:13); feast days (6:29–31); the 364-day calendar (6:32–38); circumcision on the eighth day (15:25–26); the Abrahamic "feast of the Lord" (18:14–19); the giving of the eldest daughter in marriage before younger daughters (28:6); the death sentence for "defilement," in the context of marriage to non-Jews (30:9); the blessing of Levi and his descendants (30:18–20); Isaac's blessing of his sons (31:32); a second tithe (32:10); the day of "addition" (32:28); the prohibition of incest (33:10); passover (49:7–8).[26] To be considered with this material is Jacob's vision at Bethel, in which the "Lord" appears to him with seven tablets

---

[25] The contemporaries of the author of Jubilees are "faced with arguments that Jewish ritual law and piety are no longer relevant, that it was a law and piety freely adopted in the past and subject to arbitrary change in the present" (O. Wintermute, *OTP* 2. 40).

[26] Eppel's list is similar ("Les Tables," 405–6).

containing "everything . . . which would happen to him and to his sons during all the ages" (32:21). Jacob is instructed to write down what he has seen and read (presumably on the seven tablets) in his vision (32:24–26). Joseph is depicted as abstaining from sexual relations with Potiphar's wife because he remembered the "words of Abraham" which Jacob had read (39:6).[27] In support of this idea that activities of the Patriarchs were inspired, the author of *Jubilees* also refers to special "books" which the ancients handed down: Enoch wrote a book (*Jub.* 4:21); Noah's book contained "every kind of healing" (10:13). These books were passed from Abraham to Isaac (21:10).

As Eppel notes, and I have argued in chapter 2, the foundation for the pre-existence of Torah is its association with divine Wisdom.[28] *Jubilees* has no wisdom theology, however, so heavenly tablets serve the same function. Heavenly tablets have different purposes in *Jubilees* and *1 Enoch*: in *Jubilees* they affirm the pre-existence of Torah, without recourse to wisdom. For this reason the contents of the heavenly tablets are essentially biblical, but there is also traditional material that justifies Jewish practices not biblically prescribed. In *1 Enoch* they are part of a more comprehensive program of transcending the Mosaic Torah, of accessing cosmological and eschatological knowledge not contained in Torah.

3.3 The Temple Scroll as Rival Torah

The largest Qumran Scroll presents itself as direct revelation. The *Temple Scroll* (11QT, 11QTemple) contains material from Exodus-Deuteronomy, although often in revised form, and new legislation. The main scroll is severely damaged at the beginning, end, and top. The conclusions of Yigael Yadin, who acquired the scroll, named it מגילת המקדש and published the principal edition as 11QT,[29] are typically the starting point for most of subsequent scholarship.[30] Most impor-

---

[27] The heavenly ledger is brought in here: the fornicating man will have his sin written in the "eternal books" (*Jub.* 39:6).

[28] Eppel, "Les Tables," 403. But what is done through Wisdom in rabbinic theology is accomplished in "apocalyptic" more simply by the idea of archetypes (405).

[29] Y. Yadin, *Megillat Ham-Miqdash* (3 vols. and supplement; Jerusalem: The Israel Exploration Society and the Shrine of the Book, 1977).

[30] An interesting but unimportant example of Yadin's influence is evident in the fact

tantly for this study, it was Yadin who proposed that 11QTemple was the Qumran community's Torah, perhaps written by the sect's founder, the "teacher of righteousness" (מורה הצדק).[31] Although he presents his ideas on the *"Temple Scroll"* vis-à-vis those of Yadin, Ben Zion Wacholder accepts most of Yadin's conclusions.[32] But Wacholder pushes Yadin's theses to the extreme, all the while using Yadin as his foil.[33]

Of the many internal features which suggested to Yadin that the *Temple Scroll* was regarded as scripture, perhaps the most clear and telling is his comparison of the form of the tetragrammaton (יהוה) in different kinds of Qumran texts: in biblical quotations יהוה was always rendered in Paleo-Hebrew script in texts that Qumran scholars consider sectarian (e.g., the *pesherim*), and in extra-biblical texts (*Jubilees, 1 Enoch*). In contrast, biblical scrolls from Qumran have יהוה in the same script as the rest of the text. The *Temple Scroll* has the tetragrammaton in the same form as biblical books, rather than that of sectarian documents.[34] Therefore, if the *Temple Scroll* was a native

---

that versions of the *Temple Scroll* normally begin with column 2 because Yadin thought the scroll began with a narrative of Moses' ascent up Mt. Sinai, despite the fact that there is not even a remnant of his (hypothetical) column 1. See B. Wacholder, *Dawn of Qumran: The Sectarian Torah and the Teacher of Righteousness* (MHUC 8; Cincinnati: Hebrew Union College, 1983) 13. In a later study Wacholder challenged Yadin's judgment that there ever was a (now missing) column; what Yadin labeled column 2 was for Wacholder the first column of the scroll. See "The Relationship between 11Q Torah (The Temple Scroll) and the Book of Jubilees: One Single or Two Independent Compositions," *SBLSP 1985* (ed. K. Richards; Atlanta: Scholars Press, 1985) 214–15.

[31] Y. Yadin, *The Temple Scroll: The Hidden Law of the Dead Sea Sect* (New York: Random House, 1985) 226–29. On the dating of 11QTemple see the survey of opinion in M. Wise, *A Critical Study of the Temple Scroll from Qumran Cave 11* (Studies in Ancient Oriental Civilization 49; Chicago: The Oriental Institute of the University of Chicago, 1990) 26–31.

[32] I echo here Stegemann, who claims that Wacholder "takes all his basic ideas from Yadin" ("Origins of the Temple Scroll," 235 n. 7).

[33] Wacholder even protests the name Yadin gave 11QTemple: "Temple Scroll" gives a false impression because only a portion of the surviving text is devoted to the temple architecture. The remainder of the material concerns purity topics and other *halakot*. "Temple Scroll" is like a mask that hides its identity as the Qumran sectarians' Torah. Wacholder refers to 11QT as the "Qumranian Torah," the "sectarian Torah," or "11Q Torah" in place of the accepted 11QTemple (*Dawn of Qumran*, xiii–xiv, 21).

[34] Yadin notes that one exception to this "rule" is a Psalms scroll with Paleo-Hebrew יהוה, but this may be because this scroll was used as a prayer book (*Temple Scroll*, 68).

composition of the Qumran community, it was regarded there as scripture.

Material from the Mosaic Torah is often rendered in 11QTemple with inconsistencies and other interpretive troubles omitted or corrected. Thus Yadin considered the *Temple Scroll* a type of Torah harmony which softens the rough edges of competing accounts in Exodus–Deuteronomy, and the originality of the *Temple Scroll's* author was found in "his unification of similar biblical commands and his harmonization of variant commands."[35] Wacholder admits that there is this sort of harmonizing material in 11QTemple, but only where the Scroll does not address the issues with which its author was most concerned: "The essence of 11Q Torah lies not in the passage taken more or less directly from the Mosaic *Vorlage*."[36] The material its author considered most important (i.e., new law) directly controverts the Mosaic Torah. The chief concern of the *Temple Scroll* is to "reproduce in the holy land the sacred camp in Israel as it stood before the Lord at Mount Sinai. The attainment of the highest degree of *kedusah* (sanctity) was necessary to prepare the community for the impending theophany."[37] The new statutes, as Wacholder understands them, are the standard of this greater sanctity.[38]

Although he agrees with Yadin that 11QTemple was the Qumranian Torah, Wacholder radicalizes this notion with his proposal that it was a rival Torah, "even more faithful to the word of God and more

---

[35] Yadin, *Temple Scroll*, 74. For a discussion of Yadin's "harmonization" as an exegetical principle, see J. Milgrom, "The Qumran Cult: Its Exegetical Principles," in *Temple Scroll Studies* (ed. G. Brooke; JSPSup 7; Sheffield: JSOT, 1989) 170–71. Milgrom asserts that most of Yadin's examples of harmonization are actually instances of "unification": "the fusion of the various laws on a single subject into one law" (171). Milgrom prefers the term "homogenization" for the manner by which new laws are formed from biblical laws in 11QTemple: "A law which applies to specific objects, animals, or persons is extended to other members of the same species" (171). He views this homogenization technique as the "forerunner" of the rabbinic hermeneutical principle בנין אב, "a structure (emerging out) of the father" (174–75).

[36] Wacholder, *Dawn of Qumran*, 15.

[37] Wacholder, *Dawn of Qumran*, 16.

[38] L. Schiffman, who has done much to situate Qumran halakot in early Judaism, echoes Wacholder in characterizing 11QTemple in utopian terms: it "sets forth the author/redactor's plan for a perfect society, cult, and government of the Jewish people in the land of Israel" ("Temple Scroll," *ABD* 6. 348). The purpose of 11QTemple was "to provide a system of law for the pre-messianic temple" (349).

authoritative than its Mosaic archetype."[39] The *Temple Scroll* is thus
the chief statement of sectarian theological values:

> It was the acceptance of this sectarian work as the word of God at
> Sinai in addition to the ancestral Scriptures that characterized the ide-
> ology of the sect. . . . If the traditional Torah was regarded as holy,
> the *Sep̱er Torah* was considered the holy of holies.[40]

Wacholder's exalted *"Sep̱er Torah"* ("Torah book") here is 11QTemple.

Five elements of Wacholder's thesis that 11QTemple is the Qumran
sectarian Torah merit further consideration. First, like Yadin,
Wacholder presents many texts in 11QTemple and Qumran sectarian
writings that testify to 11QTemple as a second Torah. For example, the
phrase ספר תורה החתום of CD 5:2 refers to 11QTemple.[41] Because
Wacholder's texts are extensive, and many are (frankly) ambiguous or
unpersuasive, I will focus here on the most revealing of these texts. I
am not dismissing Wacholder's (and Yadin's) use of the many texts, but
this one text exhibits self-referential interpretive activity not found
elsewhere. Since it occurs within 11QTemple, there is no problem identifying the Torah to which it refers, and it demonstrates how the
author viewed 11QTemple in relationship to the Mosaic Torah.

והיה כשבתו על כסא ממלכתו	והיה בשבתו על כסא ממלכתו
וכתב לו את <u>משנה התורה הזאת</u>	וכתבו לו את <u>התורה הזואת</u>
על ספר מלפני הכהנים הלוים	על ספר מלפני הכוהנים
(Deut 17:18)	(11QT 56:20–21)[42]

In the LXX, the phrase משנה התורה הזאת ("copy of this *torah*") is rendered τὸ δευτερονόμιον τοῦτο, "this second law." There is some war-
rant for the notion of a "second Torah," since the material given with
the first tablets (Exodus 20–33) is different from that which is given in
Exodus 34–40.[43] (The biblical text promotes confusion: although Exod

---

[39] Wacholder, *Dawn of Qumran*, 4.

[40] Wacholder, *Dawn of Qumran*, xiv.

[41] Wacholder does not comment here on the "sealed" (החתום) nature of the Torah
book, but he investigates it in the later "The 'Sealed' Torah Versus the 'Revealed'
Torah."

[42] Text of 11QTemple from F. García Martínez and E. J. Tigchelaar, *The Dead Sea
Scrolls Study Edition* (2 vols.; Leiden: Brill, 1997) 2. 1279.

[43] Noted by G. Brooke, "The Temple Scroll: a Law unto Itself?" *Law and Religion*
(ed. B. Lindars; Cambridge: James Clarke, 1988) 36.

34:1 asserts unambiguously that the second tablets were as [כ] the first, this could not be, since the first set came from Yhwh, whereas Moses brought the second set up with him; and, the commandments on the first set are different than those on the second set.) The keyword משנה is absent from 11QT 56:20–21, which otherwise replicates Deut 17:18.[44] With the omission of משנה the time-aspect of the reworked text is awkward (since it is no longer a case of a king copying the Torah in the future), but the implication is clear: התורה הזאת refers to 11QTemple.

Wacholder is further supported by the reworking of Deut 17:10–11 near the top of column 56 (11QT 56:3–5). I have arranged the two texts graphically, disregarding the versification and lines of 11QTemple in order to show the relationship between them. The line numbers are my own, for ease of reference.

	Deut 17:10–11	11QT 56:3–8a
1.	ועשית על פי הדבר אשר יגידו לך	ושיתה על פי התורה אשר יגידו לך
2.		על פי הדבר אשר יאמרו לכה
3.		מספר התורה ויגידו לכה באמת
4.	מן המקום ההוא אשר יבחר יהוה	מן המקום אשר אבחר לשכין שמי עליו
5.	ושמרת לעשות ככל אשר יורוך	ושמרתה לעשות ככול אשר יורוכה
6.	על פי התורה אשר יורוך ועל המשפט	ועל פי המשפט
7.	אשר יאמרו לך	אשר יואמרו לכה
8.	תעשה לא תסור מן הדבר	תעשה לוא תסור מן התורה
9.	אשר יגידו לך ימין ושמאל	אשר יגידו לכה ימין ושמאול

The words from the Deuteronomy text reproduced in 11QTemple are underscored. The key features of 11QTemple's rewriting are: (1) The change from יבחר to אבחר (line 4), third person singular to first person, makes Yhwh the speaker, indicating direct revelation. (2) The parallelism in Deut 17:11 (lines 5–7) is replaced by another parallelism in 11QT 56:3–4 (lines 1–3). The change subverts the sense of the original, in which תורה and משפט were functionally synonymous as singular instances of "instruction" and "commandment" (Deut 17:11). For the

---

[44] There are minor differences between Deut 17:18 and 11QT 56:20–21: the preposition כ in כשבתו is replaced by temporal ב; כתב לו, which can be read as "he [the King] will write for himself" is altered so that others (כתבו) write the Torah for the king; Deuteronomy's identification of the priests as Levites is omitted, at least at the end of column 56 of 11QTemple (column 57 is damaged at the top; see plates 71–72 in Yadin, *Megillat Ham-Miqdash*, vol. 3).

author of 11QTemple תורה and משפט were no longer equivalent because תורה was a book (ספר; 11QT 56:4) of revelation, not an item of legal instruction. (3) The special role of the community responsible for 11QTemple as tradent and interpreter of ספר תורה is indicated with יגידו לכה באמת, "they shall explain it to you accurately" (11QT 56:4; line 3). (4) In the rewrite of Deut 17:10–11, the most notable insertion is the phrase ספר התורה (11QT 56:3), which in this context must refer to the same תורה as Deut 17:18 and 11QT 56:21.

Wacholder is not given to understatement, but here he expresses little confidence in this text as a self-referential witness to 11QTemple.[45] I think the nature of the additions to, and the replacement of nonspecific language in the deuteronomic original are solid evidence that 11QTemple is to be considered the משנה התורה of Deut 17:18.[46]

---

[45] The observations on the rewrite of Deut 17:10–11 are my own, not Wacholder's. He does not scrutinize the alterations in 11QT 56:3–8a, or their significance (see *Dawn of Qumran*, 19). Wacholder notes that there is a phrase parallel to ספר התורה (11QT 56:3) in 4Q177(Catena) 1:14: ספר התורה שנית, "book of the Second Law" (*Dawn of Qumran*, 92). This is the clearest outside reference to 11QTemple.

[46] On two points Wise takes issue with the method employed here. (1) In the context of criticizing the methodology of M. Hengel, J. Charlesworth and D. Mendels' article "The Polemical Character on 'On Kingship' in the Temple Scroll: An Attempt at Dating 11Q Temple," *JJS* 37 (1986) 28–38, he asserts: "Their entire argument really rests on the prior assumption that the author of [*Torah hammelek*] had before him a *Vorlage* identical to the MT. Then, where the text of col. 56 varies from that of Deut 17, the variants are seen as deliberate alterations. This is not only a dubious, but a puzzling *a priori* in the light of the well-attested textual fluidity of the Hebrew Bible in this period" (Wise, *Critical Study*, 112). I find it hard to reconcile Wise's criticism of their method with the fact that he practices a similar method (see material on redactional methodology, pp. 161–79). Does Wise think it better to analyse redactional work on hypothetical documents rather than the Hebrew Bible (with the help of the Greek versions)? In practice, he prefers the hypothetical over the known. Wise does not recognize the fact that the nature of Deut 17:18 makes it a prime text for editorial manipulation: the combination of the ambiguous verb כתב לו with the mysterious phrase משנה התורה הזאת, and the relationship of the king to the priests. (2) Wise notes that in *Tg. Pseudo-Jonathan*, "one finds ויכתבון לה סביא, 'and the elders shall write for him. . . .' The insertion of 'elders' is clear evidence that the targumic compilers knew a plural verb in their Hebrew textual tradition, and in good targumic fashion added this word to make the subject of the verb explicit. . . . In view of the targumic text . . . no historical argument should be based on יכתבו" (Wise 112). This again is troublesome because it suggests that targumists had to have "known" a particular reading before incorporating into their paraphrase. Again, Deut 17:18 is a candidate for interpretation because of its uniqueness. But Wise argues,

Second, as a witness to the authority of 11QTemple, Wacholder notes that observance of its unique laws (תורה המשפט הזה; 11QT 29:4) is made the basis of covenant fidelity (11QT 29:5–9). He interprets the above phrase, rendered "*torah* of this ruling," along with the similar "ruling of this *torah*" (משפט התורה הזואת; 11QT 50:7, 17), as the "author's title for the whole book," and therefore concludes that, rather than the Mosaic Torah, 11QTemple is the Torah upon which the (Qumran community's notion of) covenant is conditional.[47]

Third, an example of the strategic change in the biblical original's pronouns has already been noted. 11QT 56:5 is not an isolated occurrence. In material deriving from the Mosaic Torah, 11QTemple regularly changes the pronouns of the original. For example, in 11QTemple the Sinai revelation is given in the first person, whereas it is in the third person in Exodus.[48] Yadin saw this, in Wacholder's words,

---

"the presumption is always against any suggestion of intentional change, leaving a heavy burden of proof with Hengel and his collaborators." Wise here confuses textual transmission for interpretive (i.e., targumic, midrashic) rendering.

[47] Wacholder, *Dawn of Qumran*, 18–19. The covenant in 11QT 29:9–10 is mysteriously identified as that made with Jacob at Bethel (Gen 35:10–15). Wise suggests that the now-lost material following this was ". . . and with Isaac at Gerar, and with Abraham at Haran" (cf. Exod 2:24; Lev 26:42; 2 Kgs 13:23; 2 Macc 1:2) and that scholars (following Yadin) are mistaken in scrutinizing the special sense of the Bethel covenant (*Critical Study*, 157–61, esp. 160). Wise's range of evidence is overly narrow: "God does not promise to build a future temple when he talks with Jacob at Bethel" (160 n. 15). Neither are there sites listed with occurrences of the Abraham-Isaac-Jacob formula. In fact, the only time Jacob occurs first in the formula is Lev 26:42. It is more likely that the Bethel narrative (Genesis 35) was special for the author of 11QTemple. See also J. Maier, *The Temple Scroll* (JSOTSup 34; Sheffield: JSOT, 1985) 86, and D. Swanson's interpretation of the Bethel covenant: "'A Covenant Just Like Jacob's': the Covenant of 11QT 29 and Jeremiah's New Covenant," in *New Qumran Texts and Studies. Proceedings of the First Meeting of the International Organization for Qumran Studies, Paris 1992* (ed. G. Brooke, with F. García Martinez; STDJ 15; Leiden: Brill, 1994) 273–86. Swanson argues that "like the covenant with Jacob" (11QT 29:10) is meant to negate the competing assertion "not like the covenant with their fathers" of Jer 31:32, thus opposing the interpretation of Jer 31:31–34 as something truly "new": "The author is saying that, whatever is new about the temple, there will be no new covenant" (280–81). This is an important observation for this study because, as Swanson notes, the opposition in the *Temple Scroll* establishes that some early Jewish interpreters (including Paul; see §6.3.1; 6.4) took ברית חדשה in Jer 31:31–34 as truly new, rather than "renewed."

[48] Wacholder cites 22 examples (*Dawn of Qumran*, 4–6). 11QT 55:14–21 contains an extended "rewrite" of Num 30:3–5; cf. also 11QT 55:15–17 and Deut 17:2, 11QT 56:17–18 and Deut 17:16, 11QT 60:10–11 and Deut 21:15.

as a "mere rhetorical device to add authoritativeness to the Mosaic transmission of the text," whereas Wacholder interprets it as a real claim to "divine authorship":

> The Temple Scroll is not to be characterized as an epitome attempting to paraphrase, conflate, or supplement Moses' legal corpus, but rather as a code of laws uttered by God Himself on Mount Sinai which claims at least equality to and probably superiority over the Mosaic Torah.[49]

Wacholder implicates this strategic change of pronouns with the use of an "I-thou syntax" in 11QTemple's directions for the sanctuary. These editorial procedures subtly but surely promote 11QTemple as direct revelation.

Fourth, the *Temple Scroll* contains only the prescription for the sanctuary (מקדש), without the narrative of its construction (cf. Exodus 25–34). According to Wacholder this gives the impression that the sanctuary/temple, as prescribed by God directly to Moses on Mt. Sinai, was never made according to God's instructions, and thus its building is to take place eschatologically.[50] The critical text for the eschatological מקדש is 11QT 29:7–10:

> They shall be for me a people and I will be for them for ever; and I shall dwell with them for ever and always. I shall sanctify my [te]mple with my glory, for (אשר) I shall make my glory reside over it until (עד) the day of creation, when I shall create my temple, establishing it for myself for all days, in accordance with the covenant which I made with Jacob at Bethel.

The translation reflects the two temple theory (following Yadin):[51] a future temple in which Yhwh's glory resides (akin to the deuteronomic "place for my name"), and an eschatological temple built by Yhwh.[52] Wacholder's translation is a challenge to the two temple theory:

[49] Wacholder, *Dawn of Qumran*, 6; cf. Yadin, *Temple Scroll*, 112–17.

[50] Wacholder, *Dawn of Qumran*, 8. H. Mink, though acknowledging (with most 11QTemple scholars) that 11QTemple's temple is related to Ezekiel's, comments that "there is a clear tendency on the part of the author of the scroll to avoid the 'historical' temple tradition" ("The Use of Scripture in the Temple Scroll and the Status of the Scroll as Law," *SJOT* 1 [1987] 42).

[51] Yadin, *Megillat Ham-Miqdash*, 1.140–44.

[52] Column 29 is in particularly poor shape (see Yadin, *Megillat Ham-Miqdash*, vol. 3, plate 44). The word rendered "creation" in García Martínez's translation was tran-

I shall accept them that they may be My people and I may be theirs forever; I shall dwell with them forever and shall sanctify My sanctuary with My glory *when* I make My glory dwell upon it *during* the day of blessing, *when* I shall create My sanctuary to establish it for Myself for all time, in accordance with the covenant which I made with Jacob at Bethel.[53]

Wacholder renders the two אשר clauses in 11QT 29:8–9 as future temporal, introduced by "when" (highlighted in the text above), and thus interprets them as referring to the same eschatological event. But the problem with his interpretation is that it depends on reading עד as "during" rather than "until," its accepted meaning. The competing temple theories are thus based on little more than the interpretation of a relative particle (אשר) and a preposition (עד).[54] I will not be able to

---

scribed by Yadin as הברכה, "blessing." E. Qimron reads בריה (= בריאה; "creation") rather than הברכה (*Leš* 42 [1978] 142; cited in Wacholder, *Dawn of Qumran*, 238 n. 127 and Maier, *Temple Scroll*, 86–87). Wacholder notes that בריה is observable in the "normal paragraphs" of column 29, while הברכה is from the "mirror" image from the back of column 31. בריה seems to be the preferred reading: see G. Vermes' recent translation (*The Dead Sea Scrolls in English* [4th ed. rev.; New York: Penguin, 1995] 161) and that of M. Wise, M. Abegg and E. Cook (*The Dead Sea Scrolls: A New Translation* [San Francisco: Harper, 1996] 469).

[53] Wacholder, *Dawn of Qumran*, 22. I have added the underlines to show where Wacholder differs from García Martínez's translation. Note that Wacholder follows Yadin's reading of הברכה (see above note).

[54] The nature of the temple (actual, ideal, eschatological?) prescribed in 11QTemple has been the focus of numerous studies. Most notably, J. Kampen defends Wacholder's controversial understanding of עד in "The Eschatological Temple(s) of 11QT," in *Pursuing the Text: Studies in Honor of Ben Zion Wacholder on the Occasion of his Seventieth Birthday* (ed. J. Reeves and J. Kampen; JSOTSup 184; Sheffield: Sheffield Academic, 1994) 85–97. Kampen develops Wacholder's point that the two temple theory of Yadin and his followers is based on little more than עד in 11QT 29:9 as "until," and finds support for Wacholder's interpretation in other 11QTemple texts (42:16; 63:14–15; 43:6–9; 59:9) and other Qumran writings. For example, while there are many usages in the CD which are justifiably rendered "until," ". . . this definition does not encompass the totality of the word's semantic range within its folios" (92): Kampen notes עד in a durative sense (CD 12:5; 15:15); a concurrent temporal ("while"; 12:15; 2:10; 4Q268 1:8); an inclusive atemporal (CD 10:4; 13:1). In 1QS 6:16–21 there are many uses which all "cannot designate movement toward a point in time." The phrase עד ימימה ("daily" or "annually") in 1QH 8:30 is clearly durative, as is 1QM 8:7, 4Q507 1:3 and 4Q514 1:i.8 ("and he shall also not eat *during* his uncleanness"; עד בטמאתו). So if עד (11QT 29:9) does not have to mean "until," the most reasonable interpretation of 11QTemple is that one eschatological temple is presented: "The unrealistic nature of the temple itself, for

end the debate in this study, but with either interpretation one fact is clear to all: the מקדש prescribed in 11QTemple diverges from biblical versions in a number of features. "11Q Torah prescribes characteristics of a sanctuary never recorded in the biblical tradition, such as square dimensions, a terrace, a rampart, storehouses, and three courtyards, each with gilded gates on all four sides."[55]

Fifth, Wacholder incorporates the *Book of Jubilees* into his theory for the following reasons. *Jubilees* is a rewriting of material from Genesis and pre-Sinai Exodus, the material immediately prior to that which is found in 11QTemple. Like 11QTemple, *Jubilees* is presented as God's direct revelation, though in *Jubilees* it is explicitly given to Moses on Sinai (via angelic mediation). Portions of *Jubilees* were found in five different caves.[56] This is important because the multiple copies of *Jubilees* among the Dead Sea Scrolls indicate that the book was highly valued by the community[57]—according to the prevailing paradigm in Dead Sea Scrolls scholarship which understands the Qumran ruins as the remains of a Jewish sectarian community, and the caves' scrolls as their sacred literature. In *The Dawn of Qumran* Wacholder argued that one of the purposes of *Jubilees* was to promote 11QTemple. In a few places *Jubilees* is suggestive of two laws (e.g., 1:26; 2:24), the traditional Pentateuch and 11QTemple. Texts like the following would then refer to 11QTemple: The Lord says to Moses,

> "And you write down for yourself all of the matters which I shall make known to you on this mountain: what (was) in the beginning and what (will be) at the end, what will happen in all of the division of the days which are in the Law and testimony and throughout their

---

example, its gilding and the perfection implied in its architecture, as well as the elaborate legislation for the protection of its sanctity all attest to an idealized future life to be lived in the context of a messianic temple" (95). Wacholder's one eschatological temple theory is also supported by J. Wentling, "Unraveling the Relationship between 11QT, the Eschatological Temple, and the Qumran Community," *RevQ* 14 (1989) 61–73.

[55] Wacholder, *Dawn of Qumran*, 13.

[56] Based on F. García Martínez's "List of Manuscripts from Qumran" in *The Dead Sea Scrolls Translated* (Leiden: Brill, 1994) 465–513.

[57] There are other points of similarity between the "Qumran sectarian" literature and *Jubilees*—most notably its calendar—so the relationship is more profound than I have portrayed it. My point here is to exhibit the research logic employed in Dead Sea Scrolls scholarship, that multiple attestation indicates value to the "Qumran community."

weeks (of years) according to the *Jubilees* forever, until I shall descend and dwell with them in all the ages of eternity." And he said to the angel of the presence, "Write for Moses from the first creation until my sanctuary is built in their midst forever and ever. And the Lord will appear in the sight of all." (*Jub.* 1:26–28)[58]

In a later study Wacholder suggested that 11QTemple and *Jubilees* were really two halves of one work.[59]

3.3.1 "11QTorah" and the Critics

Although many scholars think of the *Temple Scroll* as Qumran's Torah book, Wacholder has persuaded few that it was a rival to the Mosaic Torah. In this section I will summarize five other approaches that support, emend or refute 11QTemple as Qumran Torah. These studies by no means exhaust the scholarly reaction to Wacholder, but they are representative.[60]

The first approach does not directly address Wacholder's theory, but it represents an alternate way of perceiving the text-intertext relationship of 11QTemple and the Mosaic Torah. Phillip Callaway reads 11QTemple as if it were an interpretive rendering of Exodus–Deuteronomy rather than a rival version. The author of 11QTemple employed different "micro-compositional strategies" in representing the Mosaic original:

---

[58] Trans. O. Wintermute, *OTP* 2. 54.

[59] Wacholder, "The Relationship between 11Q Torah (The Temple Scroll) and the Book of Jubilees: One Single or Two Independent Compositions," *SBLSP 1985* (ed. K. Richards; Atlanta: Scholars Press, 1985) 205–16. See also J. VanderKam, "The Temple Scroll and the Book of Jubilees," in *Temple Scroll Studies: Papers Presented at the International Symposium on the Temple Scroll* (ed. G. Brooke; JSPSup 7; Sheffield: JSOT, 1989) 211–36. VanderKam argues that there is a "loose" connection between 11QTemple and *Jubilees*, but no strict relationship; they are "drawing upon the same exegetical, cultic tradition" (232). He notes that the difference between the festivals in each result from the different sections of the Torah they are concerned with: *Jubilees* with Genesis through mid-Exodus, 11QTemple with mid-Exodus through Deuteronomy (217). "*Jubilees* and the Temple Scroll operate with the same 364-day cultic calendar, never conflict with one another regarding festivals, and agree almost completely about sacrifices and procedures for their holidays" (231).

[60] For more of the scholarly reaction to Wacholder, including a list of reviews, see Wise, *Critical Study of the Temple Scroll*, 17–19.

The literary activity of the author of the Temple Scroll encompasses the gamut of compositional strategies, including verbatim and near verbatim quotations of biblical laws, varying degrees of conflation, and the production of additional, newer legislation.[61]

Additional legislation in 11QTemple is often derived by analogy to biblical laws: "The author of these laws had created a web of analogies that are not explicitly found in the biblical text, but which can be derived quite easily without violating the spirit and letter of the biblical bases."[62] As an analysis of the compositional techniques employed in 11QTemple, Callaway's study is enlightening, but he does not recognize the implications of these techniques as they subvert their Torah intertext. The difference between Callaway and Wacholder (as with Wacholder and most of Qumran scholarship) is in their divergent interpretation of the relationship between biblical law and its representation in 11QTemple. Wacholder sees a challenge to the authority of the Mosaic Torah where others find unexceptional adaptation and development.

Second, Wayne McCready generally agrees that the Qumran community had a "second Torah," but he thinks Wacholder over-stated 11QTemple's denigration of the Mosaic Torah.[63] But McCready admits that his "discomfort" with Wacholder's views owes more to his perspective than real problems with the theory. This is an important point because it exposes a tendency in scholarship to repel the idea that there were early Jewish challenges to the Mosaic Torah, without fully questioning what impact a creative post-biblical reinterpretation would have for the authority of the biblical original. When does interpretive freedom of a targumic paraphrase, or a rewritten narrative become a

---

[61] P. Callaway, "Extending Divine Revelation: Micro-Compositional Strategies in the Temple Scroll," in *Temple Scroll Studies: Papers Presented at the International Symposium on the Temple Scroll* (ed. G. Brooke; JSPSup 7; Sheffield: JSOT, 1989) 150. This article is isolated because it deals with the nature of 11QTemple vis-à-vis the Pentateuch; it does not, however, exhaust Callaway's work on 11QTemple.

[62] Callaway, "Extending Divine Revelation," 156. The "new laws" in 11QTemple that Callaway identifies are consistent with Wacholder's list: examples are the new wine (11QT 19:14; 21:10) and oil festivals (11QT 21:14–15; 43:10); purity laws (e.g., menstruation, emissions, skin disease, cemetery) for temple-area and temple city, specifically with the application of laws for the biblical "camp" to the temple; modification and supplementation of the King's law of Deut 17:14–20 (11QT 56:12–59:21); laws of rebellion.

[63] W. McCready, "A Second Torah at Qumran?" *SR* 14 (1985) 5–15.

challenge to the autonomy of the revealed text? Scholarship too often assumes the Torah monolith without asking the important questions. Whatever the strengths and weaknesses of his conception of the Qumran community and its literature, Wacholder has taken the implications of rewritten Torah to a natural conclusion. 11QTemple adds to but also changes its biblical intertext, so there is an implied affront to the Mosaic Torah's sufficiency.

Third, George Brooke goes one step beyond McCready. He views 11QTemple as an alternate Torah, but he does not replicate Wacholder's rival language: "It seems clear that the scroll is making an implicit claim to be the repository of God's authentic revelation to Moses. But it must be asked whether it is claiming to be the *sole* repository."[64] Brooke does not answer his own question. Like Wacholder, Brooke links 11QTemple with *Jubilees*; taken together they constitute an "alternate Pentateuch." Moreover, along with the Damascus Document (CD), they were the "self-expression of a group of disaffected Levites who may have been in association with a certain number of priests sympathetic to their cause."[65] Brooke's scenario is a challenge to Yadin's situating of the *Temple Scroll* within the Qumran community.[66] Brooke thereby removes the hypothetical correlation between the Qumran community as rival Judaism and 11QTemple as rival Torah. The lack of a socio-geographical entity with which to situate the *Temple Scroll* may account for Brooke's lack of commitment on the relationship between 11QTemple and the Mosaic Torah. Wacholder, on the other hand, is allowed his excesses because of the correlation between rival community and rival revelation.

Fourth, according to Michael Wise, 11QTemple is an eschatological Deuteronomy, whose "purpose was to serve as a law for remnant Israel during an earthly eschatological age, until God should usher in the 'Day of Creation'" (11QT 29:9).[67] The author of 11QTemple is primarily a redactor who used four sources: a Deuteronomy source other

[64] Brooke, "Law unto Itself," 41.

[65] Brooke, "Law unto Itself," 39. The CD "may be a rule for the group responsible for such traditions as are preserved in *Jubilees* and the Temple Scroll"—rather than a rule for lay, non-resident members of Qumran community.

[66] Brooke, "Law unto Itself?," 40.

[67] Wise, *Critical Study*, 194. Wise confirms his earlier conclusion about 11QTemple as the new Deuteronomy in the introduction to his translation of the *Temple Scroll* (Wise, Abegg, Cook, *Dead Sea Scrolls: A New Translation*, 457–59).

than biblical Deuteronomy; a Temple source; a midrash to Deuteronomy; a festival calendar. The legal material was arranged hierarchically in "concentric circles of holiness."[68] The author of 11QTemple belonged to the community of the CD. He was its Teacher of Righteousness, the new Moses of Deut 18:15.[69] Wise differentiates himself from Yadin and Wacholder, in that they treated 11QTemple as a "pseudepigraphon": "The redactor was not claiming to have found a book written by the 'old' Moses. He was much more audacious. He wrote in his own behalf as the new Moses."[70] Since 11QTemple is for him a new rather than a derivative Torah, Wise recognizes that he must account for the amount of Mosaic material incorporated into 11QTemple without alteration.

> The reason that so much of the [*Temple Scroll*] recapitulates the first Mosaic Law is simply that he believed in the verity of that revelation. From his perspective, it was only natural that, when God vouchsafed a new revelation for life in the land, much of the first revelation would remain in force. In this way he conceived of the Torah as eternal.[71]

I will not challenge Wise on whether this is an eternal Torah, and it is quite possible that the author of 11QTemple thought of it as "his" revelation. On the other hand, although Moses' name is omitted and 11QTemple is not strictly pseudepigraphical, Wise's author nowhere refers to "himself," never writes himself into the scene. Thus the self-understanding of 11QTemple's author is hidden. To the modern critic, the author's *modus operandi* is everywhere apparent in 11QTemple, but this reveals only the author's theological bent. Ultimately Wise has taken his insight that 11QTemple is a heavily redacted work intended to be an eschatological Deuteronomy, pushed it beyond the evidence and excluded other theories. By dismissing the idea of 11QTemple as

---

[68] Wise, *Critical Study*, 178. This is an adaptation of Maier's "concentric areas of holiness": the contents of 11QTemple are "increasing in their degree of holiness from zone to zone and culminating in the Holy—the place of the presence of God" (*Temple Scroll*, 5).

[69] Moses the eschatological redactor nonetheless!

[70] Wise, *Critical Study*, 188.

[71] Wise, *Critical Study*, 188–89.

another Sinai Torah kept hidden for the eschaton—the precedent for which I think the author of 11QTemple found in Deut 17:18—Wise enters into the debate about an eschatological abrogation of the Mosaic Torah, or the replacement of some of its legislation.[72] Wacholder's thesis also provokes a challenge concerning the possibility of replacing the Mosaic Torah in early Jewish theologies, but he relies on associating the scroll and the material remains of the Qumran community, whereas Wise disassociates the *Temple Scroll* from a direct link with the Qumran sect.

Fifth, unlike the preceding positions, which were variations on the theme of 11QTemple as the Qumran Torah, Hartmut Stegemann rejects the theory entirely. 11QTemple was "never the specific Law of the Qumran community." He also disputes Yadin's theory that 11QTemple was composed at Qumran: it was found at Qumran because the community copied it, not because it was uniquely valued. In other words, the *Temple Scroll* was simply part of the community's library.[73] Furthermore, 11QTemple was never meant to replace the "traditional Pentateuch," but rather to complete it; it was a "sixth book of the *Torah*," additional to Pentateuch, but of equal value.[74] Stegemann considers 11QTemple as one of many "expanded Torah scrolls" in the period.[75] He dates 11QTemple earlier than other scholars, after mid-5th century

---

[72] Wise likens the author of 11QTemple to the Matthean Jesus as new Moses, and cites Davies' *Torah in the Messianic Age*: "Yet the analogy of the Gospel of Matthew, with its clear depiction of Jesus as a new Moses, is enough to prove that some circles in ancient Judaism expected a Law sufficiently changed from that of Moses to be called new" (Wise, *Critical Study*, 188).

[73] Stegemann, "Origins of the Temple Scroll," 246; "Literary Composition of the Temple Scroll," 131. He suggests that many of the Qumran texts (paraphrases, prayers, apocryphal psalms) may have been from the "'dark' centuries of the Second Temple period" but were saved by Qumran scholars ("Origins of the Temple Scroll," 256).

[74] Stegemann, "Literary Composition of the Temple Scroll," 127; "Origins of the Temple Scroll," 254–55.

[75] Stegemann, "Origins of the Temple Scroll," 251. Stegemann's other "expanded" Torahs are 4QReworked Pentateuch (4Q 364–65) and the Samaritan Pentateuch (255 n. 106). Wacholder preemptively dismisses Stegemann's evaluation: "The contents, language, and form tend to confirm our understanding of the ancient testimony that the work before us was presented not merely as another of the pseudepigraphs that filled the caves of Qumran but as a rival to the Five Books of the Torah which God had handed down to Moses" (*Dawn of Qumran*, xiii–xiv).

B.C.E., around the time of the Chronicler; for Stegemann it could not have been composed after Sirach (ca. 200 B.C.E.).[76]

The main arguments that Stegemann offers in support of his rejection of the Yadin/Wacholder theory are: (i) Only a few copies and fragments of the *Temple Scroll* have been identified among the some 800 Qumran manuscripts. Not one copy of the Scroll was found in cave 4, despite the fact that it contained about 580 manuscripts.[77] (ii) 11QTemple would not seem to have had canonical authority for the Qumran community, since it is never quoted (or mentioned) in any "specifically Qumranic document" (CD, 1QS, etc.).[78] (iii) There are differences in halakah between 11QTemple and other Qumran documents (e.g., divorce law). (iv) In comparison with Qumran documents, "the language and style of the *Temple Scroll* are much more traditional"—that is, more biblical. (v) The Qumran documents exhibit hostility toward the practice of the priesthood, but not against temple architecture, so 11QTemple does not seem to represent the community's position on the temple.[79]

The most devastating of Stegemann's critiques is the paucity of copies or fragments of 11QTemple in comparison to biblical texts and other acknowledged sectarian documents at Qumran. Stegemann's other points are less impressive. For example, by focusing on citations of or references to 11QTemple in Qumran sectarian writings, he circumvents Wacholder's extensive presentation of linguistic, thematic and theological affinities between 11QTemple and other recognized Qumran sectarian documents.[80] And, Stegemann's argument that the language of 11QTemple is more biblical than the sectarian literature is

---

[76] Stegemann expresses an inability to conceive of a "supplementary sixth book of the *Torah*" after the Mosaic Torah became dominant, after Sirach ("Literary Composition," 129; see "Origins" 254). For Stegemann Sirach represents the dominance of the Mosaic Torah. Clearly his *a priori* assumption of the nature of early Jewish Torah theology influences his interpretation of 11QTemple.

[77] Stegemann, "Origins of the Temple Scroll," 237.

[78] Stegemann, "Origins of the Temple Scroll," 238. Stegemann challenges Yadin's identification of allusions to 11QTemple in other Qumran texts: for example, Yadin's association of ספר ההגו (CD 10:6, 13:2) with 11QTorah does not work, because this refers to a catechetical type of book, secondary to Torah (242).

[79] Stegemann, "Origins of the Temple Scroll," 239–42.

[80] See especially Wacholder's chapter, "The Sectarian Torah in Qumranic Literature" (*Dawn of Qumran*, 33–98).

immaterial because one would expect a (good) pseudepigraphical composition to mimic the semantic characteristics of its model.

3.3.2 A Rival Torah?

The evidence for 11QTemple as the Qumran group's Torah is inconclusive because of its relative scarcity of representation in the Qumran caves. Without the influx of new data,[81] the resources are lacking to resolve the tension between the stunning nature of 11QTemple (i.e., its challenge to the authority of the Mosaic Torah) and its uncertain status at Qumran (since it is underrepresented). The poor material attestation of 11QTemple is balanced somewhat by the burgeoning consensus in Qumran scholarship that links 11QTemple with *Jubilees* and the CD on the basis of common theological traits. But the latter documents' reliance on 11QTemple would account for the commonality as well, and would make superfluous the argument that all three arose within the same early Jewish group.

Wacholder has failed to persuade many that 11QTemple was the Qumran sectarian Torah rivaling the Mosaic Torah, but this failure is not wholly attributable to his thesis; the idiosyncrasies of some of his supporting exegesis and interpretation, and generally his wildly aggressive manner of communicating his conclusions are responsible as well. The issue that separates Wacholder from scholars like Yadin, Brooke and Wise is not whether 11QTemple is an early Jewish group's Torah. They differ rather over the relationship between the Pentateuch and 11QTemple, whether the latter complements, supplements or replaces the former. Wacholder's thesis stands out from the others because it correlates so well with the consensus position in Dead Sea Scrolls scholarship that the scrolls were the library of a sectarian community inhabiting the Qumran settlement. The Qumran sectarian group as rival community, and 11QTemple as its rival Torah are complementary ideas. Of course neither thesis is dependent on the other being true; 11QTemple may have been a "rival Torah" for a group other than the inhabitants of the Qumran settlement.

---

[81] In the 1995 edition of his translation of the Scrolls, Vermes refers to a rumor that "unpublished fragments from Cave 4 dating to the mid second century B.C.E. quote from either the Temple Scroll itself or possibly one of its sources" (*The Dead Sea Scrolls in English*, 152).

The correlation of the Qumranian sect as rival community and
11QTemple as rival Torah separates 11QTemple from other rewritten
biblical texts.[82] But is this the only basis for a distinction? Certainly
11QTemple is justifiably classified with *Jubilees*, *Biblical Antiquities*
(Pseudo-Philo), the *Temptation of Moses*, the *Genesis Apocryphon*
(1QapGen), and perhaps Josephus' *Jewish Antiquities*, as "rewritten
Bible."[83] Post-biblical writings classified as "rewritten Bible" fill the
intermediate position between paraphrase of (targum), and commentary (midrash; pesher) on biblical texts. Extending exegetical traditions and interpretive patterns embedded in biblical texts, these
"rewritten" texts mingle selected biblical material with traditional
and/or exegetical development.

But 11QTemple goes beyond the mere interpretive retelling of a biblical story. It blurs the line separating revelation and interpretation
unlike any other rewritten biblical text, or any (extant) document since
Deuteronomy. Thus in a limited sense I can accept Wise's contention
that 11QTemple was intended to be the new Deuteronomy, since the
audacity of Deuteronomy vis-à-vis Exodus–Numbers is its primary
precedent. The material in 11QTemple is "revealed" directly from
Yhwh, bypassing the intermediary role of Moses, and thus the Mosaic
Torah as well. *Jubilees*, to be sure, could be understood as a rival to
biblical Genesis since it often alters or embellishes the "Mosaic" original, in the same way that Chronicles could be considered a rival to its
deuteronomic antecedent. Although there is good reason to link
Jubilees theologically with 11QTemple, perhaps even to consider them
as two halves of a new Torah (Wacholder), 11QTemple's direct revelation cannot be simply equated with *Jubilees*'s interpretive revision of

---

[82] A comparative study of rewritten pentateuchal texts is necessary to establish
whether 11QTemple is distinct in its claims to be direct revelation, or in the nature of its
revisions of Mosaic material.

[83] The phrase "rewritten Bible" belongs to G. Vermes (*Scripture and Tradition in
Judaism* [SPB 4; Leiden: Brill, 1961] 67–126). See the summary discussion in D. Harrington, "Palestinian Adaptations of Biblical Narratives and Prophecies: the Bible Rewritten (Narratives)," in *Early Judaism and its Modern Interpreters* (ed. R. Kraft and G.
Nickelsburg; Atlanta: Scholars Press, 1986) 239–47. Harrington lists 11QTemple as
rewritten Bible. Although he asks the question, "What did these writers think that they
were doing when they composed their books?" (243), noticeably absent is a real answer,
especially concerning the authority of "rewritten" texts vis-à-vis their biblical subtexts.
Characteristic of many of these writings—and their most profound feature—is the presentation of interpretation as revelation.

the Genesis narratives. Whereas *Jubilees* exalts the Mosaic tradition while it supplements it,[84] 11QTemple writes Moses out; both have taken the books of Moses as their source, but after that it is difficult to draw compositional parallels.

The *Temple Scroll* is a radical rewriting of the Mosaic Torah. It is a rewriting because it is modeled on and it replicates, with varying degrees of restatement and replacement, material from the Mosaic books. It is radical because of the degree of separation it achieves from Moses and his books. The compositional strategies that I have noted do not exhaust the ways in which 11QTemple reworks Exodus–Deuteronomy, but they are sufficient to determine the character of 11QTemple. The combination of an "I-Thou syntax" that promotes 11QTemple as direct revelation, the absence (by editorial preference) of Moses' footprints, and its מקדש of symbolic proportions present 11QTemple as a "greater than" Torah. To my knowledge 11QTemple gives no greater clues that assist the uninformed reader in understanding its relationship to the Mosaic predecessor. The premise for this new Torah is not given either, but one may infer from the manner in which the author reworks the mysterious phrase משנה התורה (Deut 17:18) that 11QTemple is envisioned as משנה התורה. This insight should be coupled with the observation that the bodies of instruction in Exodus 20–33 and Exodus 34–40 differ, a fact that early Jewish exegetes would not miss. It is necessary to express reservation here because the author of 11QTemple explicitly asserts neither that the scroll was hidden and now found, nor that it was new revelation. I do not think, however, that the lack of either assertion damages Wacholder's rival Torah thesis, which depends (ultimately, I believe) on the symmetry of 11QTemple and the Qumran community.

3.4 The Visionary Wisdom of *1 Enoch* as Rival Torah

In §2.5 I cited George W. E. Nickelsburg's opinion that the specific "relationship of Enoch's wisdom to the Mosaic Torah is ambiguous."[85] This statement of restraint should not throw one off the trail. Nickelsburg regards *1 Enoch* as revelation not merely in the sense of

---

[84] For example, *Jubilees* confirms the Sinai theophany as the source of not only protology, but eschatology as well (*Jub.* 1:28–29).

[85] G. W. E. Nickelsburg, "Wisdom and Apocalypticism in Early Judaism: Some Points for Discussion," *SBLASP* (1994) 720.

making known mysteries of the heavenly realm and eschatological information, but as a Torah rival to the Mosaic Torah.[86]

By *1 Enoch* Nickelsburg means Ethiopian Enoch, the extant final form of a process of writing, interpreting, collecting, and probably adding a polemical edge to the Enoch writings. The existence of important Aramaic and Greek portions of *1 Enoch* is a problem that modern interpreters of *1 Enoch* must hold in balance with the perception of *1 Enoch* as intentionally a whole piece.

> *1 Enoch* is a consciously shaped compilation of traditions and texts, and it is appropriate to search for internal points of commonality . . . in which the compilers and editors saw the potential for a unity comprised of diversity. More fundamentally, because successive parts of the tradition developed from and built on one another, some significant unity is to be expected.[87]

Nickelsburg does not ignore the unique theological content and perspective of the individual "books" of *1 Enoch*, but he stresses the whole, the Enochic Torah. As he understands it, the Enochic Torah both presumes and surpasses the Mosaic Torah by claiming its true interpretation. Moreover, *1 Enoch* transcends because it contains cosmological, calendrical, and eschatological material lacking in the Mosaic books.

Nickelsburg's perspective on *1 Enoch* was anticipated by G. H. Dix's thesis that *1 Enoch* was intended to be the apocalyptic counterpart of the Mosaic Torah. According to Dix, for each book of the Pentateuch there was a corresponding book in Ethiopic Enoch. Book 1 is the "Enochic Genesis": it contains material on the new creation and the origin of sin and evil. Interestingly, Dix notes how Enoch's supernal journeys parallel Abraham's travels in Genesis. Book 2 (the Similitudes) is an Enochic Exodus, with the Son of Man as the deliverer greater than Moses who leads "the elect" out of oppression. Book 3, the Enochic Leviticus, reveals the laws of the heavenly bodies. Book 4 is the Enochic Numbers since it presents an eschatological version of

---

[86] A point Nickelsburg makes in many ways throughout his article, "Enoch, First Book of," *ABD* 2. 508–16.

[87] G. W. E. Nickelsburg, "The Apocalyptic Construction of Reality in *1 Enoch*," in *Mysteries and Revelations: Apocalyptic Studies since the Uppsala Colloquium* (ed. J. J. Collins and J. Charlesworth; JSPSup 9; Sheffield: JSOT Press, 1991) 52.

"the preservation of all the righteous among them as they journeyed to the Holy Land, their settlement there under Joshua, and ends with the appointment of the Cities of Refuge." Book 5, like Deuteronomy, is a sermon by a departing prophet, stressing the future blessings that obedience to the law would bring, and contrasting the futures of the godly and ungodly.[88] The "Enochites," as Dix refers to the northern Palestinian[89] group responsible for the Enochic Torah, were "manifestly religious rebels" who thought "their type of religion was older far than Mosaism."[90]

Nickelsburg does not duplicate Dix on the specific relationship of Enochic and Mosaic books, but he does regard the Epistle of Enoch as the counterpart to Deuteronomy:

> The key word "testify" (81:6; 91:3), used of Enoch's instruction to his children and of the book's function in the eschaton (104:11; 105:1), parallels the usage of Deuteronomy 30–31 and ascribes to the Enochic corpus a function that parallels the Mosaic Torah and Moses' descriptions of the future.[91]

Nickelsburg identifies a number of other ways in which *1 Enoch* presents itself as Torah: *1 Enoch* 72–82, the earliest portion of Ethiopic Enoch, is rendered in a "revelatory form" that "suggests that it is presented as a divinely ordained Torah. . . ."[92] The authors of *1 Enoch* present their revelation with the authority and immediacy of the biblical prophets.[93] To the temporal eschatology of the prophets *1 Enoch* adds a spatial dimension that intersects with "forms and traditions" of wisdom literature:

---

[88] G. H. Dix, "The Enochic Pentateuch," *JTS* 27 (1926) 29–31. Dix does not cite textual examples from *1 Enoch* to specify his assertions; in some ways Nickelsburg continues this tendency because although he writes confidently of an Enochic Torah, he seldom if ever demonstrates it textually.

[89] "And I went and sat down upon the waters of Dan—in Dan which is on the southwest of Hermon—and I read their [fallen angels] memorial prayers until I fell asleep" (*1 Enoch* 13:7). The narrative proceeds with a dream vision there. On this location as a sacred site, see G. Nickelsburg, "Enoch, Levi, and Peter: Recipients of Revelation in Upper Galilee," *JBL* 100 (1981) 575–600.

[90] Dix, "Enochic Pentateuch," 32.

[91] Nickelsburg, "Enoch, Levi, and Peter," 514.

[92] G. W. E. Nickelsburg, "Enoch, First Book of," *ABD* 2. 509.

[93] Nickelsburg, "Enoch, Levi, and Peter," 516.

Through the intersection of these currents a new phenomenon appears in *1 Enoch*. The content of Torah is broadened, and its true interpretation is specified. The revelation of God's will and of the eschatological future is supplemented by revealed knowledge of a hidden world, and together these are identified as heavenly wisdom of broad and inclusive dimensions, mediated by a primordial seer and sage.[94]

1 Enoch's status as revelation rival to the Mosaic Torah is most apparent in two features of the corpus: the prominence of Wisdom in *1 Enoch*, especially when compared and contrasted with the Wisdom/Torah tradition, and the salvific nature of Enochic revelation.

3.4.1 Revelatory Genre

1 Enoch is considered an apocalypse, or more properly a compilation of apocalypses written by a number of different authors over an extended period of time, which Nickelsburg nevertheless views as a unified work. The genre apocalypse is by nature revelatory.[95] In a paper on apocalypticism and wisdom in early Jewish literature, Nickelsburg makes the following distinction:

The claims of revelation in the wisdom literature tend to be tied to traditional texts, namely, the Mosaic Torah and prophets. The

---

[94] Nickelsburg, "Enoch, Levi, and Peter," 515.

[95] The standard definition of an apocalypse: "*Apocalypse* is a genre of revelatory literature with a narrative framework, in which revelation is mediated by an otherworldly being to a human recipient, disclosing a transcendent reality which is both temporal, insofar as it envisages eschatological salvation, and spatial insofar as it involves another, supernatural world" (J. J. Collins, "Introduction: Towards the Morphology of a Genre," *Semeia* 14 [1979] 9). Thanks largely to the narrowing of definitions in the *Semeia* 14 articles, scholarship is increasingly suspicious of casual uses of "apocalyptic" and "apocalypticism." Collins provides these guidelines for proper use: "A movement might reasonably be characterized as apocalyptic if it shares the world-view typical of the apocalypses. The most straightforward example would be a community which uses apocalypses as its typical form of expression. . . . A movement or community might also be apocalyptic if it were shaped to a significant degree by a specific apocalyptic tradition, or if its world-view could be shown to be similar to that of the apocalypses in a distinctive way" ("Genre, Ideology and Social Movements in Jewish Apocalypticism," in *Mysteries and Revelations: Apocalyptic Studies since the Uppsala Colloquium* [JSPSupp 9; ed. J. J. Collins and J. Charlesworth; Sheffield: JSOT Press, 1991] 23). Thus the community of the Dead Sea Scrolls is justifiably termed apocalyptic although they most likely produced no apocalypses.

authors of apocalyptic texts, while they actually draw heavily on the Torah and prophets, present new revelations, although they attribute them variously to pre-Mosaic authors (Enoch and Abraham), Moses himself, and post-Mosaic figures (Daniel, Ezra and Baruch). The sources of these new revelations are said to be cosmic journeys and dream visions, interpreted by angels.[96]

Thus it is characteristic of apocalyptic texts to employ and develop biblical material as well as present new revelation. One might also expect, therefore, a literary tension between the new and old revelations, the authoritative received tradition and the visionary. In *1 Enoch* celestial journeys and visions reveal heavenly secrets, or "wisdom" not contained in the Mosaic Torah. But this is not the only sense in which *1 Enoch* is revelatory for Nickelsburg, otherwise all "apocalyptic texts" would be judged as rival Torah, and indeed all rewritten biblical texts and midrashic commentaries would be as well.

3.4.2 Enochic Wisdom

In §2.5 I noted that the Similitudes of Enoch (*1 Enoch* 37–71) were the counterpart to the tradition that identified divine Wisdom with Torah. Nickelsburg finds this contrary relationship in earlier portions of Ethiopic Enoch: "Especially striking is the use of the wisdom myth of 81:1–82:4, where, in contrast to Sirach 24 and Baruch 4:1, it is Enoch's books rather than the Mosaic Torah that are the earthly repository of heavenly wisdom."[97] Wisdom is a cipher for what is also called "heavenly secrets" in *1 Enoch*. There is a heavenly repository of Wisdom, which thus must be accessed supernally, via visions and journeys. Within the Enochic corpus this "good" Wisdom can be contrasted with the "bad" wisdom of the Watchers; outside the context of *1 Enoch* the most fruitful contrast is with the Wisdom that, according to Sirach 24, materialized in Torah.

In the book of the Watchers (*1 Enoch* 6–36) the Watchers reveal to their human wives sorcery (חרשה) and magical arts (7:1; 8:3), the art of making weaponry and jewelry (8:1), and astrology (8:3).[98] These arts are subsequently referred to as "eternal secrets which are performed in

---

[96] Nickelsburg, "Wisdom and Apocalypticism," 722-23.

[97] Nickelsburg, "Wisdom and Apocalypticism," 720.

[98] Aramaic portions of *1 Enoch* from J. T. Milik's *The Books of Enoch, Aramaic Fragments of Qumrân Cave 4* (Oxford: Oxford University Press, 1976).

heaven" (9:6).[99] In a later vision Enoch is instructed to inform the Watchers that

> You were (once) in heaven, but not all the mysteries (of heaven) are open to you, and you (only) know the rejected mysteries. Those ones you have broadcast to the women in the hardness of your hearts and by those mysteries the women and men multiply evil deeds upon the earth. (1 Enoch 16:3)[100]

The remainder of the Book of the Watchers is occupied with Enoch's journeys. I assume that the secrets which Enoch views on his journeys to, for example, the cosmic mountain (1 Enoch 17) and Eden (1 Enoch 24–25; see also 17 and 30–32) are to be contrasted with the Watchers' "rejected" secrets which wrought evil on earth.

Since Wisdom in the Similitudes of Enoch was the subject of §2.5, I will assume the prior conclusions here, and only recall that the Similitudes are described as a "vision of Wisdom," and that the "Chosen One" is a revealer of Wisdom (48:7; 51:3). Despite the otherwise unattested assault on the Wisdom/Torah tradition (1 Enoch 42), the Similitudes are consistent with the rest of Ethiopian Enoch in presenting the secrets that Enoch views and hears as Wisdom. As in the Book of the Watchers' visions, Enoch is shown "all the hidden things" (40:2), and "all the secrets of heaven" (41:1). A stunning development of the Watchers myth names a new group of "chief" angels as those responsible for the misdeeds of the Semyaz-led Watchers (1 Enoch 69). Notable among these angels are Gader'el, who revealed the secrets of warfare and weaponry (69:6; compare 8:1), and especially Pinem'e, who "revealed to [the children of the people] all the secrets of their wisdom" (69:9). Pinem'e is responsible for teaching people the secret of writing, which has led many into error: "For human beings are not created for such purposes to take up their beliefs with pen and ink" (69:10). The phrasing is inexplicit, but one has to wonder what type of writing is intended here, whether it is a rebuke of written revelation in favor of Enochic visionary wisdom. Is the Mosaic Torah, as written revelation, to be associated with the Watchers' wisdom? Of course the Enochic author(s) would thus be cutting off the branch on which he is perched, since 1 Enoch belongs to the condemned category of written wisdom.

[99] So Milik, *Aramaic Fragments*, 161.
[100] English translations of *1 Enoch* are from E. Isaac, *OTP* 1. 5–89.

The final depiction of Enochic wisdom is in the last chapter of the book of Heavenly Luminaries (*1 Enoch* 72–82). Enoch hands on his book of revelation, derived at least in part from the heavenly tablets (81:1–2), to Methusaleh:

> Now, Methuselah, my son, I shall recount all these things to you and write them down for you. I have revealed to you and given you the book concerning all these things. Preserve, my son, the book from your father's hands in order that you may pass it on to the generations of the world. I have given wisdom to you, to your children, and to those who shall become your children in order that they may pass it (in turn) to their own and to the generations that are discerning. All the wise ones shall give praise, and wisdom shall dwell upon your consciousness; they shall not slumber but be thinking; they shall cause their ears to listen in order that they may learn this wisdom; and it shall please those who feast on it more than good food. (82:1–3)

This text is notable in that it parallels biblical language about Torah, especially Deuteronomy 4 and 6. Enoch's book is "wisdom" as Torah is wisdom (Deut 4:6; Ezra 7:25). Like Torah, Enochic wisdom is to be handed on from generation to generation (e.g., Deut 4:9; 6:7, 20–25). Enochic wisdom is likened to food, as is biblical wisdom (Sir 24:19; 6:19).

3.4.3 Salvation

Nickelsburg observes that the Enochic corpus is characterized by the presentation of its "wisdom" (i.e., revelation) as salvific: "This wisdom . . . is significant for its salvific function. It is Torah broadly conceived. Aspects of it reveal the laws that embody the divine will that must be obeyed if one is to be saved."[101] The saving nature of Enochic revelation is not merely a future hope. *1 Enoch* 92–105 "unfolds a revelation of an unseen heavenly realm that is *already operative* as the sphere of salvation."[102] In other words, salvation is an "already" for those who possess the Enochic wisdom, but it is also a

---

[101] G. W. E. Nickelsburg, "*1 Enoch* and Qumran Origins: The State of the Question and Some Prospects for Answers," *SBLASP* (1986) 346.

[102] G. W. E. Nickelsburg, "The Apocalyptic Message of *1 Enoch* 92–105," *CBQ* 39 (1977) 325. One line down Nickelsburg presents a picture of Enochic revelation which I think parallels Pauline mysticism well: "Because this unseen world, with its eschatologically oriented activity, is a present reality, the author's message takes on an eschatological quality."

"not yet" because they still await a future consummation of the age. The "already" aspect is present in this text from the Book of the Watchers:

> And then wisdom shall be given to the elect. And they shall all live and not return again to sin, either by being wicked or through pride; but those who have wisdom shall be humble and not return again to sin. And they shall not be judged all the days of their lives; nor die through plague or wrath, but they shall complete the (designated) number of days of their life. (*1 Enoch* 5:8–9)

The benefits of Enochic wisdom are like those of Wisdom/Torah: it rescues its adherents from sin (compare Sir 24:22; Bar 4:1; Wis 8:13).

According to Nickelsburg, the world-view of *1 Enoch* is dualistic. Thus Enochic wisdom is salvific in that it provides its adherents escape from the temporal, spatial, and ontological dualisms that oppress humanity: temporal dualism concerns the present and future; spatial dualism refers to the relationship between the heavenly and earthly, and I would add the realms visible and invisible; Nickelsburg uses "ontological dualism" for the chasm between God and world. *1 Enoch* understands humanity as existing at the "intersection" of these dualisms, which ultimately is a pessimistic position. But *1 Enoch* is optimistic since its salvation, though awaited in the future, is effected and experienced in this age by means of Enochic revelation that "presents a significant resolution" of the dualisms.[103]

3.4.4 Conclusion

It is difficult to evaluate Nickelsburg's reading of *1 Enoch* as rival Torah because he generally makes broad assertions about large portions of the book rather than performing exegeses on smaller text units that others can evaluate. And since *1 Enoch* almost never addresses the law, its relationship to the Torah must be inferred from what is said and unsaid. It is no fancy of the imagination, however, to find in *1 Enoch* an implicit yet intentional challenge to the sufficiency of Mosaic Torah. From the perspective of *1 Enoch* the Mosaic Torah is a lesser revelation: the Enochic Torah predates the Mosaic and contains all that Enoch himself saw and read in his various supernal experi-

---

[103] Nickelsburg, "Apocalyptic Construction of Reality in *1 Enoch*," 60–61.

ences.[104] The Mosaic Torah was miraculously given, but unlike the Enoch books it grants no access to the heavenly repositories of knowledge about the cosmos, the final days of this age, the identification of the elect.

1 Enoch is representative of visionary literature written and edited to be an adversary of "structure legitimating" authoritative texts.[105] There is a polar relationship between the new, yet more ancient apocalyptic revelatory text (*1 Enoch*) and the Mosaic Torah, the "landed" revelation that legitimates cult and the interpretive tradition. This tension is most observable in Nickelsburg's comparison of Ben Sira, the self-proclaimed channel of revelatory truth (Sir 24:30–34), and the visionary tradition embodied by *1 Enoch*: Ben Sira claims that "life-giving Wisdom resides in the Torah,"[106] whereas *1 Enoch* asserts that "salvation is bound up with revelation,"[107] either as inspired non-scribal interpretation of the Mosaic Torah, or as "life-giving wisdom" in itself, usually with revelation of eschatological judgment.[108] Confined to the issue of access to revelation, the polarity might be termed

---

[104] In chapter 5 I make a similar point about Paul's use of Abraham in Galatians 3–4: the Abrahamic visions and promises are preeminent because they predate the Sinai revelation.

[105] This notion of "structure legitimation" is borrowed from W. Brueggemann ("A Shape for Old Testament Theology, I: Structure Legitimation," *Old Testament Theology* [ed. P. D. Miller; Minneapolis: Fortress, 1992] 1–21).

[106] G. W. E. Nickelsburg, "Revealed Wisdom as a Criterion for Inclusion and Exclusion: From Jewish Sectarianism to Early Christianity," in *"To See Ourselves as Others See Us": Christians, Jews, and "Others" in Late Antiquity* (ed. J. Neusner and E. Frerichs; Missoula, MT: Scholars Press, 1986) 74.

[107] Nickelsburg, "Revealed Wisdom," 83.

[108] Nickelsburg, "Revealed Wisdom," on Enoch see 75–76; Qumran 79–81. He finds a similar tension between "mainstream" Torah scholarship and new revelation in early (Jewish) Christianity and the Dead Sea Scrolls. The Johannine and Pauline traditions are similar to the Enochic, although Jesus is the revealer who challenges Torah, whereas "in *1 Enoch* and the Qumran texts, the authority of revelation is invoked to support one interpretation of the Torah against other interpretations" (83). For Paul Christ's death and resurrection are the "eschatological event of salvation" that are "construed as an eschatological revelation" to which an individual's "positive or negative response . . . results in salvation or damnation" (88). In the Gospel of John, Jesus' status as revealer is asserted: "According to John, those who believe in Jesus by accepting him as the revealer have eternal life. Those who reject his claims are damned" (83). In both traditions "the incarnation of Jesus parallels the Jewish idea of the descent of Wisdom" (83).

visionary/scribe. *1 Enoch*'s dreams, visions and journeys constitute revelation that God's elect can rely on in this age and the next, an unmistakable affront to the sufficiency of Torah, cult, and scribal exegesis.

3.5 The Secret Books of 4 Ezra

The "secrets" of *1 Enoch* are paralleled in 4 Ezra 14. God identifies himself to the Seer as the one who was revealed in the bush to Moses, and who instructed Moses to publish some of what he heard publicly, and to keep some secret (14:3–6).[109] The Seer Ezra then learns about the imminent demise of the age (14:7–18), and laments to God that those born in the future will not be warned:

> For the world lies in darkness, and its inhabitants are without light. For thy law has been burned, and so no one knows the things which have been done or will be done by thee. (14:20–21)

The Seer, who is enlightened by drinking from a cup of "something like water, but its color was like fire" (14:39), then becomes the medium of a new revelation. This revelation is only new in a sense, because it is linked throughout with Moses:

> I will write everything that has happened in the world from the beginning, the things which were written in thy law, that men may be able to find the path, and that those who wish to live in the last days may live. (14:22)

It is important to note that God is the mediator in this revelation scene, rather than an angel.[110] Five men, presumably symbolizing the five "Mosaic" books, transcribe the Seer's words, and produce 94 books (14:44). Of these books 24 are "public," which may be read by both the "worthy" and "unworthy" (14:45); these are the standard books of the Hebrew Bible. The remaining 70 books are for the "wise": "Keep the

---

[109] M. E. Stone observes that Ezra is portrayed in 4 Ezra 14 in a manner paralleling Moses: "The association with Moses is very clear. Ezra receives his call in a situation similar to that of Moses and in an identical fashion. The language of the call, the double repetition of the name, and the response, although often found in call scenes . . . take on great specificity of reference because of the deliberate association with Moses" (*Fourth Ezra: A Commentary on the Fourth Book of Ezra* [Hermeneia; Minneapolis: Fortress, 1990] 410–11).

[110] Stone, *4 Ezra*, 411.

seventy that were written last, in order to give them to the wise among your people" (14:46). Secret things are commonplace in apocalyptic literature, but the secret revelation here has a special function. These 70 books are linked to the secret words of Moses (14:6), which only means that the author of 4 Ezra wanted the reader to think of them as Mosaic, rather than new.

I have not described the 70 books as "rival Torah" because, unlike the *Temple Scroll* which writes Moses out of the revelation narrative, and *1 Enoch* in which a revelation more ancient and profound than the Mosaic is given, the secret books of 4 Ezra 14 are inherently linked to the Mosaic revelation. In 4 Ezra 14, the secret revelation is qualitatively better than the written:

> For in them is the spring of understanding, the fountain of wisdom, and the river of knowledge. (4 Ezra 14:47)

As in Sirach 24 and in many texts in biblical and post-biblical literature, these fountain-figures are used for Torah, but they belong to the celestial paradise, the repository of divine wisdom. By using these symbols for the 70 secret books, 4 Ezra has figuratively presented these books—already designated as eschatological Torah—as the primordial Torah.

3.6 Conclusion: Torah in Early Jewish Literature

In *Torah in the Messianic Age and/or Age to Come*, W. D. Davies sifted through biblical and post-biblical literature for phraseology suggesting a future alteration or even abrogation of Torah. His goal was to uncover a Jewish tradition that expected a new Torah in order to illuminate Paul's characterization of Torah and the Sermon on the Mount.[111] Of course he found scant evidence for this expectation anywhere in rabbinic literature, and the scholarly consensus regards such texts as insignificant blips in a Jewish theology that persistently proclaims an eternal, immutable Torah. Moreover, these "blips" postdate the NT by centuries, so they are not considered valuable tools in deciphering the Pauline code.

---

[111] See Davies, *Setting of the Sermon on the Mount*, 109–90, which replicates the material in *Torah in the Messianic Age*, but now as the backdrop to the Sermon.

On the other hand, Davies' instinct was correct because he recognized that in his theology Paul had replaced Torah with Christ. But Davies searched for the wrong data. In this chapter I have presented an alternate portrait of early Jewish Torah theology in which the nature of Torah as revelation was modified and its sufficiency challenged. Unlike Davies I have not asked whether a document advocates a new Torah; my question, rather, has been what sort of relationship to the Mosaic Torah is represented by the heavenly tablets, the *Temple Scroll*, the visionary wisdom of *1 Enoch*, or the secret books of 4 Ezra 14? Although these theological phenomena are not directly related, they are mutually informative. Each uniquely challenges the Mosaic books as the sole repository of divine wisdom. In different ways each claims to have access to a source of wisdom superior to the Mosaic Torah.

This theological matrix does not fully explain Paul; statements like "Christ is the τέλος of the law" (Rom 10:4) or the "law of death" (Rom 8:2) are without precedent in the literature cited in this chapter. Davies' operating procedure was to seek continuity between Jewish and Pauline theology, but I do not share his disposition. I will argue in the following studies that by replacing Torah with Christ Paul *contradicted* the theological axiom that Torah was God's eternal Wisdom. Thus the eternal Torah, as a development from Torah as the embodiment of divine Wisdom, is the element of early Jewish Torah theology that is most directly relevant to Paul. But there is a sense of continuity between Paul's characterization of Torah and those texts that adduce a wisdom or revelation more essential than the Mosaic Torah. And Paul was also like the Enochic visionaries, like the author(s) of the *Temple Scroll*, like the Qumran covenanters—and like Jesus as he is portrayed in the gospels—in that he set himself as an eschatologically empowered hermeneut over Torah and even Moses. The expansions of and challenges to the Mosaic Torah investigated in this chapter are the context in which Paul's Christian view of Torah should be received.

CHAPTER 4

Torah and the Stumbling Stone in Romans 9–10

Appearing in the midst of what is alternately viewed as an obtrusive, if significant, midrashic excursus in the structure of Romans, or the pinnacle of Paul's argumentation in the letter,[1] Rom 9:30–10:13 features biblical fragments, symbols and commentary woven together to communicate a startling story: God placed an obstacle (πρόσκομμα) in Israel's path to righteousness (δικαιοσύνη) that resulted in an unanticipated redemption for an unexpected multitude. Throughout Romans

---

[1] As J. D. G. Dunn notes, Romans 9–11 appears to be a self-contained literary unit, with an identifiable beginning (9:1–5), end (11:33–36), and thesis (9:6a). Since the unit is comprised of extensive citation and commentary on biblical texts, Dunn appropriately describes Romans 9–11 as a "midrash" (*Romans 9–16* [WBC 38b; Dallas: Word, 1988] 518). The inner coherence of Romans 9–11 and its relationship to the rest of Romans is debated; see especially W. A. Meeks, "On Trusting an Unpredictable God: A Hermeneutical Meditation on Romans 9–11," in *Faith and History: Essays in Honor of Paul W. Meyer* (ed. J. T. Carroll, C. H. Cosgrove, and E. E Johnson; Atlanta: Scholars Press, 1990) 105–24. E. E. Johnson delineates four positions concerning the place and function of Romans 9–11 in Romans: two polar views in which 9–11 is (1) an appendix to chapters 1–8 or (2) the center of Romans; and two mediating views, in which these chapters (3) summarize and/or state the implications (esp. for Israel) of chapters 1–8, or are (4) "a delayed conclusion to the unfinished argument of 3:1–9" (*The Function of Apocalyptic and Wisdom Traditions in Romans 9–11* [SBLDS 109; Atlanta: Scholars Press, 1989] 110–6; quote, 115). I view Romans 9–11 as the epicenter of the letter in which Paul, using numerous biblical texts and the remnant motif, answers the questions raised in Romans 1–8 about the relationship between the historical and eschatological people of God.

Paul uses compositional strategies of ambiguity and surprise.[2] In Rom 9:30–10:13 both techniques are represented in the designification of the familiar messianic "stone" symbol, and the reorientation of Torah imagery. When his topic is Torah, Paul's compositional strategy might be termed counter-textual, since he cites from and alludes to key texts in the Wisdom/Torah tradition, but with Torah replaced in the equation by Christ and/or the gospel. This noteworthy antithesis of Torah and Christ is partially submerged in the ambiguities of Rom 9:30–10:13.

Paul's controversial statement that "Christ is the τέλος of the Law" (Rom 10:4) overshadows the rest of Rom 9:30–10:13. The sense of these words depends on the meaning of one word: does τέλος mean "end" or "goal"? "Christ the *end* of the Law" means that Christ and Torah have a discontinuous relationship, whereas "Christ the *goal* of the Law" is continuous.[3] Τέλος as "end" is more consistent with the idea that Torah would be eschatologically replaced, yet eschatological Torah theories do not depend on "end," nor are they nullified with "goal."[4] The eschatological Torah theorists generally have difficulty with what the "end" of Torah entails because they either maintain an artificial sense of continuity (Davies, Stuhlmacher), or they were unable to envision the temporal end of an eternal entity (Schweitzer).[5] Although τέλος as "goal" is preferable for philological reasons, and contextually it matches the race metaphor from Rom 9:30–33 ("pursue" and "stumble"), in this chapter I focus on the discontinuous, or disjunctive nature of the Torah/Christ relationship that is con-

---

[2] See M. D. Given, "True Rhetoric: Ambiguity, Cunning, and Deception in Pauline Discourse," *SBLSP* 1997, 526–50.

[3] R. Badenas, *Christ the End of the Law* (JSNTSup 10; Sheffield: JSOT, 1985) 3.

[4] As recognized by Badenas: "Although Davies was reluctant to interpret Rom 10.4 eschatologically, it is evident that his view influenced subsequent exegesis of this passage" (*Christ the End of the Law*, 28).

[5] But not so R. Longenecker: "The context shows that here he is specifically considering the Mosaic Law and declaring that it has been completed and abrogated by Christ on a specific level" (*Paul, Apostle of Liberty* [New York: Harper and Row, 1964] 144). Longenecker has his out, however: for Paul, only the Law in the sense of "contractual obligation" finds its "full completion and terminus in Christ" (128). H. Schoeps asserts that τέλος νόμου χριστός is "an absolutely exact inference from the standpoint of Jewish theological thought; but the rabbis did not share Paul's premise that the Messianic Age had begun with the death and resurrection of Jesus" (*Paul: The Theology of the Apostle in the Light of Jewish Religious History* [Philadelphia: Westminster, 1961] 173).

sistent with τέλος as "end."[6] But my understanding of this Pauline antithesis is not reliant on the meaning of one word, τέλος. Although I see Paul ultimately maintaining a continuity of Torah and Christ, the continuity is of the lesser-to-greater sort—that is, real supersession. The Torah that Paul envisions finds its *terminus* in Christ, in the transforming power and unmediated knowledge of God in the spirit of Christ.[7] Paul's reconfigured Torah is not the real antithesis of Christ. Rather, the eternal Torah that Paul confronts and counters in Galatians and 2 Corinthians is Christ's polar pair. In Romans, where Paul is an outsider, Paul is not rebuffing alternate gospels directly, but he does lob intertextual salvos at Torah as the embodiment of heavenly Wisdom. His gospel (see especially Rom 1:16–17) is pitted against the eternal Torah.

Paul establishes in the larger context of Rom 10:4 a Christ/Torah polarity through his configuration of biblical texts, and the resulting substructure of equivalences and dissimilarities. The goal of this chapter is to show Paul's counterpoint to the eternal Torah by analyzing his explicit biblical citations and implicit dialogue with the Wisdom/Torah tradition. The chapter focuses on the form and significance of Paul's conflated quotation of two Isaiah texts in Rom 9:33. These texts are also part of the "stone" tradition: the "stone" of Isa 8:14 and 28:16 is read as a messianic cipher elsewhere in the NT and the *targumim*.[8]

---

[6] Notwithstanding the strong lexical arguments for the teleological interpretation, τέλος is somewhat ambiguous. Moreover, the "ambiguity was intentional on Paul's part" (J. Drane, *Paul: Libertine or Legalist?* [London: SPCK, 1975] 133; cited in Badenas, *Christ the End of the Law*, 4). I will argue that the same thing holds true for λίθος in Rom 9:33.

[7] C. Bugge employed an analogy that merges the teleological and disjunctive notions of Christ as τέλος of Torah: as a river into a sea, Torah empties (*einmünden*) into Christ. The river expands into the sea; the sea contains all the particles that were in the river; and the river undergoes a reconfiguration or transformation (*Umbildung*) when it goes into the sea. Similarly, Torah expands and becomes Christ. Christ contains every element of transformed (*Umbildung*) Torah ("Das Gesetz und Christus nach der Anschauung der ältesten Christengemeinde," *ZNW* 4 [1903] 105).

[8] See Str-B, 5.276; W. Sanday and A. C. Headlam, *A Critical and Exegetical Commentary on the Epistle to the Romans* (ICC; Edinburgh: T. and T. Clark, 1958) 281; Jeremias, "λίθος," *TDNT* 4. 272–73. The witness of the targumic rendering of these stone texts verifies the place of the NT writers in the growth of an interpretative tradition. Their specific point in the trajectory is an interesting issue, which extends far beyond the confines of this chapter. The trajectory itself is noteworthy, for it shows that Paul

Paul, however, does not explicitly identify his "stone," but uses Isaiah's stone texts in Rom 9:30–10:13 as a polyvalent symbol for a sub-complex of interrelated texts concerning Torah, Abraham, and the gentiles. The special vocabulary of this sub-complex includes λίθος, πέτρα, πιστεύω, σκάνδαλον, Σιών and forms of αἰσχύνω, all of which occur in Rom 9:33.

4.1 The Messianic Stone in the New Testament

Paul's use of the two stone texts from Isaiah (8:14, 28:16) in Rom 9:33 must be differentiated from the other appearances of the stone tradition in the New Testament. Whereas for Paul the stone is something to be stumbled on, elsewhere it is a rejected stone. The theme of the stone's rejection comes from Ps 118:22: "The stone which the builders rejected has become the head of the corner." The synoptics' Jesus uses the rejected stone as a comment on the parable of the wicked tenants (Matt 21:42; Mark 12:10; Luke 20:17).[9] According to Joachim Jeremias, Jesus himself used the rejected stone: "Jesus reads His fate in the psalm."[10] In Acts it is uttered by Peter, but unlike the form of the text in Luke 20:17, which replicates the LXX of Ps 118:22, in Acts 4:11 it is οὗτός ἐστιν ὁ λίθος ὁ ἐξουθενηθεὶς ὑφ' ὑμῶν τῶν οἰκοδόμων ὁ γενόμενος εἰς κεφαλὴν γωνίας. The key difference is the identification of the builders who "despise" the stone with the audience of Peter's speech: "despised by you the builders."

One may surmise that the rejected stone of Ps 118:22 allowed early Jewish-Christian theologians to rationalize and embrace the rejection of Jesus' messiahship (and their own strife with other Jewish groups). It has been an assumption of scholarship that for some segments of

---

did not employ the Isaiah texts in a wholly unique way. Paul may be perceived as diverting from the tradition that became rabbinic Judaism, but it is not true that his use of these texts in commenting on the status of Torah in the messianic age is out of step with every movement within early Judaism.

[9] Probably a double tradition: Mark and Q or L, depending on one's solution to the textual problems of Matt 21:43–44.

[10] Jeremias, "λίθος," 274–75. According to Jeremias the phrase ראש פנה אבן signified a crown stone rather than a foundation stone, and thus this final stone was interpreted as the messianic King. The building was the eschatological temple, whether conceived literally or figuratively.

early Christianity, Jewish rejection of Jesus was the necessary justification for the gentile mission. Ps 118:22 also functions as a proof text for Christ's death and resurrection, with the phrase "the builders rejected" symbolizing Jesus' death, and "became a corner stone" his resurrection.[11] Because the rejection element of Ps 118:22 is form-fitted to NT christology rather than Jewish messianism generally, it is difficult to envision it belonging to a pre-Christian messianic stone tradition.[12] On the other hand, the stone of Isa 28:16 does not have the ready-made interface with the tradition of the rejected and crucified messiah.[13] This valuable stone is transformed into an obstacle when, in Paul's hands, it is mingled with the stumbling stone of Isa 8:14 (see below).

Although it is only echoed in the NT, Dan 2:34 may be included in the NT stone text quarry:

> A stone was cut out by no human hand, and it smote the image on its feet of iron and clay, and broke them in pieces.

Dan 2:34 seems to be a subtext in Luke 20:18, following the quotation of Ps 118:22 in Luke 20:17:

> What then is this that is written: "The very stone which the builders rejected has become the head of the corner"? Every one who falls on that stone will be broken to pieces; but when it falls on any one it will crush him. (Luke 20:17–18)

Since Daniel's stone destroyed the image by striking it, Luke 20:18 appears to be a conflation of the active smashing of Dan 2:34 and the

---

[11] Jeremias, "λίθος," 275.

[12] *Contra* Jeremias ("λίθος"), who thought Ps 118:22 was interpreted messianically outside the NT.

[13] The Isaiah Targum, which contains traditions that are regularly dated to the first century, is evidence that the stone of Isa 28:16 was understood messianically in (non-Christian) Jewish circles. It transforms the choice stone into a "mighty, strong, and powerful king." M. Albl's conclusion that "the evidence for a pre-Christian messianic interpretation of Isa 28:16 must be considered weak" (*"And Scripture Cannot Be Broken": The Form and Function of Early Christian Testimonia Collections* [NovTSup 96; Leiden: Brill, 1999] 267) rests on the difficulty in establishing dates. Accordingly, I am suggesting the *non-Christian* rather than pre-Christian use of Isa 28:16. One might also ask what Isa 28:16 would have meant in combination with other stone texts.

stone of Isa 8:14–15, over which one stumbles and breaks.[14] The stone in Daniel 2 becomes a "great mountain" that "fills all the earth" (2:35). The transformation of the stone into a world mountain is probably a development from Isa 28:16, where the stone would be placed "in Zion."

Because of its verbal similarity to Rom 9:33, the stone text in 1 Pet 2:6–8 is significant:

διότι περιέχει ἐν γραφῇ
ἰδοὺ τίθημι ἐν Σιὼν λίθον ἀκρογωνιαῖον ἐκλεκτὸν ἔντιμον καὶ
ὁ πιστεύων ἐπ᾽ αὐτῷ οὐ μὴ καταισχυνθῇ [Isa 28:16]
ὑμῖν οὖν ἡ τιμὴ τοῖς πιστεύουσιν ἀπιστοῦσιν δὲ
λίθος ὃν ἀπεδοκίμασαν οἱ οἰκοδομοῦντες οὗτος ἐγενήθη εἰς κεφαλὴν
γωνίας [Ps 118:22] καὶ λίθος προσκόμματος καὶ πέτρα σκανδάλου
[Isa 8:14] οἳ προσκόπτουσιν τῷ λόγῳ ἀπειθοῦντες εἰς ὃ καὶ ἐτέθησαν.

The underlined words are the same as in Rom 9:33. The major differences are that in 1 Peter, Ps 118:22 (rejection) is framed by Isa 28:16 and Isa 8:14, and that the Isaiah citations are not conflated, as they are in Rom 9:33. The Isaian texts in Romans and 1 Peter agree vis-à-vis the LXX: τίθημι for ἐμβαλῶ (Isa 28:16); more importantly, πέτρας σκανδάλου in place of πέτρας πτώματι (literally "rock for falling"; Isa 8:14 LXX), and parallel to λίθος προσκόμματος.[15] Isa 28:16 in the Petrine text is adjusted to be more sensible: the stone in Zion is (in order) a "corner(stone), chosen and honored," not "expensive, chosen, corner(stone), honored" as it is in Isaiah. Rom 9:33 has no clause describing the stone's value. In 1 Peter 2 the referent of the "rock of offense/stone of stumbling" is clearly Christ, whom the readers are exhorted to approach and use as an example:

Come to him, to that living stone (λίθον ζῶντα), rejected (ἀποδεδοκι-
μασμένον; Ps 118:22; 1 Pet 2:7) by men but in God's sight chosen and

[14] R. Bring suggests that Luke 2:34 reflects the stone of Isa 8:14: Simeon says, "Behold, this child is set for the fall and rising of many in Israel." The "rising and falling" is equated with Isaiah's positive and negative stone: a "sanctuary," but also a "stone of stumbling," a "rock of offense," and a "snare" ("Paul and the Old Testament: A Study of the Ideas of Election, Faith and Law in Paul, with Special Reference to Romans 9:30 – 10:13," *ST* 25 [1971] 42–43). The LXX does not maintain the polarity of the Hebrew.

[15] Σκάνδαλον is important to Paul's subtextual theological dialogue in Rom 9:33 (see below).

precious (ἐκλεκτὸν ἔντιμον; Isa 28:16); and like living stones be your-
selves built into a spiritual house, to be a holy priesthood, to offer
spiritual sacrifices acceptable to God through Jesus Christ. (1 Pet
2:4–5)

This text confirms Jeremias' observation that the stone texts were
interpreted in terms of the (eschatological) temple.[16]

Comparing the Petrine and Pauline citations of the stone texts clarifies the formal and functional differences between them, but the water
is muddied as well.[17] The similarities in text-type suggests that they are
citing from a common source, which is not the LXX, although the
three versions share the messianizing addition of ἐπ᾽ αὐτῷ, which has
no MT parallel. The obvious solution is that they are citing from a
common source, perhaps a *testimonium*.[18] Although I cannot discount
the likelihood that stone texts circulated in a written form even in this
early period, Paul's form and use of these texts is different enough
from 1 Pet 2:6–8 that it is unlikely that the authors drew from a
common written tradition.[19] An anthology of stones texts devoted to
the rejected, crucified, and exalted messiah would feature the rejection
and supervaluation theme of Ps 118:22. This theme is absent from Rom
9:33. Dependence of one on the other stimulates questions for which
positive answers are dubious. Would the author of 1 Peter have uncon-
flated Paul's Isa 28:16/8:14 citation? Could Paul have used 1 Peter, and
secondly, both follow 1 Peter's version of Isa 28:16 and 8:14, and yet con-
flate the two and ignore Ps 118:22? Although the similarity of the
Pauline and Petrine texts is conspicuous, none of the arguments for a
common source or interdependence is convincing.[20]

[16] Jeremias, "λίθος," 274–75.

[17] For the nature of Paul's use of the stone in Rom 9:33, see §4.2–4.

[18] C. H. Dodd briefly discusses the relationship between Rom 9:33 and 1 Pet 2:6–8
and sides with their dependence on a "pre-canonical" *testimonium* (*According to the
Scriptures: The Sub-structure of New Testament Theology* [London: Nisbet, 1952]
41–43).

[19] *Contra* Albl, who confidently asserts that the conclusion of a "written 'stone' text
collection" as the explanation of the unique agreement of Rom 9:33 and 1 Pet 2:6–8 is
"almost inevitable" (*Scripture Cannot Be Broken*, 274). The conflicting evidence per-
mits no quasi-necessary conclusions.

[20] Nonetheless, I cannot go the whole way with P. Dinter, who concludes from his
comparative study of Isa 8:14 and 28:16 in the MT and LXX that Paul himself was his
only source: Paul enriched his Greek texts with readings that one could find only in the
Hebrew, and he was therefore a "multi-lingual midrashist" ("The Remnant of Israel

In summary, there are two points which separate these other NT stone texts from Rom 9:33: First, outside of Paul, Christ is always the clear referent, probably because of the influence of Ps 118:22 (the rejected yet exalted stone). Non-Pauline use of the stone texts may not be superimposed onto Rom 9:33 because Paul does not cite Ps 118:22, and the identity of his "stone" is left unstated. Although there is a clearly christological use of stone/rock texts elsewhere in Paul ("and Christ was the rock"; 1 Cor 10:4), it may not be simply read into Rom 9:33. Second, the Jewish rejection of Jesus that is prominent in all other NT appearances of the stone texts is not directly apparent in Paul's use of the stone tradition.[21] As Lloyd Gaston notes, it is astonishing how often interpreters find Jewish rejection of Jesus and the gospel in Romans 9 (especially Rom 9:30–33), and then read Romans 9 as "anti-Jewish polemic" in which God in turn rejects Israel, despite the fact that Romans 11 argues against Israel's rejection by God.[22] Paul does address Israel's misstep, but not in the context of its rejection of the messiah.[23]

One final point of comparison: Paul Dinter notes how Paul's conflation of these two texts proposes a different polarity from their use in 1 Peter 2. In 1 Pet 2:6–7, Isa 28:16 (the positive valuation of the stone placed by God) is identified with the author's group, the ones who will be honored, not ashamed, whereas those who do not accept the stone are shamed because they reject what turns out to be the showcase (κεφαλὴν γωνίας; 1 Pet 2:7/Ps 118:22), and thus stumble. In Romans

and the Stone of Stumbling according to Paul" [Ph.D. diss., Union Theological Seminary, 1980] 366). Paul's polyvalent use of the stone in Rom 9:33, and its lack of common christological themes, strengthens Dinter's perception of independence but the Hebrew background does not help here. It is at least possible that Paul's language has influenced the way Christians in Rome read the Isaiah texts.

[21] *Contra* Bring: "So Israel, in rejecting him, had stumbled on the stone of offence and was threatened with destruction. Paul's great problem in Rom 9–11 was the rejection of the Messiah by the chosen people" ("Paul and the Old Testament," 43). Also J. W. Aageson, who is convinced that the christological use of the stone-tradition in the early church entails that Paul use it toward the same end ("Typology, Correspondence and the Application of Scripture in Romans 9–11," *JSNT* 31 [1987] 51–72, esp. 61–62).

[22] L. Gaston, *Paul and Torah* (Vancouver: University of British Columbia Press, 1987) 92–93.

[23] There are two viable options regarding Paul's conception of Israel's misstep: (1) investing Torah and thus observance with ζωοποίησις—that is, pursuing the wrong thing (Rom 9:30–32); (2) keeping their divine gifts to themselves (Rom 10:3).

there is no contrast in valuations of the stone: the polarity is strictly believer/unbeliever.[24] The difference between Pauline and Petrine is not as profound as Dinter makes it. In 1 Peter 2 the believer/unbeliever polarity is as prominent as it is in Romans 9–10. The main difference is the group identification. 1 Peter's exclusive you/them (ὑμῖν . . . ἡ τιμὴ τοῖς πιστεύουσιν; 1 Pet 2:7) is absent from Romans, in favor of Paul's characteristic universalism: "all who believe . . . all who call upon his name" (10:11, 13) without a Jew/Greek distinction (Rom 10:12). Paul's distinction between groups is sequential: "Jew first" (Rom 1:16) in this age, the full complement of gentiles (11:25), and then "all Israel" (11:26) last.

4.2 Paul's Stone in Context

The immediate context of Rom 9:33 is the concentration of scripture quotations in Rom 9:25–29; the finale is an exact quote from the LXX of Isa 1:9:

καὶ εἰ μὴ κύριος σαβαὼθ ἐγκατέλιπεν ἡμῖν σπέρμα ὡς Σόδομα ἂν ἐγενήθημεν καὶ ὡς Γόμορρα ἂν ὡμοιώθημεν.

The "seed" here reintroduces his exegesis of the Abraham narratives in Romans 4 and Rom 9:6b–7:[25]

οὐ πάντες οἱ ἐξ Ἰσραὴλ οὗτοι Ἰσραὴλ οὐδ' ὅτι εἰσὶν σπέρμα Ἀβραὰμ πάντες τέκνα ἀλλ' <u>ἐν Ἰσαὰκ κληθήσεταί σοι σπέρμα</u>.

The underlined phrase is from the LXX of Gen 21:12. Paul ties his exegesis of Abraham[26] to Jewish remnant theology: the "seed of Abra-

---

[24] Dinter, "Remnant," 118.

[25] Except for 1 Cor 15:36, σπέρμα in Paul occurs in the context of his exegesis of Abraham and the "promise" (Rom 4:13, 16, 18; 9:7, 8, 29; Gal 3:16, 19, 29). In addition to referring to Jesus as the "seed of David" (Rom 1:3), Paul also uses "seed of Abraham" a few times to refer to his own heredity (Rom 11:1; 2 Cor 11:22).

[26] J. Fitzmyer downplays the importance of Abraham in Romans 9 in favor of a multiplicity of OT figures (*Romans* [AB 33; New York: Doubleday, 1993] 540), but Abraham is always key in Paul's conception of his "gospel." Paul had no recourse to prophetic remnant theology without his understanding of the Abraham tradition. The other biblical characters in Romans 9 function to show that God's fiat (i.e., who receives mercy or wrath) has always been operative, so Paul's critics (rhetorical or real) cannot argue that Paul's theology takes away from the righteousness of God.

ham" is the remnant of Isa 1:9. The special terminology in Rom 9:30–32 (gentiles, righteousness, faith, works) presupposes the earlier argument concerning Abraham, and the "children of the promise." It is directly following the Isa 1:9 quotation that Paul introduces (with τί οὖν ἐροῦμεν; 9:30; also 9:14) the section in which Isaiah's stone is employed, and which features the crux: τέλος νόμου χριστός (10:4).

Paul asks a rhetorical question which appears to be the reasonable objection to the idea he has promoted with his catena of biblical citations (9:25–29):

> Surely the gentiles do not attain a righteousness they have not pursued, whereas the Jews who have pursued a Torah-righteousness have not attained it? (9:30)

His "answer" is three-fold: (1) no, Israel has not attained its goal (9:31), because (2) Israel pursued wrongly (9:32) and thus (3) "they tripped" over an obstacle that God, in fact, had placed in their path (9:33). The problem was not what Israel was seeking (νόμον δικαιοσύνης; 9:31), but how: ἐξ ἔργων rather than ἐκ πίστεως (9:32).[27] The phrase ὁ νόμος δικαιοσύνης, anomolous outside of Paul,[28] is not necessarily negative, whereas ἐξ ἔργων is. Paul's attitude toward Torah/νόμος in Romans is shaped by the words and ideas joined with it.

The phrase τί οὖν ἐροῦμεν (Rom 9:30) is clearly transitional, but Paul has not left Abraham behind. Peter Stuhlmacher argues that

> Romans 9:30–33 is a decisive turning point in the Pauline argument. It summarizes the discussion up until this point and in doing so intro-

---

[27] The meaning of ἐξ ἔργων is problematic. Is this Paul's own description of a theological position, or a term used by a group for their outlook? If it is Paul's description of Jews, what party or sect of early Judaism does it represent? Our knowledge of early Judaism is limited, but of the known sects not one saw its redemption as a reward ἐξ ἔργων νόμου. The rabbinic Judaism which emerged in the proceeding centuries did not view its covenant relationship with God as "deed-oriented." So what was Paul referring to? I think it likely that ἐξ ἔργων νόμου is Paul's phrase for (what in Judaism is called) "observance." For a Jew, Torah observance is a positive, never a negative, but for Paul it was problematic because it was exclusive to "Israel," whereas faith was inclusive. Observance separated Jews from the surrounding gentiles, which violated Paul's view of the eschatological people of God: "there is no difference between Jew and Greek" (Rom 10:12; also Gal 3:28). Gaston notes that in Romans 9–11, the contrast is not faith and deed, but deed and election (*Paul and the Torah*, 228 n. 61).

[28] The νόμος τῆς δικαιοσύνης of Wis 2:11 seems unrelated.

duces the most important catchwords for the discussion of Israel's misunderstanding of the righteousness of God.[29]

Πίστις and δικαιοσύνη are the most important of these "catchwords." They derive from the Abraham narrative that Paul treated most fully in Romans 4, but which has been a key element of his argument in Romans 9. The mingling of Abraham and Isaiah does not end with Rom 9:29, for Abraham is echoed in Paul's conflation of Isa 8:14 and 28:16 in Rom 9:33.

4.3 The Conflation of Stone Texts

Paul explains that Israel did not attain the goal because "they stumbled (προσέκοψαν) over the stumbling stone" (Rom 9:32). The explanation for this stumbling is introduced with the citation formula καθὼς γέγραπται:

ἰδοὺ τίθημι ἐν <u>Σιὼν λίθον</u> προσκόμματος καὶ πέτραν σκανδάλου καὶ <u>ὁ πιστεύων ἐπ᾽ αὐτῷ οὐ καταισχυνθήσεται</u> (9:33)[30]

The underlined elements match the LXX of Isa 28:16:

διὰ τοῦτο οὕτως λέγει κύριος ἰδοὺ ἐγὼ ἐμβαλῶ εἰς τὰ θεμέλια Σιων λίθον πολυτελῆ ἐκλεκτὸν ἀκρογωνιαῖον ἔντιμον εἰς τὰ θεμέλια αὐτῆς καὶ ὁ πιστεύων ἐπ᾽ αὐτῷ οὐ μὴ καταισχυνθῇ

לכן כה אמר אדני יהוה
הנני יסד בציון אבן
אבן בחן פנת יקרת מוסד מוסד
המאמין לא יחיש (MT)

Unlike 1 Pet 2:6, Paul does not cite the valued characteristics of this "foundation" stone. Instead, he utilizes another Isaiah stone whose value is conditional.

καὶ ἐὰν ἐπ᾽ αὐτῷ πεποιθὼς ᾖς ἔσται σοι εἰς ἁγίασμα καὶ οὐχ ὡς <u>λίθου</u> <u>προσκόμματι</u> συναντήσεσθε αὐτῷ οὐδὲ ὡς <u>πέτρας</u> πτώματι (Isa 8:14 LXX)

---

[29] P. Stuhlmacher, *Paul's Letter to the Romans* (Louisville: Westminster John Knox, 1994) 152.

[30] The minor textual variants of Rom 9:33 can be explained as attempts to enhance the symmetry of 9:33 and 10:11 with the addition of πᾶς, and to more closely match Paul's quotation of Isa 28:16 with its LXX form.

והיה למקדש ולאבן נגף ולצור מכשול
לשני בתי ישראל לפח ולמוקש ליושב ירושלם (MT)

The form of Paul's citation is unique. Like other early Jewish writers, Paul cites different texts together, sometimes with intervening commentary and/or linking formulae.[31] The term for this is חרז, figuratively applied from the field of stringing beads or pulling thread through holes.[32] But Rom 9:33 is different than the consecutive citations of different texts; it represents a form of conflation in which the components are mingled rather than strung together.[33] Paul uses the two elements he retains from Isa 28:16 (the "stone in Zion" and "belief" clauses) to frame the words he excerpts from Isa 8:14. Although he employs a standard formula for introducing biblical citations,[34] he is not merely citing the two Isaiah texts. With them Paul has created a new text, and a new set of intertextual relationships.

The justification for Paul's creative use of the sacred tradition is the strong verbal and thematic links between the texts. The most important common element is the fact that both future oriented Isaiah texts concern the אבן/λίθος.[35] Morever, in the LXX the texts have similar belief clauses that are the basis for one accessing the stone's benefits:

$$\dot{\epsilon}\grave{\alpha}\nu \,\dot{\epsilon}\pi' \,\alpha\dot{\upsilon}\tau\tilde{\omega} \,\pi\epsilon\pi\text{οι}\theta\grave{\omega}\varsigma \,\tilde{\eta}\varsigma \,\check{\epsilon}\sigma\tau\alpha\iota \,\sigma\text{οι}\; (\text{Isa } 8:14)^{36}$$

$$\dot{\text{ο}} \,\pi\iota\sigma\tau\epsilon\acute{\upsilon}\omega\nu \,\dot{\epsilon}\pi' \,\alpha\dot{\upsilon}\tau\tilde{\omega} \,\text{ο}\dot{\upsilon} \,\mu\grave{\eta} \,\kappa\alpha\tau\alpha\iota\sigma\chi\upsilon\nu\theta\tilde{\eta}\; (\text{Isa } 28:16)^{37}$$

---

[31] Compare, for example, the three stone texts of 1 Pet 2:6–8, and the stringing together of two conflicting images of the temple (Isa 59:7 and Jer 7:11) in Mark 11:17 and parallels.

[32] Although *ḥeraz* (חרז) is used in a more technical sense for citation strings with texts representing each division of *Tanak*, it generally refers to the pattern of stringing texts together, to interpret one text with another.

[33] According to K. Müller, this sort of conflation citation (*Mischzitat*) is unprecedented in Jewish literature (*Anstoss und Gericht* [Munich: Kösel, 1969] 71).

[34] See the catalog of citation formulae in J. Fitzmyer, "The Use of Explicit Old Testament Quotations in Qumran Literature and in the New Testament," *NTS* 7 (1960–61) 297–333.

[35] C. K. Barrett is oddly suspicious as to whether Paul moved from Isa 28:16 to 8:14 on the basis of λίθος/אבן alone, since Paul did not quote λίθος from Isa 28:16 ("Romans 9:30–10:21," *Essays on Paul* [Philadelphia: Westminster, 1982] 143). But what are the other options?—Barrett identifies none. The sort of creative exegesis Paul performs here must be warranted by the nature of the texts.

[36] Πεποιθώς can mean "believe" or "be persuaded" (LSJ).

[37] Paul's οὐ καταισχυνθήσεται (future indicative) diverts from the οὐ μὴ καταισχυνθῆ (aorist subjunctive) of Isa 28:16 LXX. This may be an indication of Paul's knowledge of

The MT of Isa 8:14 lacks the belief clause, whereas the targum has a conditional clause parallel to the LXX, though expressed in the negative (אם לא תקבלון).[38] Thus, in the LXX belief determines whether the stone is a positive edifice (ἁγίασμα), or a negative object (λίθου προσκόμματι/πέτρας πτώματι). Without a clarifying clause the MT maintains a profound tension between יהוה צבאות (Isa 8:13) as both a מקדש and a צור מכשול/אבן נגף. One can sympathize with the LXX for providing the criterion by which the MT's paradox is resolved: "if you believe in the κύριος, he will be your sanctuary, rather than a stone of offense or a rock of stumbling when you approach (συναντήσεσθε) him."

The consequence of Paul's selective quotation is that he has transferred the startling ambiguity of the MT's version of Isa 8:14 to the entirely positive stone of Isa 28:16.[39] In Paul's hands the valuable and precious show stone placed by God in Zion is transformed into a hindrance that one can avoid only by believing in it.[40] Normally it is diffi-

---

the Hebrew, since the MT verb is an imperfect (יחיש), and thus is open to either a future or subjunctive reading.

[38] In the targum of Isa 8:14, מקדש/ἁγίασμα is rendered suggestively as God's מימריה, which can be comparable to the Johannine λόγος. In this case it seems to be a negative word, the consequence of rejection. While I am aware of G. F. Moore's influential conclusion that מימרא in rabbinic theology is "a phenomenon of translation, not a creature of speculation" ("Intermediaries in Jewish Theology: Memra, Shekinah, Metatron," HTR 15 [1922] 54), and that similarly minimalist conclusions have been reached by A. Chester (Divine Revelation and Divine Titles in the Pentateuchal Targumim [TSAT 14; Tübingen: Mohr [Siebeck], 1986] 293–324), the categorical denial of any correlation between the targumic מימרא and the λόγος is no longer helpful, and it can be a blindfold that hinders critical inquiry. For a mediating position, sympathetic to Moore yet without the restrictions, see B. Chilton, Judaic Approaches to the Gospels (ISFCJ 2; Atlanta: Scholars Press, 1994) 177–201, and especially 271–304 on מימרא and λόγος.

[39] P. Dinter accurately summarizes the LXX's softening of Isa 8:14, and notes that Paul recovers the shock factor of the Hebrew: "Although Paul's text draws directly from the Greek Bible that he knew so well, he was in fact reaching back to the meaning of the Hebrew text of the prophet. This certain because the Septuagint translators of Isaiah were scandalized by Isa 8:14 where God himself is said to become 'a sanctuary and a stone stumbling, a rock of offense . . . a trap and a snare' to his own people. These earlier interpreters separated out the prophet and his disciples from the rest of the people, claiming that God was a sanctuary to the former and hence 'NOT a stone stumbling' but that God was to become a 'trap and a snare' to the inhabitants of Jerusalem. Paul reverses the Septuagint's attenuation of the prophetic challenge . . ." ("Paul and the Prophet Isaiah," BTB 13 [1983] 49–50.

[40] Gaston argues that commentators have paid too much attention to Isa 28:16. He bases this on the fact that Paul highlights the "stumbling stone" in Rom 9:32. Thus, Isa

cult to decide how much of a citation is important to an author—what is cited for a purpose and what is verbal packaging. Rom 9:33 is exceptional. Because Paul has taken an active role in constructing his text rather than simply citing the words and phrases from biblical texts, one may assume that each element in his conflation is significant to his overall theological goals in enlisting Isaiah's stone. While some of these elements in the transformation of the stone are recognizably Pauline, others appear to have been intended "as a pointer to another level of texts which was as determinative on Paul's theology as were the more overt references to Isa 8:14 and 28:16."[41]

4.3.1 God's Agency

In Paul's version the stone is inherently an obstacle because God alone is responsible for its position and nature, rather than an angelic or diabolical intermediary: "Paul takes the significant further step of implying that this unexpected outcome was no merely subjective vagary but was rooted in God's deliberate intent."[42] This establishes a precedent of divine intentionality in Israel's misstep to which Paul returns fully in Romans 11. Recalling the themes if not consistently the vocabulary of Rom 9:30–33, Paul states that Israel has "failed to obtain what it sought" (11:7),[43] and attributes this to a divinely instilled πώρωσις:

8:14 contains everything Paul needed to express his point (*Paul and Torah*, 128). To the contrary, it is only in the mingling of the two stones that Paul achieves his purpose.

[41] S. Pattee, "Stumbling Stone or Cornerstone? The Structure and Meaning of Paul's Argument in Rom 9:30–10:13" (Ph.D. diss., Marquette University, 1991) 108. The quotation from Pattee is actually phrased as a question, but this is the position he supports. Pattee focuses particularly on what σκάνδαλον echoes (§4.3.3).

[42] P. Meyer, "Romans 10:4 and the 'End' of the Law," in *The Divine Helmsman: Studies on God's Control of Human Events, Presented to Lou H. Silberman* (ed. J. Crenshaw and S. Sandmel; New York: KTAV, 1980) 63.

[43] The verbs of Rom 11:17 are unique in the Pauline corpus. Paul may have used them to echo biblical texts that support his argument; the volume is low, however. He uses ἐπιζητέω only one other time (Phil 4:17). It occurs in LXX texts asserting that Israel would "seek" the Lord in the eschatological restoration, or redemption of Israel: "Afterward the children of Israel shall return and seek (ἐπιζητήσουσιν) the Lord their God, and David their king; and they shall come in fear to the Lord and to his goodness in the latter days" (Hos 3:5; see also 5:15); "Behold, the Lord has proclaimed to the end of the earth: Say to the daughter of Zion, 'Behold, your salvation comes; behold, his reward is with him, and his recompense before him. And they shall be called the holy

God gave them a spirit of stupor, eyes that should not see and ears that should not hear, down to this very day. (11:8)[44]

Paul follows this with another biblical text (Ps 69:23–24 LXX) that supports the blindness theme:

Let their table become a snare and a trap, a pitfall (σκάνδαλον) and a retribution for them; let their eyes be darkened so that they cannot see, and bend their backs for ever. (11:9–10)

Paul probably read this psalm as an indication that Israel's benefits (ἡ τράπεζα αὐτῶν) would become their downfall.[45] The language of Isa 8:14–15 is again present in Paul's rhetorical question: "Have they stumbled so as to fall?" This "falling" (πέσωσιν) recalls the consequences of the stone, on which many stumble, fall (πεσοῦνται) and are broken (Isa 8:15). All this leads up to Paul's assertion that this divinely induced trip is necessary both for the salvation of the gentiles and the restoration of Israel (Rom 11:11–12).

4.3.2 Zion
The location of Paul's stone "in Zion" is potentially ambiguous because in biblical tradition Zion can mean Jerusalem generally, but

people, the redeemed of the Lord; and they shall be called Sought out (ἐπιζητουμένη), a city not forsaken'" (Isa 62:11–12). Πωρόω occurs here and 2 Cor 3:14, and πώρωσις occurs in Rom 11:25. There is no LXX background. Paul never uses ἐπιτυγχάνω elsewhere. The only relevant LXX text is Prov 12:27: "A slothful man will not catch (ἐπιτεύξεται) his prey, but the diligent man will get precious wealth."

[44] Another mingled conflation in which Deut 29:4 provides the frame and Isa 29:10 the phrase "spirit of stupor." The links are the theme of God's hardening and the presence of "eyes" in each. See C. Stanley, *Paul and the Language of Scripture* (SNTSMS 69; Cambridge: Cambridge University Press, 1992) 158–63; D.-A. Koch, *Die Schrift als Zeuge des Evangeliums: Untersuchungen zur Verwendung und zum Verständnis der Schrift bei Paulus* (BZHT 69; Tübingen: Mohr [Siebeck], 1986) 170–72.

[45] Some suspect that Paul intended τράπεζα to recall an element of temple or synagogue practice (see Dunn, *Romans*, 2. 642–43). The form of the citation reveals little of the interpretive labor that is found in Rom 9:33, and the second half of the text continues the blindness theme of 10:8. Thus it does not appear to be a specially constructed text. L. Goppelt reads τράπεζα as a figure for "the table by which Israel lives will become a snare that will cause it to fall in God's sight," specifically the Law ("τράπεζα," *TDNT* 8. 212). Yes, but τράπεζα is not readily isolated from its medium. Paul does not draw attention to it.

especially the Temple mount,[46] the cosmic mountain,[47] and/or the site of eschatological transformation.[48] Although Zion is elastic, its pervading significance is as the symbol for God's dwelling. How does Paul mean Zion? Any notion that Zion is intended as a metaphor for Israel must be dismissed.[49] Paul only uses Zion twice (Rom 9:33; 11:26), and both times it derives from an Isaiah citation (28:16; 59:20). If anything, Paul inherits the ambiguity and eschatological significance of Zion in Isaiah (46x). The most that one can argue on the basis of his two Isaiah citations is that Zion is a cipher for an eschatological event or scene.[50]

One final note on Zion that anticipates a discussion of the intertextual relationship between Sirach 24, Rom 1:16 and 9:33. Sir 24:10 states that God established (ἐστηρίχθην) Wisdom/Torah in Zion; this may itself echo Isaiah's stone established (יסד) in Zion,[51] just as Paul's use of Isa 28:14 echoes Sir 24:10.

4.3.3 Rock of Offense

I noted above that both Rom 9:33 and 1 Pet 2:8 have a form of πέτραν σκανδάλου, whereas Isa 8:14 (LXX) has πέτρας πτώματι. The presence of σκάνδαλον is especially significant in Rom 9:33, where it is not clear who or what is signified by the stone. By splicing σκάνδαλον into Isa 28:16, Paul enlists an allusive network of LXX texts identifying the gentiles as an obstacle, or a snare for Israel. Paul does not use σκάνδαλον often (6x); in Romans 9–11 it occurs twice in quotations (9:33 and

---

[46] On the significance of Zion in biblical and post-biblical tradition, see J. Levenson, *Sinai and Zion* (Minneapolis: Winston, 1985) 89–184. On Zion in spatial typologies, see M. Fishbane, *Biblical Interpretation in Ancient Israel* (Oxford: Clarendon, 1985) 368–72; *Text and Texture* (New York: Schocken, 1979) 111–20.

[47] See R. J. Clifford, *The Cosmic Mountain in Canaan and the Old Testament* (HSM 4; Cambridge, MA: Harvard University Press, 1972).

[48] For eschatological Zion in the NT, see Heb 12:22, where Zion is "the city of the living God, the heavenly Jerusalem" (compare Paul's "Jerusalem above"; Gal 4:26), and Rev 14:1, where "the Lamb" stands atop Mt. Zion with the 144,000.

[49] For example, Stanley: "Zion" is "a cipher for physical Israel in Paul" (*Paul and the Language of Scripture*, 121).

[50] The applicability of Gese and Stuhlmacher's Zion Torah (§1.2.4) to Paul is, of course, dependent on Zion as an eschatological entity. Verbally there is no clear indication of the prominence of Zion traditions in Paul, but his mission and theology seem inexplicable without the eschatological Zion texts.

[51] There is no extant Hebrew of Sir 24:10, but στηρίζω may have translated יסד. Στηρίζω is used eight times in Sirach texts for which there is a Hebrew witness; it renders יסד once (3:9), but it does not consistently translate any other word.

11:9).[52] Unique vocabulary is often a clue that Paul has in mind a biblical text, or texts.

In the LXX, both σκάνδαλον and πτῶμα are employed as translation equivalents for מכשול ("offense" or "obstacle"), but πτῶμα represents מכשול in Isa 8:14. The form of Rom 9:33 diverts from the LXX of Isa 28:16 and 8:14, so it is possible that σκάνδαλον rather than πτῶμα appeared in the Greek version Paul used. But given his creative handling of the stone texts, it is more likely that he preferred to use σκάνδαλον because it better matched his theological objective. The question then is: what end did σκάνδαλον serve that πτῶμα did not?[53]

Σκάνδαλον opens up a different set of biblical texts than does πτῶμα because σκάνδαλον, not πτῶμα, is used to render the MT's מוקש ("trap" or "snare"). I propose that Paul embraced σκάνδαλον because (1) it alluded to the function of the nations (ἔθνη) in Israel's history (מוקש), and because (2) it is featured in texts that semantically overlap with Rom 9:30–10:13 and which correlate fidelity to Torah with not falling upon σκάνδαλα. I suspect that Paul's text functioned as a countertext to these, which may have been applied to him by those who viewed him as an antinomian apostate from Torah-true Judaism.

A number of texts warn ancient Israel that the surrounding peoples pose a threat, and Israelites therefore should not mingle with them or enter into covenants with them. The surrounding peoples, represented as גוים/ἔθνη, are to be dealt with harshly:

Take heed to yourself, lest you make a covenant with the habitants of the land whither you go, lest it become a snare (מוקש) in the midst of you. (Exod 34:12)

Know assuredly that the Lord your God will not continue to drive out these nations (גוים/ἔθνη) before you; but they shall be a snare and a trap (מוקש/σκάνδαλα) for you, a scourge on your sides, and thorns in your eyes, till you perish from off this good land which the Lord your God has given you. (Josh 23:13)

---

[52] Otherwise, σκάνδαλον is something to avoid in Paul's exhortation (Rom 14:13; 16:17), and it is used twice concerning the cross/crucifixion (1 Cor 1:23; Gal 5:11).

[53] Paul does not use πτῶμα, but παράπτωμα ("trespass") occurs frequently in Romans (9x), clustered in Rom 5:15–20 and 11:11–12; otherwise Paul uses it in Rom 4:25, echoing the "Lord's prayer" (cp. Matt 6:15), Gal 6:1 and 2 Cor 5:19. It is possible that Paul avoided πτῶμα because of its closeness to παράπτωμα; he did not want the stone to be seen as an opportunity for sin.

Now the angel of the Lord went up from Gilgal to Bochim. And he said, "I brought you up from Egypt, and brought you into the land which I swore to give to your fathers. I said, 'I will never break my covenant with you, and you shall make no covenant with the inhabitants of this land; you shall break down their altars.' But you have not obeyed my command. What is this you have done? So now I say, I will not drive them out before you; but they shall become adversaries to you, and their gods shall be a snare (מוקש/σκάνδαλον) to you." (Judg 2:1–3)

This precedent for regarding the gentiles as an obstacle is adapted to a different threat in a different time:

For they will forget all of my commandments, everything which I shall command them, and they will walk after the gentiles, and after their defilement and their shame. And they will serve their gods, and they will become a scandal for them and an affliction and a torment and a snare. (*Jub.* 1:9)

For Paul these texts might suggest that the gentiles (גוים/ἔθνη) have always been a sufficient cause for Israel to stumble, that God is responsible for the gentiles' presence, and that the stumbling block is associated with Israel's misstep (Rom 11:11). The climactic inclusion of the gentiles in the eschatological people of God means that God has again placed an obstacle in Israel's midst.

In addition to the relationship between gentiles and ancient Israel, σκάνδαλον is also prominent in two texts denying that Torah can be a hindrance:

Great peace have those who love thy law (תורה);
nothing can make them stumble (מכשול/σκάνδαλον). (Ps 119:165)

He who seeks the law (תורה) will be filled with it,
but the hypocrite will stumble (יקש/σκανδαλισθήσεται) at it.
(Sir 32:15)

In the surrounding verses in Sirach 32 there is a concentration of words which are part of the vocabulary of Rom 9:30–33: σκανδαλισθήσεται (Sir 32:15); προσκόπτω (Sir 32:20); and various forms of πιστεύω (Sir 32:21–24). Again, Paul has not identified the stone, so it is quite possible that Paul is confronting the great Torah psalm and Sirach 32, which attest to the enduring value of Torah observance. The technique is using lexical resonance to recall the text(s) to which Paul's stone is the counterpoint.

4.3.4 Belief

Although Paul retains only the belief clause of Isa 28:16 (ὁ πιστεύων ἐπ' αὐτῷ) in Rom 9:33, certainly the interrelationship in both Isa 8:14 and 28:16 of the stone and belief is a key to Paul's appropriation of these texts. It is no coincidence that the elevation of belief in the LXX's version of the Isaiah stone texts is consistent with Paul's reading of the Abraham narrative in Romans 4, in which belief is the transcending value. Paul's conviction about the significance of Abraham's belief governed his selection of texts.

The belief-clause of Isa 28:16 occurs again in 10:11, but this time Paul adds πᾶς: "*All* those who believe in him (ἐπ' αὐτῷ) will not be ashamed" (Rom 10:11). Πᾶς seems to have been gleaned from Joel 2:32 (3:5 LXX), which Paul cited in Rom 10:13:

πᾶς γὰρ ὃς ἂν ἐπικαλέσηται τὸ ὄνομα κυρίου σωθήσεται.[54]

As cited, there is no verbal relationship between Joel 2:32 and Isa 28:16. Joel 2:32 is another remnant text:

> And it shall come to pass that all who call upon the name of the Lord shall be delivered; for in Mount Zion and in Jerusalem there shall be those who escape, as the Lord has said, and among the survivors shall be those whom the Lord calls.

In the larger context, then, the texts have the verbal link "Zion."[55] Paul viewed Isa 28:16 and Joel 2:32 as mutually interpretative, and on this basis he transferred Joel's one universal element to Isaiah.[56]

4.3.5 Shame

The comparison of Isa 28:16 and Joel 2:32 is a convenient segue to the significance of the verb καταισχύνω in Rom 9:33. Although beyond πᾶς there is no common vocabulary between them, these two statements are equivalent for Paul:

---

[54] Unlike Paul's quotation of Isa 28:16 and 8:14, Joel 2:32 here agrees with the LXX.

[55] The LXX of Joel 2:26 reads: οὐ μὴ καταισχυνθῇ ὁ λαός μου εἰς τὸν αἰῶνα.

[56] Joel 2 is also interpreted eschatologically in Acts 2:17–21.

πᾶς ὁ πιστεύων ἐπ᾽ αὐτῷ οὐ καταισχυνθήσεται (Rom 10:11)

πᾶς γὰρ ὃς ἂν ἐπικαλέσηται τὸ ὄνομα κυρίου σωθήσεται (Rom 10:13)

belief → not shamed (Isa 28:16) = call on name → saved (Joel 2:32)

The arrows are intended to show that belief *results in* one not being shamed, just as calling on the name *results in* one being saved. Paul presents the equivalent phrases from Isa 28:16 and Joel 2:32 in parallel expressions. The lines are parallel, but their equivalence is not simply a product of their form or proximity to each other. They are part of a larger parallelism that develops from the semantic parallelism of Rom 10:8, a citation of Deut 30:14:

> The word is near you, in your mouth (ἐν τῷ στόματι σου) and in your heart (ἐν τῇ καρδίᾳ σου).[57]

Paul structures 10:9–13 by coordinating ἐν τῷ στόματι σου with ὁμολογέω, ἐπικαλέω, and passive forms of σῴζω; similarly, ἐν τῇ καρδίᾳ σου is coordinated with πιστεύω and καταισχύνω. Paul thus creates equivalences between the phrases ἐν τῷ στόματι σου and ἐν τῇ καρδίᾳ σου from his Torah text (Deut 30:12–14), and the prophetic phrases ὃς ἂν ἐπικαλέσηται τὸ ὄνομα κυρίου (Joel 2:32) and πᾶς ὁ πιστεύων ἐπ᾽ αὐτῷ (Isa 28:16), respectively. The symmetry of Paul's language is clearest in 10:10:

> καρδίᾳ γὰρ πιστεύεται εἰς δικαιοσύνην
> στόματι δὲ ὁμολογεῖται εἰς σωτηρίαν.

Paul does not use οὐ καταισχύνω here because he is not citing a biblical text, and δικαιοσύνη is his preferred term to coordinate with πιστεύω (continuity with the Abrahamic paradigm); similarly, σῴζω is nominalized as σωτηρία in order to match δικαιοσύνη. It is nonetheless apparent in the semantic structure of 10:8–13 that Paul cited οὐ καταισχυνθήσεται (10:11; 9:33) as an analogue to both σωθήσεται (10:13; Joel 2:32) and δικαιοσύνη. For Paul, the "shame" (καταισχύνω) he finds in Isa 28:16 is therefore a cipher for eschatological judgment, as it can be elsewhere in early Jewish literature.[58]

---

[57] Paul avoids the LXX's third member of the secondary parallelism in Deut 30:14: "*and in your hands* to do them."

[58] R. Bultmann summarizes the use of αἰσχύνω in the LXX: "Its primary reference is to the shame brought by the divine judgment" ("αἰσχύνω, κτλ," *TDNT* 1. 189).

In the LXX of Isaiah, several occurrences of αἰσχύνω are open to eschatological interpretation.

> Behold, all who are incensed against you shall be put to shame (αἰσχυνθήσονται) and confounded; those who strive against you shall be as nothing and shall perish. (Isa 41:11; see also 45:24)

Idolatry is a source of shame:

> All who make idols are nothing, and the things they delight in do not profit; their witnesses neither see nor know, that they may be put to shame (αἰσχυνθήσονται). (Isa 44:9; also 42:17; 44:11; 45:16)

Those who "wait for" Yhwh will not be put to shame:

> Kings shall be your foster fathers, and their queens your nursing mothers. With their faces to the ground they shall bow down to you, and lick the dust of your feet. Then you will know that I am the Lord; those who wait for me shall not be put to shame (αἰσχυνθήσῃ). (Isa 49:23; 50:7; 65:13; 66:5)

Finally, and most importantly, an equivalence is established between salvation and not experiencing shame:

> But Israel is saved by the Lord with everlasting salvation; you shall not be put to shame (αἰσχυνθήσονται) or confounded to all eternity. (Isa 45:17).

> You shall eat in plenty and be satisfied, and praise the name of the Lord your God, who has dealt wondrously with you. And my people shall never again be put to shame (οὐ μὴ καταισχυνθῇ ὁ λαός μου εἰς τὸν αἰῶνα). You shall know that I am in the midst of Israel, and that I, the Lord, am your God and there is none else. And my people shall never again be put to shame (οὐ μὴ καταισχυνθῶσιν οὐκέτι πᾶς ὁ λαός μου εἰς τὸν αἰῶνα). (Joel 2:26–27)

Although the semantic character of Isa 45:17 (in particular) correlates with the subsequent eschatological significance of shame, I am not suggesting that these prophetic texts were intended for the apocalyptic judgment scenario. One may plot, however, their influence on early Jewish interpreters unconstrained by modern notions of authorial intent.

In early Jewish literature, the interrelationship between shame and eschatological condemnation is clear:

And many of those who sleep in the dust of the earth shall awake, some to everlasting life, and some to shame (διασπορά) and everlasting contempt (αἰσχύνη αἰώνια). (Dan 12:2)

Be confident, you righteous ones!
For the sinners are due for a shame.
They shall perish on the day of (the judgment of) oppression.
(*1 Enoch* 97:1; also 97:6; 98:3, 10)

On that day [of judgment (62:3)], all the kings, the governors, the high officials, and those who rule the earth shall fall down before him on their faces, and worship and raise their hope in that Son of Man; they shall beg and plead for mercy at his feet. But the Lord of the Spirits himself will cause them to be frantic, so that they shall rush and depart from his presence. Their faces shall be filled with shame, and their countenances shall be crowned with darkness. and the darkness grow deeper on their faces. So he will deliver them to the angels for punishment, in order that vengeance shall be executed on them. (*1 Enoch* 62:9–11)

After that their faces shall be filled with shame before that Son of Man; and from before his face they shall be driven out. And the sword shall abide in their midst, before his face. (*1 Enoch* 63:11)

In the judgment scene from the Similitudes of Enoch, the Son of Man, seated on the "throne of his glory" (62:2–3, 5), is the agent of judgment. In the NT there is a similar though less elaborate correlation of the Son of Man, condemnation and shame:

For whoever is ashamed (ἐπαισχυνθῇ) of me and my words in this adulterous and sinful generation, of him will the Son of man also be ashamed (ἐπαισχυνθήσεται), when he comes in the glory of his Father with the holy angels. (Mark 8:38//Luke 9:26)[59]

Thus shame belonged to the vocabulary of apocalyptic judgment. I contend that Paul understood the phrase οὐ καταισχυνθήσεται (Isa 28:16) in this way, and used it accordingly (Rom 9:33; 10:10).

Another group of early Jewish texts are even more relevant to how Paul would have understood οὐ καταισχυνθήσεται:

Whoever obeys me will not be put to shame (οὐκ αἰσχυνθήσεται), and those who work with my help will not sin. (Sir 24:22)

---

[59] I am arguing here neither for a one-to-one correlation between the Son of Man in the Similitudes and Synoptics, nor that the scenarios are equivalent. I am only pointing out the use of "shame" in each text's eschatological scenario.

For I resolved to live according to wisdom, and was zealous for the good; and I shall never be put to shame (οὐ μὴ αἰσχυνθῶ).[60] (Sir 51:18)

And concerning all of those, their end will put them to shame (מכדבא), and your Law which they transgressed will repay them on your day. (*2 Apoc. Bar.* 48:47)

The eschatological context is explicit only in *2 Apocalypse of Baruch* 48, where on the day of judgment the Law itself will condemn those who did not recognize Israel's Lord as creator (48:46). But Sirach 24 facilitated the sort of elevated conceptions of Torah found in later works like *4 Ezra* and *2 Apocalypse of Baruch*. The role that I envision for Torah in eschatological judgment scenarios is prepared for by the explicit assertion in Sir 24:9 of the eternal nature of Wisdom/Torah (πρὸ τοῦ αἰῶνος ἀπ' ἀρχῆς . . . ἕως αἰῶνος), when coupled with Torah's association with the fate of its adherents (§2.3).

I am drawing attention to Sirach again here not only because Rom 9:30–10:13 can be viewed as an intertextual dialogue with the Wisdom/Torah tradition in which Sirach 24 played a leading role.[61] In particular, Rom 9:33 can be understood as the countertext to the "shame" clause of Sir 24:22:

The one who obeys Wisdom/Torah will not be eschatologically ashamed

The one who believes in the stone will not be eschatologically ashamed.[62]

Paul's eternal Torah/Christ antithesis resonates even in his creative use of Isaiah's stone texts. Perhaps Paul prepared his ideal readers with an earlier echoing of Sirach:

[60] The Hebrew is ambiguous: חשבתי להיטיב ולא אהפך כי אמצאנו (Hebrew text of Sirach from F. Vattioni, *Ecclesiastico: Testo ebraico con apparato critico e versioni greca, latina e siriaca* [Naples: Pubblicazioni del Seminario di Semitistica, 1968]). הפך can be understood as "to turn," as is suggested in the parallel from 11QPs^a 21.15: ולוא אשוב (see Vattioni's apparatus, page 281). Conversely, הפך can be used more negatively, indicating destruction (i.e., "to overturn"). Both הפך and καταισχύνω are terms with eschatological connotations, depending on context.

[61] The evidence for Paul's engagement of the Wisdom/Torah becomes more overt in Rom 10:6–8 (see §4.5), as scholarship generally now recognizes. On the other hand, the subdued countertextual nature of Rom 9:33 has not been perceived.

[62] Like Isa 28:16, this text is not inherently eschatological: γενέσθω ἡμῶν ἡ θυσία ἐνώπιόν σου καὶ ἐξιλάσαι ὄπισθέν σου ὅτι οὐκ ἔστιν αἰσχύνη τοῖς πεποιθόσιν ἐπὶ σοί καὶ τελειώσαι ὄπισθέν σου (Dan 3:40 LXX). It demonstrates, however, an interrelationship between faith and "not shame" similar to that which Paul maintains in Rom 9:33 and 10:10.

If you pursue justice (διώκῃς τὸ δίκαιον), you will attain it and wear it as a glorious robe. (Sir 27:8)[63]

Israel who pursued the righteousness which is based on the law (διώκων νόμον δικαιοσύνης) did not succeed in fulfilling the law. (Rom 9:31)

By rendering the sparse εἰς νόμον οὐκ ἔφθασεν with the quasi-targumic "did not succeed *in fulfilling* the law," the RSV of Rom 9:31 obscures the relationship between the two texts.

The proposed text-countertext relationship between Paul's conflated stone text and Sirach 24 does not stand on its own. It may be considered in light of three supporting factors: (1) Rom 9:33 is leading up to a significant statement on the relationship between Torah and Christ (10:4), in which Torah is temporally and/or teleologically subordinate to Christ. (2) Paul's vocabulary also echoes Sirach 32, a Torah text that replicates many of the elements of Sirach 24 (§4.3.3), and the great Torah Psalm 119. (3) Paul subsequently superimposes Christ onto another Wisdom/Torah tradition (10:6–8; §4.5).

Moreover, Paul has already assigned "shame" a privileged position in Romans. In the thesis statement Paul says that he is "not ashamed" (οὐ ἐπαισχύνομαι)[64] of the gospel (Rom 1:16). Considered in light of Sir 24:22, Paul's εὐαγγέλιον is here an antithesis to Torah as that upon which one is "not shamed."

Wisdom/Torah → not shamed (Sir 24:22)
Gospel → not shamed (Rom 1:16)
Stone → not shamed (Rom 9:33)[65]

---

[63] Like shame, Sirach's "robe of glory" is eschatological, for in later texts the elect in heaven or paradise are depicted as wearing these garments of light (e.g., *1 Enoch* 62:15–16). See Jesus' transfiguration, in which his garments become unearthly white (Mark 9:3//Matt 17:2//Luke 9:29). The tradition of the eschatological robes of light/glory may derive from an interpretation of Gen 3:21: God took his glory away from the first couple in the form of "garments of light (אור)," and gave them "garments of skin (עור)" (see e.g., *Gen. Rab.* 20:12). In the apocalyptic *Urzeit/Endzeit* scheme, the garments of glory would be restored. The "garments of salvation" (בגדי ישע) in Isa 61:10 would influence the idea of eschatological garments as well.

[64] According to Bultmann, αἰσχύνω, ἐπαισχύνω, and καταισχύνω are "fully interchangeable" in the LXX and NT ("αἰσχύνω," 189).

[65] The arrows again represent *result* in, or *lead* to. The graphic arrangement is meant to depict the parallel ideas; it is not intended as a simple syllogism. As I argue below, the stone symbol may not be exclusively equated with any one entity—Christ, Torah, the gentiles, Abraham, the gospel (§4.4).

In Paul's only other use of ἐπαισχύνομαι, the interrelationship of (realized) eschatology and shame anticipates Rom 9:30–33 and 10:4:

> But then what return (καρπός) did you get from the things of which you are now ashamed (νῦν ἐπαισχύνεσθε)? The end (τέλος) of those things is death. But now (νυνὶ δέ) that you have been set free from sin and have been become slaves of God, the return you get is sanctification and its end (τέλος), eternal life. (Rom 6:21–22)

Paul leaves "shame" until the crucial section 9:33–10:13, in which he establishes most clearly the antithetical relationship between Christ and the vision of Torah characteristic of Sirach 24.

Rather than an accident of Paul's lexicon, "shame" is like a hypertextual link to texts that profess an elevated conception of Torah. In both Rom 1:16–17 and 9:33 an antithesis is signaled by the shame cipher, an antithesis for which Paul's reader is left to supply one element: a relationship to the eternal Torah was linked to one's status—whether termed δικαιοσύνη or οὐ καταισχύνεσθαι—before the throne of eschatological judgment. The new Pauline paradigm has devalued this insight in favor of intra-Jewish mechanisms for repentance and atonement, but only at the expense of overlooking how eschatological expectation might have conflicted with "normal religion,"[66] the effect of elevated Torah on other elements in Jewish theology, and the tension in the lives of gentile converts unsure about their δικαιοσύνη.[67]

Finally, it is notable that the theological vocabulary of Rom 1:16–17 prefigures the antithesis to the Wisdom/Torah tradition in Rom 9:30–10:13. Paul describes the gospel as the "power (δύναμις) of God for salvation (εἰς σωτηρίαν) to every who has faith" (Rom 1:16). This description of Paul's gospel resonates as text to countertext with Wis 7:25, which professes divine Wisdom as the "breath of the power (δύναμις) of God." The phrase εἰς σωτηρίαν in Rom 1:16 appears infrequently in Paul (5x), but it is also used in Rom 10:1 and parallel with δικαιοσύνη in 10:10.[68] Faith (πίστις/πιστεύω) is prominent everywhere

---

[66] This was, perhaps, A. Schweitzer's point in arguing the incompatibility of Law and eschatology (*The Mysticism of Paul the Apostle* [New York: Seabury, 1931] 189–90).

[67] This is L. Gaston's insight: the ambiguity in Jewish tradition over the status of gentiles might lead gentiles attracted to Judaism or Christianity to anxious scrupulosity in Torah observance. "Legalism—the doing of certain works in order to win God's favor and be counted righteous—arose as a Gentile problem and not a Jewish problem at all" (*Paul and Torah*, 25).

[68] In unrelated contexts, εἰς σωτηρίαν appears in 2 Cor 7:10 and Phil 1:19.

in Paul (52x in Romans), of course, but in Romans and Galatians it is clustered in contexts dominated by Paul's discussion of the Abrahamic paradigm (Rom 3:21–5:2; 9:30–10:17; Galatians 3).

In Rom 1:17 the language of Abraham is more pronounced. The δικαιοσύνη θεοῦ is revealed in the gospel. Δικαιοσύνη is the *sema* that unites for Paul the Abraham narrative with eschatological expectation. Paul then gives his Abraham principle in the form of the text by which he interprets Gen 15:6 in Gal 3:11: ὁ δίκαιος ἐκ πίστεως ζήσεται (Rom 1:17). In Galatians Paul's version of Hab 2:4 (LXX) is the polar pair of Lev 18:5: ὁ ποιήσας αὐτὰ ζήσεται ἐν αὐτοῖς. Romans is different. Paul gives only one half of the antithesis, leaving the reader to fill in the gap.[69]

4.4 The Identity of Paul's Stone

Because Paul does not identify in Rom 9:33 who or what is symbolized by the "stumbling stone and rock of offense," his use of Isaiah's stone symbol is different from the christological use of stone texts elsewhere in the NT—despite the fact that the texts are stable. It may be, as some have suggested, that he intended readers knowledgeable of the messianic interpretation of Isa 28:16 to be uncertain about whether Torah or Christ is stone.[70] In the scholarly literature there are three perspectives on the referent of "stone of stumbling, rock of offense" in Rom 9:33. The classic position is that Jesus Christ (often "Messiah") is the stone.[71] Since it interprets the stone as a mighty King (מלך תקיף גיבר ואימתן), *Tg.*

[69] "Paul's rhetorical strategies, both according to . . . Acts and his own epistles, display such a degree of intentional ambiguity, cunning, deception as to make him justifiably vulnerable to the polemical charge of perpetuating sophistries" (Given, "True Rhetoric," 531 [emphasis removed]).

[70] Given notes that "intentional ambiguity" is a "major component in sophistical argumentation" ("True Rhetoric," 538). One class of intentional ambiguity is the use of homonyms "in epistolary discourse to send two different messages to two different factions within a single audience, simultaneously protecting oneself from the ire of one while ingratiating oneself with the other" (540). Given's example of this class of ambiguity in Pauline discourse is τέλος in Rom 10:4.

[71] Sanday and Headlam: "[the Jews] have rejected the Messiah" (*Romans*, 278), "Christ" (280). C. E. B. Cranfield: "they have stumbled over Christ" (*Romans* [ICC; 2 vols.; Edinburgh: T. and T. Clark, 1975–79] 2. 511). So also M.-J. Lagrange, *Saint Paul. Epître aux Romains* (Paris: Gabalda, 1915, 1922, 1950) 251; E. Käsemann, *Romans*

Isa 28:16 adds weight to the proposed christological use of the stone.[72] Other commentators add that the stone was the cross or the crucifixion—the crucified Messiah.[73] Two Pauline texts, if applicable to Rom 9:33, suggest this interpretation:

> If I . . . still preach circumcision, why am I still persecuted? In that case the stumbling block of the cross (τὸ σκάνδαλον τοῦ σταυροῦ) has been removed. (Gal 5:11)

> But we preach Christ crucified, a stumbling block (σκάνδαλον) to Jews and folly to Gentiles. (1 Cor 1:23)

Some readers assume that Paul uses σκάνδαλον consistently for the cross, even in his stone conflation.[74]

Others follow C. K. Barrett in identifying the stone with Torah.[75] Barrett has modified his position somewhat: he maintains that the stone in Rom 9:33 is Torah, but he recognizes that Torah and Christ are brought together in Romans 10, and that in the restatement of the belief clause in Rom 10:11, ἐπ᾽ αὐτῷ is clearly Christ.[76] N. T. Wright

---

(London: SCM, 1980) 278; H. Schlier, *Der Römerbrief* (HTKNT; Freiburg: Herder, 1977) 307–8.

[72] But Stuhlmacher overstates the case: "Both passages were already being interpreted in the synagogues at the time of Paul as referring to the messiah, and Paul is simply following this custom" (*Romans*, 152). Isa 8:14 is hardly a candidate for pre-Christian messianic interpretation, and Stuhlmacher goes beyond our knowledge of the ancient synagogue. Additionally, although there are important things to learn about Paul's exegesis by observing other early Jewish exegetes, it is a mistake to force Paul to correspond to hypothetical reconstructions of their interpretive traditions. Paul did not need precedent to recreate Isaiah's stone texts.

[73] Stuhlmacher, *Romans*, 152–53.

[74] This appears to be the only explanation for J. Munck's comment that "9:30–10:4 is not concerned with the same subject as 10:5–21; it is concerned only with the earthly life of Jesus in Palestine, the Jews' rejection of him, and his crucifixion" (*Christ and Israel: An Interpretation of Romans 9–11* [Philadelphia: Fortress, 1967] 79). The "earthly Jesus" has not even been referred to in Romans 9. Munck assumes that Israel's crucifixion of the messiah (his language) is contained in Rom 9:30–10:4, but it is only present if one infers it from the presence of σκάνδαλον, which must carry with it these other uses of σκάνδαλον in connection with the cross.

[75] Barrett, "Romans 9:30–10:21," 144; Meyer, "Romans 10:4," 64; Pattee, "Stumbling Stone or Cornerstone," 109.

[76] C. K. Barrett, *The Epistle to the Romans* (2d ed.; Black's New Testament Commentaries; London: A. and C. Black, 1991) 181.

similarly argues that Paul's stone "in one sense is clearly the Torah and in another is clearly the Messiah."[77] Especially in light of Paul's reconfiguration of the Torah/Christ relationship in Rom 10:4, there is contextually good reason to see Torah as the impediment which prevents Israel from reaching its goal. But the stone in Rom 9:33 functions better as a countertext to what Paul considered misunderstandings of Torah, rather than as Torah itself—although the "stone in Zion" recalls the Torah of Sir 24:10, and perhaps the stone tablets.[78]

The third position is that the stone is Paul's message. Dinter identifies it as the "word of faith" (Rom 10:8), that is, the resurrection (10:9).[79] Following Dinter, but modifying his position, are Lloyd Gaston and Elizabeth Johnson. For Johnson, the stone is the gospel as she understands it from Rom 1:16–17: "the power of God for salvation which overturns any understanding of God's righteousness as for Jews only."[80] Gaston identifies the stone as "the gospel contained in Torah, the gospel of the inclusion of Gentiles." The "gospel contained in Torah" is the Abrahamic promises.[81]

Notwithstanding Badenas' categorical assertion that "it cannot be denied that in this context Paul explicitly applied Isa 28.16 to Christ (10.13),"[82] the stone in Rom 9:33 is not to be identified unequivocally with Christ, Torah or the gospel. Each interpretation of the stone has legitimate contextual and intertextual bases. Thus to make a one-to-one identification of Paul's stone would unnecessarily limit the power of his figure, and quiet his intended echoes. I have noted a few instances in which the reader of Romans is left to fill in important gaps, such as supplying a missing parallel pair. Similarly, at times Paul seems to be intentionally ambiguous in Romans, even provoking the

---

[77] N. T. Wright, *The Climax of the Covenant* (Edinburgh: T. and T. Clark, 1991) 240.

[78] The stone in Rom 9:33 may also reflect the use of אבנים for the tablets in Josh 8:32, set at the Mt. Ebal altar: "And there, in the presence of the people of Israel, [Joshua] wrote upon the stones a copy of the law of Moses (משנה תורת משה), which he had written." For משנה תורה, see Deut 17:18 and §3.3.

[79] Dinter, "Remnant," 119–24.

[80] Johnson, *Function*, 154.

[81] Gaston, *Paul and Torah*, 129.

[82] Badenas, *Christ the End of the Law*, 106. So also T. L. Donaldson: Christ as the stone is "virtually required by the context" (*Paul and the Gentiles: Remapping the Apostle's Convictional World* [Minneapolis: Fortress, 1997] 130).

reader to supply the wrong information.[83] For example, in Rom 1:18–32 Paul constructs an argument that appears to be directed at gentiles who do not acknowledge Israel's God as creator, whereas the subtext is Israel's experience with the golden calf.[84] The ambiguity sets up Paul's assertion of universal sinfulness in Romans 2–3.[85] In Rom 7:9–11 Paul uses the first person to narrate his own death, and the reader is left to supply the "I." Even his use of τέλος in Rom 10:4 is ambiguous enough to suggest a teleological and a temporal interpretation.[86] My point, then, is that Paul's stone is a polyvalent symbol that is consistent with other aspects of Paul's rhetoric in Romans. His stone is a comprehensive figure that integrates texts and eschatological images concerning Torah, Messiah, the gentiles.

One final note on Paul's stone text. Gaston proposes that Isa 51:1–8 is the unstated subtext to Rom 9:30–10:21.[87] His judgment has some merit because this text contains striking parallels to Paul's language and themes in Rom 9:30–10:13, and 1:16–17:

> Hearken to me, you who pursue deliverance (οἱ διώκοντες τὸ δίκαιον),
> you who seek the Lord;
> look to the rock (στερεὰν πέτραν) from which you were hewn,
> and to the quarry from which you were digged.
>
> Look to Abraham your father
> and to Sarah who bore you;

---

[83] On one level Paul is clarifying his positions for an audience unacquainted with him, yet perhaps suspicious. On another level, conversely, he is obscuring for rhetorical effect *and* to evoke. Paul's strategy parallels that of M. Sternberg's narrator: "The narrator may play games with the whole truth for the pleasure and benefit of the cunning few, but he must communicate the truth in a fashion accessible to all" (*The Poetics of Biblical Narrative* [Bloomington: Indiana University Press, 1985] 235).

[84] Christian readers of Romans may overlook the golden calf subtext because of the allure of the natural knowledge of God (Rom 1:19–21) that binds those not given Torah.

[85] Although Donaldson recognizes that Rom 1:18–32, as a statement of "Gentile sinfulness," is an "awkward fit" with Paul's assertion of universal sinfulness in Romans 2–3, he nevertheless restates the typical misreading, placing the mistake on Paul's shoulders (*Paul and the Gentiles*, 283).

[86] Ambiguities and difficulties in Romans have admittedly become a heuristic principle in this chapter, but this is not merely an embracing of textual discord. Rather, it is an admission that the critic cannot always discern authors' gaps from their traps.

[87] Gaston, *Paul and Torah*, 126–28. See also Deut 32:18, which identifies the "Rock [LXX θεός] that begot you" with the "the God who gave you birth."

for when he was but one I called him,
and I blessed him and made him many.

For the Lord will comfort Zion;
he will comfort all her waste places,
and will make her wilderness like Eden,
her desert like the garden of the Lord;
joy and gladness will be found in her,
thanksgiving and the voice of song.

Listen to me, my people,
and give ear to me, my nation;
for a law (νόμος) will go forth from me,
and my justice for a light to the peoples (ἐθνῶν).

My deliverance draws near speedily,
my salvation has gone forth,[88]
and my arms will rule the peoples (ἔθνη);
the coastlands wait for me, and for my arm they hope.

Lift up your eyes to the heavens,
and look at the earth beneath;
for the heavens will vanish like smoke,
the earth will wear out like a garment,
and they who dwell in it will die like gnats;
but my salvation will be for ever,
and my deliverance will never be ended.

Hearken to me, you who know righteousness (צדק/κρίσιν),
the people in whose heart is my law;
fear not the reproach of men,
and be not dismayed at their revilings.

For the moth will eat them up like a garment,
and the worm will eat them like wool;
but my deliverance will be for ever,
and my salvation to all generations. (Isa 51:1–8)

This extended excerpt features two verbal links to Paul's conflated Isaiah texts, "rock" (πέτρα) and "Zion"; an eschatological context (v. 6); election tied to Abraham (v. 2), from whom Paul argues for gen-

---

[88] The LXX of v. 5a differs from the MT: קרוב צדקי יצא ישעי / ἐγγίζει ταχὺ ἡ δικαιο-σύνη μου καὶ ἐξελεύσεται ὡς φῶς τὸ σωτήριόν μου.

tile inclusion in the people of God (Romans 4; 9:7–9);[89] the parallelism of תּוֹרָה/νόμος and מִשְׁפָּט/κρίσις going out to the gentiles (v. 4); and the parallelism (LXX only) of God's missionary δικαιοσύνη and σωτήριον (v. 5; cp. Rom 2:20 and 10:10).[90] Moreover, the phrase οἱ διώκοντες τὸ δίκαιον (Isa 51:1) resonates with Paul's terminology in Rom 9:30–31.

4.5 Not in Heaven

The interface with the Wisdom/Torah complex of textual associations is submerged in Rom 9:33. In Rom 10:6–8, on the other hand, Paul openly engages in countertextual argumentation with the same tradition.

> The righteousness based on faith says, Do not say in your heart, "Who will ascend into heaven?"—that is (τοῦτ᾽ ἔστιν), to bring Christ down; or "Who will descend into the abyss?"—that is, to bring Christ up from the dead. But what does it say? "The word is near you, on your lips and in your heart"—that is, the word of faith which we preach. (Rom 10:6–8)[91]

The quotation marks bracket fragments of an interpretive tradition relating to Deut 30:11–14:

> For this commandment which I command you this day is not too hard for you, neither is it far off. It is not in heaven, that you should say, "Who will go up for us to heaven, and bring it to us, that we may hear it and do it?" Neither is it beyond the sea, that you should say, "Who will go over the sea for us, and bring it to us, that we may hear

---

[89] In Paul's mind, Sarah in particular is the mother of those οἱ διώκοντες τὸ δίκαιον καὶ ζητοῦντες τὸν κύριον (Isa 51:1). The LXX's στερεὰν πέτραν is a homophone of the στεῖρα in Isa 54:1, which Paul cites is Gal 4:27. On the interpretation of Abraham the rock, Pseudo-Philo says that "Joshua rose up in the morning and gathered all the people and divided up the land among them, 'The LORD says this: "There was one rock from which I quaried out your father. And the cutting of that rock bore two men whose names are Abraham and Nahor, and out of that chiseling of that place were born two women whose names are Sarah and Melcha, and they lived together across the river"'" (L.A.B. 23:4; tr. D. J. Harrington, OTP 2. 332).

[90] The idea of the heart as locus of Torah (Isa 51:7) is paralleled in Jer 31:31–34, a foundational text in Paul's Torah theology (§6.3.1).

[91] I have altered the RSV punctuation of Rom 10:6–8 because it obscures Paul's text-comment pattern.

it and do it?" But the word is very near you; it is in your mouth and in your heart, so that you can do it.

On the surface this text appears to have been culled in support of Lev 18:5, which Paul cites in Rom 10:5: "the person who does these things will live in them." The verbal connection between Lev 18:5 and Deut 30:12–14 is the "doing" (עשׂה/ποιέω) of the divine commands.[92] But more than reinforcing a favorite text, Paul's utilization of interpreted Deuteronomy signals a return to the Wisdom/Torah tradition of Rom 9:33.[93]

In Deuteronomy 30 the parallel clause to "who will ascend to heaven" merely says "who will cross the sea," which is repeated more or less in Baruch:

> Who has gone up into heaven, and taken her, and brought her down from the clouds? Who has gone over the sea, and found her, and will buy her for pure gold? (Bar 3:29–30)

The climax of this Wisdom poem identifies "her" as Torah (Bar 4:1). Paul's "abyss"-saying in Rom 10:7 does not derive from either Deut 30:11–14 or Bar 3:29–30, but there are other texts that place Wisdom "in the abyss/depths" as the polar complement of "in heaven/heights." A good example is Sir 24:5–6, which is especially relevant because of the proposed countertextual confrontation with this chapter:

> Alone I have made the circuit of the vault of heaven and have walked in the depths of the abyss. In the waves of the sea, in the whole earth, and in every people and nation I have gotten a possession.

Whether the "abyss" here is an elaboration of the sea-clause of Deut 30:13 is ambiguous. The syntax of the Greek necessitates that the verb

---

[92] The connection in Lev 18:5 between performance of God's commands and life is paralleled in Deut 30:20, where loving and obeying Yhwh is "your life" (הוא חייך).

[93] By "interpreted Deuteronomy" I mean that, although Paul cites portions of Deut 30:12 and 14, his citations actually reference the interpretive tradition rather than the biblical text. C. Evans makes a similar point in response to Hays' somewhat undifferentiating treatment of Rom 10:6–10 (see "Listening for Echoes of Interpreted Scripture," in *Paul and the Scriptures of Israel* [ed. C. Evans and J. Sanders; JSNTSupp 83; SSEJC 1; Sheffield: JSOT, 1993] 48–50, and Hays' rejoinder in the same volume ["On the Rebound: A Response to Critiques of *Echoes of Scripture in the Letters of Paul*," 71–74] in *Echoes of Scripture*, 73–83. The scholarly debate looks back on Sanday and Headlam's oft-cited judgment that Paul is only using familiar phraseology in Rom 10:6–10, rather than interpreting Deut 30:10–14 (*Romans*, 289).

περιπατέω that goes with "abyss" does not govern "sea" in Sir 24:6, but the parallelism between "waves of the sea" and "the whole earth" seems forced, as if Deut 30:13 were dictating that a sea-clause remain in Sirach's reworked interpretive parallelism.[94] "Abyss" and "sea" are clearly parallel in Sir 24:29, as well as Job 28:14 (LXX). Thus Paul's abyss clause, whether or not it was drawn directly from any of these texts, is clearly in the orbit of Wisdom/Torah.

Bar 3:30–4:1 is the surest evidence that Deut 30:11–14 was received in Paul's day as a Wisdom text. But the version of Deut 30:11–14 in Targum Neofiti shows that Torah itself, rather than Wisdom, could be read as the "word" that is near:

> For this precept which I command you this day is not hidden from you, neither is it far away. The law (אוריתה) is not in the heavens, that one should say: Would that we had one like Moses the prophet who would go up to heaven and fetch it for us,[95] and make us hear the commandments that we might do them. Nor is the Law (אוריתה) beyond the Great Sea, that one should say: Would that we had one like Jonah the prophet who would descend into the depths of the Great Sea and bring up the law for us, and make us hear the commandments that we might do them. For the word is very near to you, in the word of your mouths and in your hearts, that you may do it.[96]

---

[94] There are three parallel pairs in Sir 24:5–6: heaven//abyss; sea//earth; people//nation. Only heaven and sea are in Deut 30:13, which seems to be the intertext. Sirach's "depths of the abyss" was a better match with "heaven" than the τὸ πέραν τῆς θαλάσσης of the deuteronomic original.

[95] M. McNamara notes that Moses' ascension is based on the idea that "where the Shekinah of the Lord was, there also was heaven. Rather than speak of Moses ascending into heaven it would be more precise . . . to say that heaven descended on Mount Sinai" (*The New Testament and the Palestinian Targum to the Pentateuch* [AnBib 27; Pontifical Biblical Institute, 1966] 75). This seems an unnecessary rationalization of the targumic tradition. If Torah were in heaven then it would take a Mosaic prophet to ascend (יסוק) and bring it down—this is the point of the targum. The bending of the heavens in *L.A.B.* 15:6 and 4 Ezra 3:18 is not a valid parallel. Another proposed parallel actually confirms that Moses was thought of as ascending into heaven, rather than heaven visiting him: "The crown of Torah is [Moses'], because he conveyed it from the heavens above, when the glory of the Lord's Shekinah was revealed to him, with two thousand myriads of angels and forty two thousand chariots of fire" (*Tg. Ps.-J.* Deut 34:5; translation by E. Levine in A. Díez Macho, *Neophyti 1: Targum Palestinense MS de la Bibleoteca Vaticana: Deuteronomy* [Madrid: Consejo Superior de Investigaciones Científicas, 1978]; cited by McNamara, 76).

[96] Text and translation in Díez Macho, *Neophyti . . . Deuteronomy*. I have maintained the varied capitalization of אוריתה. In *Tg. Neof.* Deut 30:13, אוריתה is capitalized

Paul's strategy in Rom 10:6–8 is to rework the tradition by citing an excerpt from interpreted Deuteronomy and then identifying the excerpt with Christ. Paul's commentary on the cited text is signaled by means of τοῦτ᾽ ἔστιν.[97] The result of Paul's text-commentary pattern is that he replaces Torah and/or Wisdom in the conventional reading of the textual tradition with Christ. This significant replacement—a Torah/Christ antithesis, really—is generally ignored or denied in scholarship. For example, W. D. Davies recognizes a Wisdom/Christ association in other texts (e.g., 1 Cor 1:24, 30), yet denies it here.[98] In what appears to be an act of counter-reading, M. Jack Suggs overlooks the replacement in favor of simple identification:

> In Rom. 10:6–10 Paul has taken up the familiar identification of Wisdom and Torah and added a third term: Jesus Christ. The tension between Gospel and Law is resolved by the identification of Christ with Wisdom-Torah. The apostle hopes in this way to rescue his gospel from the stigma of absolute opposition to the law. . . .[99]

Obviously Suggs' interpretation is in "absolute opposition" to the replacement that I propose. Although he does not dwell on the idea of replacement, Richard Hays perceives that Paul "hints at" an identifi-

---

as "Law," and as "la Ley" in both 30:12 and 13 of Díez Macho's Spanish translation, so the lack of capitalization in the English of 30:12 would seem to be an error.

[97] "Adopting an uncharacteristic exegetical format, Paul offers a running line-by-line pesher commentary on the passage" (Hays, Echoes of Scripture, 79). For Hays what is "uncharacteristic" is that Paul shows method, hints at formality.

[98] W. D. Davies merely echoes Sanday and Headlam: "Paul is here using words that have become proverbial" (Paul and Rabbinic Judaism [4th ed.; Philadelphia: Fortress, 1980] 153–54). Davies dismisses the claim of H. Windisch ("Die göttliche Weisheit der Juden und die paulinische Christologie," in Neutestamentliche Studien für Georg Heinrici [ed. A. Deissmann and H. Windisch; Leipzig: Hinrichs, 1914] 223–24) that Rom 10:6–8 reflects Wisdom in Bar 3:29–30 without analysis, despite the fact that he acknowledged Paul's use of Wisdom for Christ. Davies saw Christ as Wisdom, but he overlooked the inference that Torah therefore was not.

[99] J. Suggs, "'The Word is Near to You': Romans 10:6–10 within the Purpose of the Letter," in Christian History and Interpretation: Studies Presented to John Knox (ed. W. Farmer, C. F. D. Moule, and R. Niebuhr; Cambridge: Cambridge University Press, 1967) 311. Suggs begins his study of Rom 10:6–10 with the theory (G. Bornkamm and T. W. Manson) that Romans is a "testament" or "manifesto"—Paul's attempt to clarify and systematize rather than obscure. Because he assumes Paul to be wary of misinterpretation in Romans, Suggs must make noncontroversial sense of the text.

cation of Wisdom with Christ rather than Torah. The hinting takes place not at the "overt discursive level," but "in the cave of echo."[100]

In a final act of interpretive reconfiguration, Paul completes his contemporizing with the profession that the "word" (דבר/ῥῆμα) of Deut 30:14 is his τὸ ῥῆμα τῆς πίστεως (10:8).

4.6 Conclusion

Paul's two countertextual complexes in Rom 9:33 and 10:6–8, both directed at the system of signification that interprets Torah as the embodiment of divine Wisdom, can be read as the frame for his explicit reconfiguration of Torah in Rom 10:4. Paul's assertion that Christ is the τέλος of the Law tends to be interpreted alone, out of its context. This chapter has demonstrated overt and subdued countertextuality against the Wisdom/Torah tradition that will not solve the lexical problem of τέλος, but will confirm its semantic field: the elevated conception of Torah that resulted with its identification with divine Wisdom. Christ cannot be the "end" or "goal" of Torah unless Torah is not God's eternal Wisdom.

[100] Hays, *Echoes of Scripture*, 81–82.

CHAPTER 5

Abraham and Torah in Galatians 3–4

If Abraham played an important role in Romans, in Galatians he is the star. Paul uses the Genesis Abraham narratives in Galatians 2–4, focusing on the relationship between the Abrahamic promises and the Law, the covenant and circumcision, the "seed of Abraham," and the story of Sarah and Hagar.[1] My goal is to demonstrate that Paul's interpretation of the Abraham narratives is *de facto* a counterpoint to claims made for Torah in other early Jewish texts. In Galatians Abraham is a fulcrum of sorts, by which Paul supplants the eternal Torah in favor of a temporal, mediated Law that does not conflict with his gospel. For some early Jewish theologians the eternal Torah condemned the gentiles (§3.1); it is this conception of Torah that conflicts with Paul's mission to incorporate, or "graft" (Rom 11:17) the gentiles into the eschatological people of God. I am not demanding that Paul's "opponents" (οἱ ταράσσοντες; Gal 1:7) in Galatians were advocates of the eternal Torah *per se*, or that the eternal Torah alone necessitated gentile circumcision. On the other hand, the nature of Paul's response in Galatians—particularly Abraham as the recipient of pre-Sinai revelation, and Paul's reconfiguration of Torah—suggests that at least the

---

[1] Paul glossed selectively on Abraham texts. I refer here and there to the "Genesis Abraham narratives" generally, but I cite Paul's specific Genesis subtext when it is evident. The boundaries of the Abraham narratives are Genesis 12:1–25:11.

implications of the opponents' claims intersected with early Jewish Torah theology. This chapter identifies these intersections.

Abraham is the pivotal figure in Paul's opposition to the eternal Torah. As a foretaste of what is to come, I would like to draw attention to a remarkable indication of Abraham's significance:

> And the scripture, foreseeing that God would justify the Gentiles by faith, preached the gospel beforehand to Abraham, saying, "In you shall all the nations be blessed." (Gal 3:8)

On the surface, Paul's statement is a positive assertion that his gospel has its roots in Abraham's visions, and that the Abrahamic gospel concerns rendering the gentiles ἐκ πίστεως δικαιοῖ. Paul's wording of the promise does not derive directly from the LXX, but is a mingling of elements from two Genesis texts.

ἐνευλογηθήσονται ἐν σοὶ πάντα τὰ ἔθνη	(Gal 3:8)
ἐνευλογηθήσονται ἐν σοὶ πᾶσαι αἱ φυλαὶ τῆς γῆς	(Gen 12:3)
ἐνευλογηθήσονται ἐν αὐτῷ πάντα τὰ ἔθνη τῆς γῆς	(Gen 18:18)

Both Genesis texts have something to offer Paul's argumentation in Galatians: the language of Gen 18:18 would be a flag for Paul because its context is Yhwh contemplating revealing his future deeds (אֲשֶׁר אֲנִי עֹשֶׂה; v. 17)—that is, eschatological details—to Abraham (see §5.2). But it is also important for Paul that the promise was made in Gen 12:3, before the covenant of circumcision was established in Genesis 17. Paul specifically makes an argument from the chronological sequence of ἐπαγγελία and νόμος in Gal 3:17, so one knows that Paul thinks in terms of narrative sequence (§5.3; Rom 4:10).[2]

The form of the citation is not its most telling feature, however. Paul's statement that Abraham received the *gospel* beforehand is in marked contrast to the many early Jewish texts asserting that Israel's pre-Sinai patriarchs knew Torah and were observant (§3.1; 5.2). In

---

[2] On Paul's exegetical attention to narrative "mythos," or plot-line, see C. Stockhausen, "2 Corinthians and the Principles of Pauline Exegesis," in *Paul and the Scriptures of Israel*, (ed. C. A. Evans and J. A. Sanders; JSNTSup 83; SSEJC 1; Sheffield: JSOT, 1993) 143–64; also her important but unpublished paper, "The Epistle to the Galatians and the Abraham Narratives" (presented at the Catholic Biblical Association Meeting, Santa Clara, August, 1988; and, at the Midwest Regional Meeting of the SBL, Chicago, January 31, 1989).

other words, Paul's Abraham knew the gospel rather than Torah. Torah only came 430 years later and could not render the earlier promise and covenant invalid. Paul's thinking in Gal 3:17 also contains an antithesis based on the verb καταργέω (see §6.1): Torah would not supersede the pre-Sinai promise, and would not last into the eschaton. Paul's use of Abraham is a counterpoint to the eternal Torah.

5.1. Abraham in Galatians

According to many commentators, in Romans Paul alters his earlier use in Galatians of the Abraham narrative, softening his exclusiveness.[3] Certainly Paul's use of Abraham is different in Galatians and Romans, due to the polemical context of Galatians, but I do not think it is necessary to view one as a correction or explanation of the other. Both attest to the primacy of Abraham in Paul's understanding of the gospel:

> The fact that in the two letters devoted most fully to the exposition of Paul's gospel (Romans and Galatians) essentially the same line of argument is followed presumably should not be taken to indicate a lack of theological inventiveness on Paul's part. Rather it indicates just how crucial the paradigm provided by Abraham was for Paul's understanding of the gospel.[4]

It is not just the Abrahamic "paradigm" that is essential to Paul's understanding of his gospel, but the entire Abraham narrative in Genesis 12–21. In addition, Paul elicits predominately prophetic texts that assist in the interpretation of the Genesis narrative. Paul preached Abraham without preaching circumcision. One possible scenario for Galatians would have Paul's opponents aware of his reliance on the

---

[3] R. B. Hays makes the attractive proposal that τί οὖν ἐροῦμεν εὑρηκέναι Ἀβραάμ in Rom 4:1 reflects the rabbinic מה מצינו ב, and refers to Paul's exegetical conclusions in Galatians on the Abraham narrative, which may have been known to his addressees in Rome ("'Have We Found Abraham to be Our Forefather According to the Flesh?' A Reconsideration of Rom 4:1," NovT 27 [1985] 81–83).

[4] J. D. G. Dunn, "How New was Paul's Gospel? The Problem of Continuity and Discontinuity," in Gospel in Paul: Studies on Corinthians, Galatians and Romans for Richard N. Longenecker (ed. L. Jervis and P. Richardson; JSNTSup 108; Sheffield: Sheffield Academic, 1994) 372.

Abraham narrative: they highlighted the fact that Abraham's family was indeed circumcised.

The context of Paul's employment of Abraham in Galatians is the presence of "another gospel" (Gal 1:6). Paul initially dismisses his opponents' message with these words: ὅ οὐκ ἔστιν ἄλλο (1:7). Essentially this means that their message is not really "gospel" (in the Pauline sense) after all. This may be an inconsequential aside, a rhetorical repellent of the problematic ideas. On the other hand, given that εὐαγγέλιον for Paul is by nature eschatological,[5] this may be Paul's way of introducing the line of argumentation that is picked up most fully in the odd "allegorical" interpretation of the Hagar/Sarah story in Gal 4:22–31. In Paul's mind, his opponents' theology is not really new, not a gospel founded on Zion eschatology, for it is little more than the conversionist principle that some Jewish missionaries practiced vis-à-vis the non-Jewish world: to enter the Jewish covenant, gentiles must accept circumcision, and, perhaps, other aspects of Torah observance. In effect Paul condemns the alternative program on two fronts: from the pharisaic perspective it is incomplete because it requires circumcision but not Torah observance; and it is non-eschatological, not characteristic of the age to come.

One may only guess at the opponents' "or else" since it is not explicit in Galatians. Did they claim that if the Galatian converts were not circumcised, they would not be δίκαιοι, or were they merely suggesting to the gentiles that they fully follow Abraham's lead? If the former option best represents the opponents' position, Paul's vehement reply in Galatians is understandable given his conviction that gentiles are welcomed "in Christ" without circumcision. But it is entirely possible that Paul was responsible for reading implications into the opponents' claim that they did not make, specifically the inherent association of circumcision with Torah observance.

Paul stresses that he received his gospel through an ἀποκάλυψις (Gal 1:12, 16) rather than through the human mediation of the Jerusalem church's "pillars." His claim to direct revelation is consistent with how Abraham, the paradigmatic figure in Galatians, received the promise

---

[5] The origin of Paul's use of εὐαγγέλιον is debated. I am convinced that, as with many aspects of Paul's eschatology, he derives it from the Book of Isaiah (40:9; 52:7; 61:1).

of the gentiles becoming righteous through faith (3:8), and in contrast with the νόμος that is mediated by angels and Moses (3:19).[6] Without forgetting the early Jewish theological context in which direct revelation seems to be indicative of a form of realized eschatology, it functions rhetorically to allow Paul to be unyielding to alternate gospels and inconsistent application of the majority gospel, as the Antioch incident demonstrates (Gal 2:11–14). For Paul unmediated revelation is characteristic of the new age, of the new Torah inscribed on human hearts rather than tablets of stone (2 Cor 3:3). Thus the very nature of Paul's reception of the gospel is indicative of its eschatological character, in contrast (as always for Paul) to the mediated Mosaic Torah.

The substance of the alternative theology is not spelled out in Galatians, and we do not know whether it was Paul or his opponents who introduced Abraham into the argument. It is not difficult, however, to project how Abraham would have been employed by the opponents. Abraham was a convert who, after responding to God's call, was circumcised. This is a very simple principle: converts enter into the Jewish covenant through circumcision, so the Galatian converts were obliged to follow Abraham's lead. Paul's response was anything but simple. The covenant signified by circumcision of the flesh was instituted with Ishmael in Genesis 17, before Isaac, the son of the promise, was born. The inheritance of Canaan was specifically tied to this covenant (Gen 17:8). The details of the obscure reconfiguration of the relationship between Hagar/Ishmael and Sarah/Isaac in Gal 4:21–30 will be scrutinized in §5.3.2, so it is enough to note at this point that Paul associates the covenant of circumcision in Genesis 17 with the son born into slavery. Hence Paul uniquely divided what other Jewish theologians might read as one covenant into two—one historical, one eschatological.

Disregarding the eschatological element in Paul leads to a misunderstanding of his activity in the gentile world, and his argumentation in Galatians. Some view "getting in and staying in" as the main issue in Galatians.[7] The application of E. P. Sanders' "covenantal nomism" in this context is unfortunate. Covenantal nomism is an adequate concept signifying the basic attitude of early Judaism toward "getting in

---

[6] Moses is not explicitly named, but he is the likely referent of μεσίτης.

[7] For example, see J. D. G. Dunn, "The Theology of Galatians: the Issue of Covenantal Nomism," in *Pauline Theology. Volume 1* (ed. J. M. Bassler; Minneapolis: Fortress, 1991) 125–46.

and staying in," but it is not helpful as the backdrop of Galatians where Paul is concerned with eschatological peoplehood rather than normal proselytism.[8] Paul did not see himself as a missionary in any ordinary sense, so the categories of Jewish proselytism do not apply. According to his theology he was participating in the coming glory, so the axis of Galatians is Jewish eschatology: how the non-Jewish world becomes part of the eschatological people of God and escapes condemnation.

The substance of Paul's interpretation of Abraham in Galatians is threefold:[9] (1) The promises to Abraham, at least those identified with his "seed" and his "blessing to the nations" were eschatological in nature.[10] If this is accepted the historical Jewish claim to the lineage of Abraham, Isaac, and Jacob is dismissed in favor of the eschatological people of God as the children of Abraham through the promised seed, Christ. The Pauline notion of peoplehood is not based on race, gender or social status: "There is neither Jew nor Greek, there is neither slave nor free, there is neither male nor female; for you are all one in Christ Jesus" (Gal 3:28). (2) The Abrahamic promises are accessed by faith rather than circumcision and Torah observance, based on the Abrahamic model. (3) The eternal Torah is a distortion of the gospel preached beforehand to Abraham, and it conflicts with Paul's understanding of Zion eschatology. Therefore Paul occupies himself in Galatians with countering the retrojection of Torah observance onto the patriarchal narratives. The story of Abraham is no longer understood as proleptically related to the Sinai revelation and covenant, but as a prolepsis of the gospel. Paul did not construct his argument with the narrative of other patriarchs because Abraham was the pivotal figure:

---

[8] Paul's orientation in Galatians is wholly eschatological, but notice particularly the expressions "Jerusalem above" (Gal 4:26), "new creation" and "Israel of God" (Gal 6:15–16).

[9] This is in partial response to Dunn's threefold summary of Paul's argument in Galatians: (1) God's ultimate saving act would be consistent with his "initial decisive expression"—that is, Abraham, (2) that this initial expression was constituted by promise and faith, and (3) that the Law had been given a "distorted role" where it conflicted with the initial expression ("Theology of Galatians," 125).

[10] As with most elements of Abraham's figuration in early Jewish literature, the future orientation of the promises derives from the language of Genesis: Gen 18:17 attests that Yhwh would not hide from Abraham "what I am doing" (see §5.2).

a convert who received a future oriented blessing, and in the opponents' thinking, received the covenant of circumcision.[11] As I have already argued, Abraham was vital to Paul's conception of the gospel, not merely as an exemplar, since Abraham and Sarah are eschatological figures (Isa 51:1–8; §4.4).[12]

So Paul's argument in Galatians, whether or not it is a proper understanding of his opponents' claims, is against the Law. Paul does not take issue with the Law *per se*, nor is he negating it. Rather, he assigns Torah a different, entirely temporal, role. It is not difficult to understand how scholars like W. D. Davies and Peter Stuhlmacher interpret Paul's positive and negative Torah assertions in Galatians as a Pauline paradox in which Christ takes Torah's place, yet Torah remains into the coming age. Paul reassigned rather than dismissed Torah, so Davies and Stuhlmacher mistake the language of reassignment, which includes Torah's incapacity for some functions assigned to it in early Jewish literature (e.g., in ζῳοποίησις), as an endorsement. I see Paul countering an idea he disagreed with by adjusting the idea of Torah to fit his theology. His reconfiguration of Torah theology in Galatians is, in effect, an antithesis to the eternal Torah. He neither proclaimed Torah's abrogation nor assumed its endurance into the eschatological age.

Paul's reconfigured Torah is not a negative, nor an "enslaving power."[13] But Torah is inferior to his gospel: Torah was given through

---

[11] Some assume that the opponents desired "full proselytism" (E. P. Sanders, *Paul, the Law and the Jewish People* [Philadelphia: Fortress, 1983] 19) of the Galatian believers, but there is little evidence for this. In fact, Gal 5:3 would suggest that it was Paul who connected circumcision with full Torah observance: "Paul does not miss the chance to castigate the circumcisers for ritual practice less exacting than his own when he was a Pharisee. The circumcisers, for all their zeal to perform this commandment, ironically are less observant than was Paul the Pharisee" (A. F. Segal, *Paul the Convert* [New Haven: Yale University Press, 1990] 209).

[12] In Rom 1:16–17 Paul's conception of the gospel is bound to the language of Gen 15:6, thus indicating the primacy of the Abraham narrative. Hab 2:4 is actually the text cited (v. 17), but it is used only to interpret Gen 15:6.

[13] The notion that Paul considered the Law an "enslaving power" has reappeared in I. Hong's study, in which he also contends that Paul neither misrepresented the role of the Law in early Jewish theology (against Schoeps, Sanders, Räisänen), nor viewed it as entirely negative (*The Law in Galatians* [JSNTSup 81; Sheffield: JSOT Press, 1993] 190–95). Although Hong's last two points are consistent with the present study, they conflict with the first: Hong's Paul teaches an enslaving Law that has its good points—

an intermediary (3:19), whereas his gospel was revealed by God to Abraham (3:8, 18) and himself (1:12). In contrast to Ben Sira's "Law of life" (Sir 17:11; 45:5), Paul asserts that the Law was not intended to be life-giving (3:21), whereas in a different context Paul claims that the resurrected Christ (1 Cor 15:22, 45) and the Spirit (2 Cor 3:6) give life. If there is a Pauline attack on the Jewish Law here, it concerns the Law understood as an eternal entity that is more powerful than the oppressive powers of this age. This is where N. T. Wright's notion of a Pauline "exile mentality" may be enlisted:[14] Israel's subservient sociopolitical existence is itself an argument for the inability of Torah-righteousness to triumph over "this present evil age." From Paul's perspective, Israel's history disproves the life-giving nature of Torah.

Although we do not know what messages(s) Paul used to attract gentile converts, at some point Paul probably preached Abraham as the ancient convert who believed and the figure through whom gentiles receive their promised "blessing." The opponents then appropriated Abraham by pointing out that God responded to his conversion by instituting circumcision, and he submitted.[15] That Paul preached Abraham is suggested by the degree of familiarity he assumes for his audience, since they are expected to pick up on his stated and unstated use of the Abraham narratives. Because of the attention Paul gives to the Law in Galatians, it is probable that Abraham was not the substance of the opponents' theology. There is nothing about Abraham's circumcision that necessarily requires the Galatians to accept the Sinai revelation and covenant, yet Paul reacts to the opposing interpretation of the Abraham story by addressing the status of the Law. I would suggest that the opponents asserted that the Law was given beforehand to Abraham. The picture of Abraham as the model of Torah observance is consistent with the interpretation of Abraham in many early Jewish

---

Torah the virtuous tyrant. This incongruity is reminiscent of Schweitzer's position on the good/bad Law, abrogated yet eternal.

[14] N. T. Wright, *The Climax of the Covenant: Christ and the Law in Pauline Theology* (Edinburgh: T. and T. Clark, 1991).

[15] I disagree here with B. H. Brinsmead: "It is no doubt the opponents who have made Abraham a central figure in the debate" (*Galatians—Dialogical Response to Opponents* [SBLDS 65; Chico: Scholars Press, 1982] 107). What Paul finds in the Abraham story, the promise to the gentiles linked with their acceptability (δικαιοσύνη) to the Jewish God because of faith alone, is unavailable elsewhere.

texts, but I doubt whether the opponents were advocating Torah observance. They appear to have isolated the cosmic aspects of the eternal Torah.

5.2 Abraham in Early Jewish Literature

On the surface, or rhetorical, level the figure of Abraham is important to Paul's argumentation in Galatians 3–4. But Paul does not explicitly say why Abraham plays this role, so the interpreter of Galatians must fill in the details. Whether it was Paul or his opponents who introduced Abraham into the dispute, one can gain perspective by investigating how Abraham was viewed in other early Jewish writings. It is not that one must locate common Jewish theology in order to make sense of Paul, but it is helpful to know the sort of Abraham traditions that Paul may have employed or countered. Many scholars have surveyed the early Jewish use and development of Abraham, so I can afford to be selective, to isolate those aspects of Abraham's depiction that illuminate Paul's use.[16] I shall focus on Abraham as the recipient of revelation, a category that seems overlooked by scholarship but which is particularly relevant to Galatians, since Paul contends that the gospel was announced to Abraham (Gal 3:8).

---

[16] In addition to the commentaries see S. Sandmel, *Philo's Place in Judaism: A Study of Conceptions of Abraham in Jewish Literature* (Cincinnati: Hebrew Union College Press, 1956) 30–95; G. Vermes, *Scripture and Tradition in Judaism* (SPB 4; Leiden: Brill, 1961) 66–126; J. P. Schultz, "Two Views of the Patriarchs: Noachides and Pre-Sinai Israelites," in *Texts and Responses: Studies Presented to Nahum N. Glatzer on the Occasion of his Seventieth Birthday by His Students* (ed. M. Fishbane and P. Flohr; Leiden: Brill, 1975) 43–59; D. Georgi, *The Opponents of Paul in Second Corinthians* (Philadelphia: Fortress, 1986) 49–60; G. W. Hansen, *Abraham in Galatians: Epistolary and Rhetorical Contexts* (JSNTSup 29; Sheffield: JSOT, 1989) 175–99, and the literature cited in 265–66 n. 1; N. Calvert, "Abraham and Idolatry: Paul's Comparison of Obedience to the Law with Idolatry in Galatians 4.1–10," in *Paul and the Scriptures of Israel* (ed. C. Evans and J. Sanders; JSNTSup 83; SSEJC 1; Sheffield: JSOT, 1993) 222–37. Sandmel regards Abraham in the OT pseudepigrapha as common theology: "These writings do not really tell about Abraham. They allude to him as though the simple allusion is sufficient for the reader's understanding. It is implicit that he is the great ancestor who abides and whose merit abides. We see that Abraham is implicit, but we do not really see Abraham. His importance to the writers, and by inference to the readers, is such that they feel no need to go into details. Abraham has become intimately part of their assumptions and pre-dispositions" (*Philo's Place in Judaism*, 38).

A preliminary methodological principle should be established. Surveying the early Jewish Abraham material is neither a difficult nor a complicated task. It is primarily descriptive. There is an additional step that is rarely taken, yet is vital to the interpretation of Abraham. In §1.3 I introduced the question that Daniel Boyarin asked of the *Mekhilta* in order to understand its midrash on Exodus: "What in the Bible's text might have motivated this gloss on this verse?"[17] Boyarin's question is employed as a methodological tool throughout this study, but it is primary in this chapter and the next. Applied to Abraham's figuration in early Jewish texts, this means that each element and development can be and is traced back to features of the Genesis narrative. Abraham as seer, astrologer, or Torah-observant patriarch are exegetical conclusions from specific, identifiable texts, however these traditions are embellished.

In Galatians Paul views Abraham and the Law as mutually interpretive *theologoumena*. The background to this connection is found in the early Jewish idea of Abraham as the patriarch of pre-Sinai Torah observance.[18] The eternal Torah as developed in §3.1 provided a convenient theological foundation for the possibility of Abraham's knowledge of Torah, but Abraham's obedience has strong biblical support in the extended Genesis narratives, and Gen 26:5 was the specific basis for the association of Abraham's obedience with Torah:

Abraham obeyed my voice and kept my charge, my commandments, my statutes, and my laws (תורתי).[19]

---

[17] D. Boyarin, *Intertextuality and the Reading of Midrash* (Bloomington: University of Indiana Press, 1990) ix. As I noted, Boyarin's study had the advantage that the *Mekhilta* is by nature (genre) biblical commentary, whereas one has to contend for those Pauline texts that have biblical subtexts.

[18] See, for example, the recent study of B. Ego, "Abraham als Urbild der Toratreue Israels: Traditionsgeschichtliche Überlegungen zu einem Aspekt des biblischen Abrahambildes," *Bund und Tora* (ed. F. Avemaria and H. Lichtenberger; WUNT 92; Tübingen: Mohr [Siebeck], 1996) 25–40.

[19] So *m. Qid.* 4:14: "And we find that Abraham our father had performed the whole law before it was given, for it is written, 'Because that Abraham obeyed my voice and kept my charge, my commandments, my statutes, and my laws.'" In the rabbinic literature there is a difference of opinion about which Law Abraham obeyed: the majority position maintains "that the Patriarchs observed the entire law given at Sinai"; other voices believed that Abraham obeyed the Noahide laws, or that "there was a progressive increase in the number of commandments given by God to the pre-Sinai generations" (Schultz, "Two Views of the Patriarchs," 51).

In Sirach's extended praise of Jewish heroes, Abraham's Torah observance is tied to the blessing of the gentiles (as with Gen 26:4):

> Abraham was the great father of a multitude of nations, and no one
> has been found like him in glory; *he kept the law of the Most High*,
> and was taken into covenant with him; he established the covenant in
> his flesh, and when he was tested he was found faithful. Therefore the
> Lord assured him by an oath that the nations would be blessed
> through his posterity; that he would multiply him like the dust of the
> earth, and exalt his posterity like the stars, and cause them to inherit
> from sea to sea and from the River to the ends of the earth. (Sir
> 44:19–21)[20]

The more profound development of this tradition occurs in *Jubilees*
and *2 Apocalypse of Baruch*.

In *Jubilees* Abraham is presented as Torah-observant prior to the
Sinai revelation. The knowledge of the Torah by pre-Sinai generations
is a witness to the non-occasional nature of Jewish practice: Torah
observance is a participation in cosmic realities, rather than mere
custom. Concerning Abraham, *Jubilees* presents his circumcision as an
eternal statute, written on the heavenly tablets (*Jub.* 15:25). Abraham
celebrates the feast of tabernacles, also written on the heavenly tablets
(*Jub.* 16:21–31), as well as first-fruits (22:3–9).

2 Apoc. Bar. 57:1 attests to "the unwritten law . . . in force" and the
"works of commandments . . . accomplished" in Abraham's day. The
following lines of *2 Apocalypse of Baruch* 57 manifest a notable development of Abraham as the recipient of revelation: the days of Abraham were also characterized by "the belief in the coming judgment,"
"the hope of the world which will be renewed," and "the promise of
the life that will come later" (*2 Apoc. Bar.* 57:1–2). This tradition parallels 4 Ezra 3:14, which states that God revealed to Abraham secretly in
the night "the end of the times," and perhaps *L.A.B.* 23:10 as well, in
which Abraham's son Isaac is "revealed the new age." In the *Apocalypse of Abraham* he is shown many otherwise inaccessible sacred
sites: "God's mountain, glorious Horeb" (12:3; Exod 3:1), the *merkabah*
(18:12), the heavens and seventh and eighth firmaments (19:4–9), and the
garden of Eden (21:6). Chapters 23–32 of the *Apocalypse* narrate Abra-

---

[20] The Hebrew says Abraham kept מצוה, that is, one specific command (= circumcision), whereas the LXX allows for a more expansive obedience to νόμον ὑψίστου,
Torah.

ham's vision of the future: "I will explain to you what will be, and everything that will be in the last days" (24:2). Like Enoch and Moses, Abraham is a privileged seer.

The biblical basis for Abraham's special knowledge of the future is probably Gen 18:17–19, in which the narrator allows the reader to listen in on Yhwh's inner conversation:

> The Lord said, "Shall I hide from Abraham what I am about to do (אשר אני עשה), seeing that Abraham shall become a great and mighty nation, and all the nations of the earth shall bless themselves by him? No, for I have chosen him (כי ידעתיו), that he may charge his children and his household after him to keep the way of the Lord by doing righteousness and justice; so that the Lord may bring to Abraham what he has promised him."

The language would suggest to the early Jewish interpreter that Abraham was the recipient of hidden knowledge, not just of the Sinai revelation (see below) but of the future acts of God: אשר אני עשה.

In the *Damascus Document* Abraham is a "friend" of God who kept God's מצות, rather than follow the רצון רוחו ("desires of his spirit"), and passed them on to Isaac and Jacob (CD 3:2–3).[21] The *Testament of Benjamin* also portrays Abraham (along with Isaac and Jacob) handing down "the Law of the Lord and the commandments" to subsequent generations (10:3–4). Thus, in addition to his status as the receptor of Torah and eschatological knowledge, Abraham is a tradent of Torah. In *Jubilees* Abraham hands on the books of Noah and Enoch.

Abraham as seer or visionary is a development of the Genesis Abraham narrative as well. First, Yhwh (Gen 12:1; 13:14), Yhwh's angel (Gen 22:11, 15), and Elohim (Gen 21:12; 22:1) speak to Abraham directly. Secondly, Abraham has visions (מחזה; Gen 15:1). This idea is picked up in the *Genesis Apocryphon*, which depicts Abraham being informed by dreams (19.14) and visions (21.8; 22.27). In each case the dream or vision is not suggested in the Genesis version of the story; the author transfers Abraham the visionary from other Genesis episodes. Another text affirms that God used Abraham's visions for instruction:

---

[21] Abraham as God's "friend": Isa 41:8; 2 Chr 20:7; James 2:23; *Test. Abr.* passim (e.g., 1:6; 2:3; 4:7); *Apoc. Abr.* 10:5; Philo, *Sobr.* 56 (altered quote of Gen 18:17). CD 3:2–4 explains that Abraham was a friend because of his obedience.

For from the beginning of our father Abraham's laying claim to the way of truth, You led (him) by a vision, having taught (him) what at any time this world is. And his faith traveled ahead of his knowledge, but the covenant was the follower of his faith. (*Apost. Const.* 7.33.4)[22]

One might say that Abrahamic visions and revelation are bound together.

Abraham's renown as an astrologer is so nearly universal in early Jewish literature that one might suspect that Paul's reference to the Galatians' adherence to "days, months, seasons, and years" (Gal 4:10) reflects this background. The Abraham-heavy context certainly supports this reading. Little more is needed to stimulate this tradition than Gen 15:5, in which Yhwh instructs the patriarch to "Look toward heaven, and number the stars, if you are able to number them."[23] When Josephus states that Abraham taught both astronomy and arithmetic to the Egyptians (*A.J.* 1. 167), he appears to draw from both divine imperatives: "look" (הבט נא) and "count" (ספר).

Jubilees, which judges Abraham "perfect in all of his actions with the LORD and was pleasing through righteousness all of the days of his life" (23:10), provides an illuminating example of the durability of the astrologer tradition. Because it orients human behavior to the behavior of celestial bodies rather than divine command, astrology is antithetical to the theological purposes of *Jubilees*. This book proclaims a calendar that is divisible by sevens and rebukes those who follow a lunar calendar (*Jub.* 6:32–38). Given this perspective, one might expect that *Jubilees* would deny Abraham's stature as an astrologer, or render the words of Gen 15:5 differently. Instead, *Jubilees* first affirms what the reader knows. Prior to Abraham's "call" in *Jubilees* (12:22–24), he is portrayed studying the stars "from evening until daybreak so that he might see what the nature of the year would be with respect to rain" (12:16). A "word" then "came into his heart":

All of the signs of the stars and the signs of the sun and the moon are all in the hand of the LORD. Why am I seeking? If he desires, he will

---

[22] Trans. D. Darnell, "Hellenistic Synagogal Prayers," *OTP* 2. 678.

[23] The targum and LXX versions of Gen 15:5 exhibit no trace of interpretive development. They faithfully render the pivotal phrase אם תוכל, "if you can." I assume that for the early Jewish interpreter the divine command ספר הכוכבים would overwhelm any purely grammatical argument about the conditional meaning of אם תוכל.

make it rain morning and evening, and if he desires he will not send
(it) down; and everything is in his hand. (*Jub.* 12:17–18)[24]

This is subtle maneuver, but its effect is clear: Abraham has astrological ability thereafter (see *Jub.* 14:4–5), but he does not practice the art.
Abraham's "conversion" can be characterized as the renouncing of
idolatry and astrology.

The author of *Jubilees* understands that astronomical insight is a
tool by which unseen evil forces enslave humanity. In the same context
Abraham prays that God would

> Save me from the hands of evil spirits
> which rule over the thought of the heart of man
> and do not let them lead me astray from following you, O my God.
> (*Jub.* 12:20)

Paul reflects a similar perspective in Gal 4:8–9, arguing that adherence
to astronomical piety is enslaving. But Paul, in contradistinction to
Jubilees, associates the emphasis on chronologically correct practice of
holy days and religious festivals with astrology, and renders "calendrical piety" as bondage (Gal 4:10).

5.3 Paul and the Abraham Narratives

In *The Faith of Jesus Christ*, Richard Hays argues that the Christ-story
is the "narrative substructure" of Gal 3:1–4:11, and that other Pauline
texts welcome a similar interpretation.[25] Paul continually refers back
to this story as the basis of his theological argumentation and paranesis. In response to Hays, Carol Stockhausen argues that in Galatians
Paul has the entire Abraham narrative in mind (Genesis 12–22).[26] As
the first of three primary Pauline exegetical tendencies, Stockhausen
argues that "narrative texts from the Pentateuch are usually (perhaps
always) at the core of his arguments."[27] With reference to Abraham in

---

[24] I have not maintained O. S. Wintermute's poetic alignment of v. 18 (*OTP* 2. 81).

[25] R. B. Hays, *The Faith of Jesus Christ: An Investigation of the Narrative Substructure of Galatians 3:1–4:11* (SBLDS 56; Chico: Scholars Press, 1983).

[26] Stockhausen, "Principles of Pauline Exegesis"; "Galatians and the Abraham Narratives."

[27] Stockhausen, "Principles of Pauline Exegesis," 144. The other primary Pauline
exegetical principles are the use of verbally-linked (most often) prophetic texts to assist

Galatians she contends that Paul did not deal with the Abraham story in "piece-meal fashion," but most likely has the entire Genesis narrative about Abraham in mind, even where it is not cited or clearly alluded to.[28] Genesis 12–22 is therefore the "substructure of Galatians,"[29] and the structuring element for "apparently quite disparate arguments" in what Hans Dieter Betz labels the *probatio* section (Gal 3:1–4:31).[30] In fact, the goal of the *probatio* is specifically the interpretation of the Abraham narratives. Stockhausen argues that for the most part, Paul is attentive to the sequencing of the narrative.[31]

The third of Stockhausen's Pauline exegetical principles concerns the apostle's eye for contradictory biblical texts. Stockhausen refines Nils Dahl's seminal study that argued that Paul brought Gen 15:6 into his argument in Galatians as the third text which reconciles two others.[32] The use of a third text to reconcile contradictory texts is consistent with the thirteenth of Rabbi Ishmael's *middoth* (hermeneutical principles):

> The whole train of thought in Gal. 3:1–12 rests on the presupposition that Hab. 2:4 and Lev. 18:5 contradict one another, and that the two corresponding principles "by faith" and "by (works of) the law" mutually exclude one another as qualifications for justification and life.[33]

The two texts are thematically analogous, since both speak of how a person should live, but they contradict each other. Paul the exegete must determine which text is primary.[34] Contradictory scriptures of

---

in the interpretation of the Torah text, and the "location and solution of contradictions or uneasily reconciled passages" (145).

[28] Stockhausen, "Abraham Narratives," 1. Stockhausen does not believe Paul's use of the Abraham narratives is limited to Galatians 3–4, since there is a remarkable similarity between the patriarch's story and Paul's as developed in Galatians 1. Interestingly, Paul's use of ἀφορίζω in Gal 1:15 mimics the LXX of Isa 29:22 concerning Yhwh's "redeeming" (פדה) of Abraham.

[29] Stockhausen, "Abraham Narratives," 21.

[30] H. Betz, *Galatians: A Commentary on Paul's Letter to the Churches in Galatia* (Hermeneia; Philadelphia: Fortress, 1979); Stockhausen, "Abraham Narratives," 3.

[31] Stockhausen, "Abraham Narratives," 4.

[32] N. Dahl, "Contradictions in Scripture," *Studies in Paul* (Minneapolis: Augsburg, 1977) 159–77. Dahl is himself developing the suggestion of H. Schoeps, *Paul* (Philadelphia: Westminster, 1961) 177–78.

[33] Dahl, "Contradictions," 170.

[34] Dahl, "Contradictions," 171.

this sort are to be reconciled exegetically; they should be interpreted so that neither text is negated. Only in extreme cases is a third scripture employed, but a third scripture can be brought in if it suggests a resolution different from a contextual exegetical solution. The important exegetical first step, which Dahl assumes Paul knew, was to establish which text contained the "valid halakah."[35] Paul's preferred, or "valid," text is Hab 2:4, "the just live by faith," so his exegetical move is to equate Hab 2:4 with the Abrahamic promise (Gen 22:18; 28:4; see also 2 Sam 7:12).

Stockhausen questions how Gen 15:6 could have performed this function since Paul cited it first, before the contradiction was introduced. She proposes that Hab 2:4 and Lev 18:5 do not represent the primary contradiction; in fact, considered as a unit, there must be the third (reconciling) text.[36] Rather, the two "visions" (Gen 15:1; 17:1) of Abraham are contradictory:[37] the first is characterized by the language Paul positively adopts in Galatians 3–4: "seed" (Gen 15:3), "inheritance" (Gen 15:4–5), "belief" (Gen 15:6), "righteousness" (Gen 15:6), "covenant" (Gen 15:18). Yhwh appears again to Abraham (Gen 17:1), and there is another covenant (Gen 17:2) associated with circumcision "of the flesh" (Gen 17:11). Except for the hook word "seed," which is common to both visions, there is no mixing; the special vocabulary of Genesis 15 is not replicated in Genesis 17, and vice versa.[38] Paul essentially associates the first vision/covenant with his gospel, whereas the circumcision advocates are consistent with the second. The delimitation of vocabulary special to each contradictory unit is important because it exposes the extent to which Paul's argument is driven by the content of the entire Abraham narrative. In place of explicit citation of his subtext, Paul's consistent use of the terminology of the two episodes is a clear signal of his exegetical interest.[39] Those terms that many suppose are foundational to Pauline theology (e.g., πίστις, δικαιοσύνη) derive from the Abraham narratives, thus giving credence to my point that Paul preached Abraham.

Commenting on the "two covenant" language of Gal 4:21, Stockhausen argues that for Paul, the only covenant of these which could be

---

[35] Dahl, "Contradictions," 164.
[36] Stockhausen, "Abraham Narratives," 15.
[37] Stockhausen, "Abraham Narratives," 17.
[38] Stockhausen, "Abraham Narratives," 19.
[39] Stockhausen, "Abraham Narratives," 18–19.

anticipatory of the Mosaic covenant is contained in Genesis 17.[40] Early Jewish and rabbinic theologians commonly interpreted the Sinai covenant as the same one established with Abraham, so by differentiating between a covenant of promise and spirit and a covenant of circumcision and flesh, Paul is (probably intentionally) engaged in counter-reading. The first "covenant" then is that established in Genesis 15, featuring a connection of Abraham's faith and righteousness (15:6).

5.3.1 Attention to Textual Minutiae

Gal 3:16 demonstrates that Paul's interpretive eye was focused on grammatical minutia in the Genesis narratives:

> Now the promises were made to Abraham and to his offspring. It does not say, "And to offsprings," referring to many; but, referring to one, "And to your offspring," which is Christ.

Paul here differentiates between "seed" (זרע/σπέρμα) and "seeds." Paul probably had all the semantic features of the Abraham narrative in mind when he asserted that the gospel was preached to Abraham before the Torah was given. In context the "gospel" equals "In you shall all the nations be blessed" (Gal 3:8), that is, the promise to Abraham which Paul read as *Protoevangelium*. The gospel is about the gentiles becoming part of the eschatological people of God, "the blessing of Abraham" (Gal 3:14), and Gen 17:16 affirms that it would be through Sarah. Although Gen 12:2–3 is preparatory for the reading that differentiates between the two Abrahamic blessings, the particularism (גוי גדול) and universalism (כל גויי הארץ) associated with Abraham are clear in the parallelism of Gen 18:18:

> Abraham shall become a great and mighty nation
> and all the nations of the earth shall bless themselves by him.

The Abrahamic "great nation" and blessing of "all nations" are not semantic equivalents, but they may be read sequentially; Abraham's visions function as prolepses for the fruition of both "promises."[41] For

---

[40] Stockhausen, "Abraham Narratives," 19.

[41] J. L. Kugel observes that in interpretation of biblical parallelism, the rabbis viewed two (or more) parallel elements as independent expressions (see *The Idea of Biblical Poetry* [New Haven: Yale University Press, 1981] 97–102).

Paul the two clauses of Gen 18:18 would represent history and eschatology, or Israel and the church. Eschatologically, "Abraham's seed" is Christ and his family, rather than Jacob and his.

5.3.2 The Allegory

The intensity of Paul's attention to the semantic features of a narrative is exemplified in his interpretation of the story of Abraham's two sons and their mothers. Of the many Pauline enigmas, Gal 4:21–31 may be the most puzzling because it is seemingly impossible to explain or defend his argument and mode of exegesis. He introduces the story as a lesson from ὁ νόμος:

> Tell me, you who desire to be under the law, do you not hear the law? For it is written that Abraham had two sons, one by a slave and one by a free woman. (Gal 4:21–22)

Paul then identifies the story as an "allegory": "these women are two covenants" (v. 24). I will not argue here that Paul's allegorical interpretation of Genesis 16–21 does justice to the text. At best Paul's exegetical maneuvers in Gal 4:21–31 go against the trend in Jewish theology of tracing its lineage through Isaac, while at worst it is an example of Pauline misprision.[42] My goal is to think with Paul, to search out the bases for Gal 4:21–31 in his reading of biblical texts and in his "convictional world."[43]

Although Paul's reading of Genesis has proven to be inexplicable, one can learn from parallels and contrasts to Gal 4:21–31 in other early Jewish interpretations of the Hagar/Sarah narrative. Richard Longenecker notes that Philo's allegorical interpretations of the Hagar/Sarah narrative bear "several striking surface similarities to Paul's in Gal 4:21–31."[44] Both Philo and Paul orient their interpretation around the

---

[42] R. Hays (*Echoes of Scripture in the Letters of Paul* [New Haven: Yale University Press, 1989]) describes Paul's interpretation of Genesis in Gal 4:21–31 in typically colorful terms: as "counterreading" (112–13) and "strong misreading" (115), "a fancifully subversive ecclesiocentric reading of Genesis 21" (111), "hermeneutical jujitsu" (112), "a hermeneutical miracle calculated to end the argument by leaving his audience agape" (112).

[34] T. L. Donaldson, *Paul and the Gentiles: Remapping the Apostle's Convictional World* (Minneapolis: Fortress, 1997).

[44] R. Longenecker, *Galatians* (WBC 41; Dallas: Word Books, 1990) 205. The Philonic texts are: *Congr.* 9–10, 12, 14, 23; *Cher.* 9; *Leg.* 3.244; *Q. G.* 3:19. The main rabbinic texts are: *Pesiq. Rabbati* 48.2; *b. Ned.* 31a; *Gen. Rab.* 55:7; *Deut. Rab.* 4:5.

slave/free polarity, the status of the women's sons, and the expelling of Hagar and Ishmael. Hagar and her son Ishmael represent for both writers a "preliminary and preparatory stage that is superseded by something greater." Philo, for example, allegorized Hagar and Sarah in support of his distinction between lower and higher forms of wisdom. Despite Philo's separation and elevation of Sarah and Isaac, there is nothing inherently negative about Philo or Paul's depiction of Hagar and Ishmael. In rabbinic texts, however, Ishmael is portrayed as a wicked man and an idolator.[45]

For his part, Paul develops the inferior/superior relationship between these two mothers of Abraham's children to reinforce his eschatological interpretation of the Abrahamic promises. Abraham and Sarah are superior to what follows; their superior offspring (זרע) comes after the inferior. In addition, Paul's comparison of the two Jerusalems (Gal 4:25–26) is based on the superiority of the heavenly/ eschatological mountain city. But I am aware of no early Jewish text that parallels or prepares for Paul's identification of Hagar with the inferior Sinai and Jerusalem. The same thing should be maintained for Paul's representation of Hagar as the archetypal matron of slavery:[46] Paul applies the label παιδίσκη to Hagar (Gal 4:22), but this term is used to describe her in the LXX (for אמה; Gen 21:10–13); similarly, Ishmael is בן האמה, "the son of the slave woman."[47]

---

[45] For the rabbinic treatment of Ishmael, see Longenecker, *Galatians*, 201–3. In *Exod. Rab.* 1:1 the idolatry charge is founded on the word מצחק (Gen 21:9), which the MT vocalizes as a D-stem (*pi'el*) participle; in the D-stem צחק means "to play" or "joke" (KB). The LXX supplies what is gapped in the MT: Ishmael was playing (or "sporting"; παίζω) "with Isaac." The LXX replaces the יצחק/מצחק paronomasia, which would not transfer to Greek. In midrash and targum, the gap was filled in differently: Ishmael was playing *with idols*. This tradition accounts, then, for Sarah's demand that Hagar and Ishmael be expelled (Gen 21:10), and Abraham's reaction (וירע הדבר מאד בעיני אברהם; Gen 21:11).

[46] Unfortunately, Longenecker associates Paul with negative appraisals of Ishmael: "Closer parallels to Paul's contemporization in Gal 4:21–31, however, can be seen in the Qumran *War Scroll*, where in 1QM 2:13 the battle plans for the ninth year include an attack on the 'descendents of Ishmael and Keturah,' for here Ishmael is seen as one of the progenitors of the 'Sons of Darkness'" (*Galatians*, 205). Paul does not even mention Ishmael by name, and although his implicit references to the "son of the slave" (4:22; 30) and "he who was born according to the flesh" (4:29) do not flatter Ishmael, they are in no way comparable to the War Scroll's indictment of these sons of Abraham as "sons of darkness" (1QM 1:16; 2:13).

[47] Ishmael is also associated with Israel's slavery in Egypt: "Ishmaelites" buy Joseph from his brothers (Gen 37:28).

The parallels in Philo neither account for nor explain Paul's "allegory" of Hagar and Sarah.[48] Since Paul's exegetical argument occurs to no known early Jewish interpreter, it is almost certainly Paul's handiwork. But it is also possible that Paul's opponents stimulated him to explore the story in this manner because they made it relevant to the Galatians as a means of provoking believers to circumcision after the example of both the son of the slave and the son of the promise, Isaac. Isaac was circumcised on the eighth day, consistent with the biblical command (Gen 21:4; 17:12), and Ishmael was circumcised with Abraham's "house" when he was 13 years old (Gen 17:23–27). Along with Abraham, Ishmael could have been used by the opponents as the biblical precedent for gentile convert circumcision.

When Paul asserts that the story of Hagar and Sarah is allegory, does he mean that it was intended to be allegorical, or that it can be interpreted allegorically based on interpretive principles applied to the narrative?

> When Paul announces that these narrative entities are to be interpreted allegorically (v. 24), no one should be surprised. Even the conventional Jewish interpretation offered in Jubilees is allegorical, with its symbolic identification of Ishmael and Isaac as representatives of Gentiles and Jews.[49]

The *Jubilees* text Hays is referring to is 16:17–18, which differentiates between Abraham's six sons (of Keturah; Gen 25:1–2) born after Isaac who are considered gentiles, and Isaac's progeny which is a "holy seed," the "portion of the Most High," and not gentiles.[50] Hays' understanding of Paul's use of "allegory" might be termed a soft allegorism, not decidedly different from other *plenior* or "contemporiz-

---

[48] I do not dismiss, however, P. Borgen's use of Philo to explain Gal 4:21–31 ("Some Hebrew and Pagan Features in Philo's and Paul's Interpretation of Hagar and Ishmael," in *The New Testament and Hellenistic Judaism* [ed. P. Borgen and S. Giverson; Aarhus: Aarhus University Press, 1995] 151–64). Borgen contends that Hagar and Ishmael are to be understood in the context of Jewish proselytism: Hagar was an "Egyptian by blood, and a Hebrew by deliberate choice" (Philo, *Abr.* 251; cited by Borgen, 158). Borgen sees Paul condemning his opponents for making "slave-proselytes."

[49] Hays, *Echoes of Scripture*, 113.

[50] The language of *Jub.* 16:17 probably means that Ishmael, who does not appear in the context, was considered a gentile along with the sons of Keturah: "All of the seed of [Abraham's] sons would become nations. And they would be counted with the nations. But from the sons of Isaac one would become a holy seed and he would not be counted with the nations."

ing" Jewish interpretations of biblical texts. This is not an unreasonable reading of Paul, but I think it is more accurate to say that he employed the term to signify a symbolic interpretation that cannot be justified using his normal exegetical principles. Although they are אמה and בן אמה in Genesis, Paul's identification of Hagar and Ishmael as the *archetypes* of slavery is allegorical. Similarly, symbolizing the two Jerusalems by these women is allegorical. The relationship between these symbols and that which Paul claims they signify is left unstated in Gal 4:21–31.

The temptation is to say more than Paul does with the allegory, but this is unavoidable to some extent because the items compared are asymmetrical; for example, Paul does not provide a counterpart to the μέv-clause in Gal 4:24. Thus graphic arrangements like the following (which contains only items present in the text) are warranted, but they also obfuscate the suggestive nature of Paul's comparisons.

Hagar	*Sarah*
Slave	Free
Ishmael born according to flesh	Isaac born according to promise
Sinai/Present Jerusalem	Jerusalem above
Flesh	Spirit

Paul does not identify Sarah by name. Charles H. Cosgrove interprets the "missing pieces" in Gal 4:21–31 as indicative of "common ground" between author and intended audience:

> One is given the impression that Paul takes for granted the alignments on the Sarah side of the allegory, and that these alignments provide the common ground with his readers upon which the argument all along depends and from which it derives its potential force in the epistolary situation.[51]

On this point Cosgrove is consistent with my suggestion that Paul preached Abraham to the Galatians and the Genesis narratives were essential to his understanding of the gospel. But Cosgrove asserts without exegetical substantiation that an unstated Hagar/Torah "equa-

---

[51] C. H. Cosgrove, "The Law Has Given Sarah No Children (Gal. 4:21–30)," *NovT* 29 (1987) 226. Cosgrove ends the section with v. 30.

tion" is "the main point of the allegory," and that there is a Torah/ Jerusalem connection that "goes without saying."[52] In other words, Paul equates Torah with slavery. Although νόμος occurs in the introductory statement to the section—"Tell me, you who desire to be under law, do you not hear the law?" (4:21)—and to some extent the Mosaic Torah is implicated with any mention of Sinai (4:25) in Paul, the main point of the allegory is the identification of the eschatologically "free" (from this present evil age) community with the Jerusalem above. And, "covenant" and "Torah," though belonging to the same relational set of images and used in synonymous parallelism in biblical texts, were not necessarily synonymous for early Jewish exegetes, and thus Paul's assertion of "two covenants" (4:24) is not a cipher for Torah, or even two Torahs.[53]

It would also be a mistake to identify Jerusalem with its inhabitants in Paul's interpretation.[54] Unlike the author of *Jubilees*, and perhaps his opponents in Galatians, Paul does not make comparisons in Gal 4:21–31 based on ethnicity or religious group.[55] Although Isaac is associated with Paul's audience as "children of the promise" (4:28), Ishmael

[52] Cosgrove, "Law Has Given Sarah No Children," 225, 229.

[53] This is not the case with Paul's use of "new covenant" in 2 Cor 3:6, in which one subtext (Jer 31:31–34) determines his phraseology, while the other (Exod 34:29–35) determines his topic, the Torah. And, I am not arguing that covenant and Torah are unrelated in early Jewish literature: for example, "covenant of this Law" (*L.A.B.* 23:2). My point has been that covenant, unlike Torah, was not personalized, and therefore the terms were (generally) no longer an equivalent pair in parallelism.

[54] For example, K. Jobes asserts that "In a radical historical and theological reversal, Paul claims that Christians, and not Jews, are the promised sons of Abraham and the true heirs of the promises of the Abrahamic covenant" ("Jerusalem, our Mother: Metalepsis and Intertextuality in Galatians 4:21–31," *WTJ* 55 [1993] 299). In the larger context of Pauline theology there is some truth to this thinking, but Paul would never agree with Jobes' "not Jews" refrain (also 304; 306), and by using the dual Jerusalems in Gal 4:25–26, Paul explicitly shies away from racializing his argument.

[55] According to L. Martyn's survey of the "virtually normative exegesis" of Gal 4:21–31, Christian interpreters from Marcion to modern commentators have understood Paul as differentiating between Judaism as the religion of the flesh and slavery, whereas Christianity is of the spirit and freedom ("The Covenants of Hagar and Sarah," in *Faith and History: Essays in Honor of Paul W. Meyer* [ed. J. Carroll, C. Cosgrove, and E. Johnson; Atlanta: Scholars Press, 1990] 164–69). Martyn argues that Hagar represents the Law-observant mission to the gentiles, in contrast to Paul's Law-free mission symbolized by Sarah.

is not identified with a specific group, Jew or gentile. The basis of comparison is history and eschatology, or the Pauline duality of ages. Thus the holy mountains of this age, Sinai and Jerusalem, are not sites of eschatological presence or gathering; nor are they like portals through which the new age comes—except in the sense that the first climax, Jesus' death, happened in Jerusalem, and in some sense Jerusalem is the locus of nascent Christianity. For Paul the new Jerusalem, eschatological Zion, descends from heaven; it is not a renewed Jerusalem. In other words, Paul's vision of the future is closer to Enochian apocalypticism with its dualisms and access to heavenly archetypes (see §3.4) than the restoration model.

Another unstated feature of Paul's interpretation involves a discrepancy between the introduction to the allegory and his handling of the Genesis intertext. Gal 4:22 refers to Abraham and his two sons ("It is written"), yet he argues from the mothers rather than their sons. Why? I have already noted that there were established differentiations between Abraham's sons; for example, Ishmael and Keturah's sons were regarded as "sons of darkness" in 1QM 2:13. Paul uses the mothers in order to establish new relationships between biblical figure and contemporary realities. Moreover, the use of the two mothers corresponds to the two cities, as Paul makes explicit in Gal 4:26: "the Jerusalem above is free, and she is our mother." Like Hagar, Jerusalem births her children into slavery, whereas Sarah corresponds to the heavenly Jerusalem, whose children are free. The interpreter of Paul should proceed with caution here because the temptation is to view this as a slur on the inhabitants of Jerusalem, or on Jerusalem as the symbol for Judaism. This is not Paul's intent, for his salvos are usually targeted at this evil age or the parties who compromise his eschatological gospel for a decidedly "this age" version. For Paul, Jews and Judaism are in slavery not because they are bad or inordinately prone to disobedience, but because they are confined to this present evil age and because the Torah was not intended to be life-giving.

The second motivation for tracing the lineage through the mothers rather than the sons is to avoid Isaac. Isaac is not a negative figure for Paul: he is Abraham's "seed," the archetype of the "children of the promise" (Gal 4:28; Rom 9:7–9). It is not the example of Isaac that Paul is concerned to avoid, but the real-time lineage of Abraham-Isaac-Jacob. The plain sense (פשט) of the Genesis narrative is that Israel's lineage was from Abraham, through Isaac and Jacob. Paul turned the tables on a normal Jewish interpretation of patriarchal history, in which Isaac would represent Israel.[56] There is an unstated tension in Paul's reading of Genesis between Christ and Isaac because both are the promised son. Even more important for Galatians, Jacob (i.e., Israel) as the son of Isaac is the seed of Abraham. An example of the way in which Paul avoids Isaac in the narrative is seen in his quotation of Gen 21:10 in Gal 4:30:

καὶ εἶπεν τῷ Αβρααμ ἔκβαλε τὴν παιδίσκην ταύτην καὶ τὸν υἱὸν αὐτῆς οὐ γὰρ κληρονομήσει ὁ υἱὸς τῆς παιδίσκης ταύτης μετὰ τοῦ υἱοῦ μου Ισαακ. (Gen 21:10 LXX)

ἀλλὰ τί λέγει ἡ γραφή ἔκβαλε τὴν παιδίσκην καὶ τὸν υἱὸν αὐτῆς οὐ γὰρ μὴ κληρονομήσει ὁ υἱὸς τῆς παιδίσκης μετὰ τοῦ υἱοῦ τῆς ἐλευθέρας. (Gal 4:30)

Paul first writes Sarah's jealousy out by introducing the quotation as "Scripture says." And although Paul's wording faithfully represents the LXX and MT traditions, there is a significant exception: Paul replaces "my son Isaac" with "the son of the free woman." This change achieves a stylistic end by maintaining his slave/free dichotomy and knits the biblical text to the paranesis which follows in Gal 5:1.[57] But Paul also wants to read the Genesis account in such a way that the traditional linear interpretation is ignored (hence his "allegory") and Isaac is an impediment to his goal. The story is not about real sons, but about figurative sons.

But is Paul not arbitrarily reinterpreting (and thus misreading) the clear surface meaning of the Genesis narrative? To the extent that the narrative is intended to link Abraham and Isaac with the Israelite "tribes," perhaps so. Again, Paul acknowledges the allegorical nature of his interpretation, that it is symbolic rather than factual. On the other hand, if I am accurately projecting how Paul read Genesis 12–22, a different system of relationships between promise and fulfillment is apparent.

---

[56] Although in *Jubilees* Isaac's role as the beloved son of Abraham is somewhat transferred to Jacob (see e.g., 22:28). Rachel's love for Jacob (Gen 25:28) had a significant precedent: "Abraham loved Jacob, but Isaac loved Esau" (*Jub.* 19:15).

[57] Hays, *Echoes of Scripture*, 112.

In this case the peculiar phrasing in the promise regarding Sarah in Genesis 17 exposes Paul's motivation in arguing from the mothers of Abraham's two sons. In Gen 17:15–16 God speaks directly to Abraham concerning Sarah: her name is changed, a son is promised to Abraham through her, she will be blessed, and she would be לגוים (εἰς ἔθνη). The RSV translates והיתה לגוים as "she shall be a mother of nations." Both the nature of the episode—direct revelation to Abraham—and the semantic character of the message would draw Paul's interpretive eye. Abraham is an ambiguous figure because his promised blessing is for two different groups, whereas Sarah is associated with the gentiles (plural) rather than a single people.

Although Paul does not cite Gen 17:15–16 here, it is clear from the context how Paul understands Sarah:

> It is written, "Rejoice O barren one (στεῖρα) who does not bear; break forth and shout, you who are not in travail; for the children of the desolate (τὰ τέκνα τῆς ἐρήμου) are many more than the children of her that is married." (Gal 4:27; Isa 54:1 LXX)

Hays suggests that with this Isaiah text Paul "metaleptically evokes the whole rippling pool of promise found in the latter chapters of that prophetic book."[58] More specifically, Paul reads Isaiah's στεῖρα as Sarah because she is called στεῖρα (עקרה) in Gen 11:30. From the wider context one might also recall the LXX of Isa 51:1–6, which provides Paul an association of "Abraham your father" and "Sarah who gave you birth" with the passing of heaven and earth, eschatological Zion, and the transformation of the ἔρημα into the garden paradise of the Lord (v. 3).[59] Moreover, στερέα ("solid"; Isa 51:1) and στεῖρα ("barren"; Isa 54:1) would certainly not have escaped Paul's eye for paronomasia.[60] Sarah is both the barren one who bears eschatological children and, with Abraham, the solid rock of redemption (Isa 51:1, 6).

In the light of this subtextual matrix, it becomes clearer how Paul read Jesus as the promised seed of Abraham (Gal 3:16), through Sarah, through whom the gentiles receive their eschatological "blessing." It is at odds, however, with the single track Abraham-Isaac-Jacob lineage

---

[58] Hays, *Echoes of Scripture*, 120.

[59] The ἔρημος verbal analogy only works in the LXX because the MT has חרבה and מדבר in Isa 51:3, but שוממה in 54:1.

[60] Στερεός and στεῖρος meet in the form στερρός (LSJ, 1641), which makes Paul's recognition of a verbal analogy between Isa 51:1 and 54:1 more plausible.

claimed by all Jews. But it is not as if Paul dismisses the idea. For him the disassociation of Isaac (i.e., Jacob/Israel) from the second element of the Abrahamic promise is more a historically cogent datum than an *ad hoc* interpretation since Israel had not become a blessing to the gentiles.

Similar to his treatment of the mothers, Paul's association of Ishmael with Jerusalem is probably based on the phrasing of Gen 12:2 and 17:20. In the initial Abraham episode, Yhwh announces to Abraham that he will become "a great nation" (Gen 12:2). Interestingly, and I believe a flag for Paul, the very same wording—לגוי גדול/εἰς ἔθνος μέγα—is used in Gen 17:20 and 21:18 referring to Ishmael. Ishmael would be "a great nation." Ishmael would also be the father of twelve princes (נשיאם/ἔθνη). (Paul could have identified the "twelve" with the sons of Jacob were he actually making the racial argument that so many readers project onto his allegory.) The same language (לגוי גדול/ εἰς ἔθνος μέγα) is explicitly applied to Jacob in Gen 46:3, and the wilderness generation in the Sinai narrative: "of you I will make a great nation" (Exod 32:10). Granted, my hypothetical Paul is reading against the text: the immediate context speaks of the covenant established with Isaac not Ishmael (Gen 17:19, 21) and the entire patriarchal story is based on the Abraham-Isaac-Jacob/Israel lineage. But this line of argumentation is consistent with Paul's pattern of reinterpreting the promise in the light of Christ and the gentile mission, so one can at least wonder whether Paul based his contratextual figurative interpretation of the Hagar/Sarah story on the twin details of the identification of Sarah with the gentiles (Gen 17:16), and the similar wording of the initial promise to Abraham (Gen 12:2) and the promise to Ishmael (Gen 17:20).[61]

One final point on the Isa 54:1 quotation: it provides further data in support of Stockhausen's principles of Pauline exegesis. Paul characteristically uses prophetic texts to gloss Torah texts.[62]

---

[61] "Contratextuality" is T. L. Donaldson's term for Paul's reading against the text ("Abraham's Gentile Offspring: Contratextuality and Conviction in Romans 4," unpublished paper, 1992). Contratextuality is related to Hays' "counter-reading" and "misreading," and should be differentiated from my use of "countertextuality." My thanks to Prof. Donaldson for situating (in personal correspondence) his "contratextuality."

[62] Stockhausen, "Principles of Pauline Exegesis," 154–58.

5.4 Why Then the Law?

Having established in Galatians that the gospel is primary and that it predates the Law—a counterclaim to the eternal Torah—Paul must assign a new role to Torah, since his motivation is not to devalue God's Law or his tradition. The actual statements about the Law are interspersed with other related issues in Galatians but the reader knows when Paul is "on" Torah because Gal 3:19 introduces the topic:

> Why then the law? It was added because of transgressions (τῶν παραβάσεων χάριν), till the offspring should come to whom the promise had been made; and it was ordained by angels through an intermediary.

Paul understands that his previous discussion of circumcision, Abraham, and his "seed" would call into question the traditional Jewish understanding of the Torah. As I have previously asserted, it was probably Paul rather than the opponents who implicated circumcision with the Law, especially in light of Gal 5:3: "I testify again to every man who receives circumcision that he is bound to keep the whole law" (see also Gal 6:13). The opponents were advocating convert circumcision but not full Torah observance, while Paul contends that accepting circumcision means one has accepted the conditions of the covenant, notably Torah observance.

But against this notion of a lawless-circumcision party, Bernard Hungerford Brinsmead notes that other features of Paul's counter-argument in Galatians suggest that the opponents were adherents of the Law understood cosmically. In other words, the opponents held to a version of the eternal Torah, as I have argued. For Brinsmead the opponents' dependence on "calendrical piety" is consistent with the cosmic Law tradition:

> Formerly, when you did not know God, you were in bondage (ἐδουλεύσατε) to beings that by nature are no gods; but now that you have come to know God, or rather to be known by God, how can you turn back again to the weak and beggarly elemental spirits (στοιχεῖα), whose slaves you want to be once more? You observe (παρατηρεῖσθε) days, and months, and seasons, and years! (Gal 4:8–10)

The other features of Galatians that Brinsmead finds indicative of cosmic Law theology are the "mystery language" of Gal 3:1–5 and

4:8–11, and the prominence of angels in relation to the gospel in Gal 1:6–9 and the Law in 3:19.[63]

The line of interpretation advocated by Brinsmead is fruitful and consistent with my reading of Galatians, which finds Paul confronting an application of eternal Torah theology among his converts. But Brinsmead's undiscerning study of early Jewish "traditions of Law" does not provide a sufficient context for situating Paul's counter argument. On the other hand, his insight that the Galatian opposition were adherents to a cosmic Law is bolstered by the notion of Abraham receiving the gospel rather than the Law, the entirely temporal role given to Torah, the denigration by avoidance of Moses and Isaac-Jacob and therefore by extension Jews and Judaism, the stress on direct revelation, and the larger context of the eternal Torah in early Jewish literature. Unfortunately for Brinsmead, no known early Jewish group fits this profile. The literature that exhibits a "calendrical piety," particularly *Jubilees* and the Dead Sea Scrolls, tends to be more stringent in Torah observance rather than less. Scholarship has overstated the case for a hellenistic Judaism that rationalized, relativized, or generally devalued Torah observance. Perhaps one could make a case that the Galatian opposition represented a form of Jewish apocalypticism not unlike that reflected in *1 Enoch*, but if my presentation in §3.4 is correct, the Enochic profile fits Pauline Christianity better than any other known early Jewish theology.

One last point on Brinsmead's position: it is very possible that the Galatian opponents were advocates of a "calendrical piety" that in some sense attached itself to Abraham as model, or perhaps even as mediator.[64] Circumcision would then be the initiation that grants access to astrological secrets. The scenario of an advocacy of circumcision without commensurate Torah observance, the prominence of Abraham, and a religious adherence to cosmic patterns (astrology) unites Galatians' disconnected theological threads. Paul advocated direct access "in Christ" to God's expectations and empowerment, so that scrupulous adherence to cosmic laws and unseen forces is bondage to the wrong entities. These lesser intermediaries are impo-

---

[63] Brinsmead, *Galatians*, 135.

[64] Recalling the visions and heavenly ascent of the *Apocalypse of Abraham*, coupled with the tradition of Abraham as astrologer.

tent to rescue people from death in this age and condemnation in the next.

5.5 Conclusion

Like the preceding case study, this chapter has focused on both subdued and overt countertextuality against the eternal Torah. Gal 3:8 achieves its full significance only when it is set in opposition to Torah texts. Of course it is not necessary to infer that "gospel proclaimed to Abraham" is an intentional countertext to "Torah proclaimed to Abraham," but as such it coheres with the explicit reconfiguration of Torah that follows. The impotent, mediated, temporally limited, guardian Torah that Paul asserts in Galatians is prepared for by his counter-claim to the eternal Torah accessible to the patriarchs.

By isolating Abraham and basing his argumentation on the Abraham narrative, Paul in effect subverts the dominance of the Mosaic paradigm in theological debate about covenant, circumcision and Torah. Although he may be the figure symbolized as μεσίτης (Gal 3:19), Moses is not mentioned in Galatians. I see a compositional strategy in Moses' absence and the prominence of the pre-Mosaic Abraham. The absence of Moses recalls 11QTemple, but Paul's strategy with Abraham more closely resembles *1 Enoch*, in which the antediluvian Enoch is the visionary whose wisdom saves (§2.5; 3.4). Enoch's pre-Mosaic revelation is based on heavenly journeys rather than a mountain theophany: Enoch is privileged beyond Moses.[65] Similarly, with Paul the more ancient figure is the preferred. He stresses the primacy of the Abrahamic promises which predated the giving of Sinai Torah (Gal 3:17–18). One might even say that the Mosaic Torah was secondary to the revelation granted these pre-Mosaic figures, and that they were more perfect because they were further removed from later deterioration.[66] It is

---

[65] The anti-Mosaic outlook of *1 Enoch* could be attributable to socio-political factors: the apocalyptic Enochists were probably disenfranchised from the Jewish cultus by a "Mosaic" authority. But the explanation could just as well be theological in nature. The earthly Torah book was viewed as a poor representation of the heavenly tablets, and Moses' experience on Sinai paled in comparison to Enoch's heavenly journeys and visions of the throne.

[66] In the context of Paul's Abraham/Moses contrast, Betz refers to Posidonius' theory of "origin and degeneration" (*Galatians*, 139), and draws attention to M.

no coincidence that, in the early Jewish theological milieu, only Paul and the author of Enoch so forcefully asserted their independence from Moses.

Hengel's treatment: "Posidonius (*c.* 135–51/50 BC) wrote his treatise on the Jews probably about a hundred years later, after the conquest of Jerusalem by Pompey in 63 BC, but the theory of the perfection of primeval times and a later decline was a widespread one. It already appears in Hesiod and—in another form—in the Yahwist and in the Priestly codex. Ideas of this kind are likely" (*Judaism and Hellenism* [2 vols.; Minneapolis: Fortress, 1974] 1.300–301). The Abrahamic (or Enochic) was more perfect than the Mosaic. Hengel recognizes that the separation of the Mosaic from the Abrahamic differs from Ben Sira's claim that Abraham "kept the law of the most High" (Sir 44:20), and especially *Jubilees'* depiction of a Torah observant Abraham (*Judaism and Hellenism*, 302).

CHAPTER 6

The Tablets and the Veil
in 2 Corinthians 3

In the context of Paul's "Christian" view of Torah, the relevance and importance of 2 Corinthians 3 is indisputable.[1] Its γράμμα/πνεῦμα antithesis (3:6) has been regularly understood in the history of Christian thought as the quintessence of Paul's thinking on the Law.[2] Yet the word νόμος does not even occur in 2 Corinthians 3. In place of explicit references to νόμος, one finds symbols that identify Paul's main subtext in 2 Corinthians 3, the Sinai narrative in Exodus 34. Paul also employs verbal fragments from Jeremiah 31, Ezekiel 11 and 26 as hermeneutical tools in his unique reading of Moses' "veiling" (Exod 34:29–35). Despite the clear presence of these subtexts in 2 Corinthians 3, there are no formal signals that Paul is working with them. There are few clear

---

[1] *Pace* L. Gaston, who contends that 2 Corinthians 3 "has nothing to do with law or Scripture ('Old Testament') or Pharisaic Jews; rather it opposes the attempt of certain Hellenistic Jewish-Christian missionaries to develop a 'divine man' understanding of Moses as a model for their own behaviour" (*Paul and the Torah* [Vancouver: University of British Columbia Press, 1987] 29). Gaston's either/or is a misread, for elevated Torah and elevated Moses go hand-in-hand.

[2] At least since Origen the letter/spirit antithesis has been used as the grounds for a differentiation between the literal and spiritual senses of biblical texts, as well as a Law/Gospel or a NT/OT dichotomy. See W.-S. Chau, *The Letter and the Spirit: a History of Interpretation from Origen to Luther* (American University Studies 7; Theology and Religion 167; New York: Lang, 1995).

182

references to the LXX of Exodus 34 and no explicit quotations introduced with citation formulae.[3] The influence of Jeremiah and Ezekiel
is only known by inference from the semantic character of 2 Corinthians 3.

Laying further in the background, but no less significant for understanding the orientation of Paul's argument, is the conviction inspired
by the Isaian scenario of the eschatological return and universal accessibility of God's presence: "the glory (כבוד/δόξα) of the Lord shall be
revealed, and all flesh shall see it together" (Isa 40:5). In 2 Corinthians
3 Paul's diminishing of Moses' glory draws from this expectation when
coupled with the disjunctive language of Jer 31:31–34. The eschatological visions of Isaiah and Jeremiah converge on the nature of God's
future acts:

> Behold, I am doing a *new thing*. (Isa 43:19)

> I will make a *new covenant*. . . . (Jer 31:31)

Jeremiah's new covenant could also be connected with the future-oriented covenant of spirit and word in Isa 59:21. The influence of these
texts is the ground for Paul's old/new disjunction in 2 Corinthians 3, his
conviction that the eschatological antitype is superior to, and somewhat different than its historical type.[4] Rather than a restoration of
past glory, the "new" represented for Paul an eschatological replacement of the "old," even if the latter remained the model. These
replacements, and the superiority of the eschatological, permeate the
Pauline corpus, but in 2 Corinthians 3 the dissimilarity overwhelms
typological continuity.[5] Paul contends that eschatological δόξα tran-

---

[3] See the catalog of citation formulae in J. Fitzmyer, "The Use of Explicit Old Testament Quotations in Qumran Literature and in the New Testament," *NTS* 7 (1960–61)
297–333. The combination of no explicit quotations yet overt presence of subtexts can
indicate a so-called "homiletic pattern" (see P. Borgen, *Bread from Heaven* [Leiden:
Brill, 1965], especially the summary on p. 51); some find such a pattern in 2 Corinthians
3 (see below).

[4] As previously noted, for want of better terminology "history/historical" and
"eschatology/eschatological" in this study generally correspond to the rabbinic
עולם הזה and עולם הבא.

[5] It may well be, as many suppose, that these texts originally meant only a renewal,
or a restoration. Nor did "new" mean "different" for Paul and other NT theologians,
since they communicated their "new" faith often by means of typologies consistent
with Isaiah's new creation and Jeremiah's new covenant. The great events narrated in

scends even the δόξα of Moses' theophanic imprint, and the experience of this δόξα is not limited to Moses, elites, or an in-group. Hence eschatological δόξα is superior to Mosaic δόξα, and it is different in its accessibility.

Despite the lack of νόμος and a heavily figurative rhetoric, there is no doubt that Paul is manipulating conventional notions of Torah in 2 Corinthians 3. Declarations like "the γράμμα kills" (3:6), the "διακο-νία of death, carved in letters on stone" (3:7), and "not like Moses" (3:13) are directed at Torah as written revelation and Moses as its mediator. Since revelation and covenant are closely linked in the Sinai narrative and subsequent biblical and post-biblical literature, Paul's use of the suggestive terminology "new covenant," especially when he qualifies it as "not γράμμα" (3:6), directly involves the Torah as an unstated yet primary *topos*. Perhaps even more important is the association of glory with Torah in early Jewish texts. The Law was viewed as coming with, or by glory: "And your *glory* passed through the four gates of fire and earthquake and wind and ice, *to give the law* to the descendants of Jacob, and your commandment to the posterity of Israel" (4 Ezra 3:19). This idea may account for the prominence of the glory theme in 2 Corinthians 3 and 4, but it does not explain why Paul needed to address the Sinai narrative of Moses' veiling that immediately precedes his communication of Torah to the people of Israel that begins in Exod 35:1.

Pauline scholarship is divided on the implications of the "new covenant" terminology. Heikki Räisänen is the most notable critic of using Jer 31:31–34 as the subtext for Paul's theological characterization of Torah. Räisänen denies that "new covenant" in 2 Cor 3:6 has anything to do with Jer 31:31–34, and argues that even if Paul derived "new covenant" from Jeremiah, in its context ברית חדשה meant only the renewal of the Sinai covenant.[6] In Räisänen's estimation, then, Paul is reading against the text. Scott Hafemann, while confessing an inaugurated eschatology in Paul and recognizing the significance of Jer 31:31–34 in 2 Corinthians 3, denies that either feature negates the lasting

---

sacred texts (creation, paradise garden, Sinai, the righteous hero king, etc.) were symbols of even greater eschatological acts of God—hence historical-eschatological typology.

[6] H. Räisänen, *Paul and the Law* (2d ed.; WUNT 29; Tübingen: Mohr [Siebeck], 1987) 240–45.

influence of the Law for Paul.[7] Although Räisänen and Hafemann are worlds apart as Pauline interpreters, they are united in their denial of Paul's radical intention with "new covenant" and the other prophetically influenced disjunctive language in 2 Corinthians 3. This chapter is devoted to restating Paul's theological separation from Moses and Sinai that is inspired by his interpretation of prophetic disjunction.

Generally Paul uses prophetic texts to assist in the interpretation of Torah texts,[8] but this is not unique among his contemporaries. In 2 Corinthians 3, however, more than any other Pauline text, Paul uses the biblical prophets *against* the Torah and Moses.[9] The disjunctive "not like Moses" and implied "not like the Sinai Torah" are unique in early Jewish texts, paralleled only in *1 Enoch* in a less explicit form. On the other hand, as I have noted, there is biblical precedent for Paul's mode of arguing against the tradition in the Isaian "new thing" (הנני עשה חדשה; Isa 43:19) and the eschatological (הנה ימים באים) "new covenant" (ברית חדשה) of Jer 31:31. Modern commentators such as Räisänen are often content to point out that Jer 31:31–34, logically or contextually analyzed, suggests only renewal or restoration of covenant affirming Torah observance, rather than a break with the Mosaic tradition. This superimposition of original intent has little to do with the intertextual phenomenon of Jeremiah's "new covenant" in the NT. Moreover, Räisänen's position is the extreme example of an extensive scholarly inattentiveness to the impact of Jeremiah's disjunctive language on the semantic character of 2 Corinthians 3 (see §6.3.1).

Along with Ezekiel 11 and 36, Jeremiah 31 was the main prophetic text that Paul used in 2 Corinthians 3 to interpret Exodus 34, the narrative of the second giving of the tablets and Moses' veiling. The goal of this chapter is to show that in 2 Corinthians 3 Paul argues (however figuratively) that the Sinai Torah, symbolized by the figures γράμμα and πλάκες λίθιναι, was characteristic of this doomed age, whereas

---

[7] S. J. Hafemann, *Paul, Moses, and the History of Israel* (WUNT 81; Tübingen: Mohr [Siebeck], 1995) passim. Hafemann's Paul appears to be Reformed, in that he promotes the permanent place of Law in Christian theology.

[8] See especially C. Stockhausen, "2 Corinthians and the Principles of Pauline Exegesis," in *Paul and the Scriptures of Israel* (ed. C. A. Evans and J. A. Sanders; JSNTSup 83; SSEJC 1; Sheffield: JSOT, 1993) 143–64.

[9] The allegorical interpretation of Sarah and Hagar (Gal 4:21–31) is similarly disjunctive (see §5.3.2), but prophetic intertexts are not the axis of Paul's argument there.

direct revelation via the Spirit characterized the new age in which he and his converts "in Christ" were proleptically participating. If Paul is thereby attacking Torah, it is only Torah understood as an eternal, suprahistorical entity. Establishing this mode of interpretation has been one of the main points of this book.

The implications of the argumentation in 2 Corinthians 3 for Paul's Torah theology can be stated in this way: the Sinai tablets were not formed according to a heavenly archetype (i.e., heavenly tablets; 2 Cor 3:3), for Paul means that written revelation is inferior to unmediated spiritual revelation. The tablets are historical revelation, and as revelation they came with wonders and real presence (δόξα), but they are not copies of heavenly forms. Eschatological revelation is mediated only through the Spirit, and is therefore superior to historical revelation through Moses.

6.1 Letters, Apostolic Authority and Glory

The discussion to this point has had little contact with the clear themes of 2 Corinthians 3: letters of recommendation, apostolic authority, and Moses' glory and veiling. It has been necessary to provide a framework in which Paul's treatment of these themes find their meaning. The δόξα Paul has in mind in 2 Corinthians 3 is eschatological in nature, so that it is an expected δόξα, not something that he is able to manifest. So why introduce the topic δόξα, and compare his διακονία with Moses' if Paul did not in fact have a basis for comparison? What, ultimately, is Paul comparing? His eschatological mysticism provides the explanation for some of these oddities in the argumentation of 2 Corinthians 3.[10] Paul introduces the topic of letters of recommendation in order to have a basis for comparison: "letters" are characteristic of the "katargetic," in light of Paul's consistent use of καταργέω for things in the present age that are abolished or destroyed at its culmination, whereas that which is engraved upon the heart is "menic" (τὸ μένον; 2 Cor 3:11). Although the katargetic age remains, its end has dawned, and Paul's

---

[10] Recalling A. Schweitzer's notion of Pauline mysticism: "We are always in the presence of mysticism when we find a human being looking upon the division between earthly and super-earthly, temporal and eternal, as transcended, and feeling himself, while still externally amid the earthly and temporal, to belong to the super-earthly and eternal" (*The Mysticism of Paul the Apostle* [New York: Seabury, 1931] 1).

message is that the menic is available in Christ. His argument is aimed at exposing the incongruity of placing katargetic requirements on menic realities.

6.1.1 Letters

If "letters of recommendation" (2 Cor 3:1) were possessed and aggrandized by Paul's opponents, as most reasonably assume, then all of 2 Corinthians 3 can be read as a semantically playful rebuke of their claim. On the other hand, since Paul binds the request for the letters to his reconfiguration of Torah, his playfulness strikes at the heart of Jewish theology. The "letter of recommendation" (συστατικὴ ἐπιστολή) becomes the asymmetrical occasion for Paul's glosses on the narrative of Moses' veiling in Exodus 34. Paul's primary word-play is to associate letters with other things written; ἐπιστολαί becomes a subcategory of γράμμα. The movement from ἐπιστολαί to γράμμα to πλάκες λίθιναι seems arbitrary unless the opponents thought of themselves as specially connected to the Sinai tablets.

Lloyd Gaston suggests that the opponents in 2 Corinthians may have been mystifying the Corinthian Christians not only with their heavenly visions and journeys, but also with their Hebrew letters, talk of the "heavenly tablets" and the biblical tradition of the Sinai tablets written "by the finger of God" (באצבע אלהים; Exod 31:18, Deut 9:10).[11] The Sinai tablets were understood among some early Jewish interpreters to be a replica of heavenly tablets (§3.2), so Paul's apparent denigration of the Exodus 34 tablets could be directed against the idea of heavenly tablets.

Obviously Gaston's thinking is consistent with my thesis that Paul opposed the eternal Torah, since the heavenly tablets in this case would represent the otherwordly nature of Torah. But the apocalyptic visionary profile that Gaston associates with the opponents fits Paul as well. Paul claims for himself unique revelation, heavenly journeys and access to mysteries, special insight into the deep meaning of biblical texts, and for those "in Christ" a form of private revelation mediated by the Spirit and freedom from bondage to invisible forces. Paul's attitude toward those "in Christ" is most apparent by contrast: "to this day whenever Moses is read a veil lies over their minds" (2 Cor 3:15).

---

[11] Gaston, *Paul and the Torah*, 155.

Although their different genres separate them, there is much in Paul that is reminiscent of the Enochic corpus, including the disjunctive relationship to Torah as divine Wisdom (§2.5; 3.4). For these reasons I think it unlikely that the opponents in 2 Corinthians 3 were solely responsible for the language of heavenly access. If both parties were claiming apocalyptic visions, neither had any leverage. The standoff between rival visionaries may account for the significance of "letters of recommendation," since they were a form of objective validation that only one party possessed.

Paul equates the "old covenant" with the request for written letters because they do not fit the eschatological nature of his message. 2 Corinthians 3 supports the proposition that letters of recommendation are characteristic of "this fading age." Thus Hays correctly observes that Paul does not just reject the request for letters of recommendation, but he turns the concept

> into a metaphor that shifts attention from his own qualifications to the Corinthian community itself as the visible fruit of his apostolic labor.... They cannot question the legitimacy of his ministry without simultaneously questioning the legitimacy of their own origins as community.[12]

I would redirect Hays, though: the letters are a subcategory of things written (γράμμα), and the equivalences asserted in 2 Corinthians 3 are among items by nature γράμμα. Thus when Hays finds a heightening of the metaphor "letters of recommendation" in Paul's echoing of his biblical subtexts (Exodus, Jeremiah, Ezekiel), he focuses on the wrong figure.[13] Γράμμα links ἐπιστολαί and the unstated theme Torah, or written revelation; ἐπιστολαί does not do the work itself because it is a poor substitutionary figure for Torah. Since there is no inherent connection between the ἐπιστολαί and Torah, the linking category γράμμα, interposed by Paul, is all important. The equivalences in 2 Corinthians 3 belong to Paul rather than the opponents.

6.1.2 Apostolic Authority

Scholarship regularly overemphasizes the relationship between Paul's exegesis in 2 Corinthians 3 and the issue of Paul's authority. In other

---

[12] R. B. Hays, *Echoes of Scripture in the Letters of Paul* (New Haven: Yale University Press, 1989) 127.

[13] Hays, *Echoes of Scripture*, 127–28.

words, as Hans Windisch argued that 2 Cor 3:7–18 was "midrash" that digresses from the topic at hand, I am denying that Paul's exegesis bolsters his authority. The reason 2 Corinthians 3 has been significant in Christian thought is that it does not relate simply to apostolic authority *per se*. This perspective stands in contrast to Hafemann's knitting all of 2 Corinthians 3 to Paul's notion of the legitimacy (ἱκανός) and sufficiency of his ministry (διακονία). Whereas Hafemann isolates the nature of Paul's ministry, I see Paul working throughout 2 Corinthians 3 with the theme of "writing." Similarly, Stockhausen persuasively argues that γράφω is Paul's "single most important verbal and thematic hook" because it unites Exodus 34 with Jeremiah 31.[14] "Writing" thus dominates both the substructure and the surface, or rhetorical structure. Thematic evidence is located in the many images in 2 Corinthians 3 deriving from the "writing" semantic field: "letters," "engraving," "ink," "tablets." While the introductory topic "letters of recommendation" (3:1) is related to Hafeman's ministry theme, it becomes little more than the convenient occasion for Paul's "midrashic" exercise, fading into the background as Paul moves from written reputation to written revelation to the unwritten nature of the new covenant. I am not suggesting that there is no relation between Paul's conception of his ministry and his argumentation from Scripture, but the theological range of 2 Corinthians 3 transcends the ministry theme. The lingering question is why Paul correlates the tablet and veil arguments with the issue of authority.

6.1.3 Glory

In 2 Cor 3:7–11 Paul makes three arguments of the same form, with δόξα ("glory") as the topic of comparison. The items compared are separated into two columns in this graphical arrangement:

	Column A	Column B
(3:7–8)	ἡ διακονία τοῦ θανάτου	ἡ διακονία τοῦ πνεύματος
(3:9)	ἡ διακονία τῆς κατακρίσεως	ἡ διακονία τῆς δικαιοσύνης
(3:11)	τὸ καταργούμενον	τὸ μένον

The implication is that Column A, which Paul associates with condemnation, death and destruction, is that which is mediated (διακονία = agency) by the glorified Moses. Column B represents Paul's eschato-

[14] Stockhausen, *Moses' Veil*, 72–73.

logical values. Scholars note that the form of Paul's argument in 2 Cor 3:7–11 matches the rabbinic קל וחומר (lit. "light and heavy"), or reasoning *a minore ad maius*. Such arguments rest on

> perceived correspondence between two statements or events and the presumed superiority of one. The argument asserts that what is true of the inferior member of a similar pair must be true also of the superior, and to a superior degree. . . . The purpose of the inference itself is only to indicate the presence of a characteristic in the superior on the basis of its known presence in the inferior.[15]

Because of the formulaic elements εἰ . . . πῶς οὐχὶ μᾶλλον (3:7–8) and εἰ . . . πολλῷ μᾶλλον (3:9, 11), I agree with Stockhausen that the presence of this form of argument in 2 Cor 3:7–11 is "clear" and "requires no special argument." But the argument form does not itself carry the weight of Paul's argument, and there is an interpretive problem with the nature of the correspondence between the two "members." I will focus on the latter issue first.

One regularly reads in Pauline scholarship that by means of these formulaic comparisons, Paul is asserting the greater δόξα of his ministry with the lesser δόξα of the Mosaic ministry. Linda Belleville's paraphrase of Paul's argument is representative of this position:

> We do not need formal letters of recommendation because we have the permanent, inward letter written by the Spirit that goes with us no matter where we minister (vv. 1–3). . . . This ministry that we represent has a glory that far surpasses the glory of the ministry that God instituted in former times (vv. 7–11). So this explains the very open way we conduct ourselves. And if it seems that we are claiming for ourselves a glory greater than others, this is because the ministry exhibits an incomparable glory.[16]

The main problem with Belleville's paraphrase is that it equivocates on the meaning of δόξα. This will be true of any direct comparison of the δόξα actually possessed by Moses and Paul. In many ways, the Sinai narrative determines what δόξα means for Paul and his contemporaries. It is the basis and antitype for the revelation of eschatological

---

[15] Stockhausen, *Moses' Veil*, 28.

[16] L. L. Belleville, *Reflections of Glory: Paul's Polemical Use of the Moses-Doxa Tradition in 2 Corinthians 3.1–18* (JSNTSup 52; Sheffield: JSOT Press, 1991) 214.

δόξα/כבוד which "all flesh shall see" (Isa 40:5). Δόξα and its Hebrew counterpart כבוד thus have a specific biblical and post-biblical referent which can be summarized as the luminous manifestation of God's presence. Δόξα/כבוד could be used in less specific ways (e.g., "fame"), but Paul's choice of the physical imprint of Yhwh's presence on Moses' face (Exodus 34; §6.2) as the "inferior" item (column A) establishes his specific use of δόξα. Thus, if Paul's "ministry" (διακονία) possesses a greater δόξα than that manifest on Moses' face, should the apostle have to argue for it? Would it not be physically evident? The glory that Paul maintains for his διακονία is not yet manifest, so in this sense it is not comparable to Moses' δόξα. Although he believes his transformation has mystically begun (2 Cor 3:18), Paul is not arguing that he currently possesses a greater δόξα.[17] Paul envisions an eschatological mountain that is typified by Sinai, where the experience of the כבוד surpasses its biblical type in every way.[18]

Now, does the very form of Paul's argument, reasoning from inferior to superior, give the argument its teeth? On the basis of my remarks above, one could conclude that as a matter of course the eschatological δόξα outshines any δόξα present in the katargetic age. I think this is in fact Paul's position. But would the notion of a quantitatively or qualitatively superior eschatological δόξα be acceptable to his opponents, who perhaps viewed Moses' δόξα as a unique experience of heavenly reality? Similarly, would they have accepted that heavenly tablets were inferior to "tablets that are hearts of flesh" (2 Cor 3:3)?[19]

---

[17] Certainly it could be Paul and not Belleville who is the equivocator here, comparing Moses' material glory with his own glory, only evident spiritually to the Pauline in-group. Some of this material/spiritual dynamic is evident (e.g., "written in your hearts"), but it does not extend to every aspect of Paul's argumentation in 2 Corinthians 3.

[18] The superiority of the eschatological to its biblical archetype is not Paul's invention. It is implicit, for example, whenever an *Endzeit* event or scenario is depicted as qualitatively or quantitatively better than the *Urzeit* (see below). Paul's vision of eschatological Zion is informed by an interpretive tradition that transfers and expands the characteristics of all significant biblical mountains (Eden, Moriah, Sinai, Horeb, Zion, "temple-mount," Hermon) to Zion.

[19] This is M. E. Thrall's rendering of ἐν πλαχὶν καρδίαις σαρκίναις (*The Second Epistle to the Corinthians* [2 vols.; ICC; Edinburgh: T. and T. Clark, 1994] 1. 190). The translation of the phrase in the RSV, "on tablets of *human* hearts," loses some of the shock value of Paul's language.

Eschatological δόξα is already assumed in the Zion tradition, but it is possible that the opponents, if they accepted Paul's eschatology, would argue that Moses' δόξα was an anticipatory experience of eschatological δόξα. Since Moses bore the imprint of God's δόξα, it cannot be judged inferior to the eschatological experience. Paul's reasoning that the eschatological is superior to the heavenly parallels *Urzeit/Endzeit* thinking: the *Endzeit* is both a return to and an enhancing of *Urzeit* conditions. Paul's use of the *a minore ad maius* argument is then a formal attempt to make this point, but his position is probably the result of assumptions about Moses' body as a perishing host of eternal δόξα, not whether the δόξα itself was inferior.[20]

6.2 The Sinai Theophany and Moses' Veiling

The presence of "Moses" in 2 Corinthians 3 is unique within the Pauline corpus, and it may well be that the context of Paul's focus here is exceptional claims by his opponents about Moses and/or the Mosaic texts and their relation to them.[21] Except for 1 Cor 10:2, in which Paul

[20] Thus I do not think that J.-F. Collange's analogy, comparing the light of a candle (Moses' glory) to the sun's light ("vraie" glory), would work for Paul (*Énigmes de la Deuxième épître de Paul aux Corinthiens; étude exégétique de 2 Cor. 2:14–7:4* [SNTSMS 18; Cambridge: Cambridge University Press, 1972] 80). It would be an outrage to his opponents.

[21] Although Hays is more right than wrong in asserting that D. Georgi "fills the intertextual space with creatures of the imagination" (*Echoes of Scripture*, 142), Georgi's analyis of Paul's opponents is often the point of departure in studies of 2 Corinthians. Georgi argues that the Decalogue was a "heavenly letter" for the Jewish missionaries (understood in the context of "hellenistic Jewish apologetics"; esp. Philo and Josephus): "The intent in emphasizing the divine origin and significance of the Decalogue was not to show its total otherness from that which is human. Instead, the Word of God was seen as intrinsic to humans. The commandments reflected both the world order and the intrinsic structure of human existence. That which was written on the tablets did not contradict that which was written within human beings; both showed the mighty will of God, which empowers and controls the world. It has already been shown that the Apologists did not see God's order and God's power (or spirit) in opposition to one another, but understood them as synonymous. Thus what was written within human beings and what was written on stone tablets could complement each other because of the conception of the Decalogue as a heavenly letter and the inclusion of the spirit motif. All this could be used as a recommendation and could be integrated with pneumatic displays. These manifestations (and the chronicles of pneumatic deeds) reflected the relationship between God and humanity in the double form of the outer

states that "all were baptized into Moses," 2 Cor 3:13 is the only time that Paul actually comments on Moses in a biblical narrative. In Rom 5:14 he states that "death reigned from Adam to Moses," but otherwise Paul mentions Moses only in relation to his traditional authorship of the Torah. A few times "Moses" is part of an introduction to a quotation from the Torah (Rom 9:15; 10:5; 10:19; 1 Cor 9:9). In 2 Cor 3:15 this takes the form "whenever Moses is read" (2 Cor 3:14).

Paul's use of Exodus 34, the narrative of Moses' glorification and veiling, to rebuff his opponents' use of "letters of recommendation" is ungrammatical in its excess. It is like using a bazooka to do the job of a fly-swatter: if the bazooka is fired there is too much collateral damage, while it is too heavy and slow through the air to be used like a fly-swatter. Does Paul really want to hit the Sinai tradition so hard? Because Paul's mode of argument is incommensurate with the apparent issue, it looks as if he has (perhaps thoughtlessly) plugged into 2 Corinthians 3 a preformed exegetical unit that predates 2 Corinthians. I would not dispute this, for certainly Paul would have been familiar with the narrative and the prophetic texts he would employ to aid his "Christian" reading of Exodus 34. But, as in Galatians where Paul moved from the lesser issue circumcision to the nature of the Law because he found more significant implications in the elevation of circumcision, so he responds to the specific issue "letters of recommendation" with arguments directed at the Sinai tablets, Moses' δόξα and the nature of Torah. Paul's asymmetric argumentation is perhaps due to his heightened rather than diminished thoughtfulness.

Although the formal presence (explicit quotations) of Exodus 34 is low in 2 Corinthians 3, the intertextual "volume" is nevertheless high.[22] The topic in 2 Cor 3:7–18, Moses' radiant face and veiling, is narrated only in Exod 34:29–35, of which there are many excerpts in the Pauline text (see below). But כבוד, the Hebrew equivalent of Paul's

---

law and the inner law" (*The Opponents of Paul in Second Corinthians* [ET; Philadelphia: Fortress, 1986] 249).

[22] "Volume" is perhaps the most useful of Hays' seven criteria for determining intertextual "echo": "The volume of an echo is determined primarily by the degree of explicit repetition of words or syntactical patterns, but other factors may also be relevant: how distinctive or prominent is the precursor text within Scripture, and how much rhetorical stress does the echo receive in Paul's discourse?" (*Echoes of Scripture*, 30).

theme-word δόξα, does not occur in the MT of Exodus 34. I conclude two things from this absence of כבוד in the subtext:[23] one should avoid prematurely limiting the amount of text from Exodus' Sinai narrative that Paul had in mind (§6.2.1); and, Paul was familiar with a LXX version of Exodus (§6.2.2).

6.2.1 Wider Focus

Paul was not limiting his attention to the veiling narrative in Exodus 34. In Exodus 33 Moses entreats Yhwh to "show me your כבוד" (33:18); this Yhwh does under specific conditions:

> And [Yhwh] said, "I will make all my goodness pass before you, and will proclaim before you my name 'The Lord'; and I will be gracious to whom I will be gracious, and will show mercy on whom I will show mercy. But," he said, "you cannot see my face; for man shall not see me and live." And the Lord said, "Behold, there is a place by me where you shall stand upon the rock; and while my glory (כבודי) passes by I will put you in a cleft of the rock, and I will cover you with my hand until I have passed by; then I will take away my hand, and you shall see my back; but my face shall not be seen." (Exod 33:19–23)

As I will show subsequently, other features of Paul's argument in 2 Corinthians 3 derive from Exodus 33, so for now it is sufficient to note his wider intertextual focus.

6.2.2 Exodus 34 in the Septuagint

The influence of the LXX version of Exodus 34 is evident in the semantic character of 2 Corinthians 3. First, Paul's phrase οὐ δεδόξασται τὸ δεδοξασμένον mimics the language of the LXX, in which perfect passive forms of δοξάζω are used to describe Moses' face (Exod 34:29–30, 35).[24] Secondly, Paul's use of ἡνίκα in 2 Cor 3:15–16 (only here in the NT) reflects the LXX of Exod 34:34:

---

[23] I exclude from the start any discussion, however interesting, of the fluidity of the Hebrew text of Exodus in Paul's day as the explanation for his emphasizing δόξα while כבוד is missing. My two conclusions well account for Paul's language.

[24] Δεδόξασται (Exod 34:29, 35) and δεδοξασμένη (Exod 34:30) render the troublesome Hebrew term קרן. The only similar use of קרן in the MT is Hab 3:4: "His brightness was like the light, rays (קרנים) flashed from his hand; and there he veiled his power."

Whenever (ἡνίκα δ' ἄν) Moses entered the Lord's presence to speak with him, he removed the veil until he came out.

For good reason, then, Stockhausen regards the ἡνίκα δὲ ἐάν construction as a signal of "assimilated text from Exodus."[25] Stockhausen draws a parallel between 2 Cor 3:16 and Qumranian *pesher* exegesis, in which a portion of biblical text would be cited followed by a form of the word פשר and an interpretation of the text for the exegete's day and circumstance. The fragments of Exodus 34 are not limited to 2 Cor 3:16, for they characterize 2 Cor 3:12–18 and can be found as early as 2 Cor 3:7 (see below). Belleville, who locates many more examples of the text-commentary pattern in early Jewish literature other than the Qumran scrolls, identifies a Pauline form of the pattern in 2 Cor 3:12–18: "Paul cites a passage of Scripture and then comments on it phrase by phrase, picking up catchwords of his text as he goes."[26] The following graphic arrangement of text and subtext exhibits Belleville's pattern:

	2 Corinthians 3	Exodus 34
Opening	ἔχοντες οὖν τοιαύτην ἐλπίδα πολλῇ παρρησίᾳ χρώμεθα (v. 12)	
Text	καὶ οὐ καθάπερ Μωϋσῆς <u>ἐτίθει κάλυμμα ἐπὶ τὸ πρόσωπον αὐτοῦ</u> πρὸς τὸ μὴ ἀτενίσαι τοὺς υἱοὺς Ἰσραὴλ εἰς τὸ τέλος τοῦ καταργουμένου ἀλλὰ ἐπωρώθη τὰ νοήματα αὐτῶν (vv. 13–14a)	καὶ ἐπειδὴ κατέπαυσεν λαλῶν πρὸς αὐτούς <u>ἐπέθηκεν ἐπὶ τὸ πρόσωπον αὐτοῦ κάλυμμα</u> (v. 33)
Comment	ἄχρι γὰρ τῆς σήμερον ἡμέρας τὸ αὐτὸ κάλυμμα ἐπὶ τῇ ἀναγνώσει τῆς παλαιᾶς διαθήκης μένει μὴ	

---

[25] Stockhausen, *Moses' Veil*, 111.

[26] Belleville, *Reflections of Glory*, 178. Belleville does not cite Stockhausen's identification of the text-commentary pattern in 2 Cor 3:16.

ἀνακαλυπτόμενον ὅτι ἐν
Χριστῷ καταργεῖται ἀλλ᾽ ἕως
σήμερον ἡνίκα ἂν
ἀναγινώσκηται Μωϋσῆς
κάλυμμα ἐπὶ τὴν καρδίαν
αὐτῶν κεῖται (vv. 14b–15)

Text   <u>ἡνίκα δὲ ἐὰν</u> ἐπιστρέψῃ πρὸς   <u>ἡνίκα δ᾽ ἂν</u> εἰσεπορεύετο
κύριον <u>περιαιρεῖται τὸ</u>   Μωϋσῆς ἔναντι κυρίου λαλεῖν
<u>κάλυμμα</u> (v. 16)   αὐτῷ <u>περιῃρεῖτο τὸ κάλυμμα</u>
                                    ἕως τοῦ ἐκπορεύεσθαι καὶ
                                    ἐξελθὼν ἐλάλει πᾶσιν τοῖς
                                    υἱοῖς Ισραηλ ὅσα ἐνετείλατο
                                    αὐτῷ κύριος (v. 34)

Comment   ὁ δὲ κύριος τὸ πνεῦμά ἐστιν
οὗ δὲ τὸ πνεῦμα κυρίου
ἐλευθερία (v. 17)

Text +   ἡμεῖς δὲ πάντες
Comment   ἀνακεκαλυμμένῳ προσώπῳ   καὶ εἶδον οἱ υἱοὶ Ισραηλ τὸ
τὴν δόξαν κυρίου   πρόσωπον Μωϋσῆ ὅτι
κατοπτριζόμενοι τὴν αὐτὴν   δεδόξασται καὶ περιέθηκεν
εἰκόνα μεταμορφούμεθα ἀπὸ   Μωυσῆς κάλυμμα ἐπὶ τὸ
δόξης εἰς δόξαν καθάπερ ἀπὸ   πρόσωπον ἑαυτοῦ ἕως ἂν
κυρίου πνεύματος (v. 18)   εἰσέλθῃ συλλαλεῖν αὐτῷ (v. 35)

The Exodus excerpts (underlined) are clear, but Belleville's structure
will not work because she has overlooked other textual excerpts that
would subvert her order. Moreover, 2 Cor 3:18 does not belong within
the structure, although it is a summary statement.

The phrase τοὺς υἱοὺς Ἰσραήλ (2 Cor 3:7, 14) is not otherwise Pauline
(see below); it derives from Exodus 34 as well and is connected with the
people's reaction to Moses' face (Exod 34:30, 35).[27] Paul employs μὴ

---

[27] The MT and LXX of Exod 34:30 differ, with great significance: the MT has Aaron
and the בני ישראל looking at the "shining (קרן) of the skin of Moses' face," whereas the
LXX has Moses' "glorified" (δεδοξασμένη) face seen by Aaron and the πάντες οἱ πρεσβύτεροι Ἰσραήλ. Paul's language reflects the LXX, so μὴ δύνασθαι ἀτενίσαι τοὺς υἱοὺς
Ἰσραήλ (2 Cor 3:7) may be his gloss on the LXX's exclusion of the בני ישראל from the
original vision of Moses' radiant face.

ἀτενίσαι in both instances: the "sons of Israel" were not able to "gaze" at Moses' face because of their fear (Exod 34:30//2 Cor 3:7) and because Moses veiled his face (Exod 34:33, 35//2 Cor 3:13). The verb ἀτενίζω occurs only here in the Pauline corpus, but elsewhere it seems to be a preferred term for seeing in visions and looking at the wondrous.[28] In Paul's eschatological contrast to Moses' glorification and veiling in Exodus 34, he uses κατοπτρίζομαι (ix) to depict the intensification of the vision of glory: whereas the "sons of Israel" were not able even to "gaze" (ἀτενίζω) upon the "glory of the Lord" mediated by Moses' face, "we all . . . reflect as in a mirror (κατοπτριζόμενοι)" that very glory (2 Cor 3:18). In Paul's eschatological scenario the mediation and particularity of the Mosaic experience are absent.

Another excerpt from Exodus 34 in 2 Corinthians 3 is the verb ἐπιστρέφω: "When [one] turns (ἐπιστρέψῃ) to the Lord the veil is removed" (3:16). Some suppose that Paul's use of ἐπιστρέπω here is an interpretive rendering of the LXX's εἰσπορεύομαι in Exod 34:34:[29] "Whenever Moses went in (εἰσεπορεύετο) before the Lord to speak with him, he took the veil off." Although there are numerous discrepancies between text and subtext, there is good reason for thinking Paul formed his text to contemporize the paradigmatic narrative by changing εἰσπορεύομαι to ἐπιστρέφω, which signifies repentance or conversion (הׁשׁוּבה).[30] The differing verbs are framed in each text by similar adverbial phrases, ἡνίκα δ' ἄν (Exod 34:34) and ἡνίκα δὲ ἐάν (2 Cor 3:16), and similar phrasing concerning the removal of the veil,

---

[28] The only relevant LXX parallel is the interesting use in Pr Man 9 of ἀτενίζω to refer to a vision of heaven: οὐκ εἰμὶ ἄξιος ἀτενίσαι καὶ ἰδεῖν τὸ ὕψος τοῦ οὐρανοῦ ἀπὸ πλήθους τῶν ἀδικιῶν μου. In the NT ἀτενίζω is peculiarly Lukan (12x). The main parallels to 2 Cor 3:7, 13 are found in Acts concerning Stephen: ἀτενίζω is used for "gazing" at Stephen's "face like an angel" (Acts 6:15), and to narrate that he "gazes into heaven and sees the glory of God" (Acts 7:55). Similarly ἀτενίζω is used for the apostles' "gazing into heaven" after the ascension (Acts 1:10). In the rest of Luke/Acts it is used for the initial reaction to Jesus' reading of Isaiah (Luke 4:20); in the context of an angelic vision (10:4) and seeing in a vision (11:6); healing (3:4, 12; 14:9); and Paul's looking at a magician (13:9). The only usages that have nothing to do with visions or the miraculous are Luke 22:56 and Acts 23:1.

[29] For an account of the debate on the relationship between Exod 34:34 and 2 Cor 3:16, see Belleville, *Reflections of Glory*, 250–53.

[30] "The substitution of this verb interprets Moses' 'going in to the Lord' as prototypical of the conversion, in Paul's own day, of those who turn toward the Lord through the spirit" (Stockhausen, *Moses' Veil*, 112).

περιῃρεῖτο τὸ κάλυμμα (Exod 34:34) and περιαιρεῖται τὸ κάλυμμα (2 Cor 3:16). The major discrepancy is the verb.

While I agree that Paul's ἐπιστρέφω is an interpretive rendering, the explanation for its presence comes from the immediate context.[31] After the initial fearful reaction to Moses' radiant face (Exod 34:30), Moses calls and the leaders "return" (שוב/ἐπιστρέφω) to him (34:31). It is after this act of returning that Moses dons the veil for the first time (34:33). 2 Cor 3:16 is in contrast to the sequencing of the Exodus narrative: now when one "returns," the veil is removed. Paul's juxtaposition is completed with the replacement of ἐπεστράφησαν πρὸς αὐτόν (Exod 34:31) by ἐπιστρέψῃ πρὸς κύριον: the movement symbolized by תשובה is now direct, no longer to or through Moses as mediator.

Before I move on from Paul's interpretation of the veiling narrative, there is one more feature of the Exodus text that, although it does not really show itself in 2 Corinthians 3, might explain the nuances of his association of writing with engraving on tablets and the veil. The text I am thinking of is Exod 32:16:

> The tablets were the work of God, and the writing was the writing of God, graven upon the tablets.[32]

I have already noted how some scholars suppose that Paul's opponents in 2 Corinthians used Hebrew writing to "mystify" the Corinthians.[33]

---

[31] Though not necessarily as far back as Exod 33:1–10 (ἡνίκα δ᾽ ἂν εἰσεπορεύετο; v. 8), which R. Le Déaut notes was read in the *targumim* as a story of repentance/conversion (Aramaic תתובא) after the golden calf incident ("Traditions Targumiques dans le Corpus Paulinien? (Hebr 11,4 et 12,24; Gal 4,29–30; II Cor 3,16)," *Bib* 42 [1961] 46–47). In 2 Corinthians 3 Paul moves, like Exod 33:7–10, from Moses alone to a collective entity (Le Déaut, "Traditions Targumiques," 45–46). Paul's "allegorical" interpretation of the veil of Moses corresponding to the veil which accompanies the *reading of Torah* corresponds to another targumic tradition: the veil of Moses is likened to the טלית, "cloak of scholar" or "leader in prayer" (M. Jastrow, *A Dictionary of the Targumim, the Talmud Babli and Yerushalmi, and the Midrashic Literature* [New York: Judaica, 1992] 537; Le Déaut, "Traditions Targumiques," 47). If Paul knew and was drawing on the figurative correspondence of Moses' veil to the טלית, he was involved in another instance of reversal of Jewish sensibility: the cloak of honor was represented as that which materially prevented non-empowered readers of Moses from seeing things as Paul did (see A. Segal, *Paul the Convert: The Apostolate and Apostasy of Saul the Pharisee* [New Haven: Yale University Press, 1990] 151–56).

[32] The RSV translates לחת/πλάκες as "tables." I have adjusted this to "tablets."

[33] Gaston, "Paul and Torah in 2 Corinthians 3," 155; compare Georgi's concept of the Decalogue as a "heavenly letter" (*Opponents of Paul*, 249). According to Exodus the

The Hebrew letters, especially if they were biblical texts, were perhaps passed off as the "writing of God."[34] Paul's proclamation of direct access to God through the Spirit for those in Christ stands in tension with inscribed tablets and written texts as intermediaries.

My proposal, then, is that Paul's unstated but strongly implied attachment of Moses' veil to Torah is connected to the language of Exod 32:16 in the LXX. The phrase "graven upon tablets" is κεκολαμ-μένη ἐν ταῖς πλαξίν. The perfect participle κεκολαμμένη is from κολάπτω, which can be used in constructions with γράμμα to denote "inscriptions."[35] The verbs κολάπτω and καλύπτω ("to cover, veil, conceal") are candidates for paronomasia, particularly in their participial forms as the stress leaves the second vowel:

κολάπτω → κεκολαμμένη (Exod 32:16)

καλύπτω → κεκαλυμμένον (2 Cor 4:3)

Paul did not need to resort to a pun to draw together the veil and Torah, since the narrative sequence of Exod 34:29–35:1 yields this association, but such word play would have appealed to Paul not only for its aesthetical value but also as a secondary reinforcement of his exegetical and rhetorical maneuvers in 2 Corinthians 3.

6.2.3 Torah and the Veil

Once again it is the semantic features of a biblical narrative, in this case Exod 34:29–35:1, that catch Paul's exegetical eye. When Moses came down from Sinai with the second tablets, his face was radiant and Aaron and "all the sons of Israel" were afraid to approach him (34:29–30). Then Moses separates Aaron and the leaders, and speaks to them (34:31).

> Aaron and all the leaders of the congregation returned to him, and Moses talked with them. And afterward all the people of Israel came near, and he gave them in commandment all that the Lord had spoken with him in Mount Sinai. (34:31–32)

Sinai tablets, written with the "finger of God" (Exod 31:18), contained only the Decalogue. In later interpretation the tablets were envisioned as the vehicles of Torah, the Wisdom of God entrusted to Israel.

[34] The nature of the writing on the Sinai tablets—the "writing of God," "written with the finger of God"—became a problem for the early Jewish exegete once they lay in pieces on the ground after the golden calf incident (compare Exod 32:19 with L.A.B. 12:5).

[35] LSJ, 971.

The Hebrew text could be interpreted so that the privileged group (הנשאים/οἱ ἄρχοντες) are more isolated from the בני ישראל. The hinge phrase that opens this exegetical door is ואחרי כן נגשו כל בני ישראל (34:32), which is taken as a sequential clause in the RSV translation above and in the LXX (καὶ μετὰ ταῦτα). It seems to me that Paul's connection of Torah and Moses' veil is based on reading the clause introduced by אחרי כן in a different way. The phrase may have been read—however ungrammatically—as a break in the narrative, referring to what would take place in Exod 35:1: "Moses assembled all the congregation of the people of Israel (בני ישראל), and said to them, 'These are the things which the Lord has commanded you to do.'" Or perhaps the phrase was taken as Moses instructing the leaders that "after this I want you to gather all the people." Again, this interpretation arcs to Moses' delivery of the covenantal commands that begin with the gathering of the בני ישראל in Exod 35:1.[36]

In effect an alternate reading of the אחרי כן-clause establishes two sets of commands. The phrase כל אשר דבר יהוה אתו בהר סיני (Exod 34:32b) represents a reserve of Torah that is not included in Exodus 35–40. The "them" that receive this totality of the Sinai revelation are the leaders rather than כל עדת בני ישראל (Exod 35:1) who are entrusted with the explicit Torah. Nowhere in this narrative does it say that all of the Sinai Torah is delivered to the בני ישראל. In light of rabbinic tradition one might conclude that my suggested readings make room for an oral and written Torah,[37] which in turn might explain Paul's familiarity with this pattern of reading.[38] But a dual Torah is not the only product of this reading: now Moses' veiling takes place between his giving the

---

[36] Considered compositionally, my suggested readings of Exod 34:32 may appear contrived. One should remember, however, two points that inspire such speculation: (1) ancient Jewish exegesis was more syntactically and semantically playful than modern critical standards allow; (2) rabbinic tradition read its authority into the Sinai revelation.

[37] The tradents of the oral Torah were the elites in Jewish memory: "Moses received the Law from Sinai and committed it to Joshua, and Joshua to the elders, and the elders to the Prophets; and the Prophets committed it to the men of the Great Synagogue" (m. Abot 1:1).

[38] Since Exodus 34 seems amenable to the sort of interpretation that locates interpretive authority in a privileged few, Paul may have studied this isolation of the oral Torah's elite tradents during his education as a Pharisee (Phil 3:5).

leaders the whole Sinai Law (Exod 34:32b), and his delivery of Exodus 35–40 to כל עדת בני ישראל.[39]

Since a dual Torah is not part of Paul's rhetoric in 2 Corinthians 3, perhaps it is not necessary to rely upon an imaginative description of Pauline or traditional exegesis of Exodus 34–40. The narrative sequence of Exod 34:35–35:1 does most of the work. Moses' second veiling takes place immediately before his delivery of Exodus 35–40. From Paul's perspective this means that this revelation of covenantal commands is by nature veiled since Moses was veiled when he spoke the words. Paul then adds that this revelation—which he figuratively terms the "old covenant" because of the influence of Jer 31:31–34—remains veiled until the veil is removed:

> To this day, when they read the old covenant, that same veil remains unlifted, because only through Christ is it taken away. (2 Cor 3:14)

Paul's statement is a "contemporization," but this does not mean that his contemporization is a contextually inappropriate overlay of the veil upon a conventional understanding of the Sinai Torah.[40] Although his reading runs counter to what is expected, and his counter-reading is attributable to his "messianic" lenses, Paul is only extending the clues he finds in the text of Exodus concerning the nature of the Sinai revelation. Torah was delivered under a veil, and it would remain so until the veil is lifted. This pattern of viewing historical, this-worldly realities—however wonderful, as in Moses' Sinai experience of the כבוד—as secondary to the eschatological is typical of Paul.

The contemporization of Exod 34:29–35:1 continues in 2 Cor 3:15–17. Paul's contemporization here is not the "this is that" form that one finds in Qumranian *pesher* texts. He contends that the Mosaic veil remains, since it is not explicitly removed before Moses begins his

---

[39] In midrash the dual Torah was indeed read into Exodus 34, but it was not exegetically grounded on אחרי כן or the distinction between groups addressed by Moses. In *Exod. Rab.* 47.1, 3, כתב לך את הדברים האלה כי על פי הדברים האלה (God's words to Moses; Exod 34:27) suggests two groups of Torah, one written (כתב לך), the other oral (על פי). Hos 8:12 is enlisted to provide a rationale for the two forms: "were I to write for him my laws by ten thousands, they would be regarded as a strange thing."

[40] For contemporized interpretation as a characteristic of midrash, see R. Bloch's "Midrash," in *Approaches to Ancient Judaism: Theory and Practice* (ed. W. Green; BJS 1; Missoula: Scholars Press/Brown University, 1978) 29–50.

instruction in Exod 35:1. But Paul qualifies himself by identifying the Mosaic veil as a "veil upon their heart" (3:15). And in a statement that parallels rabbinic speculation that in עולם הבא there would be an enabling to more perfectly interpret and observe Torah, and, even closer, the idea of uniquely empowered exegetes (e.g., Qumran), Paul contends that this Mosaic veil is only removed eschatologically (καταργεῖται) by Christ (3:14).[41]

The force of Paul's contemporization of Moses' veiled revelation is bolstered by his appropriation of בני ישראל from Exodus 34. There can be little doubt that his οἱ υἱοὶ Ἰσραήλ (3:7, 13) signals a gloss on the Exodus subtext because this is unusual phrasing for Paul; it is otherwise found only in Rom 9:27, where Paul claims to be citing "Isaiah."[42] In Exodus 34 the בני ישראל see Moses' glorified face and are too afraid to approach him (34:30). This aspect of the narrative is reflected in 2 Cor 3:7: "the Israelites (τοὺς υἱοὺς Ἰσραήλ) could not look at Moses' face because of its brightness."[43] Although the בני ישראל are mentioned next in Exod 34:32 (see above), it seems that 2 Cor 3:13 is rather a gloss on Exod 34:35:

> Whenever Moses went in before the Lord to speak with him, he took off the veil, until he came out; and when he came out, and told the people of Israel (בני ישראל) what he was commanded, the people of Israel (בני ישראל) saw the face of Moses, that the skin of Moses' face shown; and Moses would put the veil upon his face again, until he went in to speak with him. (Exod 34:34–35)

> . . . not like Moses, who put a veil over his face so that the Israelites (τοὺς υἱοὺς Ἰσραήλ) might not see the end of the fading splendor. (2 Cor 3:13)

---

[41] This is the extent of eschatological change in Torah acknowledged by most scholars: Torah's secrets are revealed, or the exegete is better able to unearth them. This eschatological hermeneutical enabling is exhibited in the Qumran texts, NT exegesis, and the esoteric wisdom of the apocalypses.

[42] Neither the MT nor LXX of Isa 10:22 have בני ישראל/οἱ υἱοὶ Ἰσραήλ. In Rom 9:27 Paul appears to have transferred it to the Isaiah text by means of verbal analogy from Hos 2:1, which he cites in v. 26.

[43] Paul agrees with the MT of Exod 34:30 rather than the LXX: the LXX says that Aaron and οἱ πρεσβύτεροι Ἰσραήλ were afraid to approach Moses, whereas the MT identifies this group as Aaron and the בני ישראל. The LXX does have οἱ υἱοὶ Ἰσραήλ for בני ישראל in vv. 32 and 34.

This negative evaluation of Moses' veiling is probably motivated by the fact that Exodus does not explicitly connect the veiling with the people's fear. Why would Moses veil the imprint of the כבוד? Paul suggests that the veil prevents gazing (ἀτενίζω) at the δόξα κυρίου until the onset of the eschaton. The new/old contrast is heightened with the intensified vision of the δόξα κυρίου and resultant transformation in 3:18:

> We all, with unveiled face, beholding the glory of the Lord, are being changed into his likeness from one degree of glory to another.

Paul's inclusive ἡμεῖς πάντες confirms his position on the eschatological reversal of the particularity of the Mosaic experience. Whereas Moses used the veil to hide the imprint of the כבוד from the בני ישראל, all in Christ will experience eschatological δόξα (Isa 40:5).

6.3 The Influence of Jeremiah and Ezekiel

In comparison with Exodus 34, Paul draws very little from prophetic texts in 2 Corinthians 3. The semantic character of verses 2–3 and 6, however, bears the unmistakable influence of Jer 31:32, Ezek 11:19, and Ezek 36:26.[44]

ἡ ἐπιστολὴ ἡμῶν ὑμεῖς ἐστε ἐγγεγραμμένη ἐν ταῖς καρδίαις ἡμῶν γινωσκομένη καὶ ἀναγινωσκομένη ὑπὸ πάντων ἀνθρώπων φανερούμενοι ὅτι ἐστὲ ἐπιστολὴ Χριστοῦ διακονηθεῖσα ὑφ' ἡμῶν ἐγγεγραμμένη οὐ μέλανι ἀλλὰ πνεύματι θεοῦ ζῶντος οὐκ ἐν πλαξὶν λιθίναις ἀλλ' ἐν πλαξὶν καρδίαις σαρκίναις. (2 Cor 3:2–3)

. . . ὃς καὶ ἱκάνωσεν ἡμᾶς διακόνους καινῆς διαθήκης οὐ γράμματος ἀλλὰ πνεύματος τὸ γὰρ γράμμα ἀποκτέννει τὸ δὲ πνεῦμα ζῳοποιεῖ. (2 Cor 3:6)

The underlined phrases are unique in the Pauline corpus, but they have a precedent in LXX texts that are thematically related to other ele-

[44] This section summarizes, with minor revisions, Stockhausen's extensive analysis of the lexical background for the unique phraseology in 2 Cor 3:1–6, her "exegetical model" of Paul's hook-word connections and textual pooling, and the thematic impact of the text pooling (*Moses' Veil*, 42–86). Stockhausen actually proposes a wider subtextual field than Jer 31:32, Ezek 11:19, and Ezek 36:26 (and their contexts) because she tries to find a home for each of Paul's unique lexical choices.

ments of Paul's argument in 2 Corinthians 3. These are the individual LXX verses from which Paul gleaned the special vocabulary underlined above:

ἐγγράφειν ἐν ταῖς καρδίαις (Jer 31:33)[45]

πλαξές λιθίναι (Exod 31:18; 34:1, etc.)

καρδίαι σαρκίναι (Ezek 11:19; 36:26)

καινὴ διαθήκη (Jer 31:31)

The phrase πλαξές λιθίναι does not require extensive comment because it belongs to the Sinai narrative that Paul glosses in 2 Cor 3:7–16 (§6.2). In 3:3 πλαξές λιθίναι prefigures Paul's treatment of Exod 34:29–35, and thereby provides the angle from which Moses' glorification, veiling and delivery of the Torah is to be viewed. The stone tablets, highly valued in the Exodus narrative as bearing the "words of the covenant" (Exod 34:28), become the item to which Paul contrasts revelation "written . . . on tablets of hearts of flesh." The πλαξές λιθίναι thus bind (as text to countertext) the prophetic material in 3:2–3, 6 to the exegesis of Exodus which is to follow.

6.3.1 Jeremiah's New Covenant

Covenant and Torah are generally not interchangeable concepts in early Jewish literature or in Pauline thought.[46] They are complementary because in the Mosaic narratives Torah and covenant are received together and inherently linked. But in early Jewish writings that elevate Torah as a cosmic entity the parallelism of Torah with ברית (or מצוה) disappears. For example, in Sir 24:23 "covenant" is parallel to the "book of the law" rather than Torah itself. In 2 Corinthians 3, however, like Gal 4:24, the notion of covenant is key: "to this day, when they read the old covenant, that same veil remains unlifted, because only through Christ is it taken away" (3:14). The ungrammatical expression, "reading the covenant" is a clue that Paul is merging Torah with covenant because of his unstated biblical subtext.

Because καινὴ διαθήκη is an unusual phrase for Paul, and since the

---

[45] Jeremiah 31 in the MT corresponds to chapter 38 in the LXX. To simplify references I cite the Greek Jeremiah 38 as Jeremiah 31.

[46] Surprisingly, תורה and ברית rarely occur as a parallel pair (Ps 78:10; Hos 8:1).

only biblical precedent for it is found in Jeremiah, most recognize this as a subtext for Paul in 2 Corinthians 3:

> Behold, the days are coming, says the Lord, when I will make a new covenant (ברית חדשה/διαθήκη καινή) with the house of Israel and the house of Judah, not like the covenant which I made with their fathers when I took them by the hand to bring them out of the land of Egypt, my covenant which they broke, though I was their husband, says the Lord. But this is the covenant which I will make with the house of Israel after those days, says the Lord: I will put my law within them, and I will write it upon their hearts; and I will be their God, and they shall be my people. And no longer shall each man teach his neighbor and each his brother, saying, "Know the Lord," for they shall all know me, from the least of them to the greatest, says the Lord; for I will forgive their iniquity, and I will remember their sin no more. (Jer 31:31–34)

The only other occurrence of καινὴ διαθήκη in the Pauline letters concerns the eucharistic tradition: "This cup is the new covenant in my blood" (1 Cor 11:25; see Luke 22:20). Outside of Paul, in the NT it is found only in Hebrews (8:8; 8:13; 9:15; 12:24). Hebrew equivalents of καινὴ διαθήκη are found in the Qumran scrolls, the most notable of which concern the "men who entered the new covenant (ברית החדשה) in the land of Damascus" (CD 8:21; 16:19; 19:33–34; 20:12).

Those who challenge Jeremiah 31 as the subtext of Paul's καινὴ διαθήκη do so mainly because they perceive that Jeremiah's new covenant is forced to carry too much of the weight of Paul's view of Torah. Jeremiah does not anticipate a new or an abrogated Torah, the thinking goes, so Paul could not have derived either concept from the prophet. Räisänen is most outspoken on the issue:

> The distinguishing features of Jer 31.31 ff. were indeed taken up neither in Qumran nor among early Christians. We hear nothing of either the law being written in the hearts of the people or of the spontaneous knowledge of the Lord that renders all admonition superfluous. There is none of this in 2 Cor 3.6 ff. either.[47]

In an earlier chapter I suggested that in dismissing Jeremiah 31 in this manner, Räisänen confuses modern exegetical standards (authorial

---

[47] Räisänen, *Paul and the Law*, 243. The context of Räisänen's denial is Paul's possible dependence on Jer 31:31–34 for his view of Torah.

intent) with the methods practiced by Paul and his contemporaries. Now I want to challenge Räisänen's claim that Paul does not otherwise use Jer 31:31–34 in 2 Corinthians 3.

Paul's phrase "written in our hearts" (2 Cor 3:2) reflects Jer 31:33, which says "I will put my law within them, and I will write it upon their hearts."[48] But his phrasing differs from the LXX:

ἐγγεγραμμένη ἐν ταῖς καρδίαις ἡμῶν (2 Cor 3:2)

ἐπὶ καρδίας αὐτῶν γράψω αὐτούς (Jer 31:33)

Contextually and syntactically the wording of the LXX would not work for Paul, who is writing metaphorically about the Corinthian Christians as his letter of recommendation.[49] "Written on our hearts," though still figurative, bonds Paul's governing metaphor with their shared eschatological imagination. Paul may not replicate the wording of Jer 31:33, but this fact does not by itself negate the theory of Jeremiah's influence.

But is not Räisänen correct that Jeremiah speaks only about the Mosaic Torah written on the heart, rather than some sort of eschatological revelation? Yes and no. The parallel "Torah"-clauses in the MT and LXX differ:

נתתי את תורתי בקרבם

ועל לבם אכתבנה (Jer 31:33)

Although the ambiguous תורתי in the MT is clearly singular ("my torah") because the verb in the parallel clause (אכתבנה) has a corresponding feminine singular pronominal suffix, both clauses in the LXX equivalent are plural, referring to "laws":

διδοὺς δώσω νόμους μου εἰς τὴν διάνοιαν αὐτῶν

καὶ ἐπὶ καρδίας αὐτῶν γράψω αὐτούς

---

[48] I am not suggesting that Jer 31:33 is the only text containing the idea of "writing on hearts"; Prov 3:3 (MT) instructs one to "write" חסד and אמת "upon the tablet of your heart," and Prov 7:3 does the same concerning מצוה and תורה. My point would be that "writing on the heart" in 2 Corinthians 3 is one aspect of the influence of Jeremiah 31; without the presence of καινὴ διαθήκη, Jeremiah's influence would not be clear.

[49] I do not think it is necessary to resort to another Greek version of Jeremiah (although it is certainly possible, especially for Jeremiah!) to explain Paul's phrasing. The LXX version of Jer 31:33 is structurally identical to the MT, except for the difference that is addressed in the next paragraph.

That Paul read the plural "laws" written on the heart is made most clear in Rom 2:15, where he comments on gentiles who do the "things of the law" (τὰ τοῦ νόμου; v. 14), and thus "they show that what the law requires (τὸ ἔργον τοῦ νόμου) is written on their hearts." According to Paul's interpretation of the LXX, what God expects people to do (τὸ ἔργον τοῦ νόμου) is to be made internal rather than codified in written documents. Räisänen can therefore argue that Paul subverts Jer 31:33, but his argument will not hold for the LXX version.

Räisänen is blind to, and many others simply overlook, what I consider the deepest imprint of Jeremiah 31 in 2 Corinthians 3, and the most important for this study. This influence is not semantic; that is, it is not the product of hook-wording. The new covenant of Jer 31:33 is characterized as "not like the covenant which I made with their fathers." Paul does not replicate Jeremiah's formula of contrast (-כ לא/οὐ κατά), but the disjunctive relationship between new and old is evident in the following pairs:

οὐ μέλανι	πνεύματι θεοῦ ζῶντος (3:3)[50]
οὐκ ἐν πλαξὶν λιθίναις	ἐν πλαξὶν καρδίαις σαρκίναις (3:3)
οὐ γράμματος	πνεύματος (3:6)
οὐ καθάπερ Μωϋσῆς	καθάπερ ἀπὸ κυρίου πνεύματος (3:13, 18)

The γράμμα/πνεῦμα antithetical pair is typically isolated without recognition of the contrasts, but this is understandable given the stunning manner in which Paul reinforces the antithesis: "The γράμμα kills, but the πνεῦμα gives life."

The last pair (οὐ καθάπερ Μωϋσῆς/καθάπερ ἀπὸ κυρίου πνεύματος) may appear tenuous because of the distance between the items, but contextually they are clearly Paul's intended contrasts. Paul notes how, by veiling his δόξα, Moses prevented the "sons of Israel" from viewing it (3:13), whereas "we all" may gaze at and even be transformed by the "glory of the Lord." Moses as intermediary hides his δόξα, but the Spirit of the Lord shares its δόξα.

I have already noted that the inclusive language of 2 Cor 3:18 ("we all") may be traced to the eschatological vision of the כבוד יהוה in Isa 40:5, but I would be remiss if I bypassed the universalism present in the text Paul actually cites, Jeremiah 31:

---

[50] Räisänen challenges the relevancy of "ink" with reference to the tablets (*Paul and the Law*, 243), but see Stockhausen, *Moses' Veil*, 50 n. 34.

No longer shall each man teach his neighbor and each his brother, saying "Know the Lord," for they shall all know me, from the least of them to the greatest, says the Lord. (Jer 31:34)

This text makes no lexical penetration in 2 Corinthians 3, but it may have inspired his figurative statement that the Corinthians were Paul's "letter of recommendation, written on your hearts, to be known and read by all men" (3:3). "Written on your hearts" is the clue that Paul has Jeremiah 31 in mind, but the odd phrase γινωσκομένη καὶ ἀναγινωσκομένη (a juxtaposition of an expected read-then-known pattern)[51] anticipates the contrasts between the particular and veiled revelation of the γράμμα and the universal revelation of the πνεῦμα that is seen by all, known by all, and read by all. These contrasts ultimately derive from Jeremiah's disjunction, "not like the covenant I made with their fathers," which undergirds Paul's rhetoric in 2 Corinthians 3.

6.3.2 Ezekiel's Tablets

The contrasts built upon Jeremiah's new covenant extend to two similar future-oriented texts from Ezekiel. Paul's mingling of these texts' imagery is founded on the theme of return from exile, which the two prophets share, as well as a significant verbal link: "they shall be my people, and I will be their God" (Ezek 11:20; 36:28; Jer 31:33).[52] In 2 Corinthians 3 only the words καρδίαις σαρκίναις (3:3) appear to have been drawn from Ezekiel:

And I will give them one heart, and put a new spirit within them; I will take the stony heart out of their flesh and give them a heart of flesh (καρδίαν σαρκίνην), that they may walk in my statutes and keep my ordinances and obey them; and they shall be my people, and I will be their God. (Ezek 11:19–20)

A new heart I will give you, and a new spirit I will put within you; and I will take out of your flesh the heart of stone and give you a

---

[51] "Perhaps it is for stylistic reasons that the simple verb γινωσκομένη is made to precede the compound ἀναγινωσκομένη" (Thrall, Second Epistle to the Corinthians, 1. 222, noting Windisch, Der Zweite Korintherbrief, 104 n. 3).

[52] The texts are virtually identical, except that the "people" are addressed in the third person in Ezek 11:20 and Jer 31:33, but in the second person in Ezek 36:28. Also, the order of the pairs are reversed in Jeremiah: "I will be their God, and they shall be my people."

heart of flesh (καρδίαν σαρκίνην). And I will put my spirit within you, and cause you to walk in my statutes and be careful to observe my ordinances. (Ezek 36:26–27)

That Ezekiel was Paul's source for καρδίαις σαρκίναις is beyond reasonable doubt. The phrase occurs nowhere else in the LXX or NT, and "flesh" as the preferred element in 2 Cor 3:3 is inconsistent with Paul's usage in other contexts. Ezekiel's contrasts of the "stony heart" with "fleshy heart" match the disjunctive pattern that Paul employs in 2 Corinthians 3. But the leap from "stone hearts" to "stone tablets," from Ezekiel to Exodus, is groundless without the intervention of Jeremiah 31. Jeremiah provides the primary disjunction "not like the covenant with their fathers" that Paul interprets as "not like" the Mosaic experience with its tablets and veil. Paul then reads Ezekiel's "not stone" as the equivalent of "not stone tablets."

Besides the aforementioned link with Jeremiah 31, there is another parallel that could have inspired Paul to argue that the eschatological revelation of the Spirit is superior to the revelation on stone tablets:

ואת רוחי אתן בקרבכם	καὶ τὸ πνεῦμά μου δώσω ἐν ὑμῖν (Ezek 36:27)
נתתי את תורתי בקרבם	διδοὺς δώσω νόμους μου εἰς τὴν διάνοιαν αὐτῶν
ועל לבם אכתבנה	καὶ ἐπὶ καρδίας αὐτῶν γράψω αὐτούς (Jer 31:33)

In both texts an internal (בקרב) change is promised. From Paul's point of view the interiority of Torah means that God is known without the intervention of others (Jer 31:33), while the presence of the Spirit is associated with a new capacity for obedience (Ezek 36:27). He equates the transformation promised in these texts with Jeremiah's expression of contrast, "not like."

6.4 The Letter/Spirit Antithesis and Torah

The most shocking of Paul's assertions in 2 Corinthians 3 are ἡ διακονία τοῦ θανάτου (3:7) and τὸ γράμμα ἀποκτέννει (3:6). Paul does not explicitly contend that the Law kills, or that Moses kills. Yet his glosses on the Sinai narrative, his use of γράμμα as the lesser element in comparisons, and his reference to "reading" (3:14–15) leave little doubt that Paul is targeting Torah in some sense. I have argued throughout this book that Paul's intention is to controvert aspects of early Jewish

Torah theology rather than unequivocally declare Torah invalid or abrogated. Paul transfers to Christ the attributes denied to Torah. Here he seems to rebut the life-giving nature of Torah.

> And thou didst warn them in order to turn them back to your *law*. Yet they acted presumptuously and did not obey your commandments, but sinned against your ordinances, *by the observance of which a man shall live*, and turned a stubborn shoulder and stiffened their neck and would not obey. (Neh 9:29)

The underlined clause reproduces Lev 18:5 with only minor deviation:

ἃ ποιήσας αὐτὰ ἄνθρωπος (Neh 9:29)   יעשה אדם וחיה בהם
ζήσεται ἐν αὐτοῖς

αὐτὰ ἃ ποιήσας ἄνθρωπος (Lev 18:5)   יעשה אתם האדם וחי בהם
ζήσεται ἐν αὐτοῖς

In different contexts Paul uses Lev 18:5 to prove that "not life" equals "not obedience" (Gal 3:12; Rom 10:5), and argues against a Law endowed with ζωοποίησις (Gal 3:21). Paul's representation of Torah is in stark contrast to other early Jewish texts that view Torah as a source of life:

> He bestowed knowledge upon them, and allotted to them the *law of life*. (Sir 17:11; also 45:5)

> To those who live in righteousness of his commandments,
>   in the Law, which he has commanded for our life (εἰς ζωὴν ἡμῶν).
> The Lord's devout shall live by it forever;
>   the Lord's paradise, the trees of life, are his devout ones.
> Their planting is firmly rooted forever;
>   they shall not be uprooted as long as the heavens last
> For Israel is the portion and inheritance of God. (*Pss. Sol.* 14:2–5)[53]

> [the Lord speaking through Aaron] For all things were set in motion when I came down, and everything was *brought to life* when I arrived. And I did not let my people be scattered, but I gave them my *Law* and enlightened them in order that *by doing these things they would live* and have many years and not die. (*L.A.B.* 23:10)

> *Your Law is life*, and your wisdom is the right way. . . . For you know that my soul has always been associated with your Law, and that I

[53] Trans. R. Wright, *OTP* 2.663 (poetic alignment retained).

did not depart from your wisdom from my earliest days. (*2 Apoc. Bar.* 38:2, 4)[54]

I cannot resist the throne of the mighty One. But Israel will not be in want of a wise man, nor the tribe of Jacob, a son of the Law. But only prepare your heart so that you *obey the Law*, and be subject to those who are wise and understanding with fear. And prepare your soul that you shall not depart from them. *If you do this*, those good tidings will come to you of which I spoke to you earlier, and *you will not fall into the torment* of which I spoke to you earlier. (*2 Apoc. Bar.* 46:4–6)

In you we have put our trust, because, behold, your Law is with us,
1and we know that *we do not fall as long as we keep statutes*
We shall always be blessed;
at least, we did not mingle with the nations.
For we are all a people of the Name;
we, who received one Law from the One.
And that Law that is among us will help us,
and that excellent wisdom which is in us will support us.
(*2 Apoc. Bar.* 48:22–24)

. . . and received the *law of life*, which they did not keep, which you also have transgressed after them. (4 Ezra 14:30)

Many of these declarations explicitly bind Torah as a source of life to obedience to its stipulations. As such, these texts do little more than extend the deuteronomic blessings-and-curses motif, but an elevation of Torah as a life-giving entity is evident as well. It should be noted that Paul's denial of ζωοποίησις to Torah has a significant biblical precedent in the "ordinances by which they could not have life" of Ezek 20:25.

It is a giant leap, however, from "Torah is not life-giving" to "Torah kills." For good reason, then, Paul only speaks figuratively in 2 Cor 3:6–7, using the symbols that derive from his interpretation of Exodus 34: διακονία, which refers to the agency of Moses, and γράμμα, which symbolizes the complex of tablets, Torah and letters. Since his subtext is known, the explanation for Paul's strong disjunctive statements might be found within the general context of Exodus 34. Three texts reflect his negative appraisal of the Sinai covenant.

---

[54] Text of *2 Apocalypse of Baruch* from trans. of A. Klijn, *OTP* 2. 633.

(1) The axiom that no one can see God's face and live (Exod 33:20) may be what Paul is referencing with his "ministry of death" and "the letter that kills." According to this line of interpretation, the Sinai covenant is characterized by the fact that only Moses can behold the כבוד and live, whereas in the new covenant scenario all are able to access the כבוד.

(2) Yhwh is a consuming presence for those who succumbed to the golden calf idolatry:

> Go up to a land flowing with milk and honey; but I will not go up among you, lest I consume you (אכלך) in the way, for you are a stiff-necked people. . . . For the Lord had said to Moses, "Say to the people of Israel, 'You are a stiff-necked people; if for a single moment I should go up among you (אעלה בקרבך), I would consume you (כליתיך). So now put off your ornaments from you, that I may know what to do with you.'" (Exod 33:3, 5)

Again one may contrast this image of God consuming the people with 2 Cor 3:18, where Paul announces that "we all" can gaze at the glory of the Lord, without being harmed, but rather will be transformed by that image. In the Sinai narrative Paul reads that God's presence is a thing to be feared, which is the reason the wilderness generation relied so heavily on Moses as their intermediary. For Paul the new covenant is characterized by direct access of all the people.

(3) The Sinai covenant is linked with the extermination of the surrounding peoples:

> And [Yhwh] said, "Behold, I make a covenant. Before all your people I will do marvels, such as have not been wrought in all the earth or in any nation; and all the people among whom you are shall see the work of the Lord; for it is a terrible thing that I will do with you. Observe what I command you this day. Behold, I will drive out before you the Amorites, the Canaanites, the Hittites, the Perizzites, the Hivites, and the Jebusites. Take heed to yourself, lest you make a covenant with the inhabitants of the land whither you go, lest it become a snare in the midst of you." (Exod 34:10–12)

Given Paul's missionary activity on behalf of the non-Jewish world, this aspect of the covenant narrative is a striking contrast with his convictions about the new covenant and the gentiles. These verses do not state that the surrounding peoples should be killed, so the covenant here, though bad news for "the Amorites, the Canaanites, the Hittites, the Perizzites, the Hivites, and the Jebusites," is not literally a covenant of death.

6.5 Conclusion

In Exodus 34, Moses' radiant face derives from the כבוד. But in the remything of Torah that stems from the Wisdom/Torah tradition, Moses' δόξα came to signify Torah itself. Moses was touched by a divine emanation, the same emanation that creates, illuminates and sustains the world: "Moses' experience at Sinai is considered to be the reenactment of the original manifestation of the glory of God and the giving of the law at creation."[55] Moses' δόξα is also the symbol that unites the primordial paradise experience with revelation mountain: "To be like Moses in [2 Cor] 3:18 is to be brought back to the experience of Adam and Eve in the 'garden of Eden,' which is paralleled to Israel's experience of God's glory at Mt. Sinai."[56] Moses is the archetype for access to heavenly realities and the eschatological repatriation of the righteous to paradise.

In this light, Paul's approach to Moses' glorification is a denial of the symbol's full signification. Paul does not deny that Moses experienced the divine כבוד, which would be a truly contratextual reading. However, by devaluing it in comparison with eschatological glory, he assigns Moses and Torah a position secondary to "the light of the gospel of the glory of Christ, who is the image of God" (2 Cor 4:4). Torah is secondary revelation for Paul. In 2 Corinthians 3 he figuratively represents Torah as written, veiled and mediated—always in contrast to direct experience of God through the Spirit for those in Christ. His motivation for reconfiguring Torah in this manner is still somewhat mysterious, but at least his hermeneutical maneuvers are detectable.[57]

One of this study's refrains has been the eschatological character of Paul's argumentation against Torah as a cosmic entity. In 2 Corinthians

---

[55] Hafemann is amplifying "the law of life" (Sir 17:11) as it was traditionally understood (*Paul, Moses, and the History of Israel*, 433).

[56] Hafemann, *Paul, Moses, and the History of Israel*, 436.

[57] In chapter 1 the Paul-and-Torah problem is presented as a conflict of Paul's eschatology and early Jewish Torah theology. In the עולם הבא the eternal Torah condemns the gentiles who refuse Torah in עולם הזה, whereas Paul embraced an eschatological ingathering of gentiles without their acceptance of Torah and observance.

3, Paul's eschatological perspective is especially prominent, featuring his distinction between the two ages and their characteristics; the antithesis of γράμμα and πνεῦμα; the future-oriented texts from Jeremiah and Ezekiel; his antithesis between historical and eschatological glories; expectation of glorification (3:11–2, 18); and a preoccupation with the Spirit (3:3, 6, 8, 17, 18). Furthermore, Paul contends that dependence on ἐπιστολαί for authority is characteristic of the fading (katargetic) age. It is striking that Paul uses the example of a much more important subject, the Sinai tablets and Moses' iridescent face, to argue against "letters of recommendation." It appears that Paul, while thinking it important to redirect the Corinthian Christians' gaze from material authority to their inner transformation, also intended to deflect them from a focus on Moses and the Sinai tablets. He does not deny that Moses' δόξα was typologically related to their future glory. Rather, eschatological δόξα outshines its biblical antitype. And if δόξα itself is surpassed, the revelation symbolized as γράμμα will be as well. Paul moves from an issue (ἐπιστολαί) that is rather trivial in comparison to a more significant element of the katargetic, the Sinai theophany with its tablets and Moses' δόξα.

The letters are tokens of mediated revelation. They speak of an agency that must be recognized, a tapping into the legitimacy of Moses. Paul, on the other hand, does not attach to Moses, but separates himself. He thus embodies the prophetic disjunction. Figuratively, yet consistently and clearly, he contends for open access of all to God, manifest outwardly and inwardly and transforming: "known and read by all"; "it is *manifest* that you are a letter of Christ"; "we speak boldly"; "the veil is removed"; "unveiled faces gazing at the image." Letters are irrelevant when people are offered unmediated access to the transforming image.

CHAPTER 7

Conclusion

This study has attempted to set Paul-and-Torah in its theological context and then account for Paul's troubling declarations about the nature of Torah. The context of Paul-and-Torah was the early Jewish elevation of the Sinai Torah as the preeminent intermediary between God and the phenomenal world. This elevated, or eternal, Torah was the agent of creation, the final judge, the one path to the celestial world. Access to the invisible realms was gained through contemplation of Torah, discovering the secrets hidden in, with and under its letters. The eternal Torah was uniquely concentrated in Zion. If the gentile world possessed any true wisdom, it was derivative of Israel's Torah, the Wisdom that emanated from God before all else. All nations rejected the eternal Torah except the Jews; Torah would hold a grudge, for the nations would be rejected eschatologically. The Torah that condemns gentiles is incompatible with Paul's Zion eschatology, which welcomes a group of gentiles to the world mountain as fellow heirs of the Jews, irrespective of their relationship to Torah.[1] For Paul, Torah was God's time bound revelation, a gift for the Jews alone, in this "fading" age.[2]

---

[1] Paul's gentile converts may bring gifts to Zion (e.g., the collection), but it seems unlikely that Paul could have shared the outlook of those post-exilic texts that identified the convergence at Zion with Jacob's revenge, the looting or condemnation of the nations, or their enslavement (e.g., Isa 60:11–14; Joel 3:10–17). At the very least, Paul's "wild olives" (Rom 11:17–24) would not be the Jews' slaves.

[2] Although Paul did not understand the choice, arguing strenuously in Galatians against it, gentiles could accept the yoke of Torah (Gal 5:3). But Torah was a gift of the

Both the eternal Torah and Paul's Zion eschatology were exegetically engendered, which means they were theological developments based on textual interrelationships, the semantic character of specific texts, and the midrashic ingenuity of the interpreter. Paul's depreciation of Torah was a similar development, but it was addressed to the reconfiguration of the Torah image set so that Christ would fill the same theological space as the eternal Torah. Christ not Torah was Wisdom, the agent of creation, the sole intermediary between heaven and earth, the way of ascension, the eschatological revelation communicated directly through the Spirit, the conqueror of the oppressive powers of this age (Sin and Death), the unifier of Jew and gentile, the eschatological judge, and the Lord of the invisible realms. If Torah is not the means of transcendence, gentiles do not have to go through Torah to participate in the eschaton that has mystically dawned.

Paul's exegetical reconfiguration is evident in the Christ/Torah antithesis of Rom 9:30–10:13, in which he conflates two "stone" texts in a unique manner (Isa 8:14; 28:16) to form a new text with a decidedly different meaning. The new text, Rom 9:33, is an example of Pauline countertextuality: its language mimics assertions about Torah in Sirach 24 and 32, though now it is Christ who rescues his believers from eschatological "shame." This counterpoint to Sirach's identification of Wisdom with Torah is reinforced in Rom 10:6–9: Paul restates Deut 30:14 and Bar 3:29 as an affirmation of Christ rather than Torah. In Galatians 3–4 Paul realigns Abraham and the promises with Christ and the gospel. In contrast to the many early Jewish texts that assert that Israel's pre-Sinai patriarchs knew Torah and were observant (e.g., Gen 26:5; Sir 44:19–21), Paul states that Abraham received the gospel beforehand (Gal 3:8). This "gospel" is identified as the promised blessing to the gentiles (Gen 12:3; 18:18). Although it is not explicitly stated in Galatians, Paul's argumentation and theological values betray a merging of the second half of the Abrahamic promise with Zion eschatology, a move suggested by Isa 51:1–8. Paul's reconfiguration of Torah is completed in 2 Cor 3:1–4:6, where he interprets the veiling episode in Exodus 34 with the assistance of Jer 31:31–34 and Ezek 36:24–38. The

---

Jews, not the gentiles (Rom 9:4). It is likely that Torah-observant gentiles were compelled to perfect obedience since their covenantal relationship with the Jewish God was not a birthright (see L. Gaston, *Paul and the Torah* [Vancouver: University of British Columbia Press, 1987] 9–34).

Sinai Torah is inferior to its eschatological counterpart because it is written, mediated, veiled, and accompanied by death. Every person "in Christ" has access to God's כבוד, whereas only Moses could experience it at Sinai.

Paul's exegetical or intertextual reconfiguration has often been interpreted as if its target was Torah itself, and by extension the other pillars of Judaism. It seems clear from Romans that Paul battled this perception of his motives. 2 Corinthians 3 makes it difficult to think otherwise, especially since Paul distances himself from Moses. Thus Paul's affirmations of Torah's value and worth (e.g., Rom 7:12, 14), and his positive identification with it (Rom 3:31), betray a man with confused convictions, or possibly a deceiver. But if Paul's derogation is addressed to the image of Torah that condemned the gentiles and thus contradicted the one God's promise to bless the whole world in Abraham, it is unnecessary to think of Paul as an ignorant Jew who misapprehended the nature of the Jewish Law, or as an inconsistent and confused propagandist for a new religion selling itself by slandering its predecessor. Today it is reasonable to think of diverse Judaisms rather than one form of Judaism in the first century, so there should be room within this diversity for a messianic Pharisee who disagrees with some trends within the Jewish theology of his day.

Paul was not the only early Jewish author rethinking the projection of Torah into the celestial realms or challenging the sufficiency of the mosaic Torah. In *Jubilees* the heavenly tablets seem to be the source or archetype of the Sinai Torah, and therefore transcend Torah as a celestial repository of still hidden knowledge. The secret books of 4 Ezra 14 are inherently linked to the Mosaic revelation, but are presented as qualitatively better than the written Torah. Whereas the heavenly tablet image and the secret books of 4 Ezra attach themselves to Moses as they are supplementing the Mosaic Torah, the *Temple Scroll* of Qumran and *1 Enoch* separate themselves. The *Temple Scroll* (11QT) is a radical rewrite of the Mosaic Torah that achieves a degree of separation from Moses and his books. Moses is written out of this rewritten Torah, which presents itself as a "greater than" Torah. Unlike 11QTemple, *1 Enoch* does not superimpose itself on a Mosaic framework. By nature *1 Enoch* is a challenge to the sufficiency of the Mosaic Torah. Although it almost never addresses the Law, *1 Enoch* is presented as a more ancient apocalyptic revelatory text whose authority and value rivals, and perhaps was intended to surpass, the Mosaic Torah. *1 Enoch* promises access to secrets about the heavenly world and the future that are not available in the books of Moses. In creating this implied separation from Moses, *1 Enoch* is the only real parallel to the Torah perspective of the Christian Paul.[3] Of course, the vast difference between the Enochic and Pauline genres make the comparison difficult. Nevertheless both traditions challenge the adequacy of the Mosaic Torah in transcending this world.

[3] It might be argued that Paul used a Mosaic framework because he presented Christ as a new Torah, or because he viewed Christ as the Wisdom that was otherwise associated with Torah in Jewish theology. In this sense 11QTemple might be a better analogue than *1 Enoch*. But Paul mindfully distanced his gospel from Moses, particularly in 2 Corinthians 3. Moreover, Paul need not have abandoned the symbols and mode of expression of his sacred literature in order to oppose what he considered to be misinterpretations of it.

Bibliography

Aageson, J. W. "Typology, Correspondence, and the Application of Scripture in Romans 9–11." *JSNT* 31 (1987): 51–72.

Aland, Barbara, et. al., editors. *Novum Testamentum Graece*. 27th edition. Stuttgart: Deutsche Bibelgesellschaft, 1993.

Albl, Martin C. *"And Scripture Cannot Be Broken": The Form and Function of the Early Christian* Testimonia *Collections*. NovTSupp 96. Leiden: Brill, 1999.

Alexander, Phillip S. "Jewish Law in the Time of Jesus: Towards a Clarification of the Problem." In *Law and Religion*, pp. 44–58. Edited by Barnabas Lindars. Cambridge: James Clarke, 1988.

———. "Rabbinic Judaism and the New Testament." *ZNW* 74 (1983): 237–246.

———. "Retelling the Old Testament." In *It is Written: Scripture Citing Scripture. Essays in Honour of Barnabas Lindars*, pp. 99–121. Edited by D. A. Carson and H. G. M. Williamson; Cambridge: Cambridge University Press, 1988.

Allison, Dale C. *The New Moses: A Matthean Typology*. Minneapolis: Augsburg Fortress, 1993.

Alter, Robert. *The World of Biblical Literature*. New York: Basic Books, 1992.

Amir, Yehoshua. "Authority and Interpretation of Scripture in the Writings of Philo." In *Mikra: Text, Translation, Reading and Interpretation of the Hebrew Bible in Ancient Judaism and Early Christianity*, pp. 421–53. Edited by M. J. Mulder. CRINT. Assen/Maastricht: Van Gorcum; Philadelphia: Fortress, 1988.

Argall, Randal A. 1 Enoch *and Sirach: A Comparative Literary and Conceptual Analysis of the Themes of Revelation, Creation and Judgment*. SBLEJL 8. Atlanta: Scholars Press, 1995.

Avemaria, Friedrich and Lichtenberger, Hermann, editors. *Bund und Tora.* WUNT 92. Tübingen: Mohr [Siebeck], 1996.

Badenas, Robert. *Christ the End of the Law.* JSNTSup 10. Sheffield: JSOT, 1985.

Bandstra, Andrew John. *The Law and the Elements of the World: An Exegetical Study on Aspects of Paul's Teaching.* Kampen: Kok, 1964.

Banks, Robert. "The Eschatological Role of the Law in Pre- and Post-Christian Jewish Thought." In *Reconciliation and Hope*, pp. 173–85. Edited by R. Banks. Exeter: Paternoster, 1974.

————. *Jesus and the Law in the Synoptic Tradition.* SNTSMS 28. Cambridge: Cambridge University Press, 1975.

Barr, James. *Biblical Words for Time.* Naperville: Allenson, 1962.

Barrett, C. K. "The Allegory of Abraham, Sarah and Hagar in the Argument of Galatians." In *Essays on Paul*, pp. 154–70. London: SPCK, 1982.

————. *A Commentary on the Epistle to the Romans.* HNTC. New York: Harper and Row, 1967.

————. *A Commentary on the First Epistle to the Corinthians.* HNTC. New York: Harper and Row, 1968.

————. *A Commentary on the Second Epistle to the Corinthians.* HNTC. New York: Harper and Row, 1973.

————. *Freedom and Obligation: A Study of the Epistle to the Galatians.* Philadelphia: Westminster, 1985.

Barth, Markus. "Die Stellung des Paulus zu Gesetz und Ordnung." *EvTh* 33 (1973): 496–526. Reprinted in *Die Israelfrage nach Röm 9–11*, pp. 245–87. Edited by L. De Lorenzi. Rome: Abtei von St Paul, 1977.

Basser, Herbert W. "The Development of the Pharasaic Idea of Law as a Sacred Cosmos." *JSJ* 16 (1985): 104–16.

Bassler, Jouette M., editor. *Pauline Theology. Volume 1: Thessalonians, Philippians, Galatians, Philemon.* Minneapolis: Fortress, 1991.

Beal, Timothy K. "Ideology and Intertextuality: Surplus of Meaning and Controlling the Means of Production." In *Reading between Texts: Intertextuality and the Hebrew Bible*, pp. 27–39. Edited by Danna Nolan Fewell. Louisville: Westminster John Knox, 1992.

Bechtler, Steven R. "Christ, the Τέλος of the Law: The Goal of Romans 10:4." *CBQ* 56 (1994): 288–308.

Beker, J. Christiaan. *Paul the Apostle: The Triumph of God in Life and Thought.* Philadelphia: Fortress, 1980.

Bekken, Per Jarle. "Paul's Use of Deut 30,12–14 in Jewish Context. Some Observations." In *The New Testament and Hellenistic Judaism*, pp. 182–203. Edited by Peder Borgen and Soren Giverson. Aarhus: Aarhus University Press, 1995; reprinted by Hendrickson, 1997.

Belleville, Linda L. *Reflections of Glory: Paul's Polemical Use of the Moses-Doxa Tradition in 2 Corinthians 3.1–18.* JSNTSup 52. Sheffield: JSOT Press, 1991.

Berlin, Adele. *The Dynamics of Biblical Parallelism.* Bloomington: Indiana University Press, 1985.

Betz, Hans Dieter. *Galatians: A Commentary on Paul's Letter to the Churches in Galatia.* Hermeneia. Philadelphia: Fortress, 1979.

————. "In Defense of the Spirit: Paul's Letter to the Galatians as a Document of Early Christian Apologetics." In *Aspects of Religious Propaganda in Judaism and Early Christianity*, pp. 99–114. Edited by Elizabeth Schüssler Fiorenza. Studies in Judaism and Christianity in Antiquity 2. Notre Dame: Notre Dame University Press, 1976.

Betz, Otto. "The Eschatological Interpretation of the Sinai-Tradition in Qumran and in the New Testament." *RevQ* 6 (1967): 89-108.

————. "Jesus and the Temple Scroll." In *Jesus and the Dead Sea Scrolls*, pp. 75-103. ABRL. Edited James H. Charlesworth. New York: Doubleday, 1992.

Black, Matthew, editor. *Apocalypsis Henochi Graece.* Leiden: Brill, 1970.

Black, Matthew. *The Book of Enoch or 1 Enoch.* Leiden: Brill, 1985.

Bläser, Peter. *Das Gesetz bei Paulus.* NTAbh 19. Münster: Aschendorff, 1961.

Blank, Sheldon Haas. "The Septuagint Rendering of the Old Testament Terms for Law." *HUCA* 7 (1930): 259-83.

Bloch, Renée. "Methodological Note for the Study of Midrash." In *Approaches to Ancient Judaism: Theory and Practice*, pp. 51-75. Edited by William Scott Green. BJS 1. Missoula: Scholars Press, 1978.

————. "Midrash." In *Approaches to Ancient Judaism: Theory and Practice*, pp. 29-50. Edited by William Scott Green. BJS 1. Missoula: Scholars Press, 1978.

Boccaccini, Gabriele. *Middle Judaism: Jewish Thought, 300 B.C.E. to 200 C.E.* Minneapolis: Fortress, 1990.

————. "The Preexistence of the Torah: A Commonplace in Second Temple Judaism or a Later Rabbinic Development?" *Henoch* 17 (1995): 329-350.

Bockmuehl, Markus N. A. *Revelation and Mystery in Ancient Judaism and Pauline Christianity.* WUNT 2. 36. Tübingen: Mohr [Siebeck], 1990.

Borgen, Peder. *Bread from Heaven.* Leiden: Brill, 1965.

————. "Some Hebrew and Pagan Features in Philo's and Paul's Interpretation of Hagar and Ishmael." In *The New Testament and Hellenistic Judaism*, pp. 151–64. Edited by Peder Borgen and Soren Giverson. Aarhus: Aarhus University Press, 1995; reprinted by Hendrickson, 1997.

Bowker, J. W. "'Merkabah' Visions and the Visions of Paul." *JSS* 16 (1971): 157-73.

Boyarin, Daniel. *Intertextuality and the Reading of Midrash*. Bloomington: Indiana University Press, 1990.

——. *A Radical Jew: Paul and the Politics of Identity*. Berkeley: University of California Press, 1994.

Brewer, David Instone. *Techniques and Assumptions in Jewish Exegesis before 70 CE*. Texte und Studien zum Antike Judentum 30. Tübingen: Mohr [Siebeck], 1992.

Brinsmead, Bernard Hungerford. *Galatians — Dialogical Response to Opponents*. SBLDS 65. Chico: Scholars Press, 1982.

Bring, Ragnar. "Paul and the Old Testament: A Study of the Ideas of Election, Faith and Law in Paul, with Special Reference to Romans 9:30 - 10:13." *ST* 25 (1971): 21–60.

Brooke, George J. *Exegesis at Qumran: 4Q Florilegium in its Jewish Context*. JSOTSup 29. Sheffield: JSOT, 1985.

——. "The Temple Scroll: a Law unto Itself?" In *Law and Religion*, pp. 34-43. Edited by Barnabas Lindars. Cambridge: James Clarke, 1988.

——, editor. *Temple Scroll Studies: Papers Presented at the International Symposium on the Temple Scroll*. JSPSup 7. Sheffield: JSOT, 1989.

Bugge, C. "Das Gesetz und Christus nach der Anschauung der ältesten Christengemeinde." *ZNW* 4 (1903): 89–110.

Bultmann, Rudolf. "Αἰσχύνω, κτλ." *Theological Dictionary of the New Testament*, volume 1, pp. 189–91. Edited by Gerhard Kittel. Translated by G. Bromiley. Grand Rapids: Eerdmans, 1964.

——. "The History of Religions Background of the Prologue to the Gospel of John." In *Interpretation of John*, pp. 18-35. Edited by J. Ashton. London: SPCK, 1986.

——. *Theology of the New Testament*. 2 vols. New York: Charles Scribner's Sons, 1955.

Burney, C. F. "Christ as the Αρχη of Creation." *JTS* 27 (1926): 160–77.

Burton, Ernest De Witt. *A Critical and Exegetical Commentary on the Epistle to the Galatians*. ICC 35. Edinburgh: T. and T. Clark 1921.

Callan, Terrance. "Pauline Midrash: The Exegetical Background of Gal 3:19b." *JBL* 99 (1980): 549–67.

Callaway, Phillip R. "Extending Divine Revelation: Micro-Compositional Strategies in the Temple Scroll." In *Temple Scroll Studies: Papers Presented at the International Symposium on the Temple Scroll*, pp. 149–62. Edited by George J. Brooke. JSPSup 7. Sheffield: JSOT, 1989.

Calvert, Nancy. "Abraham and Idolatry: Paul's Comparison of Obedience to the Law with Idolatry in Galatians 4.1–10." In *Paul and the Scriptures of Israel*, pp. 222–37. Edited by Craig A. Evans and James A. Sanders. JSNTSup 83; SSEJC 1. Sheffield: JSOT, 1993.

Cerfaux, Lucien. *Christ in the Theology of St. Paul.* Translated by G. Webb and A. Walker. New York: Herder and Herder, 1959.

Charles, R. H. *The Book of Enoch or 1 Enoch.* Oxford: Clarendon, 1912.

Charlesworth, James H., editor. *Jesus and the Dead Sea Scrolls.* ABRL. New York: Doubleday, 1992.

———. *The Old Testament Pseudepigrapha.* 2 volumes. Garden City: Doubleday, 1983.

Chester, Andrew. "Citing the Old Testament." In *It is Written: Scripture Citing Scripture. Essays in Honour of Barnabas Lindars*, pp. 141–69. Edited by D. A. Carson and H. G. M. Williamson; Cambridge: Cambridge University Press, 1988.

———. "Jewish Messianic Expectations and Mediatorial Figures and Pauline Christology." In *Paulus und das antike Judentum*, pp. 17–89. Edited by M. Hengel and U. Heckel. Tübingen: Mohr [Siebeck], 1991.

Chilton, Bruce D. "Commenting on the Old Testament (with Particular Reference to the Pesharim, Philo, and Mekilta)." In *It is Written: Scripture Citing Scripture. Essays in Honour of Barnabas Lindars*, pp. 122–40. Edited by D. A. Carson and H. G. M. Williamson; Cambridge: Cambridge University Press, 1988.

———. *The Glory of Israel: The Theology and Provenience of the Isaiah Targum.* JSOTSup 23. Sheffield: JSOT, 1982.

———. *Judaic Approaches to the Gospels.* International Studies in Formative Christianity and Judaism 2. Atlanta: Scholars Press, 1994.

Clifford, Richard J. *The Cosmic Mountain in Canaan and the Old Testament.* HSM 4. Cambridge, MA: Harvard University Press, 1972.

Cohn-Sherbok, Dan. "Paul and Rabbinic Exegesis." In *Rabbinic Perspectives on the New Testament*, pp. 67–86. Studies in the Bible and Early Christianity 28. Lewiston: Mellen, 1990.

Collange, Jean-Francois. *Énigmes de la Deuxième épître de Paul aux Corinthiens; étude exégétique de 2 Cor. 2:14–7:4.* SNTSMS 18. Cambridge: Cambridge University Press, 1972.

Conzelmann, Hans. "The Mother of Wisdom." In *The Future of Our Religious Past: Essays in Honour of Rudolf Bultmann*, pp. 230–43. Edited by James M. Robinson. Translated by Charles E. Carlston and Robert P. Scharlemann. New York: Harper and Row, 1971.

Cosgrove, Charles H. *The Cross and the Spirit: A Study in the Argument and Theology of Galatians.* Macon: Mercer University Press, 1989.

———. "The Law Has Given Sarah No Children (Gal. 4:21–30)." *NovT* 29 (1987): 219–35.

———. "The Mosaic Law Preaches Faith: A Study in Galatians 3." *WTJ* 41 (1978): 146–64.

Cranfield, C. E. B. *Romans*. 2 vols. ICC. Edinburgh: T. and T. Clark, 1975–79.

———. "Some Notes on Romans 9:30–33." In *Jesus und Paulus: Festschrift W. G. Kummel*, pp. 35–43. Edited by E. E. Ellis and E. Grässer. Göttingen: Vandenhoeck und Ruprecht, 1975.

———. "St. Paul and the Law." *SJT* 17 (1964): 43–68.

Dahl, Nils. "Contradictions in Scripture." In *Studies in Paul*, pp. 159–77. Minneapolis: Augsburg, 1977.

———. "History and Eschatology in the Light of the Dead Sea Scrolls." In *The Future of Our Religious Past: Essays in Honour of Rudolph Bultmann*, pp. 9–28. Edited by James M. Robinson. Translated by Charles E. Carlston and Robert P. Scharlemann. New York: Harper and Row, 1971.

Danby, Herbert, translator. *The Mishnah*. Oxford: Oxford University Press, 1933.

Daube, David. "Alexandrian Methods of Interpretation and the Rabbis." In *Festschrift Hans Lewald*, pp. 27–43. Basler Juristischen Fakultät. Basel: Verlag Helbing and Lichtenhahn, 1953.

———. "ἐξουσία in Mark I 22 and 27." *JTS* 39 (1938): 45–59.

———. "Rabbinic Methods of Interpretation and Hellenistic Rhetoric," *HUCA* 32 (1949): 239–63.

Davies, W. D. "Law in First-Century Judaism." In *Interpreter's Dictionary of the Bible*, volume 3, pp. 89–95. Edited by G. A. Buttrick, et al. New York: Abingdon, 1962. Reprinted in *Jewish and Pauline Studies*, pp. 3–26. Philadelphia: Fortress, 1984.

———. "Law in the New Testament." In *Interpreter's Dictionary of the Bible*, volume 3, pp. 95–102. Edited by G. A. Buttrick, et al. New York: Abingdon, 1962. Reprinted in *Jewish and Pauline Studies*, pp. 227–42. Philadelphia: Fortress, 1984.

———. "Paul and the Law: Reflections on Pitfalls in Interpretation." In *Paul and Paulinism, FS Charles K. Barrett*, pp. 4–16. Edited by Morna D. Hooker and S. G. Wilson. London: SPCK, 1982. Reprinted in *Jewish and Pauline Studies*, pp. 91–122.

———. *Paul and Rabbinic Judaism*. 4th edition. Philadelphia: Fortress, 1980.

———. *The Setting of the Sermon on the Mount*. Cambridge: Cambridge University Press, 1964.

———. *Torah in the Messianic Age and/or Age to Come*. JBL Monograph Series 7. Philadelphia: SBL, 1952.

Dedering, S. *The OT in Syriac According to the Peshitta Version*. Peshitta Institute, 4. 3. Leiden, Brill, 1973.

Delling, Gerhard. "ἀργός, ἀργέω, καταργέω." *Theological Dictionary of the New Testament*, volume 1, pp. 452–54. Edited by Gerhard Kittel. Translated by G. Bromiley. Grand Rapids: Eerdmans, 1964.

Démann, Paul. "Moïse et la loi dans la pensée de Saint Paul." In *Moïse, l'homme de l'alliance*, pp. 189–242. Cahiers Sioniens. Paris: Desclèe, 1955.

Demsky, Aaron and Bar-Ilan, Meir. "Writing in Ancient Israel and Early Judaism." In *Mikra: Text, Translation, Reading and Interpretation of the Hebrew Bible in Ancient Judaism and Early Christianity*, pp. 1–38. Edited by M. J. Mulder. CRINT. Assen/Maastricht: Van Gorcum; Philadelphia: Fortress, 1988.

Derrett, John Duncan Martin. *Law in the New Testament*. London: Darton, Longman and Todd, 1970.

Desjardins, M. "Law in 2 Baruch and 4 Ezra." *SR* 14 (1985): 25–37.

Dey, Lala K. K. *The Intermediary World and Patterns of Perfection in Philo and Hebrews*. SBLDS 25. Missoula: Scholars Press, 1975.

Di Lella, Alexander A. "Wisdom of Ben–Sira." *Anchor Bible Dictionary*, volume 6, pp. 931–45. Edited by David Noel Freedman. New York: Doubleday, 1992.

Díez Macho, Alejandro. *Neophyti 1: Targum Palestinense MS de la Bibleoteca Vaticana*. 5 volumes. Madrid: Consejo Superior de Investigaciones Cientificas, 1968–79.

Dimant, Devorah. "Use and Interpretation of Mikra in the Apocrypha and Pseudepigrapha." In *Mikra: Text, Translation, Reading and Interpretation of the Hebrew Bible in Ancient Judaism and Early Christianity*, pp. 379–419. Edited by M. J. Mulder. CRINT. Assen/Maastricht: Van Gorcum; Philadelphia: Fortress, 1988.

Dinter, Paul E. "Paul and the Prophet Isaiah." *BTB* 13 (1983): 48–52.

———. "The Remnant of Israel and the Stone of Stumbling according to Paul." Ph. D. Dissertation. Union Theological Seminary, 1980.

Dix, G. H. "The Enochic Pentateuch." *JTS* 27 (1926): 29–42.

Dodd, C. H. *According to the Scriptures: the Sub-structure of New Testament Theology*. London: Nisbet and Co., 1952.

———. *The Bible and the Greeks*. London: Hodder and Stoughton, 1934.

———. "ENNOMOS CRISTOU." In *Studia Paulina, In hon. J. de Zwaan*, pp. 96–110. Haarlem: Bohn, 1953.

Donaldson, Terence L. "Abraham's Gentile Offspring: Contratextuality and Conviction in Romans 4." Unpublished paper, 1992.

———. "The 'Curse of the Law' and the Inclusion of the Gentiles: Galatians 3.13–14." *NTS* 32 (1986): 94–112.

———. "'The Gospel That I Proclaim among the Gentiles' (Gal. 2:2): Universalistic or Israel-Centred?" In *Gospel in Paul: Studies on Corinthians, Galatians and Romans for Richard N. Longenecker*, pp. 166–93. Edited by L. Ann Jervis and Peter Richardson. JSNTSup 108. Sheffield: Sheffield Academic, 1994.

_____. *Jesus and the Mountain. A Study in Matthean Theology*. JSNTSup 8. Sheffield: JSOT, 1985.

_____. *Paul and the Gentiles: Remapping the Apostle's Convictional World*. Minneapolis: Fortress, 1997.

_____. "Proselytes or 'Righteous Gentiles'? The Status of Gentiles in Eschatological Pilgrimage Patterns of Thought." *JSP* 7 (1990): 3–27.

_____. "'Riches for the Gentiles' (Rom. 11.12): Israel's Rejection and Paul's Gentile Mission." *JBL* 112 (1993): 81–98.

_____. "Zealot and Convert: The Origin of Paul's Christ-Torah Antithesis." *CBQ* 51 (1989): 655–82.

Dülmen, Andrea van. *Die Theologie des Gesetzes bei Paulus*. SBM 5. Stuttgart: Katholisches Bibelwerk, 1968.

Dunn, James D. G. *A Commentary on the Epistle to the Galatians*. Black's New Testament Commentaries. London: A. and C. Black, 1993.

_____. "How New was Paul's Gospel? The Problem of Continuity and Discontinuity." In *Gospel in Paul: Studies on Corinthians, Galatians and Romans for Richard N. Longenecker*, pp. 367–88. Edited by L. Ann Jervis and Peter Richardson. JSNTSup 108. Sheffield: Sheffield Academic, 1994.

_____. *Jesus, Paul and the Law*. Louisville: Westminster John Knox, 1990.

_____. "New Perspective on Paul." *BJRL* 65 (1983): 95–122.

_____, editor. *Paul and the Mosaic Law*. WUNT 89. Tübingen: Mohr [Siebeck], 1996.

_____. *Romans*. WBC. 2 vols. Dallas: Word, 1988.

_____. *The Theology of Paul's Letter to the Galatians*. Cambridge: Cambridge University Press, 1993.

_____. "Works of the Law and the Curse of the Law (Galatians 3:10–14)." *NTS* 31 (1985): 523–42.

Eckstein, Hans-Joachim. *Verheissung und Gesetz: eine exegetische Untersuchung zu Galater 2,15–4,7*. WUNT 86. Tübingen: Mohr [Siebeck], 1996.

Ego, Beate. "Abraham als Urbild der Toratreue Israels: Traditionsgeschichtliche Überlegungen zu einem Aspekt des biblischen Abrahambildes." In *Bund und Tora*, pp. 25–40. Edited by Friedrich Avemaria and Hermann Lichtenberger. WUNT 92. Tübingen: Mohr [Siebeck], 1996.

Eisenman, Robert and Wise, Michael. *The Dead Sea Scrolls Uncovered*. New York: Penguin, 1992.

Elliger, Kurt, and Rudolph, Wilhelm, editors. *Biblia Hebraica Stuttgartensia*. Stuttgart: Deutsche Bibelgesellschaft, 1984.

Ellis, E. E. "Biblical Interpretation in the New Testament Church." In *Mikra: Text, Translation, Reading and Interpretation of the Hebrew Bible in Ancient Judaism and Early Christianity*, pp. 691–725. Edited by M. J. Mulder. CRINT. Assen/Maastricht: Van Gorcum; Philadelphia: Fortress, 1988.

————. *Paul's Use of the Old Testament*. Edinburgh: Oliver and Boyd, 1957.

Endres, John C., S. J. *Biblical Interpretation in the Book of Jubilees*. CBQMS 18. Washington: Catholic Biblical Association of America, 1987.

Engberg-Pedersen, Troels, editor. *Paul in his Hellenistic Context*. Minneapolis: Fortress, 1995.

Eppel, Robert. "Les tables de la Loi et les tables célestes." *RHPR* 17 (1937): 401–12.

Feldman, Louis H. "Use, Authority and Exegesis of Mikra in the Writings of Josephus." In *Mikra: Text, Translation, Reading and Interpretation of the Hebrew Bible in Ancient Judaism and Early Christianity*, pp. 455–518. Edited by M. J. Mulder. CRINT. Assen/Maastricht: Van Gorcum; Philadelphia: Fortress, 1988.

Feuillet, André. *Le Christ Sagesse de Dieu d'après les Épîtres pauliniennes*. Études Bibliques. Paris: Gabalda, 1966.

————. "Loi de Dieu, Loi du Christ e Loi de l'Esprit. D'apres les épîtres paulieniennes: Le rapport de ces trois lois avec loi mosaique." *NovT* 22 (1980): 29–65.

Finsterbusch, Karin. *Die Thora als Lebensweisung für Heidenchristen*. SUNT 20. Göttingen: Vandenhoeck und Ruprecht, 1996.

Fishbane, Michael. *Biblical Interpretation in Ancient Israel*. Oxford: Clarendon, 1985.

————. *The Exegetical Imagination: On Jewish Thought and Theology*. Cambridge: Harvard University Press, 1998.

————. *The Garments Of Torah: Essays In Biblical Hermeneutics*. Bloomington: Indiana University Press, 1989.

————. "The Hebrew Bible and Exegetical Tradition." In *Intertextuality in Ugarit and Israel*, pp. 15–30. OTS 40. Edited by Johannes C. de Moor. Leiden: Brill, 1998.

————. "Revelation and Tradition: Aspects of Inner-Biblical Exegesis." *JBL* 99 (1980): 343–61.

————. *Text and Texture*. New York: Schocken, 1979.

————. "Torah and Tradition." In *Tradition and Theology in the Old Testament*, pp. 275–300. Edited by Douglas A. Knight. Philadelphia: Fortress, 1977.

————. "Use, Authority and Interpretation of Mikra at Qumran." In *Mikra: Text, Translation, Reading and Interpretation of the Hebrew Bible in Ancient Judaism and Early Christianity*, pp. 339–77. Edited by M. J. Mulder. CRINT. Assen/Maastricht: Van Gorcum; Philadelphia: Fortress, 1988.

————. "The Well of Living Water: A Biblical Motif and its Ancient Transformations." In *Sha'arei Talmon: Studies in the Bible, Qumran, and Ancient*

Near East Presented to Shemaryahu Talmon, pp. 3–16. Edited by M. Fishbane and E. Tov with W. W. Fields. Winona Lake, IN: Eisenbrauns, 1992.

Fitzmyer, Joseph A. *Romans*. AB 33. Garden City: Doubleday, 1994.

———. "The Use of Explicit Old Testament Quotations in Qumran Literature and in the New Testament." *NTS* 7 (1960–61): 297–333.

Flusser, David. "Durch das Gesetz dem Gesetz gestorben." *Judaica* 43 (1987): 30–46.

Fossum, Jarl. *The Name of God and the Angel of the Lord: Samaritan and Jewish Concepts of Intermediation and the Origin of Gnosticism*. WUNT 36. Tübingen: Mohr [Siebeck], 1985.

Fournier-Bidoz, Alain. "L'Arbre et la Demeure: Siracide XXIV 10–17." *VT* 34 (1984): 1–10.

Fowl, Stephen. "Who Can Read Abraham's Story? Allegory and Interpretive Power in Galatians." *JSNT* 55 (1994): 77–95.

Freedman, H, trans. *Midrash Rabbah: Genesis*. Volume 1. London: Soncino, 1983.

Fung, Ronald Y. K. *The Epistle to the Galatians*. NICNT. Grand Rapids: Eerdmans, 1988.

Furnish, Victor Paul. *II Corinthians*. AB 32A. Garden City: Doubleday, 1984.

Gammie, J. "Spatial and Ethical Dualism in Jewish Wisdom and Apocalyptic Literature." *JBL* 93 (1974): 356–85.

García Martínez, Florentino. *The Dead Sea Scrolls Translated*. Leiden: Brill, 1994.

García Martínez, Florentino, and Tigchelaar, Eibert J. *The Dead Sea Scrolls Study Edition*. 2 vols. Leiden: Brill, 1997.

Gaston, Lloyd. *Paul and the Torah*. Vancouver: University of British Columbia Press, 1987.

Georgi, Dieter. *The Opponents of Paul in Second Corinthians*. Philadelphia: Fortress, 1986.

Gese, Hartmut. *Essays on Biblical Theology*. Minneapolis: Augsburg, 1981.

———. *Vom Sinai zum Zion*. Tübingen: Mohr [Siebeck], 1974.

———. "Wisdom, Son of Man, and the Origins of Christology: The Consistent Development of Biblical Theology." *HBT* 3 (1981): 23–57.

Gilbert, Maurice. "L'éloge de la Sagesse (*Siracide* 24)." *RTL* 5 (1974): 326–48.

Given, Mark D. "True Rhetoric: Ambiguity, Cunning, and Deception in Pauline Discourse." In *SBLSP 1997*, pp. 526–50. Atlanta: Scholars Press, 1997.

Goldberg, Arnold M. *Untersuchungen über die Vorstellung von der Schekhinah in der frühen rabbinischen Literatur*. SJ 5. Berlin: Walter de Gruyter, 1969.

Goodenough, E. R. *By Light, Light: The Mystic Gospel of Hellenistic Judaism*. New Haven: Yale University, 1935.

Gross, Walter. "Erneurter oder Neuer Bund? Wortlaut und Aussageintention in Jer 31,31–34." In *Bund und Tora*, pp. 41–66. Edited by Friedrich Avemaria and Hermann Lichtenberger. WUNT 92. Tübingen: Mohr [Siebeck], 1996.

Gutbrod, W. and Kleinknecht, H. "Νόμος κτλ." In *Theological Dictionary of the New Testament*, volume 4, pp. 1022–91. Edited by G. Kittel. Translated by G. Bromiley. Grand Rapids: Eerdmans, 1967.

Hafemann, Scott J. *Paul, Moses, and the History of Israel.* WUNT 81. Tübingen: Mohr [Siebeck], 1995.

———. "Paul's Argument from the Old Testament and Christology in 2 Cor 1–9." In *The Corinthian Correspondence*, pp. 277–303. Edited by R. Bieringer. BETL 125. Leuven: Leuven University Press, 1996.

Hamerton-Kelly, R. G. *Pre-existence, Wisdom, and the Son of Man; a Study of the Idea of Pre-existence in the New Testament.* Cambridge: Cambridge University Press, 1973.

———. "The Temple and the Origins of Jewish Apocalyptic." *VT* 20 (1970): 1–15.

Hammer, Reuven, trans. *Sifre: A Tannaitic Commentary on the Book of Deuteronomy.* New Haven: Yale University Press, 1986.

Hansen, G. Walter. *Abraham in Galatians: Epistolary and Rhetorical Contexts.* JSNTSup 29. Sheffield: JSOT, 1989.

Harrington, Daniel J. "Abraham Traditions in the Testament of Abraham and in the 'Rewritten Bible' of the Intertestamental Period." In *Studies on the Testament of Abraham*, pp. 164–71. Edited by G. W. E. Nickelsburg. Missoula: Scholars Press, 1976.

———. "Palestinian Adaptations of Biblical Narratives and Prophecies: the Bible Rewritten (Narratives)." In *Early Judaism and its Modern Interpreters*, pp. 239–47. Edited by R. A. Kraft and G. W. E. Nickelsburg. Atlanta: Scholars Press, 1986.

———. "Sirach Research Since 1965: Progress and Questions." In *Pursuing the Text: Studies in Honor of Ben Zion Wacholder on the Occasion of his Seventieth Birthday*, pp. 164–76. JSOTSup 184. Edited by John C. Reeves and John Kampen. Sheffield: Sheffield Academic Press, 1994.

Hartman, Lars. *Prophecy Interpreted.* ConBNT 1. Uppsala: Almqvist and Wiksells, 1966.

Hays, Richard B. "Christology and Ethics in Galatians: The Law of Christ." *CBQ* 49 (1987): 268–90.

———. *Echoes of Scripture in the Letters of Paul.* New Haven: Yale University Press, 1989.

———. *The Faith of Jesus Christ: An Investigation of the Narrative Substructure of Galatians 3:1–4:11.* SBLDS 56. Chico: Scholars Press, 1983.

——. "'Have We Found Abraham to be Our Forefather According to the Flesh?' A Reconsideration of Rom 4:1." *NovT* 27 (1985): 79–98.

Hegermann, Harald. *Die Vorstellung vom Schöpfungsmittler im hellenischen Judentum und Urchristentum.* TU 82. Berlin: Akademie-Verlag, 1961.

Hengel, Martin. *Judaism and Hellenism.* 2 vols. Translated by J. Bowden. Minneapolis: Fortress, 1974.

——. *The Son of God.* Translated J. Bowden. London: SCM, 1976.

——. "Die Stellung des Apostels Paulus zum Gesetz in den unbekannten Jahren zwischen Damaskus und Antiochien." In *Paul and the Mosaic Law*, pp. 25–51. Edited by James D. G. Dunn. WUNT 89. Tübingen: Mohr [Siebeck], 1996.

Hengel, Martin and Heckel, Ulrich, editors. *Paulus und das antike Judentum.* Tübingen: Mohr [Siebeck], 1991.

Hickling, C. J. A. "Paul's Use of Exodus in the Corinthian Correspondence." In *The Corinthian Correspondence*, pp. 367–76. Edited by R. Bieringer. BETL 125. Leuven: Leuven University Press, 1996.

Hills, Julian. "Christ was the Goal of the Law...(Romans 10:4)." *JTS* 44/2 (1993): 585–92.

Himmelfarb, Martha. "Revelation and Rapture: the Transformation of the Visionary in the Ascent Apocalypses." In *Mysteries and Revelations: Apocalyptic Studies since the Uppsala Colloquium*, pp. 79–90. JSPSupp 9. Edited by J. J. Collins and J. H. Charlesworth. Sheffield: JSOT Press, 1991.

Hong, In-Gyu. *The Law in Galatians.* JSNTSup 81. Sheffield: JSOT Press, 1993.

Hooker, Morna D. "Paul and 'Covenantal Nomism.'" In *Paul and Paulinism, FS C. K. Barrett*, pp. 47–56. Edited by Morna D. Hooker and S. G. Wilson. London: SPCK, 1982.

Howard, George. *Paul. Crisis in Galatia: A Study in Early Christian Theology.* 2nd Edition. SNTSMS 35. Cambridge: Cambridge University Press, 1979.

Hübner, Hans. "Καταργέω." *Exegetical Dictionary of the New Testament*, volume 2, pp. 267–68. Edited by Horst Balz and Gerhard Schneider. Translated by John W. Medendorp. Grand Rapids: Eerdmans, 1990–93.

——. *Law in Paul's Thought.* Translated by J. C. G. Greig. Edinburgh: T and T Clark, 1984.

Hurtado, Larry W. *One God, One Lord: Early Christian Devotion and Ancient Jewish Monotheism.* Philadelphia: Fortress, 1988.

James, E. O. *Tree of Life.* Studies in the History of Religions 11. Leiden: Brill, 1966.

Jastrow, Marcus. *A Dictionary of the Targumim, the Talmud Babli and Yerushalmi, and the Midrashic Literature.* 2 vols. New York: Judaica, 1992.

Jenni, Ernst. "עולם." In *Theologisches Handwörterbuch zum Alten Testament*, volume 2, pp. 228–43. Edited by E. Jenni with C. Westermann. Munich: Kaiser, 1984.

Jensen, Joseph, O. S. B. *The Use of* tôrâ *by Isaiah: His Debate with the Wisdom Tradition*. CBQMS 3. Washington: Catholic Biblical Association of America, 1973.

Jeremias, Joachim. *Jesus' Promise to the Nations*. Translated by S. H. Hooke. London: SCM, 1958.

———. "Λίθος." *Theological Dictionary of the New Testament*, volume 4, pp. 268–80. Edited by Gerhard Kittel. Translated by G. Bromiley. Grand Rapids: Eerdmans, 1967.

Jervell, Jacob. "Die offenbarte und die verborgene Tora: Zur Vorstellung über die neue Tora im Rabbinismus." *Studia Theologica*. 25 (1971): 90–108.

Jocz, Jakób. *The Jewish People and Jesus Christ*. London: SPCK, 1949.

Johnson, E. Elizabeth. *The Function of Apocalyptic and Wisdom Traditions in Romans 9–11*. SBLDS 109. Atlanta: Scholars Press, 1989.

———. "The Wisdom of God as Apocalyptic Power." In *Faith and History: Essays in Honor of Paul W. Meyer*, pp. 137–48. Edited by J. T. Carroll, C. H. Cosgrove, E. E. Johnson. Atlanta: Scholars Press, 1990.

Jobes, Karen H. "Jerusalem, Our Mother: Metalepsis and Intertextuality in Galatians 4:21–31." *WTJ* 55 (1993): 299–320.

Juel, Donald. *Messianic Exegesis*. Philadelphia: Fortress, 1988.

Kalusche, M. "'Das Gesetz als Thema biblischer Theologie'? Anmerkungen zu einem Entwurf Peter Stuhlmachers." *ZNW* 77 (1986): 194–205.

Kampen, John. "The Eschatological Temple(s) of 11QT." In *Pursuing the Text: Studies in Honor of Ben Zion Wacholder on the Occasion of his Seventieth Birthday*, pp. 85–97. JSOTSup 184. Edited by John C. Reeves and John Kampen. Sheffield: Sheffield Academic, 1994.

Käsemann, Ernst. *Commentary on Romans*. Grand Rapids: Eerdmans, 1980.

Klausner, Joseph. *The Messianic Idea in Israel: From its Beginning to the Completion of the Mishnah*. Translated by W. F. Stinespring. New York: Macmillan, 1955.

Klein, Michael L. *The Fragment-Targums of the Pentateuch*. 2 vols. AnBib 76. Rome: Biblical Institute Press, 1980.

Kleinknecht, H. and W. Gutbrod. "Νόμος κτλ." *Theological Dictionary of the New Testament*, volume 4, pp. 1022–91. Edited by Gerhard Kittel. Translated by G. Bromiley. Grand Rapids: Eerdmans, 1967.

Knibb, Michael A. *The Ethiopic Book of Enoch*. 2 vols. Oxford: Clarendon, 1978.

Knox, Wilfred L. "The Divine Wisdom." *JTS* 38 (1937): 230–37.

Koch, Dietrich-Alex. *Die Schrift als Zeuge des Evangeliums: Untersuchungen zur Verwendung und zum Verständnis der Schrift bei Paulus.* BZHT 69. Tübingen: Mohr [Siebeck], 1986.

Koester, Craig R. *The Dwelling of God: The Tabernacle in the Old Testament, Intertestamental Jewish Literature, and New Testament.* CBQMS 22. Washington: Catholic Biblical Association of America, 1989.

Küchler, Max. *Fruhjudische Weisheitstraditionen: zum Fortgang weisheitlichen Denkens im Bereich des fruhjudischen Jahweglaubens.* OBO 26. Freiburg: Universitätsverlag, 1979.

Kuula, Kari. *The Law, The Covenant and God's Plan. Volume 1: Paul's Polemical Treatment of the Law in Galatians.* Finnish Exegetical Society 72. Göttingen: Vandenhoeck und Ruprecht, 1999.

Kugel, James L. *The Idea of Biblical Poetry.* New Haven: Yale University Press, 1981.

———. "Two Introductions to Midrash." In *Midrash and Literature*, pp. 77–103. Edited by Geoffrey H. Hartman and Sanford Budick. New Haven: Yale University Press, 1986.

Lagrange, M.-J. *Saint Paul, Epître aux Romains.* Paris: Gabalda, 1950.

———. *Saint Paul, Epître aux Galates.* 2nd edition. Paris: Lecoffre, 1925.

Lambrecht, Jan. "Structure and Line of Thought in 2 Corinthians 2,14–4,6." In *Studies in 2 Corinthians*, pp. 257–94. Edited by R. Bieringer and J. Lambrecht. BETL 112. Leuven: Leuven University Press, 1994.

———. "Transformation in 2 Corinthians 3,18." In *Studies in 2 Corinthians*, pp. 295–307. Edited by R. Bieringer and J. Lambrecht. BETL 112. Leuven: Leuven University Press, 1994.

Lauterbach, Jacob Z., editor and translator. *Mekilta de-Rabbi Ishmael.* 3 volumes. Philadelphia: Jewish Publication Society, 1933, 1935.

Le Déaut, R. "Traditions Targumiques dans le Corpus Paulinien? (Hebr 11,4 et 12,24; Gal 4,29–30; II Cor 3,16)." *Bib* 42 (1961): 28–48.

Lehrman, S. M. *Midrash Rabbah: Exodus.* Volume 3. London: Soncino, 1983.

Levenson, Jon D. *Sinai and Zion.* Minneapolis: Winston, 1985.

Levison, John R. "Torah and Covenant in Pseudo Philo's *Liber Antiquitatum Biblicarum.*" In *Bund und Tora*, pp. 111–27. Edited by Friedrich Avemaria and Hermann Lichtenberger. WUNT 92. Tübingen: Mohr [Siebeck], 1996.

Lichtenberger, Hermann. "Paulus und das Gesetz." In *Paulus und das antike Judentum*, pp. 361–78. Edited by M. Hengel and U. Heckel. Tübingen: Mohr [Siebeck], 1991.

———. "Das Tora-Verständnis im Judentum zur Zeit des Paulus." In *Paul and the Mosaic Law*, pp. 7–23. Edited by James D. G. Dunn. WUNT 89. Tübingen: Mohr [Siebeck], 1996.

Lim, Timothy H. *Holy Scripture in the Qumran Commentaries and Pauline Letters.* Oxford: Clarendon, 1997.

Limbeck, Meinrad. *Das Gesetz im Alten und Neuen Testament.* Darmstadt: Wissenschaftliche Buchgesellschaft, 1997.

———. *Die Ordnung des Heils: Untersuchungen zum Gesetzesverständnis des Frühjudentums.* Düsseldorf: Patmos, 1971.

Lindars, Barnabas. *New Testament Apologetic: The Doctrinal Significance of the Old Testament Quotations.* Philadelphia: Westminster, 1961.

Lloyd, G. E. R. *Polarity and Analogy: Two Types of Argumentation in Early Greek Thought.* Cambridge: Cambridge University Press, 1966.

Lohse, Eduard. *Die Texte aus Qumran.* Darmstadt: Wissenschaftliche Buchgesellschaft, 1971.

Longenecker, Richard. *Galatians.* WBC 41. Dallas: Word Books, 1990.

———. *Paul, Apostle of Liberty.* New York: Harper and Row, 1964.

McCready, Wayne O. "A Second Torah at Qumran?" *SR* 14.1 (1985): 5–15.

Mack, Burton L. *Logos und Sophia: Untersuchungen zur Weisheitstheologie im hellenistischen Judentum.* Göttingen: Vandenhoeck und Ruprecht, 1973.

———. "The Christ and Jewish Wisdom." In *The Messiah*, pp. 192–221. Edited by James H. Charlesworth. Minneapolis: Fortress, 1992.

Maher, Michael, M. S. C. "Some Aspects of Torah in Judaism." *ITQ* 38 (1971): 310–325.

Mann, Jacob. *The Bible as Read and Preached in the Old Synagogue.* The Library of Biblical Studies. New York: KTAV, 1940, 1971.

Marböck, Johannes. *Gottes Weisheit Unter Uns.* Herder Biblische Studien. BS 6. Freiburg: Herder, 1995.

———. *Weisheit im Wandel.* BBB 37. Bonn: Hanstein, 1971.

Marcus, Ralph. *Law in the Apocrypha.* New York: Columbia University Press, 1927.

Martin, Brice. *Christ and the Law in Paul.* Leiden: Brill, 1989.

Martin, Ralph P. *2 Corinthians.* WBC 40. Waco: Word, 1986.

Martyn, J. Louis. "Apocalyptic Antinomies in Paul's Letter to the Galatians." *NTS* 31 (1985): 410–24.

———. "The Covenants of Hagar and Sarah." In *Faith and History: Essays in Honor of Paul W. Meyer*, pp. 160–92. Edited by J. T. Carroll, C. H. Cosgrove, and E. E. Johnson. Atlanta: Scholars Press, 1990.

Mason, Steve. "'For I Am Not Ashamed of the Gospel' (Rom. 1.16): The Gospel and the First Readers of Romans." In *Gospel in Paul: Studies on Corinthians, Galatians and Romans for Richard N. Longenecker*, pp. 254–87. Edited by L. Ann Jervis and Peter Richardson. JSNTSup 108. Sheffield: Sheffield Academic Press, 1994.

Matlock, R. Barry. *Unveiling the Apocalyptic Paul: Paul's Interpreters and the Rhetoric of Criticism.* JSNTSup 127. Sheffield: Sheffield Academic Press, 1996.

Maurer, Christian. *Die Gesetzeslehre des Paulus nach ihrem Usprung und in ihrer Entfaltung dargelegt.* Zurich: Evangelischer, 1941.

McNamara, Martin. *The New Testament and the Palestinian Targum to the Pentateuch.* AnBib 27. Pontifical Biblical Institute, 1966.

Meeks, Wayne A. "On Trusting an Unpredictable God: A Hermeneutical Meditation on Romans 9–11." In *Faith and History: Essays in Honor of Paul W. Meyer*, pp. 105–124. Edited by J. T. Carroll, C. H. Cosgrove, and E. E. Johnson. Atlanta: Scholars Press, 1990.

Meyer, Paul W. "Romans 10:4 and the 'End' of the Law." In *The Divine Helmsman: Studies on God's Control of Human Events, Presented to Lou H. Silberman*, pp. 59–78. Edited by James L. Crenshaw and Samuel Sandmel. New York: KTAV, 1980.

Milik, Józef T. *The Books of Enoch: Aramaic Fragments of Qumrân Cave 4.* Oxford: Oxford University Press, 1976.

Mink, Hans-Aage. "The Use of Scripture in the Temple Scroll and the Status of the Scroll as Law." *SJOT* 1 (1987): 20–50.

Miscall, Peter D. "Isaiah: New Heavens, New Earth, New Book." In *Reading between Texts: Intertextuality and the Hebrew Bible*, pp. 41–56. Edited by Danna Nolan Fewell. Louisville: Westminster John Knox, 1992.

Montefiore, C. G. *Judaism and St. Paul.* London: Goschen, 1914.

Moore, George F. "Christian Writers on Judaism." *HTR* 14 (1921): 197–254.

———. *Judaism in the First Centuries of the Christian Era.* Vol. 1, 2. Cambridge: Harvard University, 1927.

———. "Intermediaries in Jewish Theology: Memra, Shekinah, Metatron." *HTR* 15 (1922): 41–85.

Mulder, Martin Jay, editor. *Mikra: Text, Translation, Reading and Interpretation of the Hebrew Bible in Ancient Judaism and Early Christianity.* CRINT. Assen/Maastricht: Van Gorcum; Philadelphia: Fortress, 1988.

———. "The Transmission of the Biblical Text." In *Mikra: Text, Translation, Reading and Interpretation of the Hebrew Bible in Ancient Judaism and Early Christianity*, pp. 87–135. Edited by M. J. Mulder. CRINT. Assen/Maastricht: Van Gorcum; Philadelphia: Fortress, 1988.

Müller, Karlheinz. *Anstoss und Gericht.* Munich: Kösel, 1969.

Munck, Johannes. *Christ and Israel: An Interpretation of Romans 9–11.* Philadelphia: Fortress, 1967.

———. *Paul and the Salvation of Mankind.* London: SCM, 1959.

Murphy, Roland E. "The Personification of Wisdom." In *Wisdom in Israel*, pp. 222–33. Edited by J. Day, R. P. Gordon, and H. G. M. Williamson. Cambridge: Cambridge University Press, 1995.

———. "Wisdom and Creation." *JBL* 104 (1985): 3–11.

Murphy-O'Connor, Jerome. *Theology of the Second Letter to the Corinthians.* Cambridge: Cambridge University Press, 1991.

Nanos, Mark D. *The Mystery of Romans: The Jewish Context of Paul's Letter.* Minneapolis: Fortress, 1996.

Neusner, Jacob. *What is Midrash?* Philadelphia: Fortress, 1987.

Nickelsburg, George W. E. "The Apocalyptic Construction of Reality in *1 Enoch.*" In *Mysteries and Revelations: Apocalyptic Studies since the Uppsala Colloquium,* pp. 51–64. JSPSupp 9. Edited by J. J. Collins and J. H. Charlesworth. Sheffield: JSOT Press, 1991.

———. "The Apocalyptic Message of *1 Enoch* 92–105." *CBQ* 39 (1977): 309–28.

———. "*1 Enoch* and Qumran Origins: The State of the Question and Some Prospects for Answers." *SBLASP* 1986: 341–60.

———. "Enoch, First Book of." *Anchor Bible Dictionary,* volume 2, pp. 508–16. Edited by David Noel Freedman. New York: Doubleday, 1992.

———. "Enoch, Levi, and Peter: Recipients of Revelation in Upper Galilee." *JBL* 100 (1981): 575–600.

———. "The Epistle of Enoch and the Qumran Literature." *JJS* (1982) 33: 333–48.

———. "Revealed Wisdom as a Criterion for Inclusion and Exclusion: From Jewish Sectarianism to Early Christianity." In *"To See Ourselves as Others See Us": Christians, Jews, and "Others" in Late Antiquity,* pp. 73–91. Edited by J. Neusner and E. S. Frerichs. Missoula, MT: Scholars Press, 1986.

———. "Salvation without and with a Messiah: Developing Beliefs in Writings Ascribed to Enoch." In *Judaisms and their Messiahs at the Turn of the Christian Era,* pp. 49–68. Edited by J. Neusner, W. S. Green and E. Frerichs. Cambridge: Cambridge University Press, 1987.

———. "Wisdom and Apocalypticism in Early Judaism: Some Points for Discussion." *SBLASP* 1994: 715–32.

Obijole, O. O. "The Pauline Concept of the Law." *ITS* 26 (1989): 22–34.

Oegema, Gerbern S. "Versöhnung ohne Vollendung? Römer 10,4 und die Tora der messianischen Zeit." In *Bund und Tora,* pp. 229–61. Edited by Friedrich Avemaria and Hermann Lichtenberger. WUNT 92. Tübingen: Mohr [Siebeck], 1996.

Oss, D. "The Interpretation of the 'Stone' Passages by Peter and Paul: A Comparative Study." *JETS* 32 (1989).

Overman, J. Andrew and Green, William Scott. "Judaism in the Greco-Roman Period." *Anchor Bible Dictionary,* volume 3, pp. 1037–54. Edited by David Noel Freedman. New York: Doubleday, 1992.

Patte, Daniel. *Early Jewish Hermeneutic in Palestine.* SBLDS 22. Missoula: Scholars Press, 1975.

Pattee, Stephen. "Stumbling Stone or Cornerstone? The Structure and Meaning of Paul's Argument in Rom 9:30–10:13." Ph.D. Dissertation, Marquette University, 1991.

Paul, Shalom M. "Heavenly Tablets and the Book of Life." *JANESCU* 5 (1973): 345–53.

Pearson, Birger. "Hellenistic-Jewish Wisdom Speculation and Paul." In *Aspects of Wisdom in Judaism and Early Christianity*, pp. 43–66. Edited by R. L. Wilken. Notre Dame: Notre Dame University Press, 1975.

Penna, Romano. *Paul the Apostle.* 2 volumes. Volume 1, *Jew and Greek Alike.* Volume 2, *Wisdom and Folly of the Cross.* Translated by Thomas P. Wahl. Collegeville: Liturgical, 1996.

Perrot, Charles. "The Reading of the Bible in the Ancient Synagogue." In *Mikra: Text, Translation, Reading and Interpretation of the Hebrew Bible in Ancient Judaism and Early Christianity*, pp. 137–59. Edited by M. J. Mulder. CRINT. Assen/Maastricht: Van Gorcum; Philadelphia: Fortress, 1988.

Pesch, Rudolf. *Römerbrief.* Die Neue Echter Bibel, Kommentar zum Neuen Testament mit der Einheitsübersetzung 6. Würzburg: Echter, 1983.

Pfeifer, Gerhard. *Ursprung und Wesen der Hypostasenvorstellungen im Judentum.* Stuttgart: Calwer, 1967.

Plummer, Alfred. *Second Epistle of St Paul to the Corinthians.* ICC. Edinburgh: T. and T. Clark, 1915.

Rahlfs, Alfred. *Septuaginta.* Stuttgart: Deutsche Bibelgesellschaft, 1935.

Räisänen, Heikki. *Jesus, Paul and Torah.* JSNTsup 43. Sheffield: Sheffield Academic, 1992.

———. *Paul and the Law.* 2nd edition. WUNT 29. Tübingen: Mohr [Siebeck], 1987.

———. "Paul's Conversion and the Development of His View of the Law." *NTS* 33 (1987): 404–19.

———. "Zion Torah and Biblical Theology: Thoughts on a Tübingen Theory." *Jesus, Paul and Torah*: 225–51.

Reinbold, Wolfgang. "Paulus und das Gesetz: Zur Exegese von Röm 9,30–33." *BZ* 38 (1994): 253–264.

Reinmuth, E. "Beobachtungen zum Verständnis des Gesetzes im Liber Antiquitatum Biblicarum (Pseudo-Philo)." *JSJ* 20 (1989): 151–70.

Renwick, David A. *Paul, the Temple, and the Presence of God.* BJS 224. Atlanta: Scholars Press, 1991.

Richard, Earl. "Polemics, Old Testament and Theology. A Study of II Cor. III,1–IV, 6." *RB* 88 (1981): 340–67.

Ringgren, Helmer. *Word and Wisdom: Studies in the Hypostatization of Divine Qualities and Functions in the Ancient Near East.* Lund: Håkan Ohlssons Boktryckeri, 1947.

Robbins, Vernon K. *The Tapestry of Early Christian Discourse.* London: Routledge, 1996.

Roon, A. van. "The Relation Between Christ and the Wisdom of God According to Paul." *NovT* 16 (1974) 207–39.

Russell. D. S. *The Method and Message of Jewish Apocalyptic*. OTL. Philadelphia: Westminster, 1964.

Rylaarsdam, J. Coert. *Revelation in Jewish Wisdom Literature*. Chicago: University of Chicago, 1946.

Sanday, William and Headlam, Arthur C. *A Critical and Exegetical Commentary on the Epistle to the Romans*. ICC. Edinburgh: Clark, 1958.

Sanders, E. P. "Law in Judaism of the NT Period." *Anchor Bible Dictionary*, volume 4, pp. 254–65. Edited by David Noel Freedman. New York: Doubleday, 1992.

———. *Paul and Palestinian Judaism*. Philadelphia: Fortress, 1977.

———. *Paul, the Law and the Jewish People*. Philadelphia: Fortress, 1983.

Sanders, James A. "Torah and Christ." *Int* 29 (1975): 372–90.

———. "Torah and Paul." In *God's Christ and His People*, pp. 36–60. Edited by Jacob Jervell and Wayne A. Meeks. Oslo: Universitetsforlaget, 1977.

Sandmel, Samuel. *The Genius of Paul*. New York: Farrar, Straus, and Cudahy, 1958.

———. *Philo's Place in Judaism: A Study of Conceptions of Abraham in Jewish Literature*. Cincinnati: Hebrew Union College Press, 1956.

Schäfer, Peter. "Die Torah der Messianischen Zeit." *ZNW* 65 (1974): 27–42.

Schechter, Solomon. *Aspects of Rabbinic Theology*. New York: Schocken, 1909.

Schiffman, Lawrence H. "Miqsat Ma'aseh Ha-Torah and the *Temple Scroll*." *RevQ* 14 (1990): 435–57.

Schimanowski, Gottfried. *Weisheit und Messias*. WUNT 2, 17. Tübingen: Mohr [Siebeck], 1985.

Schlier, H. *Der Römerbrief*. HTKNT. Freiburg: Herder, 1977.

Schnabel, E. J. *Law and Wisdom from Ben Sirach to Paul*. WUNT 2, 16. Tübingen: Mohr [Siebeck], 1985.

Schneider, Norbert. *Die rhetorische Eigenart der paulinischen Antithese*. HUT. Tübingen: Mohr [Siebeck], 1970.

Schoeps, Hans J. *Paul: The Theology of the Apostle in the Light of Jewish Religious History*. Philadelphia: Westminster, 1961.

Scholem, Gershom G. *Major Trends in Jewish Mysticism*. New York: Schocken, 1954.

———. "The Meaning of the Torah in Jewish Mysticism." *Diogenes* 14 (1956): 36–47.

Schreiner, Thomas R. *Law and its Fulfillment: A Pauline Theology of Law*. Grand Rapids: Baker, 1993.

Schultz, Joseph P. "Two Views of the Patriarchs: Noachides and Pre-Sinai

Israelites." In *Texts and Responses: Studies Presented to Nahum N. Glatzer on the Occasion of his Seventieth Birthday by His Students*, pp. 43–59. Edited by Michael A. Fishbane and Paul R. Flohr. Leiden: Brill, 1975.

Schürer, Emil. *The History of the Jewish People in the Age of Jesus Christ*. 3 vols. Revised and edited by Geza Vermes, Fergus Millar, Matthew Black, and Martin Goodman. Edinburgh: T. and T. Clark, 1973, 1987.

Schweitzer, Albert. *The Mysticism of Paul the Apostle*. Translated by W. Montgomery. New York: Seabury, 1931.

———. *Paul and His Interpreters*. Translated by W. Montgomery. New York: Schocken, 1912.

Scott, James M. *Paul and the Nations*. WUNT 84. Tübingen: Mohr [Siebeck], 1995.

———. "Throne-Chariot Mysticism in Qumran and in Paul." In *Eschatology, Messianism, and the Dead Sea Scrolls*, pp. 101–19. Edited by Craig A. Evans and Peter W. Flint. Grand Rapids: Eerdmans, 1997.

Segal, Alan F. "Conversion and Messianism: Outline for a New Approach." In *The Messiah*, pp. 296–340. Edited by James H. Charlesworth. Minneapolis: Fortress, 1992.

———. *The Other Judaisms of Late Antiquity*. BJS 127. Atlanta: Scholars Press, 1987.

———. *Paul the Convert: the Apostolate and Apostasy of Saul the Pharisee*. New Haven: Yale University Press, 1990.

———. "The Risen Christ and the Angelic Mediator Figures in Light of Qumran." In *Jesus and the Dead Sea Scrolls*, pp. 302–28. ABRL. Edited by James H. Charlesworth. New York: Doubleday, 1992.

———. "Torah and *Nomos* in Recent Scholarly Discussion." *SR* 13 (1984): 19–27. Reprinted in *The Other Judaisms of Late Antiquity*, 131–45.

———. *Two Powers in Heaven: Early Rabbinic Reports About Christianity and Gnosticism*. SJLA 25. Leiden: Brill, 1977.

———. "Universalism in Judaism and Christianity." *Paul in his Hellenistic Context*. Edited by Troels Engberg-Pedersen. Minneapolis: Fortress, 1995.

Sheppard, Gerald T. "Wisdom and Torah: The Interpretation of Deuteronomy Underlying Sirach 24:23." In *Biblical and Near Eastern Studies: Essays in Honor of William Sanford LaSor*, pp. 166–76. Edited by Gary A. Tuttle. Grand Rapids: Eerdmans, 1978.

———. *Wisdom as a Hermeneutical Construct: A Study in the Sapientializing of the Old Testament*. BZAW 151. Berlin: de Gruyter, 1980.

Siegert, Folker. *Argumentation bei Paulus gezeigt an Röm 9–11*. WUNT 34. Tübingen: Mohr [Siebeck], 1985.

Silberman, Lou H. "Paul's Midrash: Reflections on Romans 4." In *Faith and*

History: Essays in Honor of Paul W. Meyer, pp. 99–105. Edited by J. Carroll, C. Cosgrove and E. Johnson. Atlanta: Scholars Press, 1990.

Skehan, Patrick W. "Structures in Poems on Wisdom: Proverbs 8 and Sirach 24." *CBQ* 41 (1979): 365–79.

Skehan, Patrick W. and Alexander A. Di Lella. *The Wisdom of Ben Sira*. AB 39. New York: Doubleday, 1987.

Slingerland, D. "The Nature of *Nomos* (Law) within the Testaments of the Twelve Patriarchs." *JBL* 105 (1986): 39–48.

Smend, Rudolph and Luz, Ulrich. *Gesetz*. Kohlhammer Taschenbücher Biblische Konfrontationen 1015. Stuttgart: Kolhammer, 1981.

Smolar L. and Aberbach, M. *Studies in Targum Jonathan to the Prophets*. New York: KTAV; Baltimore: Baltimore Hebrew College, 1983.

Snodgrass, Klyne. "Spheres of Influence: A Possible Solution to the Problem of Paul and the Law." *JSNT* 32 (1988): 93–113.

Sperber, Alexander. *The Bible in Aramaic*. 4 volumes. Reprinted ed. Leiden: Brill, 1992.

Stanley, Christopher D. *Paul and the Language of Scripture*. SNTSMS 69. Cambridge: Cambridge University Press, 1992.

Stegemann, Hartmut. "The Literary Composition of the Temple Scroll and its Status at Qumran." In *Temple Scroll Studies: Papers Presented at the International Symposium on the Temple Scroll*, pp. 123–48. JSPSup 7. Edited by George J. Brooke. Sheffield: JSOT, 1989.

———. "The Origins of the Temple Scroll." In *IOSOT Congress Volume Jerusalem*, pp. 235–56. VTSup 40. Edited by J. A. Emerton. Leiden: Brill, 1986.

Stendahl, Krister. *Paul among Jews and Gentiles*. Philadelphia: Fortress, 1976.

———. *The School of St. Matthew and its Use of the Old Testament*. 2d ed. Philadelphia: Fortress, 1968.

Stern, Sacha. *Jewish Identity in Early Rabbinic Writings*. AGJU 23. Leiden: Brill, 1994.

Sternberg, Meir. *The Poetics of Biblical Narrative*. Bloomington: Indiana University Press, 1985.

Stockhausen, Carol K. "2 Corinthians and the Principles of Pauline Exegesis." In *Paul and the Scriptures of Israel*, pp. 143–64. Edited by Craig A. Evans and James A. Sanders. JSNTSup 83. SSEJC 1. Sheffield: JSOT, 1993.

———. "The Epistle to the Galatians and the Abraham Narratives." Paper presented at the Catholic Biblical Association Meeting, Santa Clara, August, 1988; and, at the Midwest Regional Meeting of the Society of Biblical Literature, Chicago, January 31, 1989.

———. *Moses' Veil and the Glory of the New Covenant*. AnBib 116. Rome: Pontifical Biblical Institute, 1989.

Stone, Michael E. *Fourth Ezra: A Commentary on the Fourth Book of Ezra.* Hermeneia. Minneapolis: Fortress, 1990.

Strack, H. L. and Stemberger, G. *Introduction to the Talmud and Midrash.* Translated by M. Bockmuehl. Edinburgh: T. and T. Clark, 1991.

Stuhlmacher, P. *Biblische Theologie des Neuen Testaments.* Volume 1. Göttingen: Vandenhoeck und Ruprecht, 1992.

————. "The End of the Law. On the Origin and Beginnings of Pauline Theology." In *Reconciliation, Law, and Righteousness. Essays in Biblical Theology,* pp. 134–54. Tr. E. R. Kalin. Philadelphia: Fortress, 1986.

————. "The Law as a Topic of Biblical Theology." In *Reconciliation, Law, and Righteousness. Essays in Biblical Theology,* pp. 110–33.

————. "The Pauline Gospel." In *The Gospel and the Gospels,* pp. 149–72. Edited by Peter Stuhlmacher. Grand Rapids: Eerdmans, 1992.

————. "Paul's Understanding of the Law in the Letter to the Romans." *SEÅ* 50 (1985): 87–104.

————. "Die Stellung Jesu und des Paulus zu Jerusalem." *ZTK* 86 (1989): 140–56.

Suggs, M. Jack. *Wisdom, Christology, and Law in Matthew's Gospel.* Cambridge: Harvard University Press, 1970.

————. "'The Word is Near to You': Romans 10:6–10 Within the Purpose of the Letter." In *Christian History and Interpretation: Studies Presented to John Knox,* pp. 289–312. Edited by W. R. Farmer, C. F. D. Moule and R. R. Niebuhr. Cambridge: Cambridge University Press, 1967.

Sundkler, Bengt. "Jésus et les païens." *RHPR* 16 (1936): 462–99.

Swanson, Dwight D. "'A Covenant Just Like Jacob's': the Covenant of 11QT 29 and Jeremiah's New Covenant." In *New Qumran Texts and Studies. Proceedings of the First Meeting of the International Organization for Qumran Studies, Paris 1992,* pp. 273–86. Edited by George J. Brooke (with Florentino García Martinez). STDJ 15. Leiden: Brill, 1994.

Tan, Kim Huat. *The Zion Traditions and the Aims of Jesus.* SNTSMS 991. Cambridge: Cambridge University Press, 1997.

Teeple, Howard M. *The Mosaic Eschatological Prophet.* SBLMS 10. Philadelphia: Society of Biblical Literature, 1957.

Thielman, Frank. *From Plight to Solution: A Jewish Framework for Understanding Paul's View of the Law in Romans and Galations.* NovTSup 61. Leiden: Brill, 1989.

————. *Paul and the Law: A Contextual Approach.* Downers Grove: Inter-Varsity, 1994.

Thiselton, Anthony C. "Realized Eschatology at Corinth." *NTS* 24 (1977–78): 510–526.

Thrall, Margaret E. *The Second Epistle to the Corinthians.* Volume 1. ICC. Edinburgh: T. and T. Clark, 1994.

Tobin, Thomas H., S. J. *The Creation of Man: Philo and the History of Interpretation.* CBQMS 14. Washington, D.C.: Catholic Biblical Association of America, 1983.

Toews, John E. "The Law in Paul's Letter to the Romans: A Study of Romans 9.30–10.13." Ph.D. Dissertation, Northwestern University, 1977.

Tomson, Peter J. *Paul and the Jewish Law: Halakha in the Letters of the Apostle to the Gentiles.* Compendia Rerum Iudaicarum ad Novum Testamentum. Assen: Van Gorcum; Philadelphia: Fortress, 1990.

Tov, Emmanuel. "The Septuagint." In *Mikra: Text, Translation, Reading and Interpretation of the Hebrew Bible in Ancient Judaism and Early Christianity*, pp. 161–88. Edited by M. J. Mulder. CRINT. Assen/Maastricht: Van Gorcum; Philadelphia: Fortress, 1988.

Urbach, Ephraim E. *The Sages: Their Concepts and Beliefs.* 2 vols. Translated by Israel Abrahams. Jerusalem: Magnes, 1975.

VanderKam, James C. *The Book of Jubilees: A Critical Text.* CSCO 510–11. Scriptores Aethiopici 87–88. Louvain: Peeters, 1989.

———. *Enoch and the Growth of an Apocalyptic Tradition.* CBQMS 16. Washington, D. C.: Catholic Biblical Association of America, 1984.

van Unnik, W. C. "La conception paulinienne de la nouvelle alliance." In *Litterature et theologie pauliniennes*, pp. 109–26. RechBib 5. Brussels: Desclée, 1960.

———. "Ἡ Καινὴ Διαθήκη." *Studia Patristica* 4. Edited by F. L Cross. TU 79. Berlin: Academie, 1961.

———. "'With Unveiled Face,' An Exegesis of 2 Corinthians iii 12–18." *NovT* 6 (1963): 153–69.

Vattioni, F. *Ecclesiastico: Testo ebraico con apparato critico e versioni greca, latina e siriaca.* Naples: Pubblicazioni del Seminario di Semitistica, 1968.

Vermes, Geza. *The Dead Sea Scrolls in English.* 4th edition; revised and extended. New York: Penguin, 1995.

———. *Post-Biblical Jewish Studies.* Leiden: Brill, 1975.

———. *Scripture and Tradition in Judaism.* SPB 4. Leiden: Brill, 1961.

———. "The Torah is a Light." *VT* 8 (1958): 436–38.

Vielhauer, Philipp. "Gesetzesdienst und Stoicheiadienst im Galaterbrief." In *Rechtfertigung. Festschrift für Ernst Käsemann*, pp. 543–55. Edited by J. Friedrich, W. Pöhlmann and P. Stuhlmacher. Tübingen: Mohr [Siebeck], Göttingen: Vandenhoeck und Ruprecht, 1976.

Wacholder, Ben Zion. *The Dawn of Qumran: The Sectarian Torah and the Teacher of Righteousness.* MHUC 8. Cincinnati: Hebrew Union College, 1983.

———. "The Relationship between 11Q Torah (The Temple Scroll) and the Book of Jubilees: One Single or Two Independent Compositions." In *SBLSP 1985*, pp. 205–16. Edited K. H. Richards. Atlanta: Scholars Press, 1985.

———. "The 'Sealed' Torah Versus the 'Revealed' Torah: an Exegesis of Damascus Covenant V, 1–6 and Jeremiah 32:10–14." *RevQ* 12 (1986): 351–68.

Walter, Nikolaus. "Hellenistic Jews of the Diaspora at the Cradle of Primitive Christianity." In *The New Testament and Hellenistic Judaism*, pp. 37–58. Edited by Peder Borgen and Soren Giverson. Translated by Doris Glenn Wagner. Aarhus: Aarhus University Press, 1995; reprinted by Hendrickson, 1997.

Watson, Francis. *Paul, Judaism and the Gentiles*. Cambridge: Cambridge University Press, 1986.

Weinfeld, Moshe. "God versus Moses in the Temple Scroll." *RevQ* 15 (1991): 175–80.

Weiss, Hans-Friedrich. *Untersuchungen zur Kosmologie des hellenistischen und palästinischen Judentums*. TU 97. Berlin: Akademie-Verlag, 1966.

Wentling, Judith L. "Unraveling the Relationship between 11QT, the Eschatological Temple, and the Qumran Community." *RevQ* 14 (1989): 61–73.

Westerholm, Stephen. *Israel's Law and the Church's Faith*. Grand Rapids: Eerdmans, 1988.

———. "Paul and the Law in Romans 9–11." In *Paul and the Mosaic Law*, pp. 215–37. Edited by James D. G. Dunn. WUNT 89. Tübingen: Mohr [Siebeck], 1996.

———. "Torah, Nomos, and Law: A Question of 'Meaning.'" *SR* 15 (1986): 327–36.

Wilckens, Ulrich. "Paul's View of the Law." In *Paul and Paulinism*, pp. 17–26. Edited by Morna D. Hooker and S. G. Wilson. London: SPCK, 1982.

———. "Σοφία." *Theological Dictionary of the New Testament*, volume 7, pp. 517–22. Edited by Gerhard Friedrich. Translated by G. Bromiley. Grand Rapids: Eerdmans, 1971.

———. "Zur Entwicklung des paulinischen Gesetzesverständnis." *NTS* 28 (1982): 154–90.

Wilken, Robert L., editor. *Aspects of Wisdom in Judaism and Early Christianity*. Notre Dame: Notre Dame University Press, 1975.

Williams, Sam K. "*Promise* in Galatians: A Reading of Paul's Reading of Scripture." *JBL* 107 (1988): 709–20.

Windisch, Hans. "Die göttliche Weisheit der Juden und die paulinische Christologie." In *Neutestamentliche Studien für Georg Heinrici*, pp. 220–34. Edited by A. Deissmann and H. Windisch. Leipzig: Hinrichs, 1914.

Winger, Michael. *By What Law? The Meaning of Nomos in the Letters of Paul*. SBLDS 128. Atlanta: Scholars Press, 1992.

———. "Meaning and Law." *JBL* 117 (1998): 105–10.

Wise, Michael O. *A Critical Study of the Temple Scroll from Qumran Cave 11*. Studies in Ancient Oriental Civilization 49. Chicago: The Oriental Institute of the University of Chicago, 1990.

————. "The Eschatological Vision of the Temple Scroll." *JNES* 49 (1990): 155–72.

Wise, Michael, Abegg, Martin, and Cook, Edward. *The Dead Sea Scrolls: A New Translation.* San Francisco: Harper, 1996.

Wright, N. T. *The Climax of the Covenant: Christ and the Law in Pauline Theology.* Edinburgh: T. and T. Clark, 1991.

————. "Gospel and Theology in Galatians." In *Gospel in Paul: Studies on Corinthians, Galatians and Romans for Richard N. Longenecker,* pp. 222–39. Edited by L. Ann Jervis and Peter Richardson. JSNTSup 108. Sheffield: Sheffield Academic Press, 1994.

Yadin, Yigael. *Megillat Ham-Miqdash.* 3 vols. Jerusalem: The Israel Exploration Society and the Shrine of the Book, 1977.

————. *The Temple Scroll: The Hidden Law of the Dead Sea Sect.* New York: Random House, 1985.

Ziegler, Joseph. *Isaias.* Septuaginta: Vetus Testamentum Graecum. Volume 14. Göttingen: Vandenhoeck und Ruprecht, 1967.

Index of Ancient Sources

This index is divided into two parts: the Bible and non-biblical texts. Non-biblical texts are listed in alphabetical order with the following exceptions: books with numbers as part of their titles (e. g., *2 Enoch*) are listed according to the first letter of the title; rabbinic documents are listed according to the first letter of their name (e. g., *m. Abot* is listed under A); and, known authors (e. g., Josephus and Philo) are listed according to author, not title. Thus, Plato's *Timaeus* is found under P, and 11QTorah is found under Q (Qumran caves are sorted according to cave number).

244

Index of Authors

255

Index of Subjects

The Catholic Biblical Quarterly
Monograph Series (CBQMS)

1. Patrick W. Skehan, *Studies in Israelite Poetry and Wisdom* (CBQMS 1) $9.00 ($7.20 for CBA members) ISBN 0-915170-00-0 (LC 77-153511)
2. Aloysius M. Ambrozic, *The Hidden Kingdom: A Redactional-Critical Study of the References to the Kingdom of God in Mark's Gospel* (CBQMS 2) $9.00 ($7.20 for CBA members) ISBN 0-915170-01-9 (LC 72-89100)
3. Joseph Jensen, O.S.B., *The Use of tôrâ by Isaiah: His Debate with the Wisdom Tradition* (CBQMS 3) $3.00 ($2.40 for CBA members) ISBN 0-915170-02-7 (LC 73-83134)
4. George W. Coats, *From Canaan to Egypt: Structural and Theological Context for the Joseph Story* (CBQMS 4) $4.00 ($3.20 for CBA members) ISBN 0-915170-03-5 (LC 75-11382)
5. O. Lamar Cope, *Matthew: A Scribe Trained for the Kingdom of Heaven* (CBQMS 5) $4.50 ($3.60 for CBA members) ISBN 0-915170-04-3 (LC 75-36778)
6. Madeleine Boucher, *The Mysterious Parable: A Literary Study* (CBQMS 6) $2.50 ($2.00 for CBA members) ISBN 0-915170-05-1 (LC 76-51260)
7. Jay Braverman, Jerome's Commentary on Daniel: A Study of Comparative Jewish and Christian Interpretations of the Hebrew Bible (CBQMS 7) $4.00 ($3.20 for CBA members) ISBN 0-915170-06-X (LC 78-55726)
8. Maurya P. Horgan, *Pesharim: Qumran Interpretations of Biblical Books* (CBQMS 8) $6.00 ($4.80 for CBA members) ISBN 0-915170-07-8 (LC 78-12910)
9. Harold W. Attridge and Robert A. Oden, Jr., *Philo of Byblos,* The Phoenician History (CBQMS 9) $3.50 ($2.80 for CBA members) ISBN 0-915170-08-6 (LC 80-25781)
10. Paul J. Kobelski, *Melchizedek and Melchireša'* (CBQMS 10) $4.50 ($3.60 for CBA members) ISBN 0-915170-09-4 (LC 80-28379)
11. Homer Heater, *A Septuagint Translation Technique in the Book of Job* (CBQMS 11) $4.00 ($3.20 for CBA members) ISBN 0-915170-10-8 (LC 81-10085)
12. Robert Doran, *Temple Propaganda: The Purpose and Character of 2 Maccabees* (CBQMS 12) $4.50 ($3.60 for CBA members) ISBN 0-915170-11-6 (LC 81-10084)
13. James Thompson, *The Beginnings of Christian Philosophy: The Epistle to the Hebrews* (CBQMS 13) $5.50 ($4.50 for CBA members) ISBN 0-915170-12-4 (LC 81-12295)

14. Thomas H. Tobin, S.J., *The Creation of Man: Philo and the History of Interpretation* (CBQMS 14) $6.00 ($4.80 for CBA members) ISBN 0-915170-13-2 (LC 82-19891)

15. Carolyn Osiek, *Rich and Poor in the Shepherd of Hermes* (CBQMS 15) $6.00 ($4.80 for CBA members) ISBN 0-915170--14-0 (LC 83-7385)

16. James C. VanderKam, *Enoch and the Growth of an Apocalyptic Tradition* (CBQMS 16) $6.50 ($5.20 for CBA members) ISBN 0-915170-15-9 (LC 83-10134)

17. Antony F. Campbell, S.J., *Of Prophets and Kings: A Late Ninth-Century Document (1 Samuel 1-2 Kings 10)* (CBQMS 17) $7.50 ($6.00 for CBA members) ISBN 0-915170-16-7 (LC 85-12791)

18. John C. Endres, S.J., *Biblical Interpretation in the Book of Jubilees* (CBQMS 18) $8.50 ($6.80 for CBA members) ISBN 0-915170-17-5 (LC 86-6845)

19. Sharon Pace Jeansonne, *The Old Greek Translation of Daniel 7-12* (CBQMS 19) $5.00 ($4.00 for CBA members) ISBN 0-915170-18-3 (LC 87-15865)

20. Lloyd M. Barré, *The Rhetoric of Political Persuasion: The Narrative Artistry and Political Intentions of 2 Kings 9 -11* (CBQMS 20) $5.00 ($4.00 for CBA members) ISBN 0-915170-19-1 (LC 87-15878)

21. John J. Clabeaux, *A Lost Edition of the Letters of Paul: A Reassessment of the Text of the Pauline Corpus Attested by Marcion* (CBQMS 21) $8.50 ($6.80 for CBA members) ISBN 0-915170-20-5 (LC 88-28511)

22. Craig Koester, *The Dwelling of God: The Tabernacle in the Old Testament, Intertestamental Jewish Literature, and the New Testament* (CBQMS 22) $9.00 ($7.20 for CBA members) ISBN 0-915170-21-3 (LC 89-9853)

23. William Michael Soll, *Psalm 119: Matrix, Form, and Setting* (CBQMS 23) $9.00 ($7.20 for CBA members) ISBN 0-915170-22-1 (LC 90-27610)

24. Richard J. Clifford and John J. Collins (eds.), *Creation in the Biblical Traditions* (CBQMS 24) $7.00 ($5.60 for CBA members) ISBN 0-915170-23-X (LC 92-20268)

25. John E. Course, *Speech and Response: A Rhetorical Analysis of the Introductions to the Speeches of the Book of Job, Chaps. 4 - 24* (CBQMS 25) $8.50 ($6.80 for CBA members) ISBN 0-915170-24-8 (LC 94-26566)

26. Richard J. Clifford, *Creation Accounts in the Ancient Near East and in the Bible* (CBQMS 26) $9.00 ($7.20 for CBA members) ISBN 0-915170-25-6 (LC 94-26565)

27. John Paul Heil, *Blood and Water: The Death and Resurrection of Jesus in John 18 – 21* (CBQMS 27) $9.00 ($7.20 for CBA members) ISBN 0-915170-26-4 (LC 95-10479)

28. John Kaltner, *The Use of Arabic in Biblical Hebrew Lexicography* (CBQMS 28) $7.50 ($6.00 for CBA members) ISBN 0-915170-27-2 (LC 95-45182)

29. Michael L. Barré, S.S., *Wisdom, You Are My Sister: Studies in Honor of Roland E. Murphy, O.Carm., on the Occasion of His Eightieth Birthday* (CBQMS 29) $13.00 ($10.40 for CBA members) ISBN 0-915170-28-0 (LC 97-16060)

30. Warren Carter and John Paul Heil, *Matthew's Parables: Audience-Oriented Perspectives* (CBQMS 30) $10.00 ($8.00 for CBA members) ISBN 0-915170-29-9 (LC 97-44677)

31. David S. Williams, *The Structure of 1 Maccabees* (CBQMS 31) $7.00 ($5.60 for CBA members) ISBN 0-915170-30-2

32. Lawrence Boadt and Mark S. Smith (eds.), *Imagery and Imagination in Biblical Literature: Essays in Honor of Aloysius Fitzgerald, F.S.C.* (CBQMS 32) $9.00 ($7.20 for CBA members) ISBN 0-915170-31-0 (LC 2001003305)

33. Stephan K. Davis, *The Antithesis of the Ages: Paul's Reconfiguration of Torah* (CBQMS 33) ISBN 0-915170-32-9 (LC 2001007936)

Order from:

The Catholic Biblical Association of America
The Catholic University of America
Washington, D.C. 20064